# THE Foreign Policy OF THE Third Reich 1933–1939

*To my parents,*

*without whom this work would not have been possible*

# THE Foreign Policy OF THE Third Reich 1933–1939

THOMAS X. FERENCZI

FONTHILL

Fonthill Media Language Policy

Fonthill Media publishes in the international English language market. One language edition is published worldwide. As there are minor differences in spelling and presentation, especially with regard to American English and British English, a policy is necessary to define which form of English to use. The Fonthill Policy is to use the form of English native to the author. Thomas X. Ferenczi was born and educated in Canada and now lives at Canada therefore Canadian English has been adopted in this publication.

www.fonthillmedia.com
office@fonthillmedia.com

First published in the United Kingdom
and the United States of America 2021

British Library Cataloguing in Publication Data:
A catalogue record for this book is available from the British Library



ISBN 978-1-78155-806-5



Typeset in 10.5pt on 13pt Sabon
Printed and bound in England

# CONTENTS

# Introduction

The principal aim of German foreign policy during the Third Reich was territorial expansion, and in his controversial manifesto, *Mein Kampf* (*My Struggle*), Hitler specified precisely where this territory was to be found: 'If we speak of soil in Europe today, we can primarily have in mind only Russia and her vassal border states.'[1] During one of his wartime bull sessions in August 1941, Hitler explained to his inner circle how he envisioned Russia's future under German rule. He said: 'What India was for England, the territories of Russia will be for us.'[2]

According to Hitler's *Weltanschauung* (worldview), Germany's destiny lay eastwards. Again, the pages of *Mein Kampf* explained why it was necessary for the German *Volk* (folk) to obtain *Lebensraum* (living space): '[W]e National Socialists must ... secure for the German people the land and soil to which they are entitled on this earth.'[3] This urgently needed territory, Hitler explained, would be needed to accommodate the projected German population growth in the decades to come. He predicted that the number of Germans in Europe, currently a people numbering some eighty million, would swell to over triple that figure in a century:

> Today we count eighty million Germans in Europe! This foreign policy [of ours] will be acknowledged as correct only if, after scarcely a hundred years, there are two hundred and fifty million Germans on this Continent ...[4]

Hitler believed that the German *Volk* had to discontinue their present trend of venturing into Southern and Western Europe, and instead focus their attention eastwards. Furthermore, Germany's pre-1914 Imperial policy of establishing colonies beyond the frontiers of the European Continent needed to be abandoned, and in its place substituted the procurement of vast tracts of Eastern soil:

> And so we National Socialists consciously draw a line beneath the foreign policy tendency of our pre-War period. We take up where we broke off six hundred years ago. We stop the endless German movement to the south and west, and turn our gaze towards the land in the east. At long last we break off the colonial and commercial policy of the pre-War period and shift to the soil policy of the future.[5]

How was Germany to acquire this Eastern soil? A united and strengthened German Reich had to seize land in Eastern Europe at Russia's expense, and this could only be done by conquest. In this way, too, would the historically ethnic German territories of which Germany was dispossessed at Versailles be reacquired:

> [O]ppressed territories are led back to the bosom of a common Reich, not by flaming protests, but by a mighty sword.[6]

He repeated this precept yet again:

> [T]he recovery of the lost [German] territories is not won through solemn appeals to the Lord or through pious hopes in a League of Nations, but only by force of arms.[7]

However, Hitler recognized that Germany, acting independently, might face insurmountable opposition in attempting to realize her foreign policy objectives. Thus, he proposed that Germany ally herself with two specific nations: 'In the predictable future there can be only two allies for Germany in Europe: England and Italy.'[8] Conversely, Hitler averred there was one European nation which was a thorn in Germany's side and always would be, regardless of which type of government she possessed:

> The inexorable mortal enemy of the German people is and remains France. It matters not at all who ruled or will rule France, whether Bourbons or Jacobins, Bonapartists or bourgeois democrats, Clerical republicans or Red Bolshevists: the final goal of their activity in foreign affairs will always be an attempt to seize possession of the Rhine border and to secure this watercourse for France by means of a dismembered and shattered Germany.[9]

But why should Germany seek an alliance with Britain and Italy, two states against whom Germany had fought in the Great War? Because, Hitler pointed out, it was not in Britain's interest for France to become the dominant Continental Power, for such a potent rival would inevitably threaten British global supremacy:

> England does not want a France whose military fist, unobstructed by the rest of Europe, can undertake a policy which, one way or another, must one day cross English interests. England can never desire a France which, in possession of the immense Western European iron and coal depositions, obtains the foundations of a menacing economic world position. And England, furthermore, cannot desire a France whose continental political situation, thanks to the shattering of the rest of Europe, seems so assured that the resumption of a French world policy along broader lines is not only made possible but positively forced.

Nor would it benefit Italy to have an all-powerful France on the Continent:

> And Italy, too, cannot and will not desire a further reinforcement of the French position of superior power in Europe. Italy's future will always be conditioned by a development which is geographically grouped around the Mediterranean basin.... Any further continental strengthening of France, however, is an obstacle to Italy in the future ...[10]

The establishment of an Anglo–German–Italian bloc would also isolate France and enable Germany to settle her generations-long feud with her hated Gallic foe:

> [T]he alliance would give Germany the possibility of peacefully making those preparations for a reckoning with France, which would have to be made in any event within the scope of such a coalition.[11]

Moreover, Hitler observed that the respective aims of Britain and France regarding the ascendancy of a new continental power—i.e. Germany—were incompatible: 'The ultimate aim of French diplomacy will always stand in conflict with the ultimate tendency of British statesmanship.' He explained in further detail:

> England's desire is and remains the prevention of the rise of a continental power to world-political importance; that is, the maintenance of a certain balance of power between the European states; for this seems the presupposition of a British world hegemony. France's desire [on the other hand] is and remains to prevent the formation of a unified power in Germany, the maintenance of a system of German petty states with balanced power relations and without unified leadership, and occupation of the left bank of the Rhine as the presupposition for creating and safeguarding her position of hegemony in Europe.'[12]

In simpler terms: 'England desires no Germany as a world power, but France wishes no power at all called Germany ...'[13] In view of all these points, Hitler reached the following conclusion:

> 'On soberest and coldest reflection, it is today primarily these two states, England and Italy, whose most natural selfish interests are not, in the most essential points at least, opposed to the German nation's requirements for existence, and are, indeed, to a certain extent, identified with them.[14]

Under Hitler's autocratic leadership, German foreign policy consisted of four key points, summarized here:

1. *LEBENSRAUM* and *DRANG NACH OSTEN:* the acquisition of 'living space' for the German *Volk* by a 'drive eastwards', resulting in the displacement of the native Slavic inhabitants and their replacement with German farmer-settlers;

2. *ANSCHLUSS:* the incorporation of Austria into the German Reich;

3. *GROSSDEUTSCHLAND:* the establishment of a large, homogenous Germanic bloc—a Greater German Reich—composed of all Europe's Germans (Austrian Germans, Sudeten Germans, Memel Germans, Danzig Germans, etc.) that would extend eastwards to the Ural Mountains and last a millennium; and

4. ABROGATION OF THE VERSAILLES TREATY OF 1919: (i) the abolishment of the 'War Guilt' clause, which declared that Germany was responsible for 'all the loss and damage' of the First World War; (ii) the cancellation of the provisions disallowing German rearmament; and (iii) the restoration of German land and colonies confiscated by the Allied Powers at home and abroad.

The purpose of this book is to examine how in calculated, Machiavellian phases, the Third Reich—through spidery manipulation, deliberate deception, and uncompromising coercion (and despite the best intentions of the Anglo–French democracies who first practised appeasement before finally abandoning it)—endeavoured to realize the four aims indicated above between the years 1933 and 1939.

Thomas X. Ferenczi
August 2019

PART I

# German Diplomacy and the Inaction of the Western Powers

Hitler was intensely focused on foreign policy and involved himself directly in its practice at every step. He recognized early on that he would have to gull the democratic statesmen of England, France, and America in order to further his expansionist agenda. Even before his official entrance onto the international arena, Hitler had been shrewd enough to identify the irresoluteness in his European contemporaries, in particular those statesmen with democratic inclinations. Politicians of the liberal and democratic type entertained notions of egalitarianism and humanitarianism which were anathema to Hitler. Hitler believed that once he was in office the wisest course of action would be to join forces with Fascist Italy and Imperial Japan, and to court England even if he could not establish a partnership with her.

What were the core tenets of Hitler's foreign policy? Winston Churchill (in 1948) described the 'granite pillars' of Hitler's foreign policy precisely as Hitler himself might have explained it to a National Socialist recruit:

> Foreign policy may be unscrupulous. It is not the task of diplomacy to allow a nation to founder heroically, but rather to see that it can prosper and survive. England and Italy are the only two possible allies for Germany. No country will enter into an alliance with a cowardly pacifist state run by democrats and Marxists. So long as Germany does not fend for herself, nobody will fend for her. Her lost provinces cannot be regained by solemn appeals to Heaven or by pious hopes in the League of Nations, but only by force of arms. Germany must not repeat the mistake of fighting all her enemies at once. She must single out the most dangerous and attack him with all her forces. The world will only cease to be anti-German when Germany recovers equality of

> rights and resumes her place in the sun. There must be no sentimentality about Germany's foreign policy. To attack France for purely sentimental reasons would be foolish. What Germany needs is increase of territory in Europe. Germany's pre-war colonial policy was a mistake and should be abandoned. Germany must look for expansion to Russia and especially to the Baltic States [Estonia, Latvia, Lithuania]. No alliance with Russia can be tolerated. To wage war together with Russia against the West would be criminal, for the aim of the Soviets is the triumph of international Judaism.[1]

Franz von Papen, then the latest in a long series of German Chancellors, and arguably the man most responsible for helping put Hitler into office, first encountered Hitler on 9 June 1932. He recalled his initial impressions in his post-war memoirs:

> I found him [Hitler] curiously unimpressive. Press pictures had conveyed no idea of a dominating personality and I could detect no inner quality which might explain his extraordinary hold on the masses. He was wearing a dark blue suit and seemed the complete *petit-bourgeois*. He had an unhealthy complexion, and with his little moustache and curious hair style had an indefinable bohemian quality. His demeanour was modest and polite, and although I had heard much about the magnetic quality of his eyes, I do not remember being impressed by them.
>
> After a few polite formalities I asked him for his views on the possibility of supporting my Government. He brought up his usual list of complaints—previous governments had shown a lamentable lack of statesmanship in excluding a political party with such wide support from its due share in the affairs of the State at a time when an attempt should be made to correct the errors of the Versailles Treaty and restore full German sovereignty. This struck me as a most important point, and as he talked about his party's aims I was struck by the fanatical insistence with which he presented his arguments. I realized that the fate of my Government would depend to a large extent on the willingness of this man and his followers to back me up, and that this would be the most difficult problem with which I should have to deal. He made it clear that he would not be content with a subordinate role and intended in due course to demand plenary powers for himself. 'I regard your Cabinet only as a temporary solution, and will continue my efforts to make my party the strongest in the country. The Chancellorship will then devolve on me,' he said.[2]

Kurt Ludecke, a German nationalist and ex-member of the Nazi Party, recounted in his revealing book *I Knew Hitler* the contents of a confidential talk with Hitler that took place on 12 September 1932. Hitler, just several months before being appointed Chancellor, spoke candidly:

> Can I also fool these gentlemen abroad for any length of time? That's the question. What will England say, France, the United States, once I'm Chancellor?... [W]ill I be able to rearm Germany before they get on to me with a preventative war? That depends largely, I suppose, on whether they have the leadership and guts to strike—if they can get the people to go to war again, and that I doubt....
>
> I don't care what they think and write about me abroad—better for them to keep on underrating me until I get strong—I'll be ready to strike before they know it, the fools![3]

To Ludecke, Hitler next spoke of the economic strength of the 'Versailles States' (France, Britain, and America), whom he could not then afford to alienate, and the subterfuge he would employ to convince them of his peaceful intentions:

> The economic power of the Versailles States is so enormous that I can't risk antagonizing them at the very outset. If I begin my régime with socialism, Paris, London, New York will be alarmed, the capitalists will take fright and combine, and I'll be whipped before I know it. A preventative war [against Germany] would ruin everything. No, I've got to play ball with capitalism and keep the Versailles Powers in line by holding aloft the bogey of Bolshevism—make them believe that a Nazi Germany is the last bulwark against the Red flood. That's the only way to come through the danger period, to get rid of Versailles and re-arm. I can talk peace, but mean war.
>
> If England opposes a greater Germany at all costs, all right. I still think that Mussolini might be interested in making Germany so strong that together we could force John Bull [England] to his knees. And it will be easier to overthrow Moscow and take the Ukraine if the capitalists are on my side. If the capitalists are forced to choose, believe me, they will prefer a greater Germany, even if it means the end of Moscow, to an alliance of the two [Germany and Russia] against themselves—for that would spell the finish of capitalism the world over. Never fear—faced by such an alternative, capitalism would rather have me than Stalin, and will accept my terms.[4]

So long as Germany was militarily feeble, Hitler knew he would have to tread carefully, in phases. For he had written in *Mein Kampf*:

> A shrewd victor will, if possible, always present his demands to the vanquished in installments.[5]

Hitler's concern was to ensure that he did not rouse the democratic nations into taking collective action against him, especially before Germany was armed and ready. War was the means through which Hitler sought to attain his aims, regardless of human or material cost, but he had to bide his time. It was he who would determine the moment to strike, not his adversaries.

After his appointment to the Chancellorship on 30 January 1933, Hitler immediately set about lulling the international community into a false sense of security. He realized that the most effective way of doing this was by staunchly advocating peace. This he did, repeatedly, throughout the early years of the National Socialist régime. In a proclamation to the German nation on 1 February, Hitler expounded on the Reich Government's top two priorities: elevating Germany to an equal standing with Europe's other nations, and keeping the peace:

> As regards its foreign policy the National Government considers its highest mission to be the securing of the right to live and the restoration of freedom to our nation. Its determination to bring to an end the chaotic state of affairs in Germany will assist in restoring to the community of nations a State of equal value and, above all, a State which must have equal rights. It is impressed with the importance of its duty to use this nation of equal rights as an instrument for the securing and maintenance of that peace which the world requires today more than ever before.[6]

Hitler knew perfectly well the benefits of propaganda—both subtle and explicit—which, if consistently applied, served to undermine, divide, and demoralize his enemies. Any subversive tactic that would fan the flames of chaos would do. Hitler intended to sap the strength of his adversaries abroad by eroding their willpower prior to launching an attack.

To legitimize himself to European politicians, Hitler contended that strong political measures had to be taken to stem the tide of Communism and that his actions were not intended to threaten the countries of the West. Hitler claimed that Germany was directing its fight against the Red menace and not the Western democracies, with whom he sought only friendship. Hitler averred that Germany, situated in the heart of Europe, was the nation best-equipped to keep the Red hordes—who were the arch-enemy of mankind—in check. On 26 November 1935, Hitler stated to Hugh Baillie, the head of United Press International:

> Germany is the bulwark of the West against Bolshevism and in combatting it, will meet propaganda with propaganda, terror with terror, and violence with violence.[7]

In a letter to Sir John Simon dated 26 April 1933, Sir Horace Rumbold, who had served as Britain's Ambassador to Germany since 1928, described the early stages of the new National Socialist régime in Germany. His observations were shrewd and insightful:

> Hitlerism has spread with extraordinary rapidity since the 5th March, and those who witnessed the celebration of Hitler's birthday a few days ago [20 April] must have been impressed by the astonishing popularity of the new leader with the masses. So far as the ordinary German is concerned, Hitler has certainly restored something akin to self-respect, which has been lacking in Germany since November 1918. The German people of today no longer feel humiliated or oppressed. The Hitler Government have had the courage to revolt against Versailles, to challenge France and the other signatories of the treaty without any serious consequences. For a defeated country this represents an immense moral advance. For its leader, Hitler, it represents overwhelming prestige and popularity. Someone has aptly said that nationalism is the illegitimate offspring of patriotism by inferiority complex. Germany has been suffering from such a complex for over a decade. Hitlerism has eradicated it, but only at the cost of burdening Europe with a new outbreak of nationalism.[8]

On 2 May 1933, Hitler received Sir John Foster Fraser, a journalist for the London *Daily Telegraph*, for an interview. Hitler assured Fraser that Germany sought no repetition of the Great War, that Germany no longer had any colonial ambitions extending beyond the European Continent, and that Germany had no intention of rivalling Britain in the maritime sphere. In the last sentence, however, it should be noted that Hitler openly admitted—just as he did in the pages of *Mein Kampf*—that Germany's foreign interests lay in Eastern Europe. Fraser recorded Hitler as stating:

> No one in Germany who went through the War wants to repeat that experience....
>
> The plan of German overseas expansion which perhaps existed before the War had been relinquished. Germany did not wish ... to enter into competition with England at sea. The fate of Germany was dependent not on colonies or dominions, but on its Eastern borders.[9]

In a speech to the Reichstag on 17 May, Hitler emphatically proclaimed his desire for peace:

> ... I desire to declare in the name of the National Government, and of the whole Movement of national regeneration, that we in this new Germany

> are filled with deep understanding for the same feelings and opinions and for the rightful claims to life of the other [European] nations....
>
> Our boundless love for and loyalty to our own national traditions makes us respect the national claims of others and makes us desire from the bottom of our hearts to live with them in peace and friendship.

Hitler described in detail the full extent of Germany's disarmament and the present strength of her armed forces, consisting of a token army just 100,000-strong:

> If Germany has continued for years to demand the disarmament of all, it is for the following reasons:
>
> 1. The demand for equality of rights expressed in actual facts is a demand of morality, right and reason; it is a demand which is recognized in the Peace Treaty itself and the fulfillment of which is indissolubly bound up with the demand for German disarmament, as the prelude to world disarmament.
>
> 2. On the other hand the disqualification of a great people cannot be permanently maintained, but must at some time be brought to an end. How long is it thought possible that such an injustice can be imposed on a great nation? What is the advantage of a moment as compared with the permanent development through centuries? The German nation will continue to exist exactly in the same way as the French nation and, as history has proved, the Polish nation....
>
> Germany, in demanding at present actual equality of rights such as can only be achieved by the disarmament of other nations, has a moral right to do so since she has herself carried out the provisions of the treaties. For Germany has disarmed and has carried out this disarmament under the strictest international supervision....
>
> The Rhineland was demilitarized, the German fortresses were dismantled, our ships surrendered, our airplanes destroyed, our system of military service abandoned and the training of reserves thus prevented. Even the most indispensable weapons of defence were denied us....
>
> On behalf of the German people and the German Government, I have to make the following statement: Germany has disarmed. She has complied with all obligations imposed upon her in the Peace Treaty to an extent far beyond the limits of equity and reason. Her army consists of 100,000 men. The strength and character of her police are internationally regulated.

Next, Hitler made reference to all the treaties Germany had signed in the interest of European security, but pointed out how Germany had no security for herself due to the numerous planes and vast supply of armaments in her neighbours' possession:

> Germany has thus a fully justified moral claim to the fulfillment by the other Powers of their obligations under the Treaty of Versailles. The equality of status accorded to Germany in December has not yet been given practical expression. With regard to the contention, repeated by France again and again, that the safety of France must be secured to the same extent as the equality of Germany, I would like to ask two questions:
>
> 1. Germany has so far accepted all the obligations with regard to security arising from the signing of the Versailles Treaty, the Kellogg Pact, the Treaties of Arbitration, the Pact of Non-Aggression, etc. What other concrete assurances are left for Germany to give?
>
> 2. On the other hand, how much security has Germany? According to the figures published by the League, France alone has 3,046 airplanes in service, Belgium 350, Poland 700, Czechoslovakia 670. In addition to these numbers there are innumerable reserve airplanes, thousands of tanks, thousands of heavy guns and all the necessary technical equipment for chemical warfare. Has not Germany, in her state of defencelessness and disarmament, greater justification in demanding security than the overarmed States bound together in military alliances?

Hitler talked about his willingness to voluntarily disarm what little Germany had on condition that the other European nations do likewise. If not, then Germany would have to insist on parity with the military strength of the other European nations bound by the Versailles Treaty:

> ... Germany is at any time willing to undertake further obligations in regard to international security, if all the other nations are ready on their side to do the same, and if this security is also to benefit Germany. Germany would also be perfectly ready to disband her entire military establishment and destroy the small amount of arms remaining to her, if the neighbouring countries will do the same thing with equal thoroughness. But if these countries are not willing to carry out the disarmament measures to which they are also bound by the Treaty of Versailles, Germany must at least maintain her demand for equality....

> Germany agrees in principle to a transitional period of five years during which to build up her national security, in the expectation that at the end of this period she will really be put on a footing of equality with the other States. She is also entirely ready to renounce all offensive weapons of every sort if the armed nations, on their side, will destroy their offensive weapons within a specified period, and if their use is forbidden by an international convention. Germany has only one desire: to be able to preserve her independence and defend her frontiers.[10]

Hitler trumpeted peace, time and time again. And it worked. Most foreign politicians were thoroughly hoodwinked. Nevertheless, not everyone was taken in. Rumbold, for one, saw through Hitler's deceptive assurances. He wrote:

> The task of the German Government is more complicated. They have to rearm on land, and as Herr Hitler explains in his memoirs [*Mein Kampf*], they will have to lull their adversaries into such a state of coma that they will allow themselves to be engaged one by one. It may seem astonishing that the Chancellor should express himself so frankly, but it must be noted that his book was written in 1925, when his prospects of reaching power were so remote that he could afford to be candid. He would probably be glad to suppress every copy extant today. Since he assumed office, Herr Hitler has been as cautious and discreet as he was formerly blunt and frank. He declares that he is anxious that peace should be maintained for a ten-year period. What he probably means can be more accurately expressed by the formula: Germany needs peace until she has recovered such strength that no country can challenge her without serious and irksome preparations.[11]

At this time the Western Powers were unwilling to consent to Germany's insistence on military parity. Consequently, Hitler gave official notice on 14 October that Germany was retiring from the League of Nations. In a radio broadcast to the German nation, Hitler announced that Germany wanted to be treated on an equal basis by the European community. He argued that the principle of disarmament should apply uniformly to all nations, not only to Germany, and that the Reich should be allowed to possess defensive weapons to protect herself. He bemoaned the fact that by being singled out, Germany was being deprived of her fundamental rights. Hitler explained that it was therefore impossible for Germany to retain her membership in the League of Nations, or to take part in the World Disarmament Conference (The Conference for the Reduction and Limitations of Armaments) presently underway:

> The German people has fulfilled its disarmament obligations to more than the full measure. The turn would seem to have come for armed nations to do no less than meet their analogous obligations. The German Government is not participating in this conference in order to barter for a single cannon or machine gun for the German people, but as a factor with equal rights to help in the general pacification of the world. Germany's security constitutes no inferior right to the security of the other nations....
>
> In this demand by Germany there cannot possibly be any threat to the rest of the Powers, for the defensive armament of other peoples is constructed to ward off the heaviest weapons of attack, while Germany demands no weapons of attack, but only those defensive arms which in the future are not to be forbidden, but permitted to all nations. Here, too, Germany is ready at once to content itself numerically with the minimum that is all out of proportion to the gigantic armaments of attack and defence of our former enemies.
>
> The deliberate relegation of our people to an inferior class, in that every nation of the world is conceded the self-evident right which is denied us, we feel, is the perpetuation of a discrimination unbearable to us. In my speech of last May I said that under such conditions we would regretfully no longer be able to belong to the League or to participate in international conferences....[12]

Four days later, British journalist G. Ward Price of the *Daily Mail*, a popular London newspaper, met with Hitler for an interview. Hitler spoke very plausibly on this occasion, reiterating his aversion to war and Germany's refusal to tolerate any further discrimination against her:

> Nobody here desires a repetition of war. Almost all the leaders of the National Socialist Movement were actual combatants. I have yet to meet the combatant who desires a renewal of the horrors of those four and a half years.... Our youth constitutes our sole hope for the future. Do you imagine that we are bringing it up only to be shot down on the battlefield?
>
> We are manly enough to recognize that when one has lost a war, whether one was responsible for it or not, one has to bear the consequences. We have borne them, but it is intolerable for us as a nation of sixty-five million that we should repeatedly be dishonoured and humiliated. We will put up with no more of this persistent discrimination against Germany. So long as I live I will never put my signature as a statesman to any contract which I could not sign with self-respect in private life. I will maintain this resolution, even if it means my ruin! For

> I will sign no document with a mental reservation not to fulfill it. What I sign, I will stand by. What I cannot stand by, I will not sign.[13]

On 12 November, a referendum was held in Germany on the issue of withdrawal from the League of Nations. The question on the ballot was couched almost as a marriage vow:

> Do you, German man, and you, German woman, approve of the politics of your Reich Government, and are you willing to declare that they are the expression of your own view and your own will and to bear solemn witness to this? Yes/No[14]

The widespread German anti-Versailles sentiment and nationalist fervour left little doubt that the measure would be affirmed. At the polls, over forty million Germans voted in favour, and only some two million voted against. In these early days of the Third Reich, a German citizen could still cast a negative vote or abstain from voting altogether without serious repercussion. This fact would suggest that these figures were, overall, an accurate representation of the popular will and not entirely the result of coercion or manipulation, as would happen later.

It created quite a stir in Europe when on 26 January 1934, Germany concluded a non-aggression pact with Poland (see Appendix A) intended to last ten years. The pact was signed in Berlin by representatives of the German and Polish Governments, Konstantin von Neurath and Józef Lipski respectively:

> The German Government and the Polish Government consider that the time has come to introduce a new phase in the political relations between Germany and Poland by a direct understanding between State and State. They have, therefore, decided to lay down the principles for the future development of these relations in the present declaration.
>
> The two Governments base their action on the fact that the maintenance and guarantee of a lasting peace between their countries is an essential pre-condition for the general peace of Europe....
>
> Both Governments announce their intention to settle directly all questions of whatever sort which concern their mutual relations.
>
> Should any disputes arise between them and agreement thereon not be reached by direct negotiation, they will in each particular case, on the basis of mutual agreement, seek a solution by other peaceful means ... In no circumstances, however, will they proceed to the application of force for the purpose of reaching a decision in such disputes.

> Both Governments are convinced that the relations between their countries will in this manner develop fruitfully, and will lead to the establishment of a neighbourly relationship which will contribute to the well-being not only of both their countries, but of the other peoples of Europe as well.[15]

As was his wont, Hitler touted his latest conciliatory gesture as further evidence of his peaceful intentions. To the Reichstag, Hitler announced on 30 January that 'the German Government has endeavoured in its first year to secure a new and better relationship with the Polish State'. He continued:

> Germans and Poles will have to learn to accept the fact of each other's existence. Hence it is more sensible to regulate this state of affairs ... in such a way that the highest possible profit will accrue from it for both nations....
>
> Further, it seemed to me right in such a case to attempt to deal with the problems affecting both countries by means of a frank and open exchange of views between the two parties rather than to go on entrusting third and fourth parties with this task. Moreover, whatever the differences between the two countries in the future may be, the catastrophic effects of the attempt to remove them through warlike actions would far outweigh any possible advantage gained.
>
> Thus the German Government was fortunate in finding the same general attitude in the leader of the present Polish State, Marshal Piłsudski, and in being able to incorporate this mutual recognition of the situation in a treaty which will not only be of equal advantage to the Polish and German peoples, but which also represents an important contribution to the maintenance of world peace.
>
> In the spirit of this treaty the German Government is willing and prepared to cultivate economic relations with Poland in such a way that here, too, the state of unprofitable suspicion can be succeeded by a period of useful co-operation.
>
> It is a matter of particular satisfaction to us that in this same year the National Socialist Government of Danzig has been enabled to effect a similar clarification of its relations with its Polish neighbour.[16]

After Versailles, relations between Germany and Poland had been marked by intense ill-feeling. The issues of Danzig and the Polish Corridor were sensitive ones. And although Germany had naturally been resentful against the Western Powers following Versailles, anti-Polish sentiment had been especially severe. But with this political measure, Hitler successfully brought about a *rapprochement* with Poland, then in league with France per the Franco–Polish Alliance of 1921. This strategic move by Hitler forestalled any joint opposition by both nations. As for the Poles, they were reassured by the new German régime's seemingly peaceful intentions. And from Hitler's perspective, it potentially laid the foundation for Germany to launch an aggressive war against the Soviet Union—with Poland as a military ally. It was an option Hitler initially entertained, but later (in 1939) rejected due to Polish intransigence.

It was Poland's misfortune to be situated between two aggressive nations, Nazi Germany and Soviet Russia. Both were ruled by leaders who were ruthless, cynical, and without scruple. Because of this, there was a high likelihood that Polish territory would sooner or later be encroached upon by one or both of them. For Hitler, the non-aggression pact with Poland served to secure Germany's eastern border. And now Hitler could afford to concentrate on relations with Germany's other neighbours: France, Italy, Austria, and Czechoslovakia.

On 16 February, British newsman G. Ward Price again interviewed Hitler. This time the talks concerned Austria's recent internal strife; just four days earlier a civil war had broken out. It was triggered by a clash in Linz between the Social Democratic Party's militia wing, the illegal *Republikanischer Schutzbund* (Republican Protection League), and the nationalist *Heimwehr* (Home Guard). The fighting soon extended to Vienna and other Upper Austrian and Styrian cities. The tide turned in favour of the police and right-wing forces once the Federal Army joined the conflict. In Vienna, the rebellion was crushed by the use of excessive force. Federal Chancellor Engelbert Dollfuss authorized the shelling of the Karl-Marx-Hof, an apartment complex which the socialist combatants were using as a stronghold. This posed tremendous risk to the many innocent residential tenants inside and caused much property damage. Fighting raged on throughout Styria afterwards, but the revolt was quashed just four days after it had begun.

To the speculation that German Nazis had been involved in the Austrian disorders, Hitler answered: 'We sympathize neither with Herr Dollfuss nor with his opponents. Both sides are using the wrong methods. Nothing of permanence can be achieved by the violent methods to which they have resorted.' According to Hitler, Austria's Social Democrats could never gain power by revolutionary means, just as Dollfuss could not hope to convert opponents to his cause by violent suppression. Of course, said Hitler, one could 'raze buildings using shell fire', but such tactics 'would never convince an opponent'. On the contrary, it would only strengthen his resolve. 'Persuasion' was the sole effective method of bringing an enemy into the rival camp, Hitler explained. 'That is what we have achieved in

Germany. Herr Dollfuss, on the other hand, attempted to carry out a *coup d'état*. He violated the Constitution and his methods were doomed to fail from the beginning.' Had the insurrection occurred in the Reich, Hitler stated, Germany's casualties would have been '18,000 dead and 50,000 wounded', for 'Germany's population was eleven times that of Austria's'. Hitler went on: 'What are the facts? The total number of our adversaries killed in the disturbances amounted to twenty-seven, while the number of wounded was 150. Among them was not a single woman nor a single child. Not one building was destroyed, not one shop raided. Germany's critics will say, "That may well be, but the Austrian Socialists were heavily armed!"' Germany's Communists were also well armed, Hitler added. In fact, they had stockpiled weapons of every conceivable sort. They had only held off because 'they had been won over to the cause of the National Socialists by persuasion'. This was evidenced, Hitler averred, by the election results of 12 November 1933 in which the N.S.D.A.P. had received over 92 per cent of the vote; millions of ex-Communists and ex-Socialists had been 'converted' to the National Socialist Movement. G. Ward Price then inquired if the uprising would have any bearing on the Reich's 'attitude' *vis-à-vis* Austria. Hitler responded, 'By no means; the policies I uphold are determined solely by German interests.' Of course, the recent chaotic events in Austria 'would serve to strengthen the position' of Dollfuss' conservative government. At the same time, however, 'the number of Austrian National Socialists would increase'. The Austrian working class, Hitler opined, 'would side with the National Socialist cause' due to the brutal force used by the Dollfuss régime.

Price then changed the subject to Germany's recent non-aggression pact with Poland, concluded less than a month earlier. Price noted that it had been wholly unexpected and informed Hitler that there were those who perceived it to mean that Germany and Poland intended to wage war against the U.S.S.R. together for the purpose of expropriating Russian territory. Hitler scoffed derisively at this suggestion (which was all too true). 'What? We take territory from Russia? Ridiculous!' Price then pointed out to Hitler that in his manifesto, *Mein Kampf*, first published nearly a decade ago, Hitler had advocated the seizure of Russian land for future generations of Germans settlers. However, Price observed, due to the 'decrease in the birth rate which ... had halted the growth of the German population', the acquisition of eastern lands was no longer as high a priority as was once believed.

As the interview proceeded, Hitler asserted that all past endeavours to establish a long-term peace in Europe had been fruitless, because 'public opinion had held that Poland and Germany were irreconcilable enemies'. He, however, did not personally share this outlook. In fact, after becoming

Chancellor the very first course of action he had undertaken was 'to initiate negotiations with Poland'. Hitler claimed that he had discovered Poland's leaders to be 'very magnanimous' and as equally inclined towards peace as he was. He considered the 'unbridgeable' divide between them as having 'now been crossed'. Relations had ameliorated between the two European neighbours, and Hitler expressed the 'sincere hope' that the German–Polish *rapprochement* meant that both nations had given up 'the idea of resorting to arms' not just for the duration of the ten-year non-aggression pact, 'but for all time'.[17]

Hitler flew to Venice on 14 June to discuss with Mussolini the sensitive issue of Austrian independence. It was their first meeting. Mussolini had been in power for nearly twelve years and was a respected statesman. Like Hitler, Mussolini was an intense, forceful demagogue who gestured aggressively while orating. His vision was for Fascist Italy to become the dominant power in the Mediterranean, and he wished to establish his conception of a twentieth-century version of the Roman Empire. Mussolini also glorified martial combat and believed it would toughen the Italian people and make them warlike. An extremist, Mussolini believed wholeheartedly that 'It is necessary to act, to move, to fight and, if necessary, to die.... It is blood which moves the wheels of history!'[18] But unlike Hitler, Mussolini did not espouse anti-Semitism, or at least he was not as thoroughly anti-Jewish as his German counterpart. Fascist Italy did, however, officially adopt a policy of anti-Semitism in July 1938 to placate Hitler. This was the *Manifesto della Razza* (*Manifesto of Race*), a decree disfavoured among regular Italians and even Fascist leaders. It reduced Jewish persons to the status of non-citizens and removed them from government and professional posts. Mussolini later commented that he did not give any credence to so-called 'anti-Semitic theory', but that he had implemented the policy 'for political reasons'. Mussolini stated in 1932 to the Austrian Ambassador to Italy:

> I have no love for the Jews, but they have great influence everywhere. It is better to leave them alone. Hitler's anti-Semitism has already brought him more enemies than is necessary.[19]

And in a speech to Fascists in Bari on 6 September 1934, Mussolini scorned the concept of race:

> Thirty centuries of history allow us to look with supreme pity on certain doctrines [Teutonic superiority] which are preached beyond the Alps [in Germany] by the descendants of those who were illiterate when Rome had Caesar, Virgil and Augustus.[20]

Their first meeting went badly. At the Venice–Lido airfield, Hitler deplaned. He was clad in a bland gabardine raincoat instead of his regular Brownshirt uniform, while Mussolini was decked out in a crisp military uniform bedizened with regalia. Both dictators beamed for the cameras as they shook hands together. They were driven to the Venetian town of Stra and withdrew to the Villa Pisani for a private talk. But there, behind closed doors, the friendly chitchat ceased. Mussolini brusquely told Hitler of his firm intention to continue to guarantee Austrian independence. Hitler was unaccustomed to such blunt, uncompromising opposition. Infuriated, he shouted that it was both his and the German *Volk's* will that Austria join the German Reich. Mussolini heatedly replied that Italy would not yield and would defend her position with military might, if need be. The staff waiting outside the conference room were disturbed to hear fists hammering down on the table and harsh, angry voices. Then the commotion unexpectedly stopped, the door was flung open, and Mussolini and Hitler both marched out of the room, red-faced and tight-lipped. They went outside to acknowledge the exultant crowds milling about, then returned to Venice. Following a formal dinner and a Wagner concert, Hitler and Mussolini coldly said their goodbyes. Afterwards, Mussolini mentioned to one of his aides, '*Non mi piace.*' ('I don't like the look of him.') He also stated that listening to Hitler's verbatim quotations from *Mein Kampf* had been extremely dull and that as far as he was concerned, Hitler was 'a garrulous monk'.[21] And to Filippo Bojano, the Italian press agent stationed in Berlin, Mussolini commented:

> Hitler is simply a muddleheaded fool. His head is stuffed with philosophical and political tags that are utterly incoherent. I can't make out why he waited so long to take over power, and why he played the buffoon, with his ridiculous electoral contests, in order to take legal possession of the reins of power. Either he is a revolutionary or he is not. Fascist Italy would never have come into being without a march on Rome. We [Fascists] are dynamic, and Signor Hitler is just a prater.[22]

The ascendency of the National Socialists in Germany in late January 1933 caused much political unease in neighbouring Austria. Austria's Christian Socialist Government, headed by Dollfuss, was continually being undermined by leftist and rightist extremists. Austrian Nazis were agitating, seeking to unify with the Reich. To quell them Dollfuss banned the Austrian faction of the Nazi Party, the D.N.S.A.P., on 19 June 1933. Nevertheless, it was the Communists who beat the Austrian Nazis to the punch. When violent confrontations broke out with workers in Linz in February 1934, Dollfuss promptly outlawed the Social Democratic Party.

And on 1 May, the *Maiverfassung* (May Constitution) was ratified. It introduced a new brand of authoritarianism, Austrofascism, patterned on the Italian system. It was a mixture of Catholicism, corporatism, and nationalism. Austria became a one-party state. Its sole legal political party was the right-wing *Vaterländische Front* (Fatherland Front), and the nation was renamed the 'Federal State of Austria'.

That summer, Austrian National Socialists in cahoots with German agents orchestrated a *coup d'état*. On 25 July, members of an illegal Austrian S.S. unit, S.S. Regiment 89, forced their way into the office of the Chancellor and assassinated Dollfuss. He was gunned down at close range. Mussolini was outraged at the killing of Dollfuss, and he accused Hitler of complicity:

> Hitler is the murderer of Dollfuss, Hitler is the guilty man, he is responsible for this.[23]

Mussolini telephoned Austria's Vice-Chancellor, Ernst von Starhemberg, and promised to continue upholding Austrian sovereignty:

> The independence of Austria has been and will be defended by Italy.[24]

Mussolini also sent a formal telegram to Starhemberg expressing his condolences:

> The tragic end of Chancellor Dollfuss deeply grieves me. I am bound to him by relations of personal friendship and common political views. I always admired his virtues as a statesman, his upright simplicity, and his great courage....
>
> Chancellor Dollfuss served the common people from whom he came with absolute disinterest and with defiance of peril. His memory will be honoured not only in Austria, but everywhere in the civilized world, which already has struck with its moral condemnation those responsible for his death, both near and distant.
>
> Accept the expression of my sympathy, which interprets the unanimous feeling of grief, condemnation, and regret of the Italian people.[25]

Dollfuss was replaced by Dr. Kurt von Schuschnigg, a professorial, bourgeois type, who managed to subdue the insurrectionists. The Germans were prevented from aiding the Austrian Nazis since Italy swiftly dispatched mobilized forces to the Brenner, a mountain pass through the Alps along the Italo–Austrian border. Mussolini even went so far as to warn Hitler that he would go to war in Austria's defence should Germany attempt to invade her. Mussolini backed Austrian independence because he was worried that if Germany annexed Austria, it would not be long before Hitler demanded the restoration of the South Tyrol, a province which prior to 1918 had been a part of Austria–Hungary. Mussolini also knew that Hitler had his eyes on German minorities in northern Italy.

The attempt to depose the Austrian leadership had been unsuccessful. Hitler restrained himself, for he knew that at this point Germany was not sufficiently powerful to risk military intervention by either England, France, or Italy—let alone all three of them combined.

Germany's venerable president, the elderly Paul von Hindenburg, passed away on the morning of 2 August at his Neudeck estate. According to 'The Law regarding the Sovereign Head of the German Reich' passed by the Reichstag the previous day, the offices of Reich President and Reich Chancellor were merged. Hitler was now Germany's head of state and head of government:

> The Reich Government has enacted the following law which is hereby promulgated:
>
> Section 1
>
> The office of the Reich President will be consolidated with that of the Reich Chancellor. The existing authority of the Reich President shall consequently be transferred to the Führer and Reich Chancellor, Adolf Hitler. He shall select his representative.
>
> Section 2
>
> This law is effective as of the time of the death of Reich President von Hindenburg.[26]

Now that Hitler held the reins of power, he would never release them. Just weeks earlier, as recorded in an article titled 'Germany: Second Revolution?' from *Time Magazine* dated 2 July 1934, Hitler had prophesized to a British correspondent in Berlin:

> At the risk of appearing to talk nonsense I tell you that the Nazi Movement will go on for 1,000 years!... Don't forget how people laughed at me fifteen years ago when I declared that one day I would govern Germany. They laugh now, just as foolishly, when I declare that I shall remain in power!

In his speech of 17 August at Hamburg, Hitler commented on President Hindenburg's legacy, the subsequent amalgamation of the Presidency and the Chancellorship, and the upcoming plebiscite of 19 August in which the German electorate would affirm or reject the latter:

> ... The Field Marshal and President of the Reich was a unique figure and cannot be replaced. His mission as President of the Reich reached its fulfillment in himself. No one in the future shall bear this title any more.
>
> However logical the union of the two functions is, and though the law of the Government by which the question is settled cannot be challenged on any constitutional grounds, yet I must absolutely decline to derive the right to take this most momentous step towards the new formation of the German Reich from any previous mandate. No! The people itself must decide!...
>
> The vote of 19 August will, I hope, prove to the world afresh the unquestioned stability of the German Reich today ...
>
> Not for my own sake have I asked for this vote, but for the sake of the German people. It is not I who need such a vote of confidence in order to strengthen or maintain my position; it is the German people which needs a Chancellor supported in the eyes of the whole world by such a display of confidence. For I am nothing, my fellow countrymen, but the spokesman on your behalf, and I have no desire to be anything but the representative of your life and the defender of your vital interests....[27]

Not unexpectedly, the overwhelming majority Germany's eligible voters approved the concentration of political power in Hitler's hands. 95.7 per cent of the electorate turned up at the polls. Over thirty-eight million—89.93 per cent—voted in favour, and some four and a quarter million voted against.[28]

Hitler was interviewed by G. Ward Price again on 5 August. Price's first query was regarding 'general armament and international tensions', to which Hitler replied:

> As far as Germany is concerned, there will be no new war. Germany knows the terrible consequences of war better than any other country.
>
> Almost all of the members of the National Government know its horrors. They know that it is not a romantic adventure, but rather an atrocious catastrophe. It is the conviction of the National Socialist Movement that war is of no use to anyone and can only result in ruin. We would not profit by a war. For us, 1918 was a lesson and a warning. We believe that the problems of present-day Germany cannot be solved by war. The demands it places upon the rest of Europe do not harbour the danger of such a misfortune, for they are limited to what

> the other nations consider their most elementary rights. We demand only that our present borders be maintained. We will certainly never fight again, except in self-defence. I have repeatedly reassured the French that there will be no further territorial difficulties between us once the question of the Saar has been settled; at our eastern border I have proven our peaceful intentions by concluding a pact with Poland.
>
> [Conservative Party leader] Baldwin once said that Great Britain's defensive border lay, in future, at the Rhine. Perhaps a French statesman might go even further and say that France must be defended at the Oder; Russia might perhaps claim that its national defence line runs along the Danube. In view of this situation, Germany can hardly be reproached for seeking national protection within its borders. To you as an Englishman I may say that, if England does not attack us, we will never have any differences with England, neither at the Rhine nor elsewhere. We do not have any claims upon England.

Concerning the issue of colonies abroad, Hitler explained:

> I would not demand the life of a single German in order to gain any colony in the world. We know that the former German colonies in Africa are an expensive luxury for England.

To Price's inquiries in connection with Austria and a potential *Anschluss*, Hitler answered:

> We will not attack Austria, but we cannot prevent Austrians from attempting to re-establish their former ties with Germany. These States are separated only by a line, and on both sides of this line live peoples of the same race.
>
> If one part of England were artificially separated from the rest, who would prevent its endeavouring to become united once more with the rest of the country? Germany and Austria were united until 1866.
>
> The question of the *Anschluss* is not a present day problem. I am certain that the entire affair would be settled if a secret ballot were to take place in Austria. Austrian independence is not at stake, and no one is questioning it.
>
> In the Austrian Empire of old, the various nationalities professed an affinity to their neighbours of their own race. It is only natural that the Germans of Austria are in favour of a unification with Germany. We all know that this goal is unattainable at present, for resistance in the rest of Europe would be too strong.

And when asked if Germany intended to rejoin the League of Nations, Hitler responded:

> We left the League of Nations for definite, clearly stated reasons. It was impossible for my government to continue to take part in negotiations in which we were treated on an inferior basis. When our complete equality is recognized, we will perhaps return. The British Government has declared its support of equal armaments, which constitute the major criterion, but unfortunately it has not succeeded in convincing other governments to adopt the same position.[29]

1935 marked the year Hitler first achieved a territorial objective without employing force. On 13 January, most of the Saar's inhabitants elected to re-integrate their territory with Germany. For fifteen years the Saarland had been administered by a Governing Commission membered by a Frenchman, a German, and three representatives of the Council of the League of Nations.

The purpose of the plebiscite was to determine whether the Saar, with its valuable coal-mining district, should join France or Germany. The voting process was overseen by an international force to ensure it was conducted fairly. The plebiscite offered three choices: reunify with Germany, continue to remain governed by the League of Nations, or join France.

At the polls, over 477,000 Saarlanders voted to rejoin Germany. The majority of these were ethnic Germans with strong anti-French leanings. Some 46,000 Saarlanders—many of whom were opposed to National Socialism—voted to continue under the League of Nations. And a miniscule number of some 2,000 elected for the Saar to be incorporated into France.[30] The outcome was a notable triumph for the German Reich, which re-acquired the Saar coalfields given to France by the Versailles Treaty. The results were a threefold combination of German patriotism, pro-Nazi sentiment, and a fear of Bolshevism which, it was perceived, only Hitler could stave off. Over the radio, Hitler declared on 15 January:

> An injustice that has lasted for fifteen years is approaching its end! The suffering of hundreds of thousands of folk-comrades in the Saar during this period was shared by the whole German nation. The whole German nation rejoices at the return of our comrades....
>
> There is one thing we all realize, my folk-comrades of the Saar: that we owe our joy to you. Today, a few hours from now, throughout the whole German Reich the bells will ring as an external expression of our pride and joy. We owe this to the unshakable loyalty of you Saar Germans, to your patience and your perseverance, as well as to your bravery.

> Neither force nor temptation made you waver in your faith that you are Germans, as you always have been and always will be! Therefore, as the Führer of the German people and the Chancellor of the Reich, in the name of all Germans, I now express the nation's gratitude to you. At this moment when you are once more with us, sons of our people and citizens of the new German Reich; we are filled with rejoicing....
>
> Now and in the weeks to come, you Germans of the Saar are the representatives of the German people and the German Reich....[31]

Hitler also promised that 'the German Reich has no more territorial demands on France'.[32] To the disappointment of German nationalists, this meant that he would not be seeking to re-acquire the Imperial German territory of Alsace–Lorraine, which had been annexed by the French Republic after the First World War.

Three days after the Saar plebiscite, Hitler was interviewed at Obersalzberg by Pierre J. Huss, an American journalist employed by the Hearst Press. Huss queried Hitler in connection with the plebiscite's results and the current state of Franco–German relations:

> HUSS: Herr Reichskanzler [Mr. Reich Chancellor], what is your opinion of the outcome of the Saar plebiscite?
>
> HITLER: The results of the plebiscite fill me—and every single one of my staff—with infinite pride in the German *Volk*. At the same time, this is a subsequent condemnation of the Peace Treaty of Versailles of truly historic dimensions. For in this Treaty, this region was torn from Germany on the grounds that 150,000 French lived there. After a fifteen-year rule of the League of Nations and thus ultimately of France, it has now been ascertained that not 150,000, but a scant 2,000 French reside in this region, i.e. not even four French per 1,000 inhabitants of the Saar. How can anyone be surprised no good can come of a treaty based upon such incorrect assumptions?
>
> HUSS: Herr Reichskanzler, you have frequently stated that the last obstacle to amicable relations with France would be removed when the Saar question was settled. In view of your untiring, further pursuit of this goal in the interest of world peace, do you have a specific plan in mind?
>
> HITLER: I have frequently stated that, after the return of the Saar to Germany, I would place no further territorial demands on France. I have repeated this statement definitively today before the whole world. In historical terms, it is a very difficult thing to renounce this as I am doing

in the name of the German *Volk*. But I am making this most difficult sacrifice in order to contribute to the pacification of Europe. One cannot expect more from Germany. It is now up to the rest of the world to draw the consequences of such a decision. Never shall I—and never shall the new German Reich—consent to any limitations to the rights of our people. We wish to be a peaceful *Volk*, but under no circumstances without honour.

We are willing to make a very big sacrifice, but never to renounce our freedom. We reject any differentiation between moral equality and factual equality: there is but one equality of rights, and that is the right of a sovereign state and a sovereign nation. If the world recognizes this, there is no need for grandiose plans to fortify peace in Europe.[33]

The League Council sanctioned the reunification of the Saar with Germany on 17 January, and on 1 March, the Saar was incorporated back into Germany under the rule of a Reich Commissioner, Josef Bürckel.

The day after his talk with Huss, Hitler gave another interview to the press. G. Ward Price of England questioned Hitler regarding Germany's possible return to the League of Nations, the terms of the Versailles Treaty in comparison with those of the League, the restoration of equality of rights for Germany, and the fear in France that Germany would remain peaceful only until such time as it considered itself sufficiently powerful for armed aggression:

PRICE: Under which conditions could Germany return to the League of Nations?

HITLER: Neither I nor anyone else in Germany would even consider placing any 'conditions' on our possible return to the League of Nations. Whether or not we return to this body depends exclusively upon whether we can belong to it as a completely equal nation. This is not a 'condition', but a matter of course.

Either we are a sovereign state, or we are not! As long as we are not, we have no business in a community of sovereign states....

PRICE: Will it be necessary to separate the general provisions of the League of Nations from those of the Treaty of Versailles?

HITLER: As long as the League of Nations constitutes only a treaty of guarantee for the victorious nations, it is by no means worthy of its name. The fact that, with time, this League—which was presumably designed by its founders to exist for all eternity—cannot be coupled with a Treaty the short term of which is inherent in its own weaknesses and impracticabilities, is a point which can perhaps be contested by today's interested parties, but which will one day be deemed a matter of course in history.

PRICE: Should the recognition of equality of rights be a precondition, or could granting equality of rights and rejoining the League take place simultaneously?

HITLER: German equality of rights is the prerequisite for any participation on Germany's part in international conventions and agreements. I certainly am not alone in the world with this demand; I am in the best of company. Let it be said that no self-respecting people and no responsible government would be able to think or much less act differently in such a case....

PRICE: Recently I spoke with a high-ranking political personage in France. I asked him the following: 'Why does France choose not to recognize the *fait accompli* of the restoration of German arms? We English always hold that it is more sensible not to ignore such facts.'

The politician replied to me: 'Yes, we believe that Germany will uphold a policy of reconciliation only until the Reichswehr judges itself capable of successfully waging a war. In France, there is fear that the overtures to the French associations of frontline soldiers are only a camouflage to conceal aggressive future intentions.'

What is Your Excellency's reply to this fear?

HITLER: That politician has never led a people. Otherwise how could he believe that one can talk about peace for a decade and then suddenly, with the same people, simply start a war without further ado? When I talk about peace, I am expressing none other than the innermost desire of the German *Volk*. I know the horrors of war: no gains can compensate for the losses it brings. The disastrous consequences of widespread European butchery in the future would be even worse. I believe that the madness of Communism would be the sole victor. But I have not fought this for fifteen years to elevate it finally to the throne by way of a detour. What I want is the well-being of my *Volk*! I have seen that war is not the highest form of bliss, but the contrary: I have witnessed only the deepest suffering. Hence I can quite frankly state two of my beliefs:

1. Germany will never break the peace of its own accord, and

2. He who would lay hands upon us will encounter thorns and barbs! For we love liberty just as we love peace.

> … I submit to France on behalf of the entire German *Volk* the pledge that we will place no further territorial demands upon it and thus of our own accord eliminate any grounds for revenge …[34]

For some time now, contrary to the provisions of the Versailles Treaty, Germany had been rearming, producing war planes and submarines. In early 1934, Hitler had ordered the Reichswehr to increase threefold to 300,000 men, and in June of that year he had also ordered the Navy to build two battle cruisers—the *Scharnhorst* and the *Gneisenau*—each weighing 26,000 tons (the Versailles Treaty stipulated a limit of 10,000 tons). German rearmament was a reality that could no longer escape the attention of the Western Powers, and Hitler knew it. He confided to General Ludwig Beck, Chief of the General Staff, that he would inform the European community of Germany's violations of the Versailles Treaty by 1 April 1935. He also stated to Beck that he intended to introduce conscription and disregard the Versailles Treaty's military prohibitions.

Hitler kept his word. On 16 March, 'The Law for the Building Up of the Defence Force' was promulgated. The German Armed Forces, previously known as the Reichswehr, became the Wehrmacht. The other branches of the German Armed Forces were also renamed. The Reichsheer became the Heer and the Reichsmarine became the Kriegsmarine. The Luftwaffe had already been officially established as of 26 February, although this too was contrary to the Versailles Treaty:

> Article 198
>
> The armed forces of Germany must not include any military or naval air forces.[35]

The law of 16 March introduced general compulsory service. In addition, the strength of the German Army in peacetime was set to comprise twelve corps commands and thirty-six divisions. That same day, Hitler legitimized the new measure in a radio broadcast to the German people by citing an utterance by British minister Stanley Baldwin, then Lord President of the Council (and future prime minister):

> A country, which is not willing to seize the necessary precautionary measures for its own protection will never have might in this world, neither moral nor material might.

As further justification, Hitler underscored the fact that 'for months a continually rising rearmament is taking place within the world. She [Germany] sees in the creation of a Soviet–Russian Army of 101 divisions, which means 960,000 men in present peacetime strength, an element which could not be foreseen at the time of the composition of the Versailles Treaty.' To this he added:

> She [Germany] sees further signs of rejecting the disarmament idea, proclamated in its time, in the overdoing of similar measures. It is far from the German Government to reproach any nation. However, she sees today that through the present resolved introduction of the two-year military service in France, the basic ideas of the creation of a short-service Defence Army has been abandoned in favour of a long-service organization.

Hitler explained that German rearmament was expressly to ensure the security of the Reich and for Germany to promote peace with Europe's other nations on an equal basis. Hitler promised that Germany's newly established forces would not be used for aggressive purposes but solely to protect the German nation and its people:

> What the German Government desires, as the guarding of the honour and interests of the German nation, is to guarantee the extent of those means of power which are required not only for maintaining the integrity of the German Reich, but also for the international respect and esteem of Germany as a co-guarantor of the general peace.
>
> For in this hour the German Government renews, before the German people and before the whole world, the assurance of its determination never to trespass the limit of guarding German honour and the freedom of the Reich, and especially of its determination to form, in the national German armament, not an instrument of military attack, but rather exclusively one for defence, and thus for maintaining the peace.
>
> In so doing, the German Reich Cabinet expresses the confident hope that the German people, which thus regains its honour, may be permitted, with independent equal right, to make its contribution to the pacification of the world in a free and open co-operation with the other nations and their governments.[36]

On 17 March, Hitler explained to G. Ward Price:

> One thing you must know: The German people do not want war. It simply wants equal rights for all—and that is all.[37]

Also in March, General Hermann Göring, the Reich Minister for Aviation, had these words to say about the budding Luftwaffe when he too was interviewed by G. Ward Price a week earlier:

> In the extension of our national defence, it was necessary, as we repeatedly told the world, to take care of defence in the air. As far as that is concerned I restricted myself to those measures absolutely necessary. The guiding line of my actions was, not the creation of an aggressive force which would threaten other nations, but merely the completion of a military aviation which would be strong enough to repel, at any time, attacks on Germany.

To G. Ward Price's inquiry about the hierarchy of the Luftwaffe, its uniforms, and its ranks, Göring replied:

> The Air Force is under the orders of the Reich Minister for Aviation who controls also civil aviation. His military rank is *General der Flieger* (General of the Airmen). The uniform remains similar to the uniform of the [civil] sport aviation organization but outwardly it will be marked clearly by military badges of rank. Similarly the names of rank correspond with the military designation of rank from Lieutenant upwards to General of the Airmen.

In closing, Göring once again laid emphasis on the fact that the Luftwaffe was a defensive tool to protect the Reich, and not an instrument of aggression:

> The German Air Force is just as passionately permeated with the will to defend the Fatherland to the last as it is convinced, on the other hand, that it will never be employed to threaten the peace of other nations.[38]

But in the end, despite Germany's violations of the Versailles Treaty, neither the British nor the French took any corrective measures other than to express their disapproval verbally, and on 25–26 March, the British Secretary of State for Foreign Affairs, Sir John Simon, and Foreign Affairs Minister Anthony Eden, were received by Hitler in Berlin for negotiations. To their consternation, Hitler divulged that the Luftwaffe was already equal in strength to the Royal Air Force.

At the Anglo–French–Italian Stresa Conference of 11–14 April 1935, attended by Ramsay MacDonald, Pierre Laval, and Benito Mussolini respectively, all three participants jointly censured the Reich for its rearmament policy. The objectives of the Stresa Agreement were threefold: continue to endorse the Locarno Treaties,[1*] collectively support Austrian sovereignty, and uphold the provisions of the Versailles Treaty prohibiting German rearmament.

---

1 * The Locarno Treaties negotiated in Switzerland between 5–16 October 1925 stipulated that the new borders established in Western Europe after the First World War would be respected and that future disagreements would be resolved by arbitration instead of armed conflict.

Although Hitler had assured France that Germany was no longer interested in Alsace–Lorraine, his revelation of German rearmament and introduction of compulsory military service prompted France to enter into a mutual assistance pact with the U.S.S.R. The Franco–Soviet Pact of Mutual Assistance was concluded on 2 May 1935, in Paris. The signatories were Pierre Laval, the French Minister for Foreign Affairs, and Vladimir Potemkin, the Soviet Ambassador to France. The opening preamble of the pact stated that both nations were motivated by a desire 'to consolidate peace in Europe and to guarantee its benefits to their respective countries by ensuring more completely the strict application of the provisions of the Covenant of the League of Nations, which aim at the maintenance of the national security, territorial integrity, and political independence of States ...' The first two articles stated that if either France or the Soviet Union were attacked, the other nation would immediately consult the aggrieved party and render aid:

> Article 1.
>
> In the event of France or the U.S.S.R. being threatened with, or in danger of, attack on the part of a European State, the U.S.S.R., and, reciprocally, France, undertake to proceed mutually to immediate consultation as regards the measures to be taken ...
>
> Article 2.
>
> In the event of France or the U.S.S.R. ... being the object ... of an unprovoked attack on the part of a European State, the U.S.S.R., and, reciprocally, France, shall immediately give each other aid and assistance.

The fifth article provided that the pact would 'come into force as soon as the ratifications had been exchanged'—this occurred in Moscow on 27 March 1936—and would 'remain in force for five years' thereafter, unless denounced by either side with a minimum of one year's notice.[39] But the reality was that the pact was of little value, and this was for two reasons: before either party could provide military assistance to the other, the aggrieved party was first obligated to submit notice to the League of Nations that it had been wrongfully attacked; and it was also first necessary to obtain the consent of the other three nations which had formally signed the Locarno Treaty[2*] in London on 1 December 1925: Great Britain, Italy, and Belgium.

2 * On 18 March 1936, Foreign Secretary Anthony Eden gave a concise description of the Locarno Treaty's purpose to the League Council. He said: 'What was the object of the Locarno Treaty? It was twofold. First, it aimed at preserving peace and, secondly, it aimed at creating international confidence by safeguarding the security of Western Europe.'[40]

A fortnight later, at Prague, the U.S.S.R. concluded yet another mutual assistance pact, this time with the Czechoslovak Republic. Its articles were almost identical to the Franco–Soviet pact. It was signed by President Edvard Beneš and Soviet Minister Serge Alexandrovsky. Unfortunately, it would not be long before the ineffectuality of these well-intentioned but inadequate mutual aid pacts against German aggression would be demonstrated.

Hitler delivered a major peace speech before the Reichstag on 21 May 1935 in order to alleviate any concerns German rearmament might cause around the world. As an expert propagandist, Hitler gave a speech that was moderate and reasonable, and it was remarkable how adroitly he was able to pull the wool over the eyes of the leaders of the Western Powers. According to Hitler, the German masses had appointed him as their 'representative' through the popular electoral process:

> Germany too has a 'democratic' constitution. The present German Government of the National Socialist State has also been elected by the people and feels itself in the same way responsible to the people....
> The German people has elected a single deputy as its representative with 38 million votes.... I feel myself just as responsible to the German people as would any Parliament. I act on the trust they have placed in me and I carry out their mandate.

Hitler talked very reasonably and persuasively about the senseless loss of life caused by warfare and how historically Europe's nations would have been wiser to focus their energies on tasks of construction instead of wholesale slaughter:

> The blood shed on the European Continent in the course of the last 300 years bears no proportion to the national results of the events. In the end France has remained France, Germany Germany, Poland Poland, and Italy Italy. What dynastic egoism, political passion, and patriotic blindness have attained in the way of apparently far-reaching political changes by shedding rivers of blood has, as regards national feeling, done no more than touched the skin of the nations. It has not substantially altered their fundamental characters. If these States had applied merely a fraction of their sacrifices to wiser purposes the success would certainly have been greater and more permanent....
>
> National Socialist Germany wants peace because of its fundamental convictions. And it wants peace also owing to the realization of the simple primitive fact that no war would be likely essentially to alter the distress of Europe. It would probably increase it....
>
> Germany needs peace and desires peace.

Hitler spoke of France and Poland, both with whom Germany shared a border, and re-emphasized Germany's sincere intentions towards them:

> Germany has solemnly recognized and guaranteed France her frontiers as determined after the Saar plebiscite. Without taking the past into account Germany has concluded a non-aggression pact with Poland. This is more than a valuable contribution to European peace, and we shall adhere to it unconditionally.... We did all this although we thereby finally renounced, for instance, all claims to Alsace–Lorraine, and land for which we have also fought two great wars. But we did it in particular to spare our own German nation a new and terrible sacrifice of lives. We are convinced that in doing so we are benefitting not only our own people, but also this frontier territory. We are prepared to do everything on our part to arrive at a true peace and a real friendship with the French nation. With the understanding and heartfelt friendship of genuine nationalists, we recognize Poland as the home of a great and nationally conscious people.

Hitler also cautioned the European community against the perils of Communism. This destructive ideology, which was 'diametrically opposed' to that of National Socialism, was to be ardently opposed at every turn. 'Bolshevism', Hitler warned, advocated 'the constitution of a world empire and only recognizes sections of a central International.' To this Hitler added:

> Both we National Socialists and the Bolshevists are convinced that there is a gulf between us which can never be bridged....
>
> Insofar as Bolshevism can be considered a purely Russian affair we have no interest in it whatever. Every nation must seek its salvation in its own way. So far as Bolshevism draws Germany within its range, however, we are its deadliest and most fanatical enemies....

Hitler addressed the concerns of prominent foreign statesmen throughout Western Europe to the Reich's new rearmament policy. However, he announced that Germany rejected the resolution adopted by the Council of the League of Nations at Geneva on 17 March 1935:

> 1. The German Government rejects the Geneva resolution of 17 March. It was not Germany which unilaterally broke the Versailles Treaty. The Versailles Dictate was unilaterally broken, and thereby rendered invalid as regard the points at issue, by those Powers who could not decide to carry out in their turn the disarmament which was imposed on Germany and which should have followed in their case by virtue of the Treaty.

> The new discrimination introduced at Geneva makes it impossible for the German Government to return to that institution until the preconditions for a real legal equality of all members has been established. For this purpose the German Government considers it necessary to make a clear separation between the Treaty of Versailles, which was based on a classification of the nations into victors and vanquished, and the League of Nations, which must be constituted on the basis of equal valuation and equality of rights for all the members. This equality must be extended to all functions and all property rights in international life.
>
> 2. The German Government, consequent on the failure of the other States to fulfill their disarmament obligations, has on its part renounced those articles of the Versailles Treaty which, because of the one-sided burden this laid on Germany contrary to the provisions of the Treaty, have constituted a discrimination against Germany for an unlimited period of time.

Hitler further specifically pledged that the German Government would 'unconditionally respect' the non-military articles of the Versailles Treaty, 'including the territorial provisions'; the German Government would 'uphold and fulfill all obligations arising out of the Locarno Treaty' so long as its other signatories would likewise do so; and the German Government would continue 'respecting the demilitarized zone'. Also, the Reich was prepared to abide by any terms restricting the production of armaments so long as Europe's other nations were bound by the same restrictions:

> 8. The German Government has announced the extent of the expansion of the new German Defence Force [Wehrmacht]. Under no circumstances will it depart from this. It does not regard the fulfillment of its program in the air, on land, or at sea, as constituting a menace to any nation. It is ready at any time to limit its armaments to any degree that is also adopted by the other Powers.
>
> The German Government has already spontaneously made known the definite limitations of its intentions, thereby giving the best evidence of its good will to avoid an unlimited armaments race. Its limitation of the German air armaments to parity with the individual Great Powers of the West makes it possible at any time to fix a maximum which Germany will be under a binding obligation to observe with the other nations.

Hitler also stated that Germany would be satisfied with possessing an air force on par with Britain and restricting its naval forces to thirty-five per cent of the Royal Navy:

> The limitation of the German Navy is placed at thirty-five per cent of the British Navy ... For Germany this demand is final and abiding.

Hitler ended his peroration with an expression of good will. Although his words were, of course, disingenuous, at the time they made an extremely positive impression on his listeners at home and abroad, particularly in England. He solemnly declaimed:

> Whoever lights the torch of war in Europe can wish for nothing but chaos. We, however, live in the firm conviction that in our time will be fulfilled, not the decline but the renaissance of the West. That Germany may make an imperishable contribution to this great work is our proud hope and our unshakable belief.[41]

Few could resist the appeal of Hitler's compelling, eloquent speech. Virtually everyone who heard it was profoundly struck by the ring of sincerity it conveyed, and the British were greatly affected by it.

21 May was also the day Germany passed 'The Reich Defence Law' (see Appendix B). Signed by Hitler, War Minister Werner von Blomberg, and Interior Minister Wilhelm Frick, it was divided into three parts. Part I stipulated that Hitler would be empowered to 'declare a state of defence for the area of the Reich' in the event of war; Part II provided that Hitler had the authority to order mobilization if hostilities with a foreign power were inevitable; and Part III warned that anyone who acted 'in violation of a decree issued by authority of this law' would be punished with incarceration, a fine, or both.[42]

At this time Hitler's admiration for the British Empire was considerable. He still sought an alliance with England, and he wished to reach an understanding that would allow him to acquire *Lebensraum* unfettered. In an attempt to improve German–British relations, Hitler authorized Joachim von Ribbentrop, then Ambassador-Plenipotentiary at Large, to fly to London. He arrived on 2 June, and diplomatic talks commenced two days later. On 18 June, the Anglo–German Naval Agreement (see Appendix C) was ratified, but not before Ribbentrop threatened to withdraw the entire German delegation from London if the German terms were not accepted in full. In spite of this gross diplomatic blunder, Ribbentrop's mission was successful. The terms of the naval agreement specified that, per the suggestion made by Hitler during his peace speech of 21 May, Germany would henceforth be permitted to enlarge its navy—but only up to a maximum of thirty-five per cent of British naval forces. It was Samuel Hoare, the British Foreign Secretary, who formally informed Ribbentrop in a note that the latter's proposal to permit Germany to possess such a fleet had been approved by the British Government:

> I have now much pleasure in notifying Your Excellency of the formal acceptance by His Majesty's Government in the United Kingdom of the proposal of the German Government discussed at those conversations that the future strength of the German Navy in relation to the aggregate naval strength of the Members of the British Commonwealth of Nations should be in the proportion of 35:100....
>
> (*a*) The ratio 35:100 is to be a permanent relationship, i.e., the total tonnage of the German fleet shall never exceed a percentage of 35 of the aggregate tonnage of the naval forces, as defined by treaty, of the Members of the British Commonwealth of Nations ...
>
> (*c*) Germany will adhere to the ratio 35:100 in all circumstances ...[43]

When Hitler learned of the British Government's decision, he was convinced that a new era of Anglo–German collaboration had begun. Overjoyed, he declared that 18 June was 'the happiest day of his life'.[44]

Britain's leaders felt that the new concord restricting the total naval tonnage of the German Kriegsmarine was a key step in preserving a long-lasting European peace. But the Italians and the French were not of the same opinion, since the British had not bothered to check with them beforehand. They were appalled. In their eyes it was a gross violation of the Versailles Treaty and amounted to express British approval for the Germans to considerably increase the strength of their navy. Moreover, the Anglo–German Naval Agreement had the twofold effect of shaking the stability of the British–French–Italian coalition and emboldening the Germans. It was unlike the Stresa Conference of 11–14 April, where British, French, and Italian leaders had been united in their position against German rearmament. To the chagrin of the French and Italians, this time around the British had (as the Poles did before them in 1934) acted independently and concluded an ill-advised, separate deal with the Reich. This was especially egregious because less than five months earlier, at a summit meeting in London between British Prime Minister MacDonald and French Premier Laval, both sides had pledged to deal jointly on issues concerning German armaments.

But on 3 October, the attention of the Western Powers abruptly switched from German rearmament to Italian aggression when the Italians invaded Ethiopia. Italian forces under the commands of Marshal Emilio De Bono and General Rodolfo Graziani crossed into Ethiopia from Italian Eritrea and Italian Somaliland respectively. They made rapid progress. Italy's Ethiopian campaign seriously undermined the authority and credibility of the League of Nations. And in the end, the League's condemnation of Italian aggression and imposition of economic sanctions on raw materials, arms, and loans in November made little difference.

Just a few days before the Italian adventure, Churchill addressed a gathering of notables at London's Carlton Club. In his speech, he gave a few words of caution to the Italian dictator:

> To cast an army of nearly a quarter of a million men, embodying the flower of Italian manhood, upon a barren shore two thousand miles from home, against the good will of the whole world and without command of the sea, and then in this position embark upon what may well be a series of campaigns against a people and in regions which no conqueror in four thousand years ever thought it worthwhile to subdue, is to give hostages to fortune unparalleled in all history.[45]

On 2 October, the day before the invasion, Mussolini made a patriotic speech in Rome. He began by exalting Fascist unity:

> Blackshirts of revolution, men and women of all Italy, Italians all over the world, beyond the mountains, beyond the seas, listen. A solemn hour is about to strike in the history of the country. Twenty million Italians are at this moment gathered in the squares of all Italy. It is the greatest demonstration that human history records. Twenty millions, one heart alone, one will alone, one decision.
>
> This manifestation signifies that the tie between Italy and Fascism is perfect, absolute, unalterable. Only brains softened by puerile illusions, by sheer ignorance, can think differently, because they do not know what exactly is the Fascist Italy of 1935.
>
> For many months the wheel of destiny and of the impulse of our calm determination moves towards the goal. In these last hours the rhythm has increased and nothing can stop it now.
>
> It is not only an army marching towards its goal, but it is forty-four million Italians marching in unity behind this army. Because the blackest of injustices is being attempted against them, that of taking from them their place in the sun. When in 1915 Italy threw in her fate with that of the Allies, how many cries of admiration, how many promises were heard? But after the common victory, which cost Italy six hundred thousand dead, four hundred thousand lost, one million wounded, when peace was being discussed around the table only the crumbs of a rich colonial booty were left for us to pick up. For thirteen years we have been patient while the circle tightened around us at the hands of those who wish to suffocate us.
>
> We have been patient with Ethiopia for forty years. It is enough now.

Mussolini criticized the League of Nations for having the effrontery to threaten Italy with paltry punitive measures, and dismissed the prospect of any armed Anglo–French intervention. He also took a gibe at Ethiopia, asserting contemptuously that it had no place amidst modern countries:

> The League of Nations instead of recognizing the rights of Italy dares talk of sanctions, but until there is proof to the contrary I refuse to believe that the authentic people of France will join in supporting sanctions against Italy. Six hundred thousand dead whose devotion was so heroic that the enemy commander justly admired them—those fallen would now turn in their graves.
>
> And until there is proof to the contrary, I refuse to believe that the authentic people of Britain will want to spill blood and send Europe into a catastrophe for the sake of a barbarian country, unworthy of ranking among civilized nations. Nevertheless, we cannot afford to overlook the possible developments of tomorrow.
>
> To economic sanctions, we shall answer with our discipline, our spirit of sacrifice, our obedience. To military sanctions, we shall answer with military measures. To acts of war, we shall answer with acts of war.

Mussolini promised to do all he could to prevent the Ethiopian campaign from transforming into a conflict of continental proportions:

> A people worthy of their past and their name cannot and never will take a different stand. Let me repeat, in the most categorical manner, that the sacred pledge which I make at this moment before all the Italians gathered together today, is that I shall do everything in my power to prevent a colonial conflict from taking on the aspect and weight of a European war.

And lastly Mussolini extolled Italy, a great cultured nation renowned worldwide for its innumerable contributions to mankind:

> This conflict may be attractive to certain minds which hope to avenge their disintegrated temples through this new catastrophe. Never, as at this historical hour, have the people of Italy revealed such force of character, and it is against this people to which mankind owes its greatest conquest, this people of heroes, of poets and saints, of navigators, of colonizers, that the world dares threaten sanctions.
>
> Italy! Italy! Entirely and universally Fascist! The Italy of the Blackshirt revolution, rise to your feet, let the cry of your determination rise to the skies and reach our soldiers in East Africa. Let it be a comfort to those

> who are about to fight. Let it be an encouragement to our friends and a warning to our enemies. It is the cry of Italy which goes beyond the mountains and the seas out into the great world. It is the cry of justice and of victory.[46]

As of November, Marshal Pietro Badoglio headed the invasion. He initiated (with Mussolini's permission) the aerial bombardment of helpless civilians and medical installations, and the use of deadly chemical agents, including mustard gas. And on 28 December, Mussolini transmitted a message to Badoglio authorizing him to employ against the Ethiopian combatants both poison gas and flamethrowers.

While the Italo–Ethiopian conflict raged on, the Reich did not endorse or take part in the punitive economic measures taken by the League of Nations against Italy's imperialist designs. Germany instead remained neutral. Foreign Secretary Eden was in favour of adopting oil sanctions against Italy and put forth a proposal to this effect on 2 March 1936. An oil stoppage would have gravely impacted Italy's modern, mechanized forces and perhaps even forced the Italians to put an early end to their colonial campaign. But for such a scheme to have worked, it would have been necessary for the United States, a non-member of the League, to participate in the oil embargo as well. In any event, the British and French Governments were strongly opposed to Eden's initiative. As for Mussolini, he had nothing but contempt for the foppish Eden, at one point describing the dapper Englishman as 'the best-dressed fool in Europe'.

Mussolini felt extremely antagonized by the League's actions against Italy. He became disaffected from the British and French and decided instead to turn towards a new potential ally, Nazi Germany. Italo–German relations had been at a low ebb for years, particularly since the failed July *Putsch* of 1934 in Austria. But in 1936, Italo–German relations were to change significantly—for the better. The balance of power in Europe was to shift dramatically as a result. Mussolini desired to effect some kind of reconciliation with Germany. Accordingly, on 7 January 1936, Mussolini informed a stunned Ulrich von Hassell, Germany's Ambassador to Italy, that he now wished to put Austria in a position where she would be compelled to pursue a foreign policy that would be in alignment with that of Germany. Hassell's recollection of the conversation was recorded in a telegram:

> Since we [the Germans] had always declared that we did not wish to infringe Austria's independence, the simplest method would be for Berlin and Vienna themselves to settle their relations on the basis of an Austrian independence, e.g., in the form of a treaty of friendship with a non-

> aggression pact, which would in practice bring Austria into Germany's wake, so that she could pursue no other foreign policy than one parallel with that of Germany. If Austria, as a formally quite independent State, were thus in practice to become a German satellite, he [Mussolini] would have no objection. He saw in this great advantages for Germany as well as for Italy, in that Germany, as already stated, would acquire a reliable satellite, while at the same time German–Italian mistrust would be eliminated and all Danubian Pact machinations frustrated. Should this not come about, then it was to be feared that Austria, who was beginning to doubt Italy's ability to help her at the decisive moment, would be driven to side with Czechoslovakia and thus with France.[47]

During another talk with Hassell, Mussolini informed him that he deemed the Anglo–French–Italian coalition of the Stresa Conference 'dead'. He further asserted that if Germany were to contravene the terms of the Locarno Pact, Italy would do nothing to support Britain and France. This was precisely what Nazi politicians wished to hear, especially Hitler. By formally acknowledging Nazi Germany's interest in Austria as being legitimate, Mussolini had removed the main barrier between them. However, at first German officials were unsure if Mussolini's new attitude was sincere, for such a *volte-face* seemed too good to be true. In light of this new development, Hitler dispatched his personal lawyer, Hans Frank, to Rome. Frank delivered to Mussolini a missive expressing Hitler's personal approval of Italy's Ethiopian campaign and Mussolini's anti-Bolshevik convictions. After this the discord between the Nazi and Fascist nations abated.

Italian forces inevitably crushed determined but unsuccessful Ethiopian resistance and seized Addis Ababa in early May 1936. King Haile Selassie was forced into exile, and Mussolini proclaimed Ethiopia an Italian province with King Victor Emmanuel III its new Emperor. Germany officially recognized Italian Ethiopia in October 1936, which Mussolini did not fail to appreciate. The British, however, did not officially recognize the Italian conquest of Ethiopia until April 1938; the French, not until October 1938. The sanctions imposed on Italy by the League of Nations ceased as of 15 July; the League had elected to discontinue them eleven days before. In 1938, Mussolini criticized the League of Nations' impotence with a cynically astute observation: 'The League is very well when sparrows [small countries] shout, but no good at all when eagles [Major Powers] fall out.'

On 21 February, Hitler was interviewed by Bertrand de Jouvenel on behalf of the *Paris-Midi*, a French daily newspaper. Jouvenel was a celebrated young French writer. During the conversation, Hitler vowed that he wanted 'to prove to my people that the idea of hereditary enmity between France and Germany is an absurdity'. Hitler added: 'The German people have understood this. I have been successful in a far more difficult task of reconciliation, the reconciliation of Germany and Poland.' After these placatory words by Hitler, Jouvenel broached the subject of Hitler's numerous declarations of peace:

> DE JOUVENEL: We Frenchmen certainly read your declarations of peace with great pleasure, but we are nevertheless disturbed on account of other, less encouraging things. For instance, you have said very bad things about France in your book *Mein Kampf*. Now, this book is regarded throughout Germany as a kind of political Bible. It is sold without the successive editions being in any way subjected to revision as regards the passages dealing with France.
>
> HITLER: When I wrote this book, I was in prison. It was the time when the French troops were occupying the Ruhr. It was at the moment of greatest tension between our two countries ... Yes, we were enemies, and I stood for my country, as is fitting, against yours; just as I stood for my country for four and a half years in the trenches. I should despise myself if I were not first of all a German in the moment of a conflict. But today there is no longer any cause for a conflict. You want me to correct my book, like a man of letters bringing out a new and revised edition of his works. But I am not a man of letters. I am a politician. I undertake my corrections in my foreign policy, which aims at an understanding with France. If I succeed in bring about the Franco–German *rapprochement*, that will be a correction which will be worthy to be made. I enter my corrections in the great book of history![48]

Next it was the Germans' turn for a *fait accompli*. On the morning of 7 March 1936, German soldiers marched into the Rhineland. Three Wehrmacht battalions crossed the Rhine River into the demilitarized zone. However, German forces had been ordered to withdraw immediately if the large French Army intervened. The German troops, some 32,000 men armed with rifles, were utterly outclassed and outnumbered by powerful French forces comprising one hundred divisions. The reoccupation of the Rhineland, known as *Unternehmen Weserübung* ('Operation Winter Exercise'), was in direct breach of Section III, Articles 42 and 43, of the Versailles Treaty:

> Article 42
>
> Germany is forbidden to maintain or construct any fortifications either on the left bank of the Rhine or on the right bank to the west of a line drawn fifty kilometres to the East of the Rhine.

> Article 43
>
> In the area defined above the maintenance and the assembly of armed forces, either permanently or temporarily, and military manoeuvres of any kind, as well as the upkeep of all permanent works for mobilization, are in the same way forbidden.

Article 44 went on to say that if Germany breached the terms of Articles 42 and 43, then Germany would 'be regarded as committing a hostile act against the Powers signatory of the present Treaty and as calculated to disturb the peace of the world'.[49]

The reoccupation of the Rhineland was also in contravention of the first two articles of the Locarno Pact of 16 October 1925:

> Article 1
>
> The High Contracting Parties [Belgium, France, Germany, Great Britain, and Italy] collectively and severally guarantee, in the manner provided in the following Articles, the maintenance of the territorial *status quo* resulting from the frontiers between Germany and Belgium and between Germany and France, and the inviolability of the said frontiers as fixed by or in pursuance of the Treaty of Peace signed at Versailles on 28 June 1919, and also the observance of the stipulations of Articles 42 and 43 of the said treaty concerning the demilitarized zone.
>
> Article 2
>
> Germany and Belgium, and also Germany and France, mutually undertake that they will in no case attack or invade each other or resort to war against each other.
>
> This stipulation shall not, however, apply in the case of:
>
> 1. The exercise of the right of legitimate defence, that is to say, resistance to a violation of the undertaking contained in the previous paragraph or to a flagrant breach of Articles 42 or 43 of the said Treaty of Versailles, if such breach constitutes an unprovoked act of aggression and by reason of the assembly of armed forces in the demilitarized zone immediate action is necessary.[50]

Although the argument could be made that Germany had been coerced into signing the Versailles Treaty, the same could not be said of the Locarno Pact, for Germany had entered into it voluntarily. To the House of Commons on 9 March, Eden expounded:

> The course taken by the German Government in unilaterally repudiating obligations into which they have freely entered, and in simultaneously

> acting as if they did not exist, both complicates and aggravates the international situation. The abrogation of the Locarno Treaty and the occupation of the demilitarized zone have profoundly shaken confidence in any engagement into which the Government of Germany may in future enter. There can be no one in this House or this country who would wish to condone or excuse such a step. It strikes a severe blow at that principle of the sanctity of Treaties which underlies the whole structure of international relations.[51]

And a little over a fortnight later, Eden remarked:

> We have heard much, more particularly since the advent of the present régime in Germany, about the *Diktat* of Versailles, but nobody has ever heard of the *Diktat* of Locarno.[52]

On 7 March, Hitler announced that Germany had dispatched a token number of its armed forces into the Rhineland in view of the fact that the Locarno Pact was void. In a speech before his Reichstag deputies, he began by speaking of the late Great War era and American President Woodrow Wilson's fourteen points outlining the prerequisites for long-term peace:

> It [Germany] had the honour to be compelled to fight against a world in arms and the misfortune to have lost the struggle. As a vanquished foe, the blame for the responsibility of the struggle was laid on the shoulder of the German people although they had never wished or looked forward to the war or desired it. The Germans believed in those 14 points with all the force of a people who were in despair both in regard to themselves and the world at large.... For many years past we all have been the victims of this fantastic belief and therewith have been the objects of its terrible consequences. It is not within the scope of my explanations here to describe the terrible disillusion that came upon our people in ever increasing measure. I will not speak of the despair and the suffering and the misery which those years brought upon the German people and upon us. We had been dragged into a war for the outbreak of which we were no more guilty or innocent than the other nations.

Hitler then briefly described the modern-day armaments race and alluded to the worldwide instability of the present era:

> In each year that has gone by since then [the First World War] we hear the rattle of weapons rather than the bells of peace sounding throughout the world.... History will one day record that since the end of the Great War

> the Earth has been a prey to mental, political, and economic revolutions such as usually occur only once in a thousand years …[53]

And in a memorandum intended for the other signatories of the Locarno Pact—also dated 7 March—Hitler justified his brazen action by claiming that France, instead of accepting Germany's sincere overtures, preferred to take up a policy of encirclement targeting Germany. This was demonstrated, Hitler averred, by the recent ratification of the Franco–Soviet Mutual Assistance Pact by the French Government in February 1936:

> The repeatedly friendly offers and peaceful assurances of Germany have been met by France with a military pact with the Soviet Union exclusively directed against Germany and in violation of the Locarno Pact.

Consequently, Hitler denounced the Locarno Pact:

> The Locarno Pact has thereby lost its significance and practically ceased to be. Germany regards herself, therefore, as no longer bound by this extinct pact.

He next stated that the Franco–Soviet Mutual Assistance Pact, and the subsequent Soviet–Czechoslovak Pact, endangered Germany's security. The Reich was therefore (according to Hitler) fully within its rights to reoccupy the Rhineland as a precautionary step:

> The German Government are now compelled to meet the new situation created by this pact, a situation which is aggravated by the fact that the Franco–Soviet Pact is amplified by an exactly parallel treaty of alliance between Czechoslovakia and Soviet Russia. In the interests of the natural right of a nation to protect its frontiers and preserve its means of defence, the German Government have therefore restored once more, as from today, the full and unrestricted sovereignty of the Reich in the demilitarized zone of the Rhineland.

Hitler further asserted that:

1. Germany was prepared to be re-admitted to the League of Nations on an equal basis;

2. Germany was prepared to sign non-aggression pacts of a twenty-five-year duration with both France and Belgium;

3. Germany was also prepared to conclude non-aggression pacts with all neighbouring States, including Lithuania;

4. Germany was prepared to set up demilitarized zones with France and Belgium, providing they were willing to do likewise; and

5. Germany was in favour of establishing among the Major Powers a Western European air defence pact in which they would collectively bombard the lands of any rogue nation seeking to invade or attack the others. He concluded with two emphatic assurances, the first regarding German honour and the second concerning the Reich's peaceful intentions:

> First, we swear an oath that we will yield before no power and before no coercion in our determination to restore the honour of our nation. And we swear to succumb with honour to the gravest distress rather than capitulate before it.
>
> And, secondly, we proclaim now more than ever before our wish to further the cause of mutual understanding between the nations of Europe and particularly an understanding among our western nations and neighbours.[54]

Hitler had ordered the operation on his own initiative and had disregarded the dire warnings of his top generals that the risk was too great, most notably those of Field Marshal Blomberg. But as it turned out, Hitler's daring gambit had succeeded, for there had been no active opposition from any quarter. Despite the fact that the British and French were obliged to enforce the provisions of the Versailles Treaty and the Locarno Pact, both had failed to honour their commitments. The reality was that the French Government and their military chiefs were divided and reluctant to act, not least in part due to an internal economic crisis, but especially since the British were unwilling to aid them militarily. Had the French taken military action to expel the Germans from the Rhineland, not only could they have done so with relative ease, they could have marched onwards into Berlin and toppled the National Socialist régime. Hitler crowed:

> I know what I would have done, if I'd been the French; I should have struck and I would not have allowed a single German soldier to cross the Rhine.[55]

In spite of its success, however, the military venture had been extremely stressful for Hitler, particularly its aftermath. In private he confessed:

> The forty-eight hours after the march into the Rhineland were the most nerve-racking in my life. If the French had then marched into the Rhineland we would have had to withdraw with our tails between our legs, for the military resources at our disposal would have been wholly inadequate for even a moderate resistance.[56]

On 27 January 1942, Hitler boasted to his inner circle during a table-talk session how he had gambled everything on a bluff six years earlier and emerged a winner:

> What would have happened if anybody other than myself had been at the head of the Reich! Anyone you care to mention would have lost his nerve. I was obliged to lie, and what saved us was my unshakable obstinacy and my amazing aplomb. I threatened unless the situation eased to send six extra divisions into the Rhineland. The truth was, I only had four brigades. Next day, the English papers wrote that there had been an easing of the situation.[57]

To the rest of the world, which had awaited developments with bated breath, it was evident that the resolve of the British and French had deteriorated. The British were largely indifferent. No less a personage than Lord Lothian made the following comment:

> After all, they [the Germans] are only going back into their own back-garden.[58]

But Anthony Eden strongly disapproved. In a statement to the League Council on 18 March, he reiterated on behalf of the British Government the opinion that the Versailles Treaty had unquestionably been violated:

> I have already stated before the Council the view of His Majesty's Government in the United Kingdom that a patent and incontestable breach of the provisions of the Treaty of Versailles relating to the demilitarized zone [Articles 42 and 43] has been committed.[59]

Belgium withdrew from the Locarno Pact and thereafter chose to remain neutral in European affairs. It was the last time the Western Powers were in a position to curb German expansionism without a major armed conflict. But this would no longer be possible, for now Hitler had effectively reinforced Germany's flanks. The German–Polish Non-Aggression Pact served to protect Germany's eastern border, and the construction of the West Wall, the German version of the French Maginot Line conceived in

1936, began in 1938. The 390-mile line of defensive fortifications was to run along the Reich's western frontier, safeguarding it from France and the Low Countries.

On 9 March, Hitler once more granted British correspondent G. Ward Price an interview. The latter wished to know, now that Germany had reoccupied the Rhineland, if Hitler intended to reduce the strength of his forces in the area to eliminate the possibility of there being any German aggression towards France:

> PRICE: Now that the Führer has reclaimed total sovereignty over the entire German territory, is he willing to restrict the forces deployed in the Rhineland to a number that would preclude any offensive actions directed against France on the part of Germany?
>
> HITLER: It was not our intention to commit an act of aggression against France as we occupied the so-called 'demilitarized' zone....
>
> The area is merely being furnished with garrisons to protect its freedom precisely as in the other parts of the Reich—no more and no less! There cannot be any talk of massing troops along the border for offensive purposes because:
>
> a) Germany no longer has anything to demand of France and it will not demand anything anymore;
>
> b) Germany itself has called for the establishment of non-aggression pacts, expressing the desire that England and Italy might become signatory powers and guarantors of these agreements;
>
> c) massing troops along the border would be unnecessary from a military point of view and, as a matter of fact, it would be senseless!
>
> Moreover, we want to create a future in which these two countries no longer feel threatened by one another. When [French Interior Minister] M. [Albert] Sarraut declares that he cannot support the sight of German cannons threatening the Strasbourg fortress, it ought to be quite obvious that we too cannot support the sight of French fortress cannons threatening our open cities Frankfurt, Freiburg, Karlsruhe, etc. Such a sense of threat could be prevented by finding a mutual solution to the question of the 'demilitarized' zone.[60]

On 24 March, Ambassador Ribbentrop was also interviewed by G. Ward Price. He made the following statements concerning Germany's rights, her peaceful intentions, and the Rhineland affair:

> I can assure you that the German nation will no longer tolerate this Versailles spirit [i.e. the notion that European countries should be divided into two groups, the victors and the vanquished]. It will submit no longer to any discrimination in the matter of its rights between Germany and other nations. The world must understand that all that kind of thing is over and done with.
>
> It follows, therefore, that the German Government will never accept any one-sided limitation of its sovereign rights within its own frontiers....
>
> I believe that the day will come when it is universally recognized that the step taken by the German Government in reoccupying the Rhineland was a definite advance towards the consolidation of Europe.
>
> I base these claims upon the following arguments:
>
> (1) Quite apart from the fact that it is and must be intolerable for any nation not to be master in its own house, it was impossible, after the conclusion of an anti-German military alliance between France and Russia, to leave the densely populated western provinces of Germany any longer without military protection.
>
> (2) Previous experience had taught us that it was quite useless to hope that an agreement about the restoration of German sovereignty in the Rhineland might be reached by way of negotiations.
>
> (3) Is it conceivable that the mere restoration of full sovereignty in any one country should prevent the consolidation of peace in a whole continent?
>
> The German Government therefore believes that its actions in reoccupying the Rhineland on 7 March has opened the way to negotiations for a lasting peace because such negotiations can succeed only if they are carried on between equal and free peoples.[61]

A plebiscite held on 29 March inquired of the German electorate if they approved of the remilitarization of the Rhineland. Voter turnout was extremely high at 99 per cent; 45,001,489 out of 45,453,691 qualified voters went to the polls. The official figures were: positive—44,461,278 (98.8 per cent); negative or invalid—540,211 (1.2 per cent).[62] Hitler's popularity soared throughout the Reich after the Rhineland *coup*, and its success emboldened him. He began to regard himself as infallible. In a Munich speech on 14 March, before 300,000 frenzied Bavarians, he proclaimed:

> Neither threats nor warnings will prevent me from going my way. I follow the path assigned to me by Providence with the instinctive

> sureness of a sleepwalker. My destination is the peace rooted in the equal rights of the nations. We are one of Europe's major powers and wish to be respected as a major power.[63]

In a preface to a collection of historical documents concerning Locarno written on 19 May 1936, Ribbentrop criticized the Locarno Treaty by pointing out that it had not achieved its intended results; namely, disarmament in Europe. Instead, the Western Powers continued to increase in strength while the Reich, Ribbentrop claimed, remained vulnerable. Only when Germany reintroduced military conscription and rearmed of her own volition was the European balance of power restored:

> The demilitarization of the Rhineland [in 1919 per the Versailles Treaty] should by the Locarno Treaty [of 1925] have resulted in the disarmament of Europe, which was an obligation undertaken by those party to the treaty. The demilitarization of the Rhineland need not have represented a serious weakening of German security if Europe had shown its peaceful intentions by completely disarming. It was a faith in this possibility which explains and justifies the German acceptance of a completely undefended Rhineland zone.
>
> Unfortunately, just the opposite occurred. Instead of France and Europe disarming, the armies surrounding a defenceless and disarmed Germany, equipped with the most modern weapons grew stronger and stronger and not until Germany restored her own military sovereignty was the military equilibrium in Europe re-established.

Ribbentrop also touched on the German reoccupation of the Rhineland. He opined that the Reich was fully justified in doing so in order to safeguard its territorial integrity:

> On 7th March Germany in her geographically exposed position in the heart of Europe, confronted by a powerful military coalition did no more than claim the most primitive prerogative of every nation namely that of securing and defending her own frontiers.[64]

On 11 July, the German and Austrian Governments entered into an agreement designed to reduce the political friction between them and restore 'relations of a normal and friendly character' thereby. Known as the July Agreement, it was drafted by Austrian Chancellor Kurt von Schuschnigg and German Ambassador Franz von Papen, and its provisions met with Hitler's approval. The new *détente* between Germany and Austria also reassured Mussolini. In the agreement, Germany promised to respect Austria's independence; the two nations would each refrain from interfering in the domestic affairs of the other; Austria would adopt a policy in congruity with that of Germany; and the Rome Protocols of 1934—along with Austria's relations with Italy and Hungary—would remain unchanged:

*Austro–German Agreement of 11 July 1936*

1. The German Government recognizes the full sovereignty of the Federate State of Austria in the spirit of the pronouncements of the German Führer and Chancellor of 21 May 1935.

2. Each of the two Governments regards the inner political order (including the question of Austrian National Socialism) obtaining in the other country as an internal concern of that country, upon which it will exercise neither direct nor indirect influence.
The Austrian Federal Government will constantly follow in its policy in general, and in particular towards Germany, a line in conformity with leading principles corresponding to the fact that Austria regards herself as a German State.
By such a decision neither the Rome Protocols of 1934 and their additions of 1936, nor the relationship of Austria to Italy and Hungary as partners in these protocols, are affected. Considering that the *détente* desired by both sides cannot become a reality unless certain preliminary conditions are fulfilled by the Governments of both countries, the Austrian Federal Government and the German Government will pass a number of special measures to bring about the requisite preliminary state of affairs.[65]

Also, Austrian National Socialists, as members of the 'National Opposition', would be permitted to become part of the Austrian Government, and those imprisoned for their political activities would be released.

Just six days after the July Agreement was signed, civil war erupted in Spain. General Francisco Franco, leader of the Nationalists, was determined to oust the leftist Spanish Republican Government. He intended to replace it with a Fascist government, with himself as military dictator. Soon after the civil war began, Germany and Italy sent military aid to Spain in support of Franco. Germany sent the Condor Legion, an aerial unit headed by Luftwaffe commander Hugo Sperrle. Italy's contributions were greater. She sent two expeditionary units, the *Aviazione Legionaria* (Legionary Air Force) and the *Corpo Truppe Volontarie* (Corps of Volunteer Troops). Luftwaffe chief Göring was very much in favour of assisting the Spanish Fascists. As a leading National Socialist his *prima facie* reason was to halt the expansion of Communism, but he also had a personal motive: he wanted to test the proficiency of his new air force in battle. On 14 March 1946, at his post-war trial at Nuremberg, Göring shed some light on the matter:

> When the civil war broke out in Spain, Franco sent a call for help to Germany and asked for support, particularly in the air. One should not forget that Franco with his troops was stationed in Africa and he could not get the troops across, as the fleet was in the hands of the Communists, or, as they called themselves at the time, the competent Revolutionary Government in Spain. The decisive factor was, first of all, to get his troops over to Spain.
>
> The Führer thought the matter over. I urged him to give support under all circumstances; firstly, in order to prevent the further spread of Communism in that theatre and, secondly, to test my young Luftwaffe at this opportunity in this or that technical respect.[66]

Not unexpectedly, the U.S.S.R. sided with the left-wing Republican Government and provided it with ordnance, planes, and tanks. International Brigades also fought for the Republican side. These were anti-Fascist paramilitary forces of many nationalities, composed of socialists, communists, radicals, and anarchists. At the same time, the British Government vigorously advocated neutrality. As for France, she presently shared a border with two Fascist nations, Italy and Germany. To share another with a Fascist Spain would be a most unwelcome development, as democratic France would then be surrounded by a hostile Fascist bloc. What made the situation even worse was the fact that France was politically divided. The French Government, headed by socialist Prime Minister Léon Blum, supported the Spanish Republic. Meanwhile, French rightist elements backed Franco's Nationalists. This kind of domestic disunity in France and elsewhere fit precisely into Hitler's agenda.

Throughout the Spanish Civil War, the British and French made ongoing attempts to prevent interference in Spain's internal affairs, but to no avail. They recognized the Francoist régime as of 27 February 1939. The Spanish Civil War lasted nearly three years. The internecine conflict was characterized by brutality and atrocities on both sides, with over half a million fatalities. The Nationalists captured Barcelona and Madrid in the final months of the war (January and March 1939 respectively), and Franco emerged victorious on 1 April 1939. Spain became a one-party police state, with Franco as Caudillo (Leader).

The direct intervention of Germany and Italy in the Spanish Civil War made them appear dynamic in the eyes of the European community—much more so than the Western democracies. Germany benefitted considerably from her contribution to the Spanish Civil War. And for the new generation of recently conscripted German soldiers, it was their first exposure to actual warfare. But undoubtedly the greatest gain for Germany was political in nature: closer ties with Italy. Although Britain and France sought to bring Italy back into the fold after sanctions had been abandoned by the League of Nations, it was too little, too late. And the mutual aims of Fascist Italy and Nazi Germany in connection with Spain solidified their bond even further.

In his Milan speech of 1 November 1936, Mussolini made denigrating references to the 'great shipwreck' of 'Wilsonian ideology'. He disparaged the 'illusion' of disarmament, which he described as 'impossible and absurd'; the 'illusion' of collective security, which 'never existed, does not exist, and will never exist'; the 'platitude' of invisible peace, which was 'necessary to reject'; the 'absurdity' of the League of Nations, which as far as the Fascists were concerned, could 'perish in peace'; and the 'diabolical' application of sanctions 'against the people of Italy ... men, women, and children'. It was during this speech that Mussolini, for the first time, used the term 'axis' in reference to the new Italo–German alliance. He proclaimed:

> The meetings at Berlin had as a result an understanding between two countries on definite problems, some of which are particularly troublesome these days. But these understandings which have been consecrated verbally and duly signed—this Berlin–Rome protocol is not a barrier. It is rather an axis around which all European States animated by a desire for peace may collaborate.[67]

By this Mussolini meant that Germany and Italy were the dominant nations of Europe and that Europe's other, lesser nations would rotate around them on an axis, subject to their will, like moons orbiting a planet.

In his 1925 manifesto, Hitler had specified that there were only two European nations with whom the Reich could align herself: England and Italy. Thus far, Hitler had managed to bring Italy into the fold. But despite the cajoling of Ribbentrop, Germany's new Ambassador to Britain as of August, and the Reich Government's endless vilification of Bolshevism—to which the British and French were understandably receptive—the British continued to resist Germany's efforts to entice them into a partnership.

As it turned out, Germany concluded a pact with the Japanese, rather than the British. On 25 November, German and Japanese plenipotentiaries Ribbentrop and Kintomo Mushakoji signed in Berlin the Anti-Comintern Pact (see Appendix D), an 'Agreement Against the Communist International'.

The bilateral concord was to all outwards appearances a preventative measure aimed against the Comintern[3*] yet was in actuality directed against the U.S.S.R. The preamble and first article of the Anti-Comintern Pact described its purpose. Germany and Japan were to confer with one another and work in concert against the Comintern's revolutionary agenda:

> The Government of the German Reich and the Imperial Japanese Government, recognizing that the aim of the Communist International, known as the Comintern, is to disintegrate and subdue existing States by all the means at its command, convinced that the toleration of interference by the Communist International in the internal affairs of the nations not only endangers their internal peace and social well-being, but is also a menace to the peace of the world, desirous of co-operating in the defence against Communist subversive activities, have agreed as follows:
>
> Article 1
>
> The High Contracting States agree to inform one another of the activities of the Communist International, to consult with one another on the necessary preventative measures, and to carry these through in close collaboration.

The second article of the pact invited 'third States whose internal peace is threatened by the subversive activities of the Communist International' to join. Consequently, two other Fascist nations, Spain and Italy, signed the pact on 6 November 1937. And the third article stipulated that the pact was to 'remain in force for a period of five years'.[69]

The ramifications of the Anti-Comintern Pact for the peoples of Europe could not have been more plain. It aligned the belligerent Axis Powers and imperilled those countries which were militarily feeble or neutral. And to further solidify his alliance with Japan, Hitler announced on 20 February 1938 that Germany officially recognized the Japanese puppet state of Manchukuo (Manchuria). The reason for this policy, Hitler explained, was to halt the spread of Bolshevism:

> I believe a Japanese defeat in the Far East would never be any good to Europe or America, but would exclusively benefit Bolshevist Soviet Russia.... In this connection the two States [Germany and Italy] with Japan represent the most formidable obstacle against the further advance of the Russian Bolshevik force.[70]

---

3 * The Comintern was a worldwide revolutionary organization. According to its revised Constitution, its program was 'to struggle with all means, even with weapon in hands, for the overthrow of the international bourgeoisie, and the creation of an International Soviet Republic'.[68]

On 26 February 1937, Hitler received Edmund Schulthess at the Reich Chancellery in Berlin for an interview. Schulthess had served as a member—and four times as President—of Switzerland's Federal Council between the years 1912 and 1935. To Schulthess Hitler remarked that Switzerland's 'continued existence' was 'a European necessity' and that the Germans sought 'to live as good neighbours on the best terms with her and to come to fair agreements on all matters'. Hitler also gave his assurance that no matter what the future held, the Reich would never breach Swiss neutrality:

> In my recent Reichstag speech [of 30 January 1937], when I spoke of the neutrality of two other countries [Belgium and Holland],[4*] I intentionally refrained from mentioning Switzerland because of the traditional neutrality which she practices and which has always been recognized by the Powers including ourselves, is in no way questioned. At all times, whatever may happen, we shall respect the inviolability and neutrality of Switzerland. I say this most definitely. I have never given cause for any other view.[72]

On 24 September 1937, Mussolini travelled to Germany for a highly-publicized and celebrated state visit. Along with an entourage of dozens, the Duce was accompanied by three of his top Fascist cronies: Foreign Minister Galeazzo Ciano, Press and Propaganda Minister Dino Alfieri, and Party Secretary Achille Starace. The occasion represented the 'unshakable' alliance of the Fascist and Nazi dictators and their combined peoples—some 115 million—against the 'decadent' democracies of the West and the Communist hordes of the East. Together, they would inaugurate a new era and establish a New Order on the Continent.

Mussolini's train reached Munich at midmorning on 25 September. He was warmly welcomed by Hitler and numerous leading Nazi officials, most notably Reichsführer-S.S. Heinrich Himmler and Propaganda Minister Dr. Joseph Goebbels. Indulging Mussolini's vanity (which was considerable), Hitler ensured that his Italian guest was welcomed with much pomp—deferent handshakes, stiff saluting, low bowing, and endless flag-waving. During the day Mussolini visited various palaces and monuments in Munich, including the Führerhaus, the Feldherrnhalle, and the Museum of German Art. Mussolini even conferred upon Hitler a commission: an honorary rank of Corporal in the Fascist Militia. To reciprocate, Hitler awarded Mussolini the Grand Cross of the German Eagle in Gold with Diamonds. Mussolini was the sole recipient of this extremely prestigious and distinctive award.

---

4 * On 30 January 1937, Hitler had solemnly stated: 'The German Government has assured Belgium and Holland of its readiness to recognize and guarantee these States as untouchable and neutral regions for all time.'[71]

On 26 September, Mussolini observed spectacular army manoeuvres. He also observed impressive Luftwaffe exercises, including a remarkable demonstration of the slow-flying Storch aircraft. Next day the Axis leaders travelled to the Reich's industrial region, the Ruhr, to inspect the Krupp munitions plant at Essen. Mussolini was extremely interested in learning the truth about Germany's military strength, and he was not disappointed. Armaments factories were busy mass-producing tanks and artillery at an astonishing rate.

The highlight of the state visit was a massive rally at the *Olympiastadion* (Olympic Stadium) in Berlin on 28 September. It was a grandiose display of Fascist–Nazi solidarity. Large posters prominently displayed throughout the city advertised in bold gothic font that Hitler and Mussolini would speak at 18:30 o'clock on the *Maifeld* (May Field). By evening some 700,000 people had congregated on the *Maifeld* (Hitler claimed it was one million), the imperial sports field adjoining the *Olympiastadion*, to hear the Axis leaders address them. Goebbels gave a preliminary address in which he boastfully announced that the speeches were being broadcast throughout the Reich and internationally. He added:

> More than 100,000,000 people in Germany and Italy are at the loudspeakers, connected with us through the air.

Next, Goebbels warmly welcomed Mussolini:

> We greet your beautiful country and your brave nation. Seeing you shoulder to shoulder with our beloved Führer is the most joyful event of our lives.[73]

Of the two dictators, Hitler spoke first. He described Mussolini as 'one of the lonely men in history who are not put to trial by historic events but determine the history of their country themselves'. He continued:

> The ideals of liberalism and democracy have not preserved the German nation from the worst depression history has ever seen. National Socialism was thus forced to create a new ideal and a more effective one, according all human rights to our people which had been denied the nation for fifteen long years.
>
> During this time of bitter experience Italy, and Fascist Italy especially, refused to take part in the humiliation Germany was subjected to. I must make it a point to say this tonight before the German people and the whole world. In the course of these years, Italy has shown understanding for the demands of a great nation claiming equal rights with other

> peoples in the endeavour to provide the means of subsistence and, above all, to save its honour....
>
> The common trend of ideas expressed in the Fascist and National Socialist Revolutions has developed today into a similar course of action. This will have a salutary influence on the world, in which destruction and deformation are trying to win the upper hand. Fascist Italy has been transformed into a new *Imperium Romanum* by the ingenious activities of a compelling personality.
>
> You, Benito Mussolini, will have realized that in these days, due to the National Socialist State, Germany has become a Great Power, thanks to her racial attitude and her military strength. The inherent strength of the two countries is the best guarantee for the preservation of Europe, which is inspired by a sense of responsibility in the discharge of its cultural mission. It is not willing to allow destructive elements to cause its decline and dissolution....
>
> Every attempt to interfere with the understanding between the two nations or to play one up against the other by casting suspicion and by obscuring the real aims in order to dissolve the ideal partnership will be of no avail because of the innermost desire of one hundred and fifteen million people, who are united at the manifestation of this very hour, and because of the determination of the two men who are standing here to address you....[74]

Mussolini, fluent in several languages, delivered his speech in German. He proclaimed his personal sentiments of political and spiritual unity with the National Socialist revolution:

> I came not only as the head of a government, but also as leader of the Fascist revolution, wishing to express solidarity with your revolution.

Mussolini also underscored his and Hitler's desire to work in the interests of a genuine European peace:

> The Nazis and the Fascists want peace and are determined always to work together for peace—a real, fruitful peace. Behind this visit to Germany there are no secret intentions and no attempt to split further an already badly divided Europe. If we are asked whether the result of this visit will be peace or war, I and the Führer can answer in a loud voice: 'Peace!'

Fascism and National Socialism, Mussolini averred, were the truest, purest forms of democracy, for these revolutionary movements truly represented the will of their respective peoples:

> There is no dictatorship either in Germany or Italy, but only organizations serving the welfare of the people. No governments have greater support from their peoples. The best democracies are Germany and Italy.

Still nursing a grudge, Mussolini could not refrain from hurling a last reproach at the League of Nations for its imposition of economic sanctions against Italy from November 1935 to June 1936. He also expressed his gratitude to Germany for her abstention in this regard:

> No nation having military strength can be the victim of an economic blockade. Fifty-two nations decided on 'criminal' sanctions at Geneva but they were unable to overcome Italy. It even strengthened Italy ... Germany never participated in sanctions. We shall never forget this.[75]

At the end of Mussolini's oration, the exultant crowds cheered themselves hoarse. Mussolini was ecstatic by the overwhelming response of the German masses. Not even a sudden downpour near the end of the rally, which thoroughly drenched him, could dampen his enthusiasm.

On 29 September, Mussolini viewed an impressive eighty-minute military procession along the Charlottenburger Chaussee of some 14,000 Wehrmacht troops with General Erwin Witzleben at their forefront. By the time the state visit was over, Mussolini believed wholeheartedly that he could do no better than to join forces with Hitler. So impressed was Mussolini by the martial exhibitions he had witnessed that he was certain the Reich had overtaken the Western Powers and was now Europe's most potent power.

5 November 1937 was a key date in the annals of the Third Reich. In Berlin, Hitler convoked a top secret meeting in which he outlined his plans for launching a European war of conquest and the prerequisites to be met beforehand. The conference was attended by senior officials: War Minister Werner von Blomberg, Foreign Minister Konstantin von Neurath, Army chief Werner von Fritsch, Luftwaffe chief Hermann Göring, and Navy chief Erich Raeder. Minutes were taken by Colonel Friedrich Hossbach, Hitler's Wehrmacht adjutant. The protocol, transcribed on 10 November, was thereafter known as the Hossbach Memorandum (see Appendix E). It was a crucial and incriminatory document used as evidence at the post-war Nuremberg trials of Germany's culpability in the 'planning, preparation, initiation, or waging of a war of aggression, or a war in violation of international treaties, agreements, or assurances, or participation in a common plan or conspiracy for the accomplishment of any of the foregoing ...'[76]

At the beginning of the conference, Hitler adjured the attendees that total confidentiality was critical, and instructed them that what he said was to be regarded as his will and testament in case of his death. These sombre words made a deep impact on those present. Next, Hitler stressed Germany's need for *Lebensraum* in Eastern Europe, and asserted that it would be necessary to wage war in order to acquire it:

> The aim of German policy was to make secure and to preserve the racial community [*Volkmasse*] and to enlarge it. It was therefore a question of space.
>
> The German racial community comprised over 85 million people and, because of their number and the narrow limits of habitable space in Europe, constituted a tightly packed racial core such as was not to be met in any other country and such as implied the right to a greater living space than in the case of other peoples. If, territorially speaking, there existed no political result corresponding to this German racial core, that was a consequence of centuries of historical development, and in the continuance of these political conditions lay the greatest danger to the preservation of the German race at its present peak. To arrest the decline of Germanism [*Deutschtum*] in Austria and Czechoslovakia was as little possible as to maintain the present level in Germany itself. Instead of increase, sterility was setting in, and in its train disorders of a social character must arise in course of time, since political and ideological ideas remain effective only so long as they furnish the basis for the realization of the essential vital demands of a people. Germany's future was therefore wholly conditional upon the solving of the need for space, and such a solution could be sought, of course, only for a foreseeable period of about one to three generations.

However, Hitler warned that there remained two barriers to be overcome, namely 'two hate-inspired antagonists, Britain and France, to whom a German colossus in the centre of Europe was a thorn in the flesh ... both were opposed to any further strengthening of Germany's position either in Europe or overseas ... Germany's problem could only be solved by means of force ...' Hitler highlighted the fact that Germany could not afford to delay, for the future was uncertain and the German Armed Forces could not be allowed to become out of date:

> Nobody knew today what the situation would be in the years 1943–45. Only one thing was certain, that we could not wait longer. On the one hand there was the great Wehrmacht, and the necessity of maintaining it at its present level....

Other pressing factors included 'the aging of the [National Socialist] Movement and its leaders; and on the other, the prospect of lowering the standard of living and of a limitation of the birthrate, which left no choice but to act'. Hitler also considered whether it would be feasible for

Germany to become autarkic, or if the Reich should instead participate in the 'world economy'. Ultimately it was decided that Germany had to acquire raw materials from its neighbouring nations, not from colonies abroad, and they had to be seized by force. Hitler explained:

> The history of all ages—the Roman Empire and the British Empire—had proved that the expansion could only be carried out by breaking down resistance and taking risks; setbacks were inevitable. There had never been spaces without a master, and there were none today; the attacker always comes up against a possessor.
>
> The question for Germany ran: where could she achieve the greatest gain at the lowest cost?

But before proceeding, it was essential for the Reich to deal with Austria and Czechoslovakia in order 'to remove the threat to our flank in any possible operation against the West'. Hossbach recorded that Hitler was determined 'to solve Germany's problem of space at the latest by 1943–45' before Germany's adversaries were ready. Germany was 'obliged to take the offensive' and had to do so 'while the rest of the world was still preparing its defences'.[77]

After the meeting, Blomberg, Fritsch, and Neurath[5*] tried to remonstrate with Hitler. They contended that his plans for launching a series of localized wars in Eastern Europe would unduly endanger the Reich, since Germany was not yet sufficiently strong. Furthermore, they were of the opinion that the 'contingencies' which Hitler cited as a precondition for launching a war—such as war between France and Italy in southern Europe, or a civil uprising in France—were highly improbable. They also felt that any offensive action on Germany's part in the East would provoke a military response from France due to the collective security agreements in place there. This preventative measure of the French, designed to stem German aggression, was known as the *cordon sanitaire*. Plus, it was almost a certainty that should Germany and France become embroiled in a war, Britain would enter the conflict on the side of the French. Germany was not yet ready for a showdown with her Anglo–French enemies. The trio therefore recommended to the Führer that he defer his large-scale plans of conquest. Germany should hold off at least until she was militarily prepared to hold her own in localized conflicts that would almost certainly develop into a major war spanning Continental Europe. Of course, Hitler had no intention of putting his plans on hold. On the contrary, he wanted to accelerate them, and it was not long before these three naysayers, with their inconvenient objections, were swept aside.

---

5 * In his post-war testimony at Nuremberg, Neurath claimed that Hitler's war plans had so disturbed him that he 'suffered several heart attacks'.[78]

At Augsburg on 21 November, Hitler delivered a speech regarding Germany's lost colonies. These had been stripped from the Reich per Article 119 of the Versailles Treaty. Hitler declared that sooner or later, Germany's former 'oversea possessions' would have to be restored to her, regardless of any opposition:

> The world will have to return the property of which we have been robbed. The principal objections to our demands must be silenced. We must make our demands louder and louder. I know the world will not refuse all of them.[79]

As Germany had done in the autumn of 1933, Italy withdrew from the League of Nations on 11 December 1937. This decision was publicly revealed to the Italian population the following day, after a brief meeting of the Fascist Grand Council. Before an ebullient crowd of 100,000 people in Rome's *Piazza di Venezia*, Mussolini inveighed against the League of Nations. His chief complaint against the League of Nations was for penalizing Italy with economic sanctions after invading Ethiopia in 1935, and for failing to compensate Italy accordingly:

> The historic decision, which the Fascist Grand Council has acclaimed and you have enthusiastically received, could not be longer delayed. We have for many years offered the world the spectacle of unexampled patience.
>
> We have not forgotten, and we shall not forget, the shameful attempt at the strangulation of the Italian people that was perpetrated at Geneva.
>
> The League has not made the reparation which was our due. The good intentions of certain Governments were drowned immediately their delegates made contacts in the fatal surroundings of Geneva's Sanhedrin, which is manipulated by dark and hidden forces and enemies of Italy and our revolution.

Because of the unacceptable way Italy had been treated, Mussolini declared, she would no longer hold herself accountable to an ineffectual democratic entity worthy of nothing save contempt:

> Consequently our presence at the door at Geneva is no longer tolerable. As soldiers we had to choose. Were we to stay in? Were we to get out?
>
> That is why we shout 'It is enough', and leave without regret, the tottering temple in which men do not work for peace, but prepare for war.
>
> It is grotesque to believe that pressure was exerted on us to decide. Our comrades of the Berlin–Tokyo Axis have shown absolute discretion.

> Italy's withdrawal from the League is an event of great historical importance, which has drawn the attention of the world. The consequences of it cannot be foreseen, but we will not abandon our fundamental policy of aiming at collaboration for peace, of which we have furnished a luminous example in the last few days by the consecrating of peace in the Adriatic.
>
> The threatening voices which have been raised from time to time perhaps will be again raised from the flocks of the great democracies, but they will leave us perfectly indifferent. They can do nothing against people like the Italians, who are capable of any sacrifice.
>
> We have the arms of the sky, land, and sea, both numerous and tempered by two victorious wars. Above all, we have the heroic spirit of our revolution, which no human force in the world will ever be able to bend.[80]

Mussolini's speech was not received abroad as gravely as it might have been. This was due to the fact that most non-Italians thought Mussolini would have made additional pronouncements intended to exacerbate the current European state of affairs. Also that day, Hitler made a formal statement regarding Italy's departure from the League of Nations. He lambasted the League for its impotence and emphasized that Germany would never rejoin it because of its venality.

On 3 May 1938, Hitler journeyed to Italy aboard his *Sonderzug* (special train) for an historic state visit. He was accompanied by a vast entourage of Party bosses and Nazi ministers, including Hess, Ribbentrop, and Goebbels. Disembarking at the train station in Rome, Hitler was personally welcomed by King Emmanuel III and Mussolini. On the way to the *Quirinale*, where he lodged as an honoured guest, the Führer was driven across a specially constructed street, the *Via Adolf Hitler*. The Italians had spared no effort or expense in preparing for the Führer's arrival. During his week-long tour Hitler and his retinue enjoyed the sight of Fascist demonstrations on an epic scale in Rome, Naples, and Florence. Together, Hitler and Mussolini inspected many notable cultural and architectural sites. As in September 1937, the occasion was a stunning spectacle of Axis unity, not only for the Germans and Italians to marvel at but all Europeans. Hitler's diplomatic state visit took place in the wake of Austria's annexation just seven weeks earlier. Together with a series of recent victories in the Spanish conflict by Franco's Nationalist forces, it was evident that at this stage Fascism was on the rise.

In Rome on 7 May, Hitler delivered a speech in which he highlighted the common aims and purpose of both the German and the Italian peoples:

> The National Socialist Movement and the Fascist Revolution have created two new powerful States which today in a world of unrest and

> disintegration stand as creations of order and healthy progress. Germany and Italy have thus like interests and through sharing in a common *Weltanschauung* are closely bound together. In this way there has been created in Europe a bloc of 120,000,000 people who are determined to safeguard their eternal vital rights and to defend themselves against all those forces which might venture to oppose their natural development.
>
> Out of this fight against a world which rejects and refuses to understand their claims, a fight which Germany and Italy have had to wage shoulder to shoulder, there has gradually grown up a warm friendship between the two peoples.... It is therefore only natural that our two peoples should in the future continue to build up and deepen in constant co-operation this friendship which in recent years has ever proved of increasing value.

Next, Hitler assured Mussolini of the inviolability of the Italo–German border, which nature had defined—the Alps:

> Now today after nearly two thousand years, thanks to your historic activity, Benito Mussolini, the Roman State arises from remote traditions to new life, and north of you there arose, formed out of numerous tribes, a new Germanic Reich. Now that we have become immediate neighbours, taught by the experience of two millennia, we both wish to recognize that natural frontier which Providence and history have clearly drawn for our two peoples. That frontier will then render possible the happiness of a permanent co-operation peacefully secured through the definite separation of the living-spaces of the two nations, but it will also serve as a bridge for mutual help and support. It is my unalterable will and my bequest to the German people that it shall accordingly regard the frontier of the Alps, raised by Nature between us both, as for ever inviolable.

Hitler promised Mussolini that Germany would stand by Italy through thick and thin:

> Duce, just as you and your people have maintained your friendship with Germany in days of crisis, so I and my people will show the like friendship towards Italy in times of difficulty.

The rebirth of Italian grandeur and the might of the Italian Armed Forces had greatly impressed Hitler:

> The stupendous impressions I have just received of the youthful strength, the will to work, and the proud spirit of the new Italy will remain for

> me an imperishable memory. Unforgettable, too, was the sight of your soldiers and Blackshirts covered with the glory of their recent operations [in Spain], of your well-tried fleet, and of the élan of your magnificent air force. They give me the certainty that your admirable constructive work which I follow with the sincerest well-wishing will in the future as in the past lead to great successes.[81]

Henceforth the world was confronted by an increasingly powerful Axis coalition that would, in the span of a few short years, permanently destroy the Old Order of Europe.

PART II

# Annexation and Expansion

After the First World War, the relationship between Germany and Austria was governed by the exacting provisions of both the Versailles Treaty and the Treaty of St. Germain. Article 80 of the Versailles Treaty stated unequivocally that Germany was required to 'respect strictly the independence of Austria ... this independence shall be inalienable, except with the consent of the Council of the League of Nations.'[1] And it was the Treaty of St. Germain, signed by Austria and the Allied Powers on 10 September 1919, that definitively set Austria's frontier with Germany as 'The frontier of 3 August 1914'.[2]

Just as Germany was forbidden to violate Austrian independence, Austria was likewise prohibited from violating her own independence. Article 88 of the Treaty of St. Germain stipulated that Austria's independence was 'inalienable otherwise than with the consent of the Council of the League of Nations' and that she was obliged to 'abstain from any act which might directly or indirectly or by any means compromise her independence, particularly, and until her admission to membership of the League of Nations, by participation in the affairs of another Power [i.e. Germany]'.[3] Other significant consequences of the Treaty of St. Germain for Austria was the dissolution of the Austro–Hungarian Empire, the loss of greater than half of the Austrian Empire's pre-war territory, the abolition of military conscription in Austria, and the restriction of the Austrian Army to a token peacetime strength of 30,000 men.

On the subject of Austro–German relations, Hitler announced to his Reichstag deputies on 30 January 1934:

> It is ... a matter of great regret to the German Government that the relations of the Reich to the present Austrian Government are by no

> means satisfactory. The fault does not lie with us. The assertion that it is the intention of the German Reich to coerce the Austrian State is absurd, and cannot be substantiated or proved.[4]

In his peace speech to the Reichstag on 21 May 1935, Hitler gave the following assurance in connection with Austria:

> Germany neither intends nor wishes to interfere in the internal affairs of Austria, to annex Austria, or to conclude an *Anschluss*. The German people and the German Government have, however, the very comprehensible desire, arising out of the simple feeling of solidarity due to a common national descent, namely, that the right to self-determination should be guaranteed not only to foreign nations but to the German people everywhere. I myself believe that no régime which does not rest on public consent and is not supported by the people can continue permanently.[5]

And on 1 May 1936, Hitler again spoke of alleged German aggression towards Austria:

> The lies that Germany will pounce upon Austria tomorrow or the day after are being spread again. I ask myself: Who are these elements who do not want peace and mutual understanding, who must stir up and sow distrust continuously, who are they in reality?[6]

However, these two-faced utterances were intended solely for public consumption. In truth, Hitler had long had his eyes on his Austrian homeland and bringing about a union of the two Germanic nations was uppermost in his mind. At Augsburg on 21 November 1937, Hitler spoke of the Reich's need to secure further *Lebensraum* and Germany's ever-increasing might:

> Today we are faced with new tasks, for the living space of our people is too narrow. The world seeks to evade the examination of these problems and the answering of these questions. But that it will not be able to do so. One day the world will have to pay attention to our demands. I do not for one second doubt that just as we have been able to raise up the nation at home, so, too, abroad we shall secure the same vital rights as other peoples. I do not doubt that this vital right of the German people will in its turn one day be understood by the whole world. I am convinced that the most difficult part of the preparatory work has already been achieved. It only remains for all National Socialists ever and again to

> recall the principles by which we have grown great. If the whole Party and also the whole nation stand united behind the leadership, then this leadership, relying on this common strength of a people of sixty-eight millions expressed in the last resort by its army, will be able both to defend with success the nation's interests and successfully to accomplish the tasks which are set before us.[7]

The Hossbach Conference of 1937 established unequivocally that Hitler's next conquests were to be Austria and Czechoslovakia. And in late 1937 and early 1938 Hitler managed to dispose of several of his closest collaborators: military chiefs Blomberg and Fritsch, and ministers Schacht and Neurath. These conservative types were not in accord with Hitler's plans to wage an aggressive war—certainly not so soon, anyway—and were instead urging moderation. For the first two men, scandals were engineered to defame them. For the latter two, Schacht was compelled to resign and Neurath was 'bumped upstairs' to the nominal post of President of the 'Privy Cabinet Council'.

Blomberg resigned his posts on 27 January 1938 when it came to Hitler's attention that the young woman Blomberg had recently married had posed for indecent photographs in 1932. The fifty-nine-year-old Blomberg, a lonely widower, became enamoured with a twenty-six-year-old secretary, Erna Gruhn. Following a brief engagement, the two had married on 12 January. Soon afterwards, an investigation uncovered Gruhn's salacious past and was reported to the Gestapo and to Göring. Although Göring had been best man at Blomberg's wedding, he had long coveted Blomberg's position. Seizing the opportunity to blacken his rival's name, Göring rushed to Hitler to break the news. Hitler himself had attended the wedding as a witness, and he was appalled, for marriage by a German officer of high rank to a woman of disreputable background was considered unacceptable. At first, disdainful of the pretentious affectations of the military's upper crust, Hitler had personally endorsed the wedding of his highest field marshal to a woman of rather pedestrian background. But now, Hitler insisted that Blomberg annul the marriage to protect the Wehrmacht's reputation. This Blomberg was unwilling to do. But after Göring threatened to tarnish Blomberg's reputation by publicizing the fact that his wife had a police record for obscenity, Blomberg chose to step down permanently.

Meanwhile Fritsch, a career officer without a family, was forced to resign due to trumped-up allegations of homosexuality fabricated by Himmler's Gestapo to discredit him. The accusations were untrue, as established in a later hearing. Now that Blomberg was out of the picture, Göring also wanted Fritsch out of the way so that he would not succeed

Blomberg. As for Himmler, he wanted to elevate the standing of his S.S. in Hitler's eyes at the military's expense. A file fabricated by S.D. chief Reinhard Heydrich containing 'evidence' of Fritsch's homosexual activities was brought out into the open. Fritsch strongly denied the allegations, but his protestations of innocence were not enough to save him. He was pressured to resign on 4 February. Afterwards, the Wehrmacht's top brass petitioned for an impartial hearing, and an honour court was convoked to look into the matter. It was soon revealed that the homosexual acts concerned an individual named Rittmeister von Frisch, who was a different person altogether. Even the last name was spelled differently. Fritsch was officially exonerated on 18 March, but by then the damage was done. His good name was ruined, and Hitler decided not to reinstate him. On 18 December, Fritsch ruefully declared to Ulrich von Hassell, who had recently been dismissed from his post as Ambassador to Italy in the aftermath of the Blomberg–Fritsch Affair:

> This man—Hitler—is Germany's destiny for good and for evil. If he now goes over the abyss ... he will drag us all down with him. There is nothing we can do.[8]

Dr. Hjalmar Schacht was persuaded to resign from his offices as General Plenipotentiary and Economics Minister in November 1937 by Göring. The latter had grown weary of Schacht's continuous objections to his excessive military expenditures. Neurath, the old-school diplomat, was succeeded by Ribbentrop as Foreign Minister. An ex-champagne salesman, Ribbentrop had managed to get into Hitler's good graces after concluding the Anglo–German Naval Agreement of 1935. Few, if any, had anything positive to say about Ribbentrop, who was rude, arrogant, and overbearing. According to Göring, Ribbentrop was 'Germany's No. 1 parrot'; Papen described him as 'a husk with no kernel'; and André François-Poncet, the French Ambassador to Germany, observed that 'One could not talk to Ribbentrop, he only listened to himself.' But the assessment of Nevile Henderson, Britain's Ambassador to Germany, was the most damning of all. In his view, Ribbentrop was 'a combination of vanity, stupidity, and superficiality'.[9]

With all these personnel changes taking place, Hitler decided to assume total control of the German Armed Forces. He abolished the post of War Minister, dissolved the *Reichskriegsministerium* (Reich War Ministry), and replaced it with a new organization, the *Oberkommando der Wehrmacht* (High Command of the Armed Forces). Its new chief was General Wilhelm Keitel. He was widely regarded with contempt by his contemporaries for his shameless sycophancy to Hitler. And on 4 February, Hitler issued the 'Decree concerning the Leadership of the Armed Forces' wherein he arrogated to himself full command powers over the Wehrmacht:

> From now on I take over directly the command of the whole Armed Forces.
> The Armed Forces Office with its functions as High Command of the Armed Forces, hitherto within the Reich War Ministry, will come directly under my command and as my military staff.
> At the head of the staff of the High Command of the Armed Forces is the former Chief of the Armed Forces department as 'Chief of the High Command of the Armed Forces'. He [Keitel] is equal in rank to a Reich Minister.
> At the same time, the High Command takes the responsibility for the affairs of the Reich Ministry of War, and by my order the Chief of the High Command of the Armed Forces exercises the authority formerly belonging to the Reich Minister.
> It is the High Command of the Armed Forces' duty to carry out in peacetime, in accordance with my instructions, the preparation of the defence system of the Reich.[10]

The hierarchy of the German Armed Forces was restructured. Blomberg was gone, and Hitler had personally taken over his old post as Supreme Commander. Fritsch too was gone, and he was replaced by a likely candidate to whom he had given a favourable recommendation, Walther von Brauchitsch. Göring had hoped to succeed Blomberg as the new head of Germany's armed forces, but this was not to be. To placate him, he was instead elevated to the lofty rank of field marshal. What the reshuffling ultimately meant was that the military was further subordinated to Hitler and was less able to oppose him.

By this time Hitler was prepared to expand the Reich's borders by backing his bluster and bravado with the threat of military force. The success of Germany's foreign policy thus far had utterly convinced Hitler of the righteousness of his cause and of the 'divine mission' he believed Providence had chosen for him. He now turned to the matter of ethnic Germans in two neighbouring nations, Austria and Czechoslovakia. In a speech to the Reichstag on 20 February 1938, Hitler declared:

> There are more than 10,000,000 Germans in States adjoining Germany which before 1866 were joined to the bulk of the German nation by a national link. Until 1918 they fought in the Great War shoulder to shoulder with the German soldiers of the Reich. Against their own free will they were prevented by peace treaties from uniting with the Reich. This was painful enough, but there must be no doubt about one thing: Political separation from the Reich may not lead to deprivation of rights, that is the general rights of racial self-determination ...

> In the long run it is unbearable for a world power, conscious of herself, to know there are citizens at her side who are constantly being inflicted with the severest sufferings for their sympathy or unity with the total nation, its faith, and philosophy.
>
> We well know there can scarcely be a frontier line in Europe which satisfies all. It should be all the more important to avoid the torture of national minorities in order not to add to the suffering of persecution on account of their belonging to a certain people....
>
> It cannot be denied that Germany herself, as long as she was powerless and defenceless, was compelled to tolerate many of these continual persecutions of the German people on our frontier.
>
> But ... present-day Germany will know how to guard its more restricted interests. To these interests of the German Reich belong also the protection of those German people who are not in a position to secure along our frontiers their political and philosophical freedom by their own efforts.[11]

It was plain from Hitler's words that he next intended to direct his aggression towards Austria and Czechoslovakia. True, the *putsch* in Austria four years earlier had miscarried. But Hitler and Mussolini now saw eye to eye on the Austrian question. Mussolini would not send his troops to the Austro–Italian frontier this time around. As for Federal Chancellor Schuschnigg, leader of the Fatherland Front since 1936, he had long since banned all other political parties, including the Social Democrats, Communists, and National Socialists. He had done so in order to prevent them from undermining his government. It was also his top priority to preserve Austrian sovereignty against external threats; namely, Hitler's Germany.

The July Agreement of 1936 established a tentative reconciliation between Germany and Austria. But in spite of the agreement, behind the scenes Hitler made every effort to bolster National Socialism within Austria, while Schuschnigg tried to fend off these unwelcome machinations. Franz von Papen, then Germany's Ambassador to Austria, insisted that he was attempting to effect an *Anschluss* with Austria using diplomatic methods. Nevertheless, the threat of Austrian National Socialists carrying out another *coup d'état*, or of Hitler launching an invasion, remained ever-present. Numerous revolutionary acts were perpetrated by Austrian Nazis in 1937, which Schuschnigg described as follows:

> Towards the end of 1937 the Nazi underground terror was again in full swing. Telephone booths exploded, tear-gas bombs were thrown, and mass demonstrations were arranged in order to induce the Austrian

> police to intervene. Once the police dispersed the crowds, Berlin protested that we did not keep our share of the bargain [i.e. per the Agreement of 11 July 1936] and allowed the persecution of National Socialism.[12]

But Schuschnigg was ardently opposed to Nazism, and on 5 January 1938 he proclaimed:

> There is no question of ever accepting Nazi representatives in the Austrian Cabinet. An absolute abyss separates Austria from Nazism. We do not like arbitrary power, we want law to rule our freedom. We reject uniformity and centralization.... Christendom is anchored in our very soil, and we know but one God: And that is not the State, or the Nation, or that elusive thing, Race. Our children are God's children, not to be abused by the State. We abhor terror; Austria has always been a humanitarian State. As a people, we are tolerant by predisposition. Any change now, in our *status quo*, could only be for the worse.[13]

On 25 January, Austrian police raided the *Teinfaltstrasse* apartment of Dr. Leopold Tavs, the leader of an underground organization known as the 'Committee of Seven'. There, they uncovered evidence of a scheme involving the assassination of Ambassador Papen and a *putsch* to be carried out in April. Tavs, who was also the deputy to Austrian Gauleiter Josef Leopold, was arrested for treason. In light of the tense situation, Schuschnigg was willing to try to ameliorate Austro–German relations by meeting directly with Hitler. Accordingly, Papen set up an interview between Hitler and Schuschnigg at Berchtesgaden.

On 11 February, Schuschnigg set off from Vienna to Salzburg by train. With him was Guido Schmidt, the Austrian Foreign Minister. The following day they crossed over the German border and were driven up to the Berghof, Hitler's mountain retreat in the Bavarian Alps. Upon arrival the Austrian politicians were met by Hitler on the front steps. He was ominously accompanied by three military men: General Keitel, the O.K.W. chief; General Walther von Reichenau, in charge of Army forces along the Austro–German frontier; and General Sperrle of the Luftwaffe. Schuschnigg followed Hitler to the large study on the second level of the Berghof. Once inside, Schuschnigg walked over to the panoramic window, thirty-five yards wide. Gazing outwards, he spoke in glowing terms of the impressive lofty view and pleasant weather. Hitler immediately retorted to Schuschnigg that they 'did not get together to speak of the fine view or of the weather'. Hitler then launched a verbal onslaught intended to browbeat Schuschnigg into submission. The experience made such an indelible impression on him that years later Schuschnigg was able to recall the entire conversation from memory. In his memoirs he dryly described it as 'somewhat unilateral':

> HITLER: ... Austria has never done anything that would be of any help to Germany. The whole history of Austria is just one uninterrupted act of high treason. That was so in the past, and is no better today. This historical paradox must now reach its long-overdue end. And I can tell you here and now, Herr Schuschnigg, that I am absolutely determined to make an end of all this. The German Reich is one of the Great Powers, and nobody will raise his voice if it settles its border problems.

Schuschnigg informed Hitler that contrary to how the Führer felt, the Austrian people considered their history to be a significant part of German history, and he emphasized that 'Austria's contribution in this respect is considerable'. Hitler contemptuously replied that Austria's contribution was nil, and blamed the Hapsburg Dynasty and the Catholic Church for undermining Germany:

> HITLER: Absolutely zero—I am telling you—absolutely zero. Every national idea was sabotaged by Austria throughout history; and indeed, all this sabotage was the chief activity of the Hapsburgs and the Catholic Church.

To this Schuschnigg responded that numerous Austrians had significantly contributed to German culture; Beethoven, for example. Hitler replied that Beethoven was born a Rhinelander. Schuschnigg then called attention to the fact that Beethoven (who had lived in Vienna from the age of twenty-one to his death) had considered himself an Austrian:

> SCHUSCHNIGG: All the same, Herr Reichskanzler, many an Austrian contribution cannot possibly be separated from the general picture of German culture. Take for instance a man like Beethoven ...
>
> HITLER: Oh—Beethoven? Let me tell you that Beethoven came from the lower Rhineland.
>
> SCHUSCHNIGG: Yet Austria was the country of his choice, as it was for so many others.
>
> HITLER: That's as may be. I am telling you once more that things cannot go on in this way. I have a historic mission; and this mission I will fulfill because Providence has destined me to do so.... Who is not with me will be crushed.... I have chosen the most difficult road that any German ever

took; I have made the greatest achievement in the history of Germany, greater than any other German. And not by force, mind you. I am carried along by the love of my people.

SCHUSCHNIGG: Herr Reichskanzler, I am quite willing to believe that.

Hitler then emphasized his Austrian origins, and dared Schuschnigg to hold a federal election in which the two Chancellors would campaign against one another. Schuschnigg pointed out that this was constitutionally impossible. He asked Hitler to list in detail his complaints, and promised him that the Austrian Government would strive to rectify them, if it could:

HITLER: And you know, I could call myself an Austrian with just as much reason—in fact, with far more reason—than you, Herr Schuschnigg. Why don't you try a plebiscite in Austria in which we two run against each other? You just try that.

SCHUSCHNIGG: Well, if that were possible. But you know yourself, Herr Reichskanzler, that this is impossible. My views differ radically from yours. There is nothing we can do but live together, side by side, the little State next to the big one. We have no other choice. And so I would ask you to enumerate your complaints. We will do everything to remove obstacles to a better understanding, as far as it is possible.

HITLER: That is what you say, Herr Schuschnigg. But I am telling you that I am going to solve the so-called Austrian problem one way or the other. Do you imagine that I don't know that you are fortifying your border against the Reich?

Schuschnigg knew that the Austrian Government was well within its rights to reinforce its borders if it chose to do so. However, Hitler's claim was false, and Schuschnigg said as much:

SCHUSCHNIGG: That is not true.

HITLER: Listen. You don't really think that you can move a single stone in Austria without my hearing the most accurate details about it the very next day, do you?

SCHUSCHNIGG: ... We have taken these measures on all our borders, and nobody can object if we prepare a defence against illegal intrusions on our territory.

HITLER: I have only to give an order, and in one single night all your ridiculous defence mechanisms are blown to bits. You don't seriously believe that you can stop me, or even delay me for half an hour, do you? Who knows? Perhaps you will wake up one morning in Vienna to find us there—just like a spring storm. And then you'll see something. I would very much like to save Austria from such a fate, because such an action would mean blood. After the Army, my S.A. and the Austrian Legion would move in, and nobody could stop their just revenge—not even I. Do you want to make another Spain of Austria? I would like to avoid all that—if possible.

Schuschnigg promised Hitler that he would look into it, and if need be halt the construction of the alleged defensive barriers along the Austro–German border, should they exist. He further cautioned Hitler that if he invaded Austria, armed conflict would ensue, pitting Austrian against German:

SCHUSCHNIGG: I shall investigate the matter and will have any defence work on the German border stopped. I am fully aware that you can invade Austria; but Herr Reichskanzler, whether we like it or not, that would mean bloodshed. We are not alone in this world, and such a step would probably mean war.

HITLER: It is easy enough to talk of war while we are sitting here in our comfortable easy-chairs. But war means endless misery for millions. Do you want to take this responsibility upon yourself, Herr Schuschnigg? Don't think for one moment that anybody on earth is going to thwart my decisions. Italy? I see eye to eye with Mussolini, the closest ties of friendship bind me to Italy. And England? England will not move one finger for Austria.... And France? Well, three years ago we marched on the Rhineland with a handful of battalions. That was the time I risked everything. If France had stopped us then we would have had to retreat perhaps sixty kilometres or so, and even then, we could have stopped them there. But now it is too late for France. The world must know that it is unbearable for a great power like Germany to have every little State on her borders believe that it can provoke her. I have watched it long enough without interfering because I hoped that in the end reason would triumph. But it is simply an impossible state of affairs when people are thrown into jail in Austria merely because they sing a song that you don't like or because they salute each other with 'Heil Hitler'. The persecution of National Socialists in Austria must have an end, or else I shall put an end to it.

SCHUSCHNIGG: Nobody is persecuted in Austria who abides by the law....

> HITLER: ... I give you once more, and for the last time, the opportunity to come to terms, Herr Schuschnigg. Either we find a solution now, or else events will take their course. And we shall see whether you will like those events.... Think it over, Herr Schuschnigg, think it over well. I can only wait until this afternoon. If I tell you that, you will do well to take my words literally. I don't believe in bluffing. All my past is proof for that. I have achieved everything that I set out to do, and have thus become perhaps the greatest German in all of history. It is not my habit to talk much or to give warning of things to come ...
>
> SCHUSCHNIGG: Herr Reichskanzler, you know my views on this question. They are my personal views as well as those which duty towards my country dictates. Now what exactly are your wishes?
>
> HITLER: That we can discuss this afternoon.

After Hitler's two-hour tirade, the Chancellors broke for lunch. Schuschnigg noted that Hitler was now in a very good humour. That afternoon, Ribbentrop handed Schuschnigg a two-page typed copy of Hitler's specific demands. These included the appointment of Arthur Seyss-Inquart, a Viennese Nazi and lawyer, to the post of Interior Minister; the appointment of a second Nazi, Edmund Glaise-Horstenau, to the post of War Minister; the appointment of a third Nazi, the banker Hans Fischböck, to the post of Finance Minister; a 'systematic exchange' of up to one hundred officers; the release from prison of Austrian Nazis; the reinstatement of dismissed Nazi officials, and the right for Austrians to endorse Nazism without the threat of persecution. To Schuschnigg's dismay, it was clear that the terms of the Berchtesgaden Agreement all but meant the takeover of Austria by the Nazis. When Schuschnigg was once again summoned into Hitler's study, Hitler was pacing to and fro, seemingly preoccupied.

> HITLER: Herr Schuschnigg, I have decided to make one last attempt. Here is the draft of the document. There is nothing to be discussed about it. I will not change one single iota. You will either sign it as it stands or else our meeting has been useless. In that case I shall decide during the night what will be done next.

Schuschnigg advised Hitler that he had reviewed the text of the 'Agreement' and that although he could sign it, he had to point out that legally the authority to accept its provisions lay in the hands of Austria's President, and therefore he could not guarantee that the 'Agreement' would, in fact, be accepted:

> SCHUSCHNIGG: I have been informed of the contents of the document and can do nothing under the circumstances but take cognizance of it. I am also willing to sign it, but I want to make it quite clear that my signature alone can be of no value whatsoever to you ... Consequently I can in no way guarantee that the time limits stipulated in the document—as, for instance, the three days for the amnesty—will be observed.
>
> HITLER: You have to guarantee that.
>
> SCHUSCHNIGG: I could not possibly, Herr Chancellor.

Hitler angrily stood up, rushed to open the double doors, and hollered, 'General Keitel!' He then snapped at Schuschnigg, 'I shall have you called later.' Alarmed, Keitel hurried into Hitler's study to receive his instructions, but to his astonishment found Hitler standing there, cool and collected. Amused, Hitler informed Keitel that he had no orders for him. Meanwhile, Schuschnigg and Schmidt waited anxiously outside, expecting to be arrested. A half-hour later, however, Schuschnigg was called back to confer with Hitler yet again.

> HITLER: I have decided to change my mind—for the first time in my entire life. But I warn you—this is your very last chance. I have given you three more days before the agreement goes into effect.

Facing the prospect of what he perceived to be an imminent invasion of Austria, Schuschnigg—under tremendous pressure—signed the Berchtesgaden Agreement. He hoped he would be able to remedy the situation as soon as possible upon his return to Austria. Meanwhile Hitler, satisfied that Schuschnigg had capitulated to his demands, adopted a more conciliatory tone:

> HITLER: Well, now that we have come to an agreement, the Austrian problem is solved. Believe me, Herr Bundeskanzler [Federal Chancellor], it is for the best. Now we can abide by this agreement for the next five years. That is a long time and in five years the world will look different, anyway.

Schuschnigg suggested to Hitler that they should inform the press that during their talks they had reaffirmed the July Agreement, but Hitler would have none of it. He replied:

> Oh, no! First you have to fulfill the conditions of our agreement. This is what is going to the press: 'Today the Führer and Reichskanzler conferred with the Austrian Bundeskanzler at the Berghof.' That's all.

Schuschnigg turned down Hitler's offer to remain for supper, and he and Schmidt returned to Salzburg. Papen went with them to the border, noting that they drove in 'oppressive silence'. Trying to lighten the mood, he said:

> Well, now you have seen what the Führer can be like at times. But the next time I am sure it will be different. You know the Führer can be absolutely charming.[14]

But Schuschnigg was not persuaded by Papen's palliative words. There was no doubt in his mind that disaster was imminent. In his memoirs he recalled that 'there was little room for any hope'.[15] The Führer had given Schuschnigg until 15 February to confirm with a 'binding reply' that the terms of the Berchtesgaden Agreement would be met, and until 18 February to carry them out. And, in fact, although certain—but not all—of the Berchtesgaden Agreement's terms were approved by Austrian President Wilhelm Miklas soon thereafter (such as the provision for releasing incarcerated National Socialists), the situation nonetheless deteriorated. Schuschnigg referred to the interval between his interview with Hitler and the German invasion of Austria—12 February to 11 March—as 'The Four-Weeks' Agony'. *Hakenkreuz* flags began to be prominently displayed, and badges were everywhere available for purchase. Government and police officials began to engage in non-violent opposition to the Schuschnigg régime. Throughout Austria, marches and rallies were held. In Styria, Nazi agitators besieged the *Grazer Rathaus* (Graz Town Hall) and hoisted up a *hakenkreuz* flag.

Eight days after his meeting with Schuschnigg, Hitler addressed the Reichstag. It was a postponement of his annual speech of 30 January marking the anniversary of the Nazi 'seizure of power'. The speech was broadcast throughout Germany and also over the Österreichischer Rundfunk (Austrian Radio). Hitler explicitly proclaimed:

> The German Reich is no longer willing to tolerate the suppression of ten million Germans across its borders.[16]

This blunt statement was directed towards both Austria and Czechoslovakia (the latter with its sizeable Sudeten German population). Hitler went on to describe his meeting with Schuschnigg as if it had been a cordial occasion with the two Chancellors working closely together in a spirit of mutual understanding to find common ground, and not a one-sided harangue:

> Now I turn to Austria. It is not only the same people but above all a long communal history and culture which bind together the Reich and Austria.

> Difficulties which emerged in the carrying out of the agreement of 11 July 1936 made essential an attempt to remove misunderstandings and obstacles to final reconciliation. It is clear that whether we wished it or not an intolerable position might have developed that would have contained the seeds of a catastrophe. It does not lie in the power of man to stop the rolling stone of fate which through neglect or lack of wisdom has been set moving.
>
> I am happy to say that these ideas correspond with the viewpoint of the Austrian Chancellor, whom I invited to visit me. The underlying intention was to bring about a *détente* in our relations which would guarantee to National Socialist sympathizers in Austria within the limits of the law the same rights enjoyed by other citizens.
>
> In connection with it there was to be an act of conciliation in the form of a general amnesty and better understanding between the two States through closer and friendlier relations in the various spheres of cultural, political, and economic co-operation. All this is a development within the framework of the treaty of 11 July.
>
> I wish to pay tribute to the Austrian Chancellor for his efforts to find together with me a way which is just as much in the interests of both countries as in that of the entire German people whose sons we all are regardless of where we came from. I believe we have thus made a contribution to European peace.[17]

The speech was received with consternation by both Austrian Nazis and non-Nazis alike. In response, four days later Schuschnigg convoked a session of the Bundestag (Austrian Federal Diet). Alluding to the July Agreement with Germany, Schuschnigg vowed, 'Austria will go so far and no farther!'[18] He then reaffirmed Austrian independence with a fiery catchphrase, 'True German and red white red until we're dead!'[19] On 3 March, Schuschnigg dispatched a note to Mussolini explaining that he planned to hold a national plebiscite to reinforce Austria's political stance. Mussolini, however, believed that such a ploy was a 'mistake'. He opined:

> If the result is satisfactory, people will say that it is not genuine. If it is bad, the situation of the [Austrian] Government will be unbearable; and if it is indecisive, then it is worthless.[20]

Nevertheless, Schuschnigg was resolved to proceed. On 9 March, he conferred with his ministers. He was desperate. From Innsbruck he proclaimed that a national plebiscite would be held in four days. The Austrians themselves would determine, with a 'Yes' or 'No' vote, whether they wished to remain independent, Christian, and free. That same day,

Hitler learned of Schuschnigg's planned plebiscite. He was concerned that the Austrian people—if not subject to Nazi coercion—might in fact elect to maintain the Schuschnigg Government, and this he could not permit. He promptly summoned his military commanders, and plans were swiftly drafted for the occupation of Austria by the Wehrmacht.

Hitler also dispatched an urgent letter to Mussolini about the imminent invasion. It was personally delivered to the Duce on 10 March by Prince Philipp von Hesse, the husband of the Italian Princess Mafelda. Seeking his Axis partner's understanding, Hitler explained to Mussolini the circumstances compelling him to react: the thousands of Austrian refugees seeking asylum in the Reich; the repression of a specific segment of Austrians by an oppressive government hostile to National Socialism; the resultant political instability; the alleged breach of the July Agreement by Chancellor Schuschnigg; and the fact that he, Germany's Führer—as a native Austrian—could no longer afford to remain inactive. Lastly, Hitler reassured Mussolini that Italy's frontiers were sacrosanct to him, would never be violated by Germany, and would forever be demarcated by the Brenner:

> In a fateful hour I am turning to you, Excellency, to inform you about a decision, occasioned by the circumstances and irrevocable from today on. For years the Germans in Austria have been forced and mistreated by a régime which lacks all lawful foundation. The immeasurable sufferings to which they are exposed have no limits. Germany alone has as of now accepted 4,000 refugees who had to leave their fatherland although the great majority of Austria's population shares their political view. In order to eliminate this tension which became increasingly unbearable, I decided to undertake a last attempt with the Chancellor of the Confederation Schuschnigg, to reach an agreement whereby full equality for all under the law should be guaranteed once and for all. During one conference at Berchtesgaden I directed the Austrian Confederation's Chancellor's attention to the fact that Germany could not for long bear it that a majority in Austria would be mistreated by a minority on account of its national ideology. I myself am a son of this earth, Austria is my country, and I know from the circle of my own relations what great adversities and sufferings the great majority of this people who serve these national ideas have to endure. I pointed out to the Austrian Chancellor that such a condition could not be tolerated by a great nation. I dare say that it would be a unique fact in the world if one had to stand by idly while men of the same blood, the same descent and of the same common historical past are being persecuted and deprived of rights for these very reasons. In addition, I told Schuschnigg that in case the equality of right of all Germans in Austria would not be restored we should be compelled some day to take over ourselves the

protection of our brothers, forgotten by everybody. My demands were more than moderate. According to all principles of reason, right and justice and the democratic ways, Schuschnigg really should have resigned to make room for a government which enjoys the confidence of the whole nation.

I did not go that far. I was satisfied with a number of assurances according to which in the future all inhabitants of Austria would be entitled to the same rights and the same duties and that from the military aspect a certain security would be created within the framework of the Austrian laws which, though not righteously decreed, were nevertheless in force. Chancellor of the Confederacy Schuschnigg solemnly assured me this and made an agreement in this sense. But from the first moment on he did not keep it. Today he struck a new blow against this agreement by instituting a pretended plebiscite which should become a really distorted picture of a plebiscite. The consequences which this new violation created among the majority of the people were those I feared: the Austrian people are now finally revolting against the constant pressure which necessarily would lead to new measures of force. Therefore, the representatives of the oppressed population as well as the government and of the other organizations retired.

Since day before yesterday the country is increasingly driving towards anarchy. By authority of my responsibility as Führer and Chancellor of the German Reich, but also as a son of this earth, I can no longer watch idly the course of these events.

I have decided, therefore, to restore in the future in my country peace and order and to give to the will of the people the opportunity to clearly, openly and unequivocally decide for themselves their own future.

I want, therefore, to assure you, the Duce of the Italian people, and Fascist Italy, most solemnly the following:

1. Consider this procedure as an act of native self-defence and, accordingly, as a deed which every man of character would have done in my place in the same manner. You, too, Excellency, could not act differently if the fate of the Italians would be at stake. As Führer and National Socialist I could not do otherwise.

2. In an hour critical for Italy [during the Italo–Ethiopian War], I have proved to you the firmness of my sympathy. Do not doubt that not the least will be changed about this is in the future.

3. Whatever the consequences of the coming events may be, I have drawn a clear borderline against France and am now drawing an equally clear one against Italy. This border is the Brenner. This decision will never

be doubted or attacked. I did not decide this in 1938, but immediately after the World War, and I never made a secret out of it.

Adolf Hitler[21]

At 2 a.m. on 11 March, Hitler issued Directive No. 1 for the invasion of Austria, '*Unternehmen Otto*' ('Operation Otto'—see Appendix F). The invasion was to be carried out by Army, Luftwaffe, and S.S. personnel on 12 March. The invasion plan stated:

1. If other measures prove unsuccessful, I intend to invade Austria with Armed Forces to establish constitutional conditions and to prevent further outrages against the pro-German population....

4. The forces of the Army and Air Force detailed for this operation must be ready for invasion and/or ready for action on 12 March 1938 at the latest from 1200 hours.
I reserve the right to give permission for crossing and flying over the frontier, and to decide the actual moment for invasion.

5. The behaviour of the troops must give the impression that we do not want to wage war against our Austrian brothers. It is in our interest that the whole operation shall be carried out without any violence but in the form of a peaceful entry welcomed by the population. Therefore any provocation is to be avoided. If, however, resistance is offered it must be broken ruthlessly by force of arms.
Austrian units who come over to us, immediately come under German command.[22]

General Jodl issued a supplementary directive on the policy to be followed should the invading Wehrmacht come across any Czechoslovakian or Italian forces in Austria:

1. If Czechoslovakian troops or militia units are encountered in Austria they are to be regarded as hostile.

2. The Italians are everywhere to be treated as friends, especially as Mussolini has declared himself disinterested in the solution of the Austrian question.[23]

Meanwhile, Schuschnigg was resolved to do everything within his power—so long as it was legal and non-violent—to maintain Austrian independence. Above all, Schuschnigg was determined to avoid bloodshed between the German and Austrian peoples. By 10 a.m. Schuschnigg had received Hitler's ultimatum to call off the plebiscite scheduled for 13 March, and soon after midday he acquiesced. At 2 p.m. Göring began telephoning from Berlin to issue orders to Seyss-Inquart, and another ultimatum was given: Schuschnigg must step down as Chancellor and Arthur Seyss-Inquart must be appointed the new head of the Austrian Government. Although the Austrian Nazis were an unscrupulous, opportunistic lot, even they seemed affected by the German Government's coercive methods. Seyss-Inquart was agitated, and Minister Glaise-Horstenau, who was instrumental for relaying Hitler's instructions to Seyss-Inquart, stated:

> I don't know whether one can continue under these circumstances as a gentleman.[24]

President Miklas was unwilling to submit to the German demands. Under no circumstances would he name Seyss-Inquart Chancellor. As for Schuschnigg, he was unwilling to let the situation escalate into a civil war, and so he chose to resign. He knew that Nazism was a temporary phenomenon that would eventually come to an end:

> Austria was a German state, and would be a German state when the confusing nightmare of National Socialism was long past, a historical memory of blood and tears.[25]

He added ruefully:

> My task was finished. I had done my duty to the best of my knowledge, and I refused to be instrumental—directly or indirectly—in the preparations for Cain once more to slay his brother Abel.[26]

Shortly before 8 p.m. Schuschnigg broadcast his final speech as Chancellor over the Austrian radio:

> The German Government sent President Miklas an ultimatum that unless my Government fell in with the German Government's proposals, German troops would march into Austria. I yield to brute force.
>
> I declare before the world that all reports of workers' unrest in Austria, that blood is flowing in the streets, are complete fabrications.
>
> President Miklas asked me to inform the Austrian people that we yield to superior force.

> We have ordered the Austrian Army to offer no resistance and to retire, because we do not wish to spill German blood....
>
> So I take farewell, in this hour, of the Austrian people with a German word and a greeting, 'God protect Austria.'[27]

At 8:45 p.m. Hitler gave the order to proceed with the invasion of Austria in a second top secret directive:

> *Directive No. 2*
>
> 1. The demands of the German ultimatum to the Austrian Government have not been fulfilled.
>
> 2. The Austrian Armed Forces have been ordered to withdraw in front of the entry of German troops and to avoid fighting.
>
> The Austrian Government has ceased to function of its own accord.
>
> 3. To avoid further bloodshed in Austrian towns, the entry of the German Armed Forces into Austria will commence, according to Directive No. 1, at daybreak on 12.3.
>
> I expect the set objective to be reached, by exerting all forces to the full, as quickly as possible.
>
> Adolf Hitler[28]

To justify the imminent invasion, Göring gave orders over the telephone to Wilhelm Keppler, Secretary at the German Embassy in Vienna, that Seyss-Inquart was to send a fabricated telegram to the German Government. The text of the spurious telegram was to read:

> The provisional Austrian Government [the interim post-Schuschnigg Government headed by Seyss-Inquart] ... sends to the German Government the urgent request for support in its task of preventing bloodshed. For this purpose, it asks the German Government to send German troops as soon as possible.[29]

Also that night, Hitler spoke to Prince Philipp von Hesse, Oberpräsident of Hesse-Nassau, in a short yet important telephone conversation lasting from 10:25 to 10:29 p.m. As the son-in-law of Italy's monarch, Victor Emmanuel III, the Prince often served as an intermediary between Hitler and Mussolini. Von Hesse had recently returned from the *Palazzo Venezia*, a fifteenth century renaissance palace in Rome's city centre. There he had met with Mussolini for talks regarding the Austrian situation. Inside the palace was Mussolini's office, the imposing *Sala del Mappamondo* (World Map Room). Hitler's great relief is evident throughout, for he knew that the Wehrmacht could now enter Austria without the worrisome prospect of armed Italian opposition. Mussolini's abandonment of his former role as guarantor of Austrian independence further cemented German–Italian relations:

> VON HESSE: I have just come back from the *Palazzo Venezia*. The Duce accepted the whole thing in a very friendly manner. He sends you his regards. He had been informed from Austria, Schuschnigg gave him the news. He had then said it would be a complete impossibility, it would be a bluff, such a thing could not be done. So he was told that it was unfortunately arranged thus and it could not be changed any more. Then Mussolini said that Austria would be immaterial to him.
>
> HITLER: Then, please, tell Mussolini, I will never forget him for this.
>
> VON HESSE: Yes.
>
> HITLER: Never, never, never, whatever happens. I am still ready to make a quite different agreement with him.
>
> VON HESSE: Yes, I told him that, too.
>
> HITLER: As soon as the Austrian affair has been settled, I shall be ready to go with him through thick and thin, nothing matters.
>
> VON HESSE: Yes, my Führer.
>
> HITLER: Listen, I shall make any agreement—I am no longer in fear of the terrible position which would have existed militarily in case we had gotten into a conflict. You may tell him that I do thank him ever so much, never, never shall I forget that.
>
> VON HESSE: Yes, my Führer.
>
> HITLER: I will never forget it, whatever will happen. If he should ever need any help or be in any danger, he can be convinced that I shall stick to him whatever might happen, even if the whole world were against him.
>
> VON HESSE: Yes, my Führer.[30]

President Miklas stubbornly held out as long as possible. To his dismay it became clear that neither England nor France were going to intervene in the rape of Austria. Shortly before midnight he caved in and reluctantly appointed Seyss-Inquart Chancellor, along with his clique of Nazi ministers. Nevertheless, Hitler was resolved to invade and Miklas' late acceptance of the German Government's ultimatum did not deter him. The occupation of Austria by German forces began at 5:30 a.m. on 12 March. Shortly before 4 p.m. Hitler traversed the Austro–German frontier at Braunau, his birthtown, and delivered a speech in Linz:

> If Providence once called me forth from this town to be the leader of the Reich, it must, in so doing, have given to me a commission, and that commission could be only to restore my dear homeland to the German Reich. I have believed in this commission, I have lived and fought for it, and I believe I have now fulfilled it. You are all witnesses and sureties for that. I know not on what day you will be summoned, I hope it will not be far distant. Then you must make good your pledge with your own confession of faith, and I believe that then before the whole German people I shall be able to point with pride to my own homeland. And this must then prove to the world that every further attempt to tear this people asunder will be in vain.[31]

In Germany, Hitler's proclamation of 12 March for the unification of Austria with Germany was broadcast over the radio. It was read by Goebbels to foreign press correspondents:

> ... the German Reich will not suffer that henceforth in this territory [Austria] Germans should still be persecuted because they belong to our nation or because they profess their belief in certain [National Socialist] views. It desires calm and order! I determined therefore to place the help of the Reich at the service of the millions of Germans in Austria. Since this morning the soldiers of the German Army are on the march across all the frontiers of German–Austria. Tanks, infantry divisions, bands of S.S. on the ground, and the German Air Arm in the blue heaven—summoned by the New National Socialist Government in Vienna—will be the guarantee that as soon as possible the opportunity will be given at last to the German people itself to fashion its own future and its own destiny by a real plebiscite. Behind these troops stand the will and the resolution of the whole German nation!
>
> I myself as Leader and Chancellor of the German people shall be happy now once more as a German and a free citizen to be able to tread the soil of the country which is also my homeland. The world must convince itself that the German people in Austria is experiencing in these

> days hours of bliss and deep joy. It sees in the [German] brothers coming to its help its saviours from profound distress.
>
> Long live the National Socialist Reich!
>
> Long live National Socialist German–Austria![32]

The Wehrmacht was received with tremendous acclaim by the Austrian population. *Hakenkreuz* flags flew everywhere and flowers were joyfully given to the invading German troops. The invasion became known as the '*Blumenkrieg*' ('War of Flowers'). No resistance was offered by either the Austrian Army or the military forces of neighbouring nations. Himmler's S.S. and Gestapo went to work immediately. In Vienna, some 76,000 people were arrested within days of 12 March. Anti-Nazi Austrian officials and politicians were the first to be rounded up. Schuschnigg himself did not escape the dragnet. He was taken into custody by the Gestapo and remained imprisoned for seven long years. For five of those years he was kept in solitary confinement, first at Sachsenhausen concentration camp, then at Dachau. Expecting to be shot at any moment, Schuschnigg was finally liberated on 4 May 1945 by an American detachment.

Hitler, overwhelmed by the ecstatic reception he had received from the Austrian population, and the successful progress of the occupation thus far, sent a short emotional telegram to Mussolini thanking him for his support: 'Mussolini, I shall never forget this. Adolf Hitler.' In return, Mussolini sent Hitler a formal reply: 'Hitler, Vienna. My attitude is determined by the friendship between our two countries, which is consecrated in the Axis.'[33]

Meanwhile, it was necessary for the German Government to reassure Britain's leaders, who were understandably alarmed at the events taking place in Austria. Thus on 13 March, Göring contacted Ribbentrop, who was then in London, and briefed him on what he should say to the British regarding the German invasion of Austria. (Hitler, who had returned to his homeland, had temporarily left control of the Reich Government in Göring's hands.) It should be noted that the language used by Göring and Ribbentrop during the call was carefully calculated to deceive anyone listening in. Ribbentrop was certain that the British were monitoring his calls, and he tailored his dialogue accordingly. The telephone conversation was recorded in an Air Ministry transcript:

> GÖRING: As you know, the Führer has entrusted me with the administration of the current government procedures [*Führung der Regierungsgeschäfte*], and therefore I wanted to inform you. There is overwhelming joy in Austria, that you can hear over the radio.
>
> RIBBENTROP: Yes, it is fantastic, is it not?

GÖRING: Yes, the last march into the Rhineland is completely overshadowed. The Führer was deeply moved, when he talked to me last night. You must remember it was the first time that he saw his homeland again. Now, I mainly want to talk about political things. Well, this story that we [the German Government] had given an ultimatum is just foolish gossip. From the very beginning the National Socialist Ministers and the representatives of the people (*Volksreferenten*) have presented the ultimatum. Later on more and more prominent people of the Movement participated, and as a natural result, the Austrian National Socialist Ministers asked us to back them up so that they would not be completely beaten up again and be subjected to terror and civil war. Then we told them we would not allow Schuschnigg to provoke a civil war, under any circumstances. Whether by Schuschnigg's direct order or with his consent, the Communists and the Reds had been armed and were already making demonstrations, which were photographed with 'Heil Moskau' and so on. Naturally, all these facts caused some danger for Wiener-Neustadt. Then you have to consider that Schuschnigg made his speeches, telling them the *Vaterländische Front* [Fatherland Front] would fight to the last man. One could not know that they would capitulate like that, and therefore Seyss-Inquart, who already had taken over the Government, asked us to march in immediately. We had already marched up to the frontier before this, since we could not know whether or not there would be a civil war. These are the actual facts which can be proved by documents.

Göring next instructed Ribbentrop to inform the British ministers that: the German Government had not issued an ultimatum to Schuschnigg and that it was Seyss-Inquart and his cabal who had done so; Lieutenant-General Wolfgang Muff, Papen's military attaché in Vienna, had only been present to address a technical query; and Seyss-Inquart had specifically requested, via telephone and telegram, German military reinforcements to maintain order in Austria:

GÖRING: ... Tell the following to Halifax and Chamberlain: It is not correct that Germany has given an ultimatum. This is a lie by Schuschnigg, because the ultimatum was presented to him by Seyss-Inquart, Glaise-Horstenau, and [Hugo] Jury. Furthermore, it is not true that we have presented an ultimatum to the Federal President, but that it also was given by the others, and as far as I know, just a military attaché came along, asked by Seyss-Inquart, because of a technical question. He was supposed to ask whether, in case Seyss-Inquart would ask for the support of German troops, Germany would grant this request.

Furthermore, I want to state that Seyss-Inquart asked us expressly, by phone and by telegram, to send troops because he did not know about the situation in Wiener-Neustadt, Vienna, and so on; because arms had been distributed there. And then he could not know how the Fatherland Front might react since they always had had such a big mouth.

Ribbentrop then asked Göring if the situation in Vienna had stabilized. Göring responded that Austrian and German troops were carrying on in a spirit of comradeship:

RIBBENTROP: Herr Göring, tell me, how is the situation in Vienna; is everything settled yet?

GÖRING: Yes. Yesterday I landed hundreds of airplanes with some companies, in order to secure the airfields, and they were received with joy. Today the advance unit of the 17th Division marches in, together with the Austrian troops. Also, I want to point out that the Austrian troops did not withdraw, but that they got together and fraternized immediately with the German troops, wherever they were stationed.

Finally, Göring invited Ribbentrop to return to the Reich. He commented on the crisp, clear weather and the excitement of the Austrian people which he was able to make out on the radio now and again:

GÖRING: Well, do come! I shall be delighted to see you.

RIBBENTROP: I shall see you this afternoon.

GÖRING: The weather is wonderful here—blue sky. I am sitting here on my balcony—all covered with blankets—in the fresh air, drinking my coffee. Later on I have to drive in. I have to make the speech. And the birds are twittering, and here and there I can hear over the radio the enthusiasm, which must be wonderful over there.

RIBBENTROP: That is marvellous.[34]

Also that day, the German Government enacted 'The Law concerning the Reunion of Austria with the German Reich'. Signed by Hitler, Göring, and other top ministers, its first five sub-articles were the most crucial:

Article 1. Austria is a province of the German Reich.

> Article 2. On Sunday, 10 April 1938, a free and secret plebiscite shall be held for German men and women of Austria over twenty years of age on the question of reunion with the German Reich.
>
> Article 3. In the plebiscite the majority of the votes cast shall decide the issue.
>
> Article 4. The necessary regulations for the implementation and supplementing of this Federal Constitutional Law shall be provided by decree.
>
> Article 5. This Federal Constitutional Law shall enter into force on the day of its proclamation. The Federal Government is entrusted with the execution of this Federal Constitutional Law.[35]

Hitler immediately ordered the Austrian Federal Army to be placed under his command with Infantry General Fedor von Bock, Commander-in-Chief of the 8th Army, at its head. All its members were to swear an oath of allegiance to Hitler at once. And on 15 March, all Austrian officials were required to swear the following oath of office:

> I swear that I shall be loyal and obedient to Adolf Hitler, the Führer of the German Reich and People, and that I shall observe the laws and conscientiously fulfill the duties of my office, so help me God.[36]

Those who refused to comply were dismissed. Jewish persons were excluded from the oath-taking. Also, Nazi Germany's present laws were introduced in Austria, including: 'The Law Against Formation of New Parties of 14 July 1933'; 'The Law for the Preservation of Unity of Party and State of 1 December 1933'; 'The Law Concerning Reich Governors of 30 January 1935'; 'The Reich Flag Law of 15 September 1935'; 'The Order for Implementation of the Four-Year Plan of 18 October 1936'; and 'The Reich Law Concerning the Compulsory Registration of Members of the German State Abroad of 3 February 1938'. And two days later, Hitler ordered that Austria's National Bank be liquidated and its assets deposited into the German Reichsbank.

Hitler's motorcade finally entered Vienna on the afternoon of 14 March. He was welcomed by euphoric crowds. That evening, with the seventy-five-year-old Infantry General Alfred Krauss at his side, Hitler saluted the assembled Viennese masses from the balcony of the Imperial Hotel on the *Ringstrasse* (Ring Street).

During the four-week period between the annexation of Austria and the scheduled April plebiscite, Hitler travelled throughout Germany and

Austria, promoting himself and the National Socialist régime. While campaigning he harshly denounced Schuschnigg, describing him as an evildoer:

> I see in Herr Schuschnigg one of those forces who wish to create evil, but by the dispensation of Providence are yet ordained at the last to work for the good.[37]

In a speech to the Reichstag at the Kroll Opera House on 18 March, Hitler took the opportunity to publicly express his gratitude to Mussolini for remaining inactive during the Austrian invasion:

> I should like to express to the great Italian statesman in the name of the German people and my own name our warmest thanks. We know what Mussolini's attitude has meant for Germany in these days. If there could have been a strengthening of the relations between Italy and Germany it took place then.
>
> The ideological unity of our interests has become for us Germans an indissoluble friendship. The land and frontiers of this friend are to us inviolable. I repeat I shall never forget Mussolini's attitude. The Italian people know that the German nation supports my word. Thus on this occasion as before, the axis that connects our two countries proves of the greatest service to the peace of the world.[38]

And at Königsberg on 25 March, Hitler related a grossly distorted version of his discussion with Schuschnigg:

> I said to the Austrian Chancellor: 'Herr Schuschnigg, you are oppressing a country. You have no right to do so. This country is my homeland as much as it is yours. How comes it that you are continually doing violence to it? I am ready to stand with you before the people at an election. Both of us will stand as candidates. The people shall decide.' He objected that that was impossible on constitutional grounds. But I warned him to seek a peaceful way of lessening the tension, as otherwise no one could guarantee that a people's tortured soul would not cry aloud. I could not let there be any doubt that on the frontiers of Germany no more fellow-countrymen [Austrians] could be shot.
>
> And I tried to make it clear to him in all seriousness that this was the last way which perhaps might lead to a peaceful solution of this crisis. I left him in no doubt that, if this way should fail, in one way or another matters would not end there. I begged him to have no doubt that I was serious in my intention to place the help of the Reich at the service of my

> oppressed fellow-countrymen and not to doubt my resolution ... He did not believe the seriousness of my assurances and for this reason, one may suppose, he broke the agreement.

Hitler further explained his motivations and spoke scornfully of the foreign press' interpretation of events:

> I wanted to spare this country [Austria] the horrors of Spain and then I *had* to help: I had been summoned. I could not have borne the responsibility before the history of Germany if I had not given the order to march.
>
> Certain foreign newspapers have said that we fell on Austria with brutal methods. I can only say: even in death they cannot stop lying. I have in the course of my political battle won much love from my people, but when I crossed the former frontier [into Austria] there met me such a stream of love that I have never experienced a greater. Not as tyrants have we come, but as liberators.[39]

In Vienna on the evening of 9 April, Hitler listed five motivations, either personal, political, or economic, for effecting the *Anschluss* between Austria and the Reich. The first was on the grounds of ethnic ties, for the Austrians were a German people:

> In the first place this [Austria] is a German country, its inhabitants are German. It was the Reich which long ago founded this East March. It was men of the old Reich who long ago migrated hither. For countless centuries they have fulfilled their task as the East March of the Reich, and in so doing they have not merely remained Germans, they have indeed, on many an occasion, proved the shield of the Reich.

Hitler argued that Austria urgently needed Germany; her ills of disproportionate unemployment, low birthrate, and high mortality rate needed to be corrected:

> In the second place this country cannot, in the long run, live without the Reich. What do 32,175 square miles mean today? In the world of today, nothing! What do six and a half million people mean? Nobody takes any notice of them! Here is a perfect example for the German tribes of the truth of 'United we stand, divided we fall!' Actual facts have proved that this land and these six and a half million could not live here. When a tiny country has more than 300,000 unemployed on relief together with 100,000 who have drawn the maximum amount of unemployment relief

> to which they are entitled, and is no longer able to solve the problem, then it is clear proof that such a creation is not capable of independent existence. A further proof of this is to be seen in Austria's vital statistics. No one can deny that she has the lowest percentage of births and the biggest percentage of deaths.

The Austrians themselves, Hitler averred, had never wished to be detached from Germany, and after the Great War had sought unification with their German brethren. But the democratic Powers, in their zeal to penalize the vanquished Central Powers, had obstructed the realization of this goal:

> In the third place this people had no desire to be separated from the Reich. In the moment when its mission as the leading people in a huge empire ceased, the inner voice of blood immediately made itself felt. After the collapse in 1918 German Austria immediately wished to rejoin the Reich. The fatal ruling houses were now done with and the people had no desire to identify itself with the values and formations of its erstwhile dynasties. But the world prevented the fulfillment of its wishes. The democratic world outside prevented the *Anschluss* between German Austria and Germany. But the people turned against this world. And in the period when the banner of National Socialism was rising in Germany, in this country too people came to look to it more and more, and, as I well know, hundreds of thousands belonged to the Movement in their hearts. Then came mistreatment of this people by a group that had no right, either by virtue of its numbers or of its value, to lead this people and country.

Austria was his homeland, Hitler declared, and therefore he had personal motivations for effecting a reunion of his country of birth with Germany:

> And if this third reason is not a sufficient explanation of the fact that I am addressing you here today, then I only need to give the fourth. This is my home! Years ago, as a mere boy, I left Linz and came to this city. Then something drove me from here to the great Reich. Then came the War, and I was so thankful that I, poor and unimportant man though I was, was able to do something for this great Germany. I fought as a decent German soldier. Then, after the end of the War, I went on my way through Germany and won this dearest land of all for myself, finding hundreds of thousands and millions who believed in me because I in turn believed in them. At a time when all began to have doubts of Germany because the need in which she lay was so great, I was proud to be a German. I clung fast to this people, I fought and struggled for it, and

> won its confidence. I would be a bad German if I had not all my life so thought and acted.

Hitler believed that Austria would be better off with himself at the helm than with Schuschnigg:

> Finally, if that reason still leaves some people cold, then I must advance a fifth: I stand here because I am of the opinion that I can do more than Schuschnigg. I am not presumptuous when I say this. If I had not believed in it, I would not be here today; but Germany would not be where she is either.
>
> I have shown by my life that I can do more than this dwarf who ruined this country. I do not know whether in a hundred years anyone will remember the name of my predecessor; but my name will remain as that of one of the greatest sons of this country.

Hitler attributed his tremendous political success to the will of Providence:

> And I believe that it was the will of God to send a boy from here into the Reich, to let him grow up there, to elevate him to Führer of the nation, and to make it possible for him then to bring his home into the Reich.

And in his peroration, Hitler declared:

> I now proclaim for this land its new mission. Its mission answers to the call which once summoned hither German settlers from all parts of the old Reich. From now on the oldest East March of the German people shall be the newest bastion of the German nation and thus of the German Reich. For centuries in the troublesome years of the past the storms of the East broke on the frontiers of the old march. For centuries more to come she is to be once more an iron guarantor of the security and freedom of the German Reich, and thus yet another surety for the happiness and peace of our great people. And I know that the old East March of the German people will fulfill its new task just as it solved and mastered its old task.
>
> I am speaking in the name of the millions of this beautiful German land, in the name of the Styrians, the Upper Austrians, the Lower Austrians, the Carinthians, the Salzburgers, the Tyrolese, and, above all, in the name of the city of Vienna, when I assure your sixty-eight million fellow Germans who are at this very moment listening to me throughout our broad Reich that this land is German, that it has grasped its mission, that it will fulfill it, and that no one will ever surpass it in its faithfulness to the great community of the German nation.

> But our task will now be by work, industry, common action and co-operation to solve the great social, cultural and economic tasks, and above all to make Austria more and more a fortress of the National Socialist way of thinking and of National Socialist determination to develop and construct.
>
> As Führer and Chancellor of the German nation and of the German Reich I now report to history the entry of my homeland into the German Reich.[40]

Now that Austria had come *Heim ins Reich* (Home to the Reich), Goebbels' Propaganda Ministry took every conceivable measure to ensure that the plebiscite of 10 April was an historic event. Austria was plastered with propaganda posters and *hakenkreuz* flags, and Nazi troops marched to the tune of stirring martial music. Almost one-tenth of the Austrian electorate—chiefly Jews, Socialists, and Communists—were stripped of their voting rights. The single question posed to the voters on the ballot read:

> Do you agree with the reunification of Austria with the German Reich that was enacted on 13 March 1938 and do you vote for the party of our leader, Adolf Hitler?[41]

The ballot could be marked with an 'x' either 'Yes' or 'No'. Under the totalitarian system of the Third Reich, the plebiscite's results were a foregone conclusion. In Germany, 99.08 per cent of the electorate endorsed the *Anschluss*. In Austria, 99.75 per cent were in favour. When Hitler was informed of the plebiscite's results, he declared to the press that it was 'the proudest hour' of his life.[42]

Czechoslovakia was Hitler's next target, for Czechoslovakia's position in Central Europe was a strategic one and as such would be very useful to him. Hitler was not alone in recognizing Czechoslovakia's value in a geopolitical context. Over a half-century earlier the Prussian statesman and 'Iron Chancellor' Otto von Bismarck had said:

> He who possesses Bohemia holds the key to Europe.[43]

However, Hitler harboured a strong antipathy towards the Czechs themselves, for many reasons:

1. They were a non-Germanic people, and therefore in his view, of lesser racial value;
2. Czechoslovakia was the product of the post-war peace treaties;
3. The Czechoslovak Republic, presently headed by the well-respected President Edvard Beneš, was politically moderate and democratic;

4. Czechoslovakia was a member and staunch proponent of the League of Nations;
5. Czechoslovakia had mutual assistance pacts with both France and the U.S.S.R.;
6. Czechoslovakia possessed a strong, well-trained, well-equipped army;
7. Czechoslovakia had the notable Škoda Works, a major arms manufacturer;
8. Czechoslovakia was a 'natural fortress' and had nearly impenetrable defensive fortifications strategically positioned along the Czecho–German border; and
9. Czechoslovakia's bomber aircraft could travel from Western Bohemian bases and strike at Berlin without difficulty.

Therefore, a nation as potent and 'dangerous' as Czechoslovakia had to be neutralized. As early as 21 April, barely five weeks after the *Anschluss*, a meeting between General Keitel and Hitler took place in Berlin concerning the necessity to amend '*Fall Grün*' ('Case Green'), the German plan for the conquest of Czechoslovakia (see Appendix G), on account of the successful non-violent military occupation of Austria and its incorporation into the Reich. The document summarizing the meeting, dated 22 April, was prepared by Lieutenant-Colonel Rudolf Schmundt, Hitler's Wehrmacht adjutant:

Bases of the Dissertation on *Grün*

Summary of discussion between Führer and General Keitel of 21 April:

A. Political Aspect.

1. Strategic surprise attack out of a clear sky without any cause or possibility of justification has been turned down. As result would be: hostile world opinion which can lead to a critical situation. Such a measure is justified only for the elimination of the last opponent on the mainland.

2. Action after a time of diplomatic clashes, which gradually come to a crisis and lead to war.

3. Lightning-swift action as the result of an incident (for example, assassination of German ambassador in connection with an anti-German demonstration).

B. Military Conclusions.

1. The preparations are to be made for the political possibilities (2 and 3). Case 2 is the undesired one since '*Grün*' will have taken security measures.

2. The loss of time caused by transporting the bulk of the divisions by rail—which is unavailable, but should be cut down as far as possible—must not impede a lightning-swift blow at the time of the action.

3. 'Separate thrusts' are to be carried out immediately with a view to penetrating the enemy fortification lines at numerous points and in a strategically favourable direction. The thrusts are to be worked out to the smallest detail (knowledge of roads, composition of the columns according to their individual tasks). Simultaneous attacks by the Army and Air Force.
   The Air Force is to support the individual columns (e.g. dive-bombers: sealing off installations at penetration points, hampering the bringing up of reserves, destroying signal communications traffic, thereby isolating the garrisons).

4. Politically, the first four days of military action are the decisive ones. If there are no effective military successes, a European crisis will certainly arise. Accomplished facts must prove the senselessness of foreign military intervention, draw allies into the scheme (division of spoils) and demoralize '*Grün*'.
   Therefore: bridging the time gap between first penetration and employment of the forces to be brought up, by a determined and ruthless thrust by a motorized army....

C. Propaganda.

1. Leaflets on the conduct of Germans in Czechoslovakia (*Grünland*).

2. Leaflets with threats for intimidation of the Czechs (*Grünen*).[44]

It should be noted that Article 3 of Section A ('Political Aspect') indicates that the Nazis were even considering orchestrating the assassination of the German Ambassador in Prague (Ernst Eisenlohr) to justify aggressive action against Czechoslovakia!

That spring, Hitler once again began to clamour for the rights of 'persecuted Germans abroad'. This time his attention was focused upon those Germans located in the Sudetenland, the mountainous and westernmost region of the Czech province of Bohemia. These German Sudeteners, over three million, were nearly one-fourth of Czechoslovakia's entire population. Their representative was Konrad Henlein, an ex-gymnastics instructor and the head of the pro-Nazi *Sudetendeutsche Partei* (Sudeten German Party). The S.d.P. had a membership of some 1.3 million and received funding and aid from Germany.

At a confidential meeting (their first) in Berlin on 28 March, Hitler instructed his stooge Henlein to deliberately make demands of the Czech Government that were so excessive that Prague could not possibly consent to them. (Throughout the summer Henlein repeatedly visited the Reich to receive orders from Hitler personally: Munich on 9 July, Berchtesgaden on 1–2 September, Nuremberg on 8 September.) Accordingly, per Hitler's orders and on behalf of the S.d.P., Henlein revealed to the Czech Government the so-called *Karlsbader Programm* (Carlsbad Program) on 24 April. It consisted of eight points and insisted upon the following terms:

1. Full equality of status for Czechs and Germans;
2. A guarantee of this by the recognition of the Sudeten Germans as a legal body incorporate;
3. Delimitation and legal recognition of the German-speaking areas within the State;
4. Full self-government for the German areas;
5. Legal protection for every citizen living outside the area of his own nationality;
6. Removal of injustices inflicted since 1918, and reparation for them;
7. Recognition of the principle 'Within the German area German officials'; [and]
8. Full liberty to profess German nationality and political philosophy.[45]

In turn, the Czech Government stated it would agree to grant the German Sudeteners further minority rights, but was unwilling to accede to the other demands as yet.[6*] To the rest of European community it seemed as if the matter was purely a domestic issue between the Czechs and the Sudeteners. But this was not the case, for Hitler intended to create conditions that would preclude a mutually acceptable resolution between the two parties and destabilize Czechoslovakia internally.

6 * It was not until 30 June that Henlein's demands were eventually accepted by Prague in full.

The lack of armed response to the annexation of Austria demonstrated that the Western Powers, with their vivid memories of the carnage of the First World War, would do their utmost to avoid a repetition of the years 1914–18. And although France was contractually obligated to support Czechoslovakia by treaty, her aversion to war was as great as that of Britain—perhaps even more so. After giving the matter careful consideration, Chamberlain concluded that the Sudeteners' complaints were not illegitimate. He therefore recommended to the Czech Government that they submit to Henlein's demands, and the French followed suit, echoing the advisement of their Anglo-Saxon partners. But on 20 May, the Czech Government discovered—possibly through faulty intelligence disseminated by the Soviets calculated to provoke an armed conflict—that German forces were assembling along the German–Czech frontier. Anticipating a potential German attack from the west, the Czech Government ordered a partial mobilization. When Hitler learned of the precautions taken by Prague to ward off German aggression, he was furious. He categorically denied having any aggressive designs against Czechoslovakia, and denounced Beneš. But the truth was that Hitler was resolved to destroy Czechoslovakia, regardless of his public assurances. To secure his western flank, on 28 May he ordered 'serious measures', i.e. the expansion of the Luftwaffe and the construction of additional 'gigantic fortifications' overseen by his top engineer, Dr. Fritz Todt.

On 30 May, Hitler prepared another 'most secret' directive[7*] for a 'Two-front war with main effort in the south-east'. It read in part:

> *1. Political Prerequisites.*
>
> It is my unalterable decision to smash Czechoslovakia by military action in the near future. It is the job of the political leaders to await or bring about the politically and military suitable moment.
>
> *2. Political Possibilities for the Commencement of the Action.*
>
> The following are necessary prerequisites for the intended invasion:
> *a.* suitable obvious cause and, with it
> *b.* sufficient political justification,
> *c.* action unexpected by the enemy, which will find him prepared to the least possible degree.

7 * A previous iteration had been prepared on 20 May titled 'Draft for the New Directive "*Grün*"'. In this earlier version—unlike the one dated 30 May—it was *not* contemplated to 'smash Czechoslovakia without provocation, in the near future through military action'.[46]

> From a military as well as a political standpoint the most favourable course is a lightning-swift action as the result of an incident through which Germany is provoked in an unbearable way for which at least part of world opinion will grant the moral justification of military action.
>
> But even a period of tension, more or less preceding a war, must terminate in sudden action on our part—which must have the element of surprise as regards time and extent—before the enemy is so advanced in military preparedness that he cannot be surpassed.[47]

Keitel attached a covering note to the directive, which specified that 'Its execution must be assured by 1 October 1938 at the latest.' The bulk of the German Army was to be used in the operation against Czechoslovakia. It was to penetrate the Czech border defences 'with speed and decision'. A small force would be kept in the rear to safeguard Germany against any hostile action taken by the French. Also, a 'Propaganda War' was to be launched concurrently; its purpose was to 'intimidate Czechoslovakia by threats and soften her power of resistance ...'[48]

On 18 June, Hitler informed Keitel in a directive of his intention to proceed against Czechoslovakia on the condition that the Western Powers remain inactive:

> ... I will decide to take action against Czechoslovakia only if I am firmly convinced, as in the case of the demilitarized zone and the entry into Austria, that France will not march and that therefore England will not intervene.[49]

As of 11 July, the German Press once again began printing grossly distorted accounts of excesses perpetrated by the Czechs against the Sudeteners, and for a time there was a surge of virulent anti-Czech propaganda throughout the Reich. Next day in Paris, in a public speech, Prime Minister Édouard Daladier vowed to uphold France's obligations to Czechoslovakia. The French statesman proclaimed:

> The solemn undertakings we have given to Czechoslovakia are sacred and cannot be evaded.[50]

It was evident to all—the British, the French, and the Soviets—that the Sudetenland was Hitler's next target. During the summer months Hitler relentlessly put the squeeze on Czechoslovakia. The Nazis kept trying to impress upon the British and French Governments the purported intractability of the Czechoslovak Government in refusing Germany's supposedly reasonable demands. Germany's Ambassador to England,

Herbert von Dirksen, reported to the German Foreign Ministry on 18 July his assessment of present Anglo–German relations. He recognized that the British would go to considerable lengths to help settle the Sudeten problem, but only if Germany kept the peace:

> The present British Cabinet is the first one since the war to make a settlement with Germany one of the most important points on its program; it thus shows the greatest understanding for Germany that is possible in any group of British political leaders of Cabinet calibre. The present Cabinet possesses sufficient strength at home to carry out this task. In essential points it has approached the guiding principles represented by Germany: elimination of the Soviet Union from decisions on the fate of Europe; elimination of the League of Nations from the same task; advisability of bilateral negotiations and treaties. It is showing growing understanding for the demands of Germany in the Sudeten question. It would be willing to make great sacrifices to satisfy Germany's other legitimate demands—on the *one* condition that these objectives are sought by peaceful means.[51]

On 22 July, the British and French Governments turned down an offer by Germany for a four-Power conference to settle the Sudeten affair, since Czech representatives were not invited to take part. A week later in Breslau (today Wrocław), Henlein brazenly declared that all ethnic Germans, regardless of the country in which they happened to be domiciled, were first and foremost citizens of the Reich and were thus bound by its laws. With these and other inflammatory words, Henlein persisted in doing his utmost to trigger a Sudeten uprising that would precipitate an extreme reaction from the Czech Government, giving Germany the excuse it needed to step in. Germany was also urging Czechoslovakia's other neighbours, Hungary and Poland, to turn the screws on Czechoslovakia by pushing forwards their claims on Czechoslovak territories containing large numbers of Hungarians and Poles respectively.

To gain a better understanding of the Sudeten situation, Chamberlain sent his colleague Lord Walter Runciman to Czechoslovakia as a special envoy. He arrived in Prague on 3 August. By this measure the British Government was openly acknowledging that the German Sudeteners' cause had merit. Consequently, the Czechs could not help but feel that perhaps they could not count on their democratic allies after all. Runciman's task was twofold: to ascertain the true facts of the conflict between the Czech Government and Henlein's S.d.P., and to mediate between them (and if possible, to help them reach an understanding). Runciman met with Beneš and Henlein on several occasions. He also spoke with various other

Czech and S.d.P. officials, and to both Nazi and non-Nazi Sudeteners. During his meetings with Beneš, Runciman repeatedly pressured the Czech President to accept the terms of the Sudeten separatists. In the end, however, Runciman's attempts to negotiate a settlement between Prague and Henlein's S.d.P. were unsuccessful. For unbeknown to him, Henlein had been expressly directed by Hitler not to come to terms with the Czech Government, and on 16 September, Runciman was asked to return to England at Chamberlain's request.

The next day Runciman reported to the British Cabinet the findings of his unorthodox mission. Runciman was 'disappointed that he had not been able to bring about a solution by agreement between the parties concerned'. Nonetheless, he had been informed by Foreign Affairs Secretary Lord Halifax at the time of his departure to Prague that 'time gained was of importance'. His initial impression in Prague was that the Czechoslovak Government was 'blind to what was going on around them'. The Czech President, Dr. Beneš, 'was a man of great ability, [but] so agile that he made those about him distrust him'. As for Dr. Milan Hodža, he 'was an excellent Prime Minister, but with rather limited experience'. The rest of the Czech Cabinet, according to Runciman, 'were of poor quality and did not count'. Of Henlein, Runciman remarked that he 'lived at Asch, four hours' motor journey away from Prague, and could only be seen occasionally. He was a genial, good-tempered person, but nothing much could be got out of him.' Runciman had also discovered that 'even before his own arrival in Prague, Herr Henlein had been in frequent communication with Berlin'.[52]

Four schemes had been suggested to resolve the Sudeten crisis. Unfortunately, each one of them had certain features that the opposite side found objectionable. They were:

1. The creation of a new and independent Sudeten German State;
2. A plebiscite [on incorporating the Sudetenland into Germany];
3. A Four-Power conference [with British, French, German, and Czech participants]; and
4. A federal solution [i.e. the establishment of a federal Czechoslovakia].[53]

Runciman also explained that he had been hesitant to 'produce a plan of his own', since it might 'draw upon himself and possibly on the British Government the fire of criticism'. In the final analysis, Runciman was of the opinion that 'Czechoslovakia could not continue to exist as she was today. Something would have to be done, even if it amounted to no more than cutting off certain [German-populated] fringes.'[54] Several days later Runciman sent a letter to Beneš summarizing his conclusions on the

Sudeten matter. Chamberlain was given an advance copy, which included a few minor alterations to the text. Runciman began by recognizing the longstanding antagonism between the Germanic and Slavic peoples in Central Europe:

> The problem of political, social, and economic relations between the Teuton and Slav races in the area which is now Czechoslovakia is one which has existed for many centuries, with periods of acute struggle and periods of comparative peace. It is no new problem, and in its present stage there are at the same time new factors and also old factors which would have to be considered in any detailed review.

Runciman asserted that he had 'much sympathy, however, with the Sudeten case'. He went on to explain:

> It is a hard thing to be ruled by an alien race, and I have been left with the impression that Czechoslovak rule in the Sudeten areas for the last twenty years, though not actively oppressive, and certainly not 'terroristic', has been marked by tactlessness, lack of understanding, petty intolerance and discrimination, to a point where the resentment of the German population was inevitably moving in the direction of revolt.

He noted that 'the feeling among the Sudeten Germans until about three or four years ago was one of hopelessness'. But the advent of National Socialist Germany had given the Sudeteners 'new hope', and Runciman stated that he regarded the Sudeteners 'turning for help to their kinsmen [in Germany] and their eventual desire to join the Reich as a natural development in the circumstances'. Runciman then enumerated the numerous grievances of the Sudeteners:

> Czech officials and Czech police, speaking little German, were appointed in large numbers to purely German districts; Czech agricultural colonists were encouraged to settle on land transferred under the Land Reform in the middle of German populations; for the children of these Czech invaders Czech schools were said to have been built on a large scale; there is a very general belief that Czech firms were favoured as against German firms in the allocation of State contracts and that the State provided work and relief for Czechs more readily than for Germans. I believe these complaints to be in the main justified. Even as late as the time of my Mission, I could find no readiness on the part of the Czechoslovak Government to remedy them on anything like an adequate scale.

It was plain that Runciman felt, overall, that the Sudeten Germans were in the right and that the Czech Government was at fault. Runciman then opined that 'those frontier districts between Czechoslovakia and Germany where the Sudeten population is in an important majority should be given full right to self-determination at once. If some cession [of Sudeten territory] is inevitable', he added, 'as I believe it to be, it is as well that it should be done promptly and without procrastination.' Lastly, Runciman shared his recommendations for establishing peace in the heart of Europe, which were fourfold:

1. That those parties and persons in Czechoslovakia who have been deliberately encouraging a policy antagonistic to Czechoslovakia's neighbours should be forbidden by the Czechoslovak Government to continue their agitations; and that if necessary legal measures should be taken to bring such agitations to an end.

2. That the Czechoslovak Government should so remodel her foreign relations as to give assurance to her neighbours that she will in no circumstances attack them or enter into any aggressive action against them arising from obligations to other States.

3. That the principal Powers, acting in the interests of the peace of Europe, should give to Czechoslovakia guarantees of assistance in case of unprovoked aggression against her.

4. That a commercial treaty on preferential terms should be negotiated between Germany and Czechoslovakia if this seems advantageous to the economic interests of the two countries.[55]

In the second week of September the situation worsened. On 7 September, the S.d.P. abruptly discontinued their negotiations with Prague. On 11 September, a bloody uprising initiated by the S.d.P. broke out. There were violent altercations between pro-Nazi Sudeteners and police in Eger, Reichenberg, and Teplitz. And on 12–13 September, the disruptions continued throughout the Sudetenland, with numerous fatalities. On 10 September, Göring delivered a vituperative speech at the annual National Socialist Party Congress at Nuremberg. Before a crowd of some thirty-thousand members of the Labour Front, he denounced the Czechoslovak nation for 'oppressing' its Sudeten minority. Göring stated that Germany intended to thoroughly resolve the Sudeten problem and that no foreign nations would deter her from this aim. He gave a grim warning:

> If fate should win and another world war come, Germany would not lose but win.[56]

Göring next bragged of the incomparable might of the Luftwaffe, the unassailable fortifications of the West Wall (an enormous defensive barrier facing the French Maginot Line), and the Reich's ability to withstand a naval blockade like the one conducted by the British against Imperial Germany during the Great War. So confident was he of Germany's autarkic efficiency that he claimed the Reich could hold out for thirty years if necessary, should war break out. In his ugly rant Göring also belittled the Czech people and ascribed the underlying cause of Central Europe's political disorders to be the machinations of Soviet Jewry which, naturally, were abetted by the Western democracies:

> I do not deny that heavy clouds are gathered on the horizon and that terrific political tension grips Europe and the world. A small part of European humanity today treats with chicanery the minorities entrusted to it and thereby has become a kernel of unrest for all Europe. Unfortunately, one does not see the root of the disturbance. One seeks everywhere on the periphery to find tension there instead of at its point of origin. We know what is going on. We know it is intolerable that a cultureless little people over there—no one knows where they came from—endlessly oppresses and annoys people of culture. We know that it is not the laughable pygmies in Prague but that behind them hides Moscow, and the eternal Jewish-Bolshevist demons of destruction. From there comes the agitation, the promises, the unrest, the rumours, the lies. And the democracies are all for it. It cannot be otherwise.[57]

Two days later Hitler spoke at a Nazi rally at Nuremberg much in the same vein. He aggressively demanded the right of self-determination for the German Sudeteners and blamed President Beneš personally for their woes:

> In no circumstances shall I be willing any more to regard with endless tranquility a continuation of the oppression of German compatriots in Czechoslovakia.
>
> Herr Beneš indulges in tactics and speeches. He is trying to organize negotiations to clear up questions of procedure on the lines of Geneva and to make small concessions. This cannot go on forever. This is not a matter of phrases; it is of right—that is, of violated right.
>
> What the [Sudeten] Germans demand is the right of self-determination, which every other nation also possesses. It is not up to Herr Beneš to give

> the Sudeten Germans gifts. They have the right to claim a life of their own just as much as any other people.
>
> If the democracies, however, should be convinced that they must in this case protect with all their means the oppression of Germans, than this will have grave consequences. I believe I am serving peace the more if I do not leave any doubts about this.... I demand that the oppression of 3,500,000 Germans in Czechoslovakia shall cease and be replaced by the free right of self-determination.... It is up to the Czechoslovak Government to discuss matters with the authorized representatives of the Sudeten Germans and bring about an understanding ...
>
> The Germans of Czechoslovakia ... are neither defenceless nor deserted. I believe I must state this especially at this party convention at which for the first time representatives of our German Austrian Legion take part. They know best how much pain it causes to be separated from a mother country. They, too, will first understand the meaning of my statements today. They will also agree with me most enthusiastically if I state before the entire nation that we would not deserve to be Germans if we were not willing to adopt such an attitude ...[58]

Hitler's speech so agitated the Sudeteners that there were further incidents of civil unrest and on 13 September the Czechoslovak Government proclaimed a state of martial law. In response, the Sudeten National Socialists demanded it be lifted. Next day the Prague Government declared that they had successfully quelled the Sudeten disturbances. The French Government were greatly distressed by the ongoing Sudeten–Czech clashes, frequently fatal, and the ever-growing threat of war. Under the circumstances, Daladier suggested to Chamberlain that he confer with Hitler to secure as favourable a compromise as possible. Chamberlain agreed to do so and on 14 September his urgent personal message was sent by telegram to Henderson at the British Embassy in Berlin for conveyance to Hitler:

> In view of increasingly critical situation I propose to come over at once to see you with a view to trying to find peaceful solution. I propose to come across by air and am ready to start tomorrow.
>
> Please indicate earliest time at which you can see me and suggest place of meeting. Should be grateful for very early reply.
>
> NEVILLE CHAMBERLAIN[59]

Hitler was astounded at Chamberlain's unexpected initiative. The Prime Minister of England, leader of the world's greatest colonial empire, would come crawling! Hitler could scarcely believe it. For in 1939, Britain was still the number one world power. At this time the British Empire controlled, both politically and economically, over one-fourth of the Earth's population and nearly one-third its territory. Hitler swiftly responded that he would be 'very ready' to meet with Chamberlain at Berchtesgaden on the afternoon of 15 September.

At 8:35 a.m. on the 15th Chamberlain flew from Heston Airport to Germany to discuss with Hitler the Sudeten affair. It was the very first time the elderly prime minister had ever travelled by air. After landing at Oberwiesenfeld Airport in Munich at midday, Chamberlain—who was accompanied by Sir Horace Wilson, his close advisor, and Sir William Strang, head of the Foreign Office's Central Department—was received by Ribbentrop. The Anglo–German party boarded a train to complete their journey, which lasted three hours. Lunch was served in the dining cart. Throughout the trip, the train passed numerous German troop carrier vehicles, ostensibly on their way to German–Czech frontier. The train reached Berchtesgaden at 5 p.m., by which time dark clouds had obscured the mountaintops and rain had begun to fall.

After a brief stop at the Berchtesgaden's Grand Hotel, before which a half-dozen Blackshirts stood stiffly at attention, Chamberlain was cordially welcomed by the Führer on the front steps of his alpine retreat. Hitler was clad in his usual black pants and brown jacket with *hakenkreuz* armband. After taking tea in the vast hall of the Berghof, during which the British and German delegates chatted amongst themselves, Chamberlain and Hitler withdrew to the latter's study for their confidential talk. Dr. Paul Schmidt, an expert in modern languages, served as interpreter. It had been decided in advance that Ribbentrop, although present at Berchtesgaden, would be excluded from the summit meeting, for he was perceived by both parties as being a potentially 'disturbing element' on account of having formerly served as Germany's Ambassador to England.

The conversation was held in the exact same room in which Hitler had hounded Chancellor Schuschnigg the previous winter. Chamberlain began with a sincere expression of his desire to ameliorate Anglo–German relations since becoming prime minister. In turn, Hitler thanked him for taking 'so much trouble to come all the way to see him' and, as was customary for him, proceeded to recapitulate his numerous diplomatic and political achievements since assuming the chancellorship. In his detailed exposition Hitler did not neglect to speak of the Versailles Treaty, the League of Nations, disarmament, the Great Depression, and Germany's National Socialist rebirth. Hitler then admonished Chamberlain about the anti-German tone of the British Press, and criticized the British policy of 'interference' in German matters and the Reich's relations *vis-á-vis*

Austria. But then he got to the heart of the matter: the German Sudeteners were *Volksdeutsche*, and as such it was essential that they rejoin their brethren in Germany proper. Czechoslovakia had to agree to cede its western borderland territory, the Sudetenland, to the Reich. However, Hitler emphatically declared that he had no intention of bringing any Czechs into Germany; he did not want them. Chamberlain responded that he would entertain any reasonable proposal on condition that force was not employed. The two statesmen then discussed the finer points of incorporating the Sudeten region into Germany. As the technical conversation wore on, Hitler exclaimed irritably:

> But all this seems to be academic; I want to get down to realities. Three hundred Sudetens have been killed and things of that kind cannot go on; the thing has got to be settled at once. I am determined to settle it; I do not care whether there is a world war or not. I am determined to settle it and to settle it soon and I am prepared to risk a world war rather than allow this to drag on.

Chamberlain angrily interrupted:

> If the Führer is determined to settle this matter by force without waiting even for a discussion between ourselves to take place, what did he let me come here for? I have wasted my time.

Hitler paused; perhaps he had gone too far. He replied that 'if the British Government were prepared to accept the idea of secession in principle' with regard to the German Sudeteners, then they could next discuss how to go about putting this into practice. Chamberlain advised Hitler that he would take up with his colleagues the subject of Sudeten self-determination and the transfer to Germany of Sudeten territory. Once this was done, he would return to Germany to advise Hitler of the outcome. Lastly, Chamberlain requested of Hitler that he refrain from taking military action against Czechoslovakia before he returned for further negotiations. Hitler gave him an assurance to this effect.[60]

The meeting finished at approximately 8 p.m. with Chamberlain under the impression that he had bought himself more time to resolve the Sudeten crisis. He returned to the Grand Hotel fifteen minutes later, weary and tousled. He paused momentarily to oblige the press photographers, then withdrew to his room where he spent the night. At 9 p.m. Henderson descended to the lobby to disclose the text of the official communiqué, which contained three curt sentences—far from sensational—to the effect that the two politicians had had 'a full and frank exchange of views', that Chamberlain would confer with the British Cabinet in London the following day, and that another conference between the statesmen would be held several days later. It soon became known that the subsequent talks would take place at Godesberg, a picturesque spa town some twenty miles from Cologne. By 5:30 p.m. on the 16th Chamberlain was back in England.

To his Cabinet peers, Chamberlain gave an account of his first encounter with Hitler. He erroneously believed that Hitler's aims were 'strictly limited' and that the Führer would be appeased once the Sudeten question was resolved to his satisfaction. But what did Chamberlain truly think of Hitler, in terms of character? He said:

> In spite of the hardness and ruthlessness I thought I saw in his face, I got the impression that here was a man who could be relied upon when he had given his word.[61]

On 17 September, Hitler sounded off to newsman G. Ward Price with a one-sided denunciation of all things Czech. He condemned the 'oppression' of ethnic German Bohemians; bemoaned the fact that the Czechs people had never been independent until the victorious Allies had made them so; inveighed against Czechoslovakia itself as being an ill-conceived creation of Versailles that gave the Czechs undeserved ascendancy over minority peoples with a 'superior' culture; accused the Prague Government of playing off the Western Powers against each other to prolong the existence of the 'artificial' Czech State; and berated President Beneš for not having the sense to allow the Sudeteners to unite with their racial brethren in Germany:

> This Czech illness must be dealt with once and for all, immediately. It is like a cancer in the entire organism of Europe: if allowed to grow, it will infect international relations until they finally break down.
>
> This situation has lasted for twenty years. No one can estimate how much it has cost the peoples of Europe in this time. As an ally of the Soviet Union, Czechoslovakia points like a dagger at the heart of Germany....
>
> The Czechs have never been an autonomous peoples; it was not until peace treaties raised them to an unmerited and artificial supremacy over minorities which are more numerous than they themselves. Bohemia was a German electorate in the Middle Ages. The first German university was founded in Prague two hundred years before the days of Queen Elizabeth. The modern German language itself was derived from the language of the diplomats who served in the governmental offices of that

city, the site that the German Emperor had made his capital for a time. Only in the course of the Hussite Wars were the Czechs independent for any period of time. They made use of their independence in the same manner the Bolshevists do, plundering and pillaging until the Germans roused themselves and fought back.

The creation of this heterogeneous Czechoslovakian Republic after the war was complete insanity. It does not have any characteristics of a nation, either from an ethnological or linguistic point of view, or from an economic or strategic one.

It was a deed of insanity and ignorance to have a handful of obviously inferior Czechs rule over minorities which belong to the German, the Polish and the Hungarian people, people who can look back upon a culture one thousand years old. The Sudeten Germans have absolutely no respect for the Czechs and will not submit to their rule....

The Czechoslovakian Government is making a desperate attempt to pit the European superpowers against one another—else the Czech State would no longer exist. But it is impossible to maintain such an unnatural configuration through political and diplomatic trickery!

If Henlein is imprisoned, I will be the leader of the Sudeten Germans, and then let us see for how long Dr. Beneš will manage to issue his decrees. Hopefully, he will not have me jailed as well! Had the Czechs a great statesman, he would long have permitted the Sudeten Germans to link up with the Reich and would have been glad to have secured continued autonomy for the Czechs themselves. But Dr. Beneš is a politician, not a statesman.[62]

Also on the 17th, Hitler issued orders for the creation of the *Sudetendeutsches Freikorps* (Sudeten German Free Corps). The S.F. was a pro-Nazi militia patterned on Germany's S.A. It was membered by Sudeteners loyal to S.d.P. leader Konrad Henlein who had fled to Germany. These men were given training and weapons by the Germany Army. Their purpose was to instigate the disintegration of Czechoslovakia from within by acts of violence and terror. The S.F. unleashed 'The Undeclared German–Czechoslovak War'. It began in the early morning hours of 18 September. Bloody battles between the S.F. and the Czech *Stráž Obrany Státu* (State Defence Guard) resulted in dozens of violent deaths. Lynchings, kidnappings, and arson were the order of the day. The conflict ended in the opening days of October.[8*]

8 * Having served its purpose, the *Sudetendeutsches Freikorps* was dissolved on 10 October. Illegal actions committed by the *Sudetendeutsches Freikorps* against the Czechs were amnestied by Hitler per a legislative order of 7 June 1939.

On 18 September, five German armies—the 2nd, 8th, 10th, 12th, and 14th—were ordered to place themselves strategically at the German–Czechoslovak frontier in anticipation of a breakout of hostilities. That morning Daladier and Foreign Minister Georges Bonnet flew from Paris to London, landing at Croydon Airport at 9:30 a.m. There the Frenchmen were met by Chamberlain and Halifax, and the quartet set off almost at once for 10 Downing Street. Their discussions lasted throughout the afternoon and evening and concluded at 12:08 a.m. on 19 September. In what was termed the 'Anglo–French Plan', the four statesmen decided to permit the incorporation of Sudeten territory into the Reich. At noon on 19 September, the decisions made in London were relayed to the Czech Government by British and French diplomats at Prague. These were:

1. the cession of specific Sudeten frontier areas to Germany, i.e. those with an ethnic German population of seventy-five per cent or greater;

2. the establishment of a cantonal system elsewhere in the Sudetenland, where the local population would elect the type of government it desired;

3. guarantees by England, France, Germany, Italy, Poland, Hungary, and Romania to assure the integrity of Czechoslovakia's remaining territory; and

4. the nullification of Czechoslovakia's alliances with both France and the U.S.S.R.

Later, an official description of the talks was released:

> After a full discussion of the present international situation, representatives of France and Britain are in complete agreement regarding the policy to be adopted with a view to promoting a peaceful solution of the Czechoslovak question. The two Governments hope thereafter that it be possible to consider a more general settlement in the interests of European peace.[63]

The Czech Government turned down the Anglo–French Plan on 20 September. They believed that to accede to its exacting provisions would inevitably place Czechoslovakia 'under the complete domination of Germany'. But on 21 September, British and French representatives gave President Beneš an ultimatum: either the Czechs accept the Anglo–French Plan as is, or else they would have to deal with Germany on their own, without the assistance of the Western Powers. In view of this grim prospect, the Czech Government reconsidered and reluctantly agreed to accept it. The following day, under pressure, Hodža resigned. He was replaced as head of the Czech Government by Jan Syrový, a one-eyed general.

Hitler met with Hungarian Prime Minister Béla Imrédy at Berchtesgaden the same day the Czechs had initially rejected the Anglo–French Plan. Also present were Foreign Affairs Minister Kálmán de Kanya and General Lajos Keresztes-Fischer. The proceedings began with Hitler upbraiding the Hungarian party for their 'undecided attitude' towards Czechoslovakia. The Führer addressed the Hungarians as would a stern headmaster to non-compliant schoolboys. He curtly explained that he was determined to resolve the Sudeten matter and he did not care if it triggered a general war. Nothing less than the cession of the Sudetenland in full would suffice now, and he was certain that the Western Powers would remain inactive. Hitler warned that this was Hungary's last chance to take advantage, along with Germany, of Central Europe's present restructuring. Otherwise he would have to disregard Hungary's territorial claims altogether. As far as Hitler was concerned, the optimal solution would be to eliminate the Czechoslovak nation once and for all, for the Reich could not continue to allow a well-armed, democratic nation of non-Germanics to penetrate deep into its vitals like an arrow. Hitler instructed the Hungarian visitors to undertake a twofold course of action, namely:

(1) that Hungary should make an immediate demand for a plebiscite in the territories which she claimed, and

(2) that she should not guarantee any proposed new frontiers for Czechoslovakia.[64]

Hitler also advised that it might prove advantageous for Hungary to threaten to leave the League of Nations and set up a paramilitary force of its own, along the lines of the *Freikorps*. Hitler stated that he would put an end to the Czech matter within a few weeks at most. He would inform Chamberlain of the Reich's escalated demands concerning the Sudetenland with unsparing candour. In his estimation it would be best for Czechoslovakia to be dealt with militarily. Still, there was always the unexpected; the Czechs might actually yield to pressure and grant to the Germans all they wanted. Hitler repeated to the Hungarians that he would present Chamberlain with his new demands the next time they met. If the Czechs resisted, he would crush them by force. However, Hitler acknowledged that it would be best if the Czechs gave him a justifiable excuse to do so. Imrédy assured Hitler that he would submit to Hitler forthwith a comprehensive list of Hungary's claims on Czechoslovakia.

In a speech at Treviso on 21 September, during his Venetian tour, Mussolini commented wryly about Czechoslovakia's multiethnic composition. Not only should the rights of the Sudeten German minority in Czechoslovakia be addressed and resolved, contended Mussolini, but so should those of the Hungarians, Poles, Ruthenians, and Slovaks:

> If Czechoslovakia is facing a situation which we may call delicate it is because it was—we say 'was', having in mind that a solution has been reached—not merely Czechoslovakia but 'Czecho–Germano–Magyaro–Polono–Rutheno–Slovakia'. I insist that since this problem has been faced we must settle it in integral fashion.

Mussolini continued with a metaphorical reference to Chamberlain's proactive efforts:

> At this moment the British Prime Minister, who took the political initiative, is directing the ship of peace into port.[65]

On 22 September, Chamberlain travelled back to Germany for a second conference with Hitler. Before departing from Heston Airport, Chamberlain gave a brief statement to the British Press:

> A peaceful solution of the Czechoslovakia problem is an essential preliminary to a better understanding between the British and German peoples; and that, in turn, is the indispensable foundation of European peace.
>
> European peace is what I am aiming at, and I hope this journey may be the way to get it.[66]

Around noon, several hours before Chamberlain had reached his destination, Hitler summoned his generals for a conference. They examined a detailed map of Czechoslovakia, with Czechoslovakia's numerous strategic fortifications plainly indicated. The generals cautioned their Supreme Commander that in the event of war, bypassing these formidable structures would result in the deaths of hundreds of thousands of troops. On top of everything else, it would take time to overrun the Czech fortifications. Meanwhile, the Anglo–French democracies and the U.S.S.R. would attack Germany from the west and east respectively. But Hitler brushed aside these inconvenient objections. He ordered:

> I want all measures taken for an immediate invasion of Czechoslovakia. We shall march in even if it means a world war. I have pledged my word

to the whole German people. I am not going to be intimidated by Czech fortresses or by anybody.[67]

For another twenty minutes the conference went on, during which Hitler and his generals discussed technical matters. Afterwards they departed, subdued and quiet. The generals realized full well that if Germany invaded Czechoslovakia, and if the Western Powers and Soviet Russia intervened, the unenviable responsibility to win a major war would fall on their shoulders.

Hitler and Chamberlain met in Godesberg at the Hotel Dreesen, along the bank of the Rhine River, at 4:30 p.m. Godesberg was adorned with *hakenkreuz* and union jack flags in anticipation of Chamberlain's arrival. Chamberlain began the conference by apprising Hitler of the progress he had made over the past week since their last encounter. Pleased with himself, he informed Hitler that after 'laborious negotiations' he had succeeded in convincing not only his own government, but also those of France and Czechoslovakia, to consent to the transfer of the Sudeten region to the Reich. No plebiscite would be necessary, and a three-man, German–Czech–Neutral commission would determine the disposition of its multiethnic parts. In place of the mutual assistance pacts presently in force between Czechoslovakia and the U.S.S.R., a new 'international guarantee' would prevent any wrongful, unilateral aggression against the remainder of the Czechoslovak State. But when it was his turn to speak, Hitler—who could scarcely believe that the Prague Government would cave in so quickly, and whose preparations for Case Green were well underway—rejected this arrangement:

HITLER: Do I understand that the British, French, and Czech Governments have agreed to the transfer of the Sudetenland from Czechoslovakia to Germany?

CHAMBERLAIN: Yes.

HITLER: I am terribly sorry, but after the events of the last few days, this plan is no longer of any use.[68]

Chamberlain was stunned. He had not anticipated such a reversal. Indignant, Chamberlain informed Hitler that he was 'disappointed and puzzled', for the Führer had received everything he had asked for a week ago at Berchtesgaden, and more besides. Chamberlain added that he had put his entire political career on the line to see to it that Hitler's demands were accepted in full. But Hitler was not interested in Chamberlain's troubles. He now demanded that German forces be permitted to occupy the Sudeten district no later than 1 October. And if the Czechs tried to impede the German troops' entry onto Sudeten soil, it would mean war. Under the circumstances, Chamberlain decided—for the time being—to discontinue the conversation. In escalating his demand from annexation to outright military occupation without warning, Hitler had caught Chamberlain off guard. With a heavy heart, Chamberlain returned to his room at the Hotel Petersberg, No. 109, to consider his options.

The following morning Chamberlain wrote a placatory letter which was delivered to Hitler straightaway. He tactfully restated to Hitler that if Germany were to attack Czechoslovakia, the latter would be left with no alternative other than to defend itself with all means at its disposal. The British Prime Minister stressed that there was no need for violence, for the Czechoslovak Government had in principle agreed to cede the Sudetenland to the Reich in conformity with Germany's wishes. It was only necessary that the process be conducted correctly and peaceably:

> I am ready to put to the Czech Government your proposal as to the areas, so that they may examine the suggested provisional boundary. So far as I can see, there is no need to hold a plebiscite for the bulk of the areas, i.e. for those areas which, according to statistics upon which both sides seem to agree, are predominantly Sudeten German areas.
>
> I have no doubt, however, that the Czech Government would be willing to accept your proposals for a plebiscite to determine how far, if at all, the proposed new frontier need be adjusted.
>
> The difficulty I see about the proposal you put to me yesterday afternoon arises from the suggestion that the areas should in the immediate future be occupied by German troops. I recognize the difficulty of conducting a lengthy investigation under existing conditions, and doubtless the plan you propose would, if it were acceptable, provide an immediate ceasing of the tension.
>
> But I do not think you have realized the impossibility of my agreeing to put forward any plan, unless I have reason to suppose that it will be considered by public opinion in my country, in France, and indeed in the world generally, as carrying out the principles already agreed upon in an orderly fashion and free from the threat of force.
>
> I am sure that an attempt to occupy forthwith by German troops areas which will become part of the Reich at once in principle, and very shortly afterwards by formal delimitation, would be condemned as an unnecessary display of force.
>
> Even if I felt it right to put this proposal to the Czech Government, I am convinced that they would not regard it as being in the spirit of

the arrangement which we and the French Government urged them to accept, and which they have accepted [The Anglo–French Plan].

In the event of German troops moving into the areas, as you propose, there is no doubt that the Czech Government would have no option but to order the forces to resist, and this would mean the destruction of the basis upon which you and I a week ago agreed to work together—namely, an orderly settlement of this question rather than a settlement by the use of force.

It being agreed in principle that the Sudeten German areas are to join the Reich, the immediate question before us is how to maintain law and order pending the final settlement of the arrangements for the transfer.[69]

Hitler dictated a response upon receipt of Chamberlain's note. He repeated his endless denunciations of the Czechoslovak Government, which he alleged had for almost twenty years relentlessly persecuted the Sudeten Germans. The most heinous outrage of all, Hitler accused, was that the Czechs had hindered the Sudeteners in their righteous struggle for self-determination. But he would now quash these Czech excesses. Hitler also wrote that he distrusted the Czechs and their 'insincere assurances'. He believed they were just stalling for time in order to be able to find a way 'by one means or another' to obstruct a transfer of Sudeten territory to Germany. But Germany was resolved to settle the problem, if not 'by way of negotiation', then by the only other method remaining—namely, the use of force:

For nearly two decades the Germans, as well as the various other nationalities in Czechoslovakia, have been maltreated in the most unworthy manner, tortured, economically destroyed, and above all prevented from realizing for themselves the right of nations to self-determination.

All attempts of the oppressed to change their lot failed in the face of the brutal will to destruction of the Czechs. The latter were in possession of the power of the State, and did not hesitate to employ it ruthlessly and barbarically. England and France have never made an endeavour to alter this situation.

If formerly the behaviour of the Czechoslovak Government was brutal, it can only be described during recent weeks and days as madness. The victims of this madness are innumerable Germans.

In a few weeks the number of refugees who have been driven out has risen to over 120,000. This situation as stated above is unbearable, and will now be terminated by me.

What interests me, Your Excellency, is not the recognition of the principle that this territory is to go to Germany, but solely the realization which both puts an end in the shortest time to the sufferings of the unhappy victims of Czech tyranny, and at the same time corresponds to the dignity of a Great Power.

For England it is a question at most of political imponderables, whereas for Germany it is a question of primitive right, of the security of more than three million human beings and the national honour of a great people.[70]

Hitler's letter reached Chamberlain at 3 p.m. It was translated to him verbally since there had been insufficient time to prepare a written translation, and within the space of three hours Chamberlain had composed and dispatched to Hitler a reply. He advised Hitler that as the intercessor between the Germans and Czechs, he would present the Führer's new terms to Prague. He also asked Hitler to have ready for him a memorandum outlining these terms, along with a map of the Sudeten areas in question clearly marked:

My dear Reichskanzler,

I have received Your Excellency's communication in reply to my letter of this morning and have taken note of its contents.

In my capacity as intermediary, it is evidently now my duty—since Your Excellency maintains entirely the position you took last night—to put your proposals before the Czechoslovak Government.

Accordingly, I request Your Excellency to be good enough to let me have a memorandum which sets out these proposals, together with a map showing the area proposed to be transferred, subject to the result of the proposed plebiscite.

On receiving this memorandum, I will at once forward it to Prague and request the reply of the Czechoslovak Government at the earliest possible moment.

In the meantime, until I can receive their reply, I should be glad to have Your Excellency's assurance that you will continue to abide by the understanding, which we reached at our meeting on the 15th September and again last night, that no action should be taken, particularly in the Sudeten territory, by the forces of the Reich to prejudice any further mediation which may be found possible.

Since the acceptance or refusal of Your Excellency's proposal is now a matter for the Czechoslovak Government to decide, I do not see that I can perform any further service here, whilst, on the other hand, it has become necessary that I should at once report the present situation to my colleagues and to the French Government. I propose, therefore, to return to England.

Yours faithfully,
Neville Chamberlain[71]

The Hitler–Chamberlain talks resumed at 10:30 p.m. that evening at the Hotel Dreesen. There Hitler handed Chamberlain the memorandum and map he had requested. This was the peremptory 'Godesberg Memorandum', as it was thereafter known. Hitler's stiff new terms stipulated that Czech forces had to commence their evacuation from the Sudetenland at 8 a.m. on 26 September, and the evacuation had to be finished by 28 September. Chamberlain was appalled, and he strongly protested:

> CHAMBERLAIN: But this is nothing less than an ultimatum!
>
> HITLER: Nothing of the sort.

To this Chamberlain countered that the Godesberg Memorandum was what the Germans would consider a *Diktat*, whereupon Hitler retorted:

> HITLER: It is not a *Diktat* at all. Look, the document is headed by the word 'Memorandum'.

Just then an adjutant hurried in, interrupting the meeting. He held in his hand a crucial note stating that President Beneš had declared in a radio broadcast the mobilization of the entire Czech Army.[9*] Hitler was momentarily startled, but he controlled himself and quietly said:

> Now, of course, the whole affair is settled. The Czechs will not dream of ceding any territory to Germany.[72]

Chamberlain disagreed. He held the view that the mobilization of Czech forces 'was a precaution, but not necessarily an offensive measure'. Hitler's interpretation was different. He responded that if the Czechs truly intended to keep their word and cede the Sudetenland to the Reich, they would not have mobilized. This led to a heated dispute between Hitler and Chamberlain about who had, in fact, been the first to mobilize. Hitler argued that Czechoslovakia had been the first to mobilize its forces (this was actually the second time for the Czechs, the first being the partial mobilization of 20 May). Chamberlain countered that Germany had done so first. Lying through his teeth, Hitler angrily retorted that Germany had not mobilized at all!

9 * The full mobilization ordered by Beneš was to be completed in under six hours. This meant that by sunrise two million Czechs would be ready for war. The Czech Army comprised 800,000 men, plus 1.2 million reservists. All were called up without exception. France, greatly alarmed at this turn of events, ordered a partial mobilization the following day.

It was after midnight when Chamberlain asked Hitler if the Godesberg Memorandum 'was really his last word'. He was almost at his wits' end. Hitler affirmed that it most certainly did. Discouraged, Chamberlain regretfully stated that to carry on further negotiations under the circumstances would be futile. He had tried to the best of his ability to keep the peace, but it had all been in vain. At that moment Hitler unexpectedly relented with an offer, one which Chamberlain mistakenly believed was a generous compromise:

> You are one of the few men for whom I have ever done such a thing. I am prepared to set one single date for the Czech evacuation—October first—if this will facilitate your task.[73]

With that, Hitler crossed out '28 September' with a pencil and replaced the date with '1 October'. It must be noted that the extra three days given for the Czechs to withdraw from the Sudetenland was not really a compromise on Hitler's part, since the original date set for the military conquest of Czechoslovakia had been 1 October all along (as specified in the covering note affixed to Hitler's Case Green directive of 30 May). The six articles of the Godesberg Memorandum read:

1. Withdrawal of the whole Czech Armed Forces, the police, the *gendarmerie*, the customs officials and the frontier guards from the area to be evacuated as designated on the attached map, this area to be handed over to Germany on the 1st October.

2. The evacuated territory is to be handed over in its present condition (see further details in appendix). The German Government agree that a plenipotentiary representative of the Czech Government or of the Czech Army should be attached to the headquarters of the German military forces to settle the details of the modalities of the evacuation.

3. The Czech Government discharges at once to their homes all Sudeten Germans serving in the military forces or the police anywhere in Czech State territory.

4. The Czech Government liberates all political prisoners of German race.

5. The German Government agrees to permit a plebiscite to take place in those areas, which will be more definitely defined, before at latest the 25th November. Alterations to the new frontier arising out of the plebiscite will be settled by a German–Czech or an international commission. The plebiscite itself will be carried out under the control

of an international commission. All persons who were residing in the areas in question on the 28th October, 1918, or were born there prior to this date will be eligible to vote. A simple majority of all eligible male and female voters will determine the desire of the population to belong to either the German Reich or to the Czech State. During the plebiscite both parties will withdraw their military forces out of areas which will be defined more precisely. The date and duration will be settled by the German and Czech Governments together.

6. The German Government proposes that an authoritative German–Czech commission should be set up to settle all further details.

The Memorandum's appendix expressly forbade the destruction or dismantlement of any of the Sudetenland's installations, or the removal of its resources:

Appendix

The evacuated Sudeten German area is to be handed over without destroying or rendering unusable in any way military, commercial or traffic establishments (plants). These include the ground organization of the air service and all wireless stations.

All commercial and traffic materials, especially the rolling-stock of the railway system, in the designated areas, are to be handed over undamaged. The same applies to all utility services (gas-works, power stations, etc.).

Finally, no food-stuffs, goods, cattle, raw materials, etc., are to be removed.[74]

Hitler's last-minute alteration had the welcome effect of easing the tension, and the three-hour conference ended at 1:30 a.m. in a friendly spirit. Chamberlain expressed his gratitude for 'the Führer's consideration' and told Hitler he would forward the latter's modified terms to the Prague Government. He also told Hitler that after their recent talks, he felt as though a 'relationship of confidence' had developed between them. Hitler thanked the Prime Minister and repeated 'with great earnestness' the bald-faced lie that the Sudetenland was his final European territorial demand. Hitler's final words to Chamberlain concerned a German–British understanding for Anglo non-intervention on the Continent; in exchange Germany would not infringe upon Britain's overseas empire:

Between us there need be no differences. We will not stand in the way of your extra-European interests, and you can, without harm to

> yourselves, leave us a free hand on the European Continent in middle and southeastern Europe.[75]

Hitler was at this moment torn between two alternatives: he could either send his armies into Czechoslovakia, or acquire the Sudetenland through negotiations. Naturally he preferred to strike, although the second choice, a viable one, remained open. Chamberlain withdrew across the Rhine River to the Hotel Petersberg. When a reporter outside inquired if the situation was 'hopeless', Chamberlain replied:

> I would not like to say that. It is up to the Czechs now.[76]

Before boarding his plane in Königswinter, destination England, Chamberlain solemnly pronounced:

> During the next few days there is grave responsibility upon everyone concerned to consider very carefully the issues that are at stake. We must still make great efforts to save the peace of Europe.[77]

Once back in London on 24 September, Chamberlain's next task was to present Hitler's memorandum and map to his Cabinet ministers and the French Government for consideration. After deplaning at Heston airport, Chamberlain first shook hands with the towering Lord Halifax, then declared to those awaiting him:

> My first duty now that I have come back is to report to the British and French Governments the result of my mission, and until I have done that, it would be difficult for me to say anything about it. I will only say this: I trust that all concerned will continue their efforts to solve the Czechoslovakia problem peacefully, because on that turns the peace of Europe in our time.[78]

But as it turned out, the British Cabinet—most notably War Secretary Duff Cooper and to a lesser extent Lord Halifax—could not be convinced to accept Hitler's new proposals. The French Government also turned them down. And the following day, Jan Masaryk, the Czech Ambassador to England (and the son of Czechoslovakia's first President, Tomáš Masaryk), presented to Lord Halifax the Czech Government's official rejection of Hitler's Godesberg Memorandum:

> My Government now has studied the document and map. It is a *de facto* ultimatum of the sort usually presented to a vanquished nation and not

> a proposition to a sovereign State which has shown the greatest possible readiness to make sacrifices for the appeasement of Europe. Not the smallest trace of such readiness for sacrifices has yet been manifested by Herr Hitler's Government. My Government is amazed at the contents of the memorandum. The proposals go far beyond what we agreed to in the so-called Anglo–French Plan. They deprive us of every safeguard for our national existence. We are to yield up large portions of our carefully prepared defences, and admit German armies deep into our country before we have been able to organize it on a new basis or make any preparations for its defence. Our national and economic independence would automatically disappear with acceptance of Herr Hitler's plan....
>
> My Government wish me to declare in all solemnity that Hitler's demands in their present form are absolutely and unconditionally unacceptable to my Government.[79]

On September 26, Sir Horace Wilson—acting in the capacity of a special emissary—called on Hitler at the Reich Chancellery. (Along with Chamberlain, Wilson was a strong proponent of appeasement and one of the key architects of Munich.) With Wilson were two diplomats: Nevile Henderson, Ambassador to Germany, and Ivone Kirkpatrick, First Secretary of the British Embassy in Berlin. The interview began at 5 p.m. It was an especially tempestuous one, for Wilson had brought with him a letter from Chamberlain—which was read aloud—informing Hitler of the categorical rejection of the Godesberg Memorandum by Prague:

> The Czechoslovak Government now inform me that, while they adhere to their acceptance of the proposals to the transfer of the Sudeten German areas on the lines discussed by my Government and the French Government, and explained by me to you on Thursday last, they regard as wholly unacceptable the proposal in your Memorandum for the immediate evacuation of the areas and their immediate occupation by German troops, these processes to take place before the terms of cession have been negotiated or even discussed.
>
> Your Excellency will remember that in my letter to you of Friday last I said that an attempt to occupy forthwith by German troops areas which will become part of the Reich at once in principle, and very shortly afterward by formal delimitation, would be condemned as an unnecessary display of force, and that, in my opinion, if German troops moved into the areas that you had proposed, I felt sure that the Czechoslovak Government would resist, and that this would mean the destruction of the basis upon which you and I agreed a week ago to work together—namely, an orderly settlement of this question rather than a settlement by the use of force.

> I referred also to the effect likely to be produced upon public opinion in my country, in France, and indeed in the world generally. The development of opinion since my return confirms me in the views I expressed to you in my letter and in our subsequent conversation ...
>
> I learn that the German Ambassador in Paris has issued a communiqué which begins with stating that, as a result of our conversations at Godesberg, Your Excellency and I are in complete agreement as to the imperative necessity to maintain the peace of Europe. In this spirit I address my present communication to you.
>
> A settlement by negotiation remains possible and, with a clear recollection of the conversations which you and I have had, and with an equally clear appreciation of the consequences which must follow the abandonment of negotiations and the substitution of force, I ask Your Excellency to agree that representatives of Germany shall meet representatives of the Czechoslovakian Government to discuss immediately the situation by which we are confronted with a view to settling by agreement the way in which the territory is to be handed over.
>
> I am convinced that these discussions can be completed in a very short time, and, if you and the Czechoslovakian Government desire it, I am willing to arrange for the representation of the British Government at the discussions.
>
> In our conversation, as in the official communiqué issued in Germany, you said that the only differences between us lay in the method of carrying out an agreed principle. If this is so, then surely the tragic consequences of a conflict ought not to be incurred over a difference in method.[80]

Incensed by what he was hearing, Hitler erupted like a landmine. '*Es hat keinen Sinn weiter zu verhandeln!*' ('There is no sense in continuing to negotiate!') After he had composed himself, Hitler gave an ultimatum: the Czechs had to accept the terms of the Godesberg Memorandum, including the occupation of the Sudeten region by German forces, no later than 1 October. The deadline Hitler gave for the Czechs to acquiesce to his conditions was 2 p.m. on 28 September—less than two days away—or else there would be war.

That evening Hitler addressed the German *Volk* at the Berlin Sports Palace. It was a disturbingly violent speech. Inside the indoor arena a prominent banner displayed the stark message, 'Sudeten Germans are neither defenceless nor deserted!'[81] Hitler made his entrance at 8:09 p.m. The thousands of Berliners packed in the great hall received him with tremendous applause, which continued unabated for three minutes. The speech was broadcast internationally. At 8:16 p.m. Goebbels gave a brief introduction:

> In this historic hour, which keeps all Europe in breathless suspense, you [Adolf Hitler] speak for Europe and the whole world. Your people are united. No threat and no pressure from anywhere could change your and our position.[82]

At 8:20 p.m. Hitler spoke. He first explained that the objective of Germany's foreign policy was not to oppress or subjugate foreign peoples, but to protect the German *Volk*:

> Our foreign policy is not determined by *Weltanschauung*. Our aim is the preservation of the German people. We are not interested in the suppression of other people, nor to having other people among us. Let them be happy in their way and let us be happy in ours. This limits our foreign policy; but the aims of [German] foreign policy are neither unlimited nor erratic.

Hitler adamantly insisted that the Czech Government cede the Sudetenland to Germany by 1 October. If not, Germany would take it by force, come what may. The rest of his offensive tirade was replete with unsparing insults and slander directed at President Beneš, the Czechoslovak State, and the Western democracies:

> Europe was torn up [at Versailles] under the slogan of self-determination and re-divided by [democratic] madmen regardless of historical nationalities. That is how Czechoslovakia came into being. Czechoslovakia began with a lie, the father of which was Beneš. I sympathize with the Hungarians, the Poles, and the Ruthenians, but I speak only of the fate of my own countrymen.
>
> My effort for peace is not a mere phrase, but confirmed by facts, which no democratic liar may deny. There are two problems left. Ten million Germans are living outside the Reich and want to return there. There is a point where conciliation must end, because it would be weakness. I would not have the moral right to be the leader of the German people if I renounced this. It was the limit of complacency. The history of the union with Austria confirmed that I had the right. There is a last problem [the Sudetenland], which must and will be settled. It is the last territorial demand I make on Europe, but one which I will never give up.
>
> When Beneš lied this state together, he promised a cantonal system on the Swiss model, but instead he started a régime of terrorism. Germans tried to protest, but were shot and then a war of extermination began. Six hundred thousand Germans had to leave Czechoslovakia because they would have been starved.

Beneš resolved to exterminate the German race and succeeded in intimidating them and muzzling them. It became clear that the *raison d'être* of Czechoslovakia was only to attack Germany. Bolshevism used Czechoslovakia as a roadway to Central Europe....

Finally, at Nuremberg, I demanded self-determination [for the German Sudeteners]. Beneš' answer was new deaths and imprisonments. Then Britain came. I told Mr. Chamberlain of the only solution we would consider. I left no doubt that German patience had ended. France and Britain saw that the only solution was to cede the Sudetenland.

I am grateful and thankful to Mr. Chamberlain for his efforts. I assured him that Germany wants only peace. I gave repeated proof of this. I repeated that after this problem had been solved Germany would not have a territorial problem in Europe. I told him that after the Czechs had peacefully settled the problem with other minorities we were ready to guarantee Czechoslovakia, but I also told him that my patience has ended.

When Beneš saw that Britain and France would not help him unless the territories were ceded, he agreed, but what did he do. He is hanging Germans. The military oppression was aggravated immediately Beneš spoke. He did not cede the territories, but expelled Germans. Here the game ends.

I first demanded a plebiscite for the whole of Czechoslovakia, but I yielded, and told Mr. Chamberlain that I would agree to a vote only in some parts. I also agreed to the plebiscite being conducted under international supervision and for an international commission to determine the frontier.

Beneš rejects the proposals. He says that my memorandum created a new situation. What new situation? That he keeps his promise. He must hand us the territory on Saturday [1 October]. Now it is two men against each other. Beneš and I, with me and Germany.

We don't want the Czechs. Our demand for the [German] Sudetens is irrevocable. Beneš can choose peace or war. He will either accept my demands or I will go to liberate the Germans. I am the first soldier. Let the world know that behind me the people marches in step. Let the world know it is a different people from 1918.

When such patience was shown as we showed, it cannot be said that we thirst for war. My [Godesberg] memorandum, which is my last and final word, was nothing but the realization of what Beneš promised. Its essence is that territory [the Sudetenland] which belongs to Germany, which Germany wants, shall become German, not after Beneš has succeeded in exterminating half a million Germans, but now, immediately.

> Let us unite in swearing this holy oath: 'Our will shall be stronger than our need and danger. Our will shall break that need and danger.' We have decided that we are ready. Let Beneš choose![83]

After Hitler finished, the assembled Berliners cheered for ten minutes without pause. The raucous applause was interspersed with frenzied shouts of 'Lead us on to victory!' Goebbels concluded the rally by promising Hitler that 'the German nation stands as one man behind you' and would carry out the Führer's orders 'enthusiastically and obediently'. He added that the shameful events of November 1918 would never happen again and that the German *Volk* would 'defend the life and honour of our nation to the last breath'.[84]

Next day at 12:10 p.m. Wilson brought to Hitler a new message from Chamberlain. The British Prime Minister wished to advise Hitler that due to the latter's distrust of the Czech Government, the British Government would ensure that the Czechs upheld their end of the bargain in any deals made. This offer did not interest Hitler. He countered that the final responsibility lay with the Czechs. They could either agree to the Godesberg Memorandum, or not. If they refused, he would 'destroy Czechoslovakia'. Wilson was appalled by Hitler's brutality. He stood and in a dispassionate voice relayed to Hitler the crux of Chamberlain's position: if France was compelled to come to Czechoslovakia's defence (per the Franco–Czechoslovak Mutual Assistance Treaty of 1925) and become 'actively engaged' in an armed conflict with Germany, Britain would 'feel obliged' to side with its French ally. Hitler took this to mean that if France chose to attack Germany, then Britain would do likewise. Wilson replied that Hitler had misunderstood and that on the contrary, whether or not there would be a general war depended entirely on the Führer. Hitler furiously retorted that if England and France were so keen on attacking Germany, they were welcome to do so. He was not concerned, and if in a week's time they were all at war, so be it.[85] But this was bluster, for in the autumn of 1938 Germany was not sufficiently powerful to take on Czechoslovakia, the Western democracies, and possibly even the Soviet Union (which was allied by treaty with both France and Czechoslovakia), all at once.

After the stormy thirty-minute meeting, Wilson flew back to England to deliver to Chamberlain Hitler's written reply to his letter of 26 September. In London, several hours later, Chamberlain discussed Hitler's letter in confidence with a few of his Cabinet ministers. It appeared from the text that a peaceful solution might still be possible, but only if the Czech Government was willing to be amenable:

> The Government in Prague feel justified in maintaining that the proposals in my Memorandum of 23rd September went far beyond the

concessions which it made to the British and French Governments, and that the acceptance of the Memorandum would rob Czechoslovakia of every guarantee of its national existence.

This statement is based on the argument that Czechoslovakia is to give up a great part of her prepared defensive system before she can take steps elsewhere for her military protection. Thereby the political and economic independence of the country is automatically abolished.

Moreover, the exchange of population proposed by me would turn out in practice to be a panic-stricken flight.

I must openly declare that I cannot bring myself to understand these arguments, or even admit that they can be regarded as seriously put forward.

The Government in Prague simply passes over the fact that the actual arrangements for the final settlement of the Sudeten German problem in accordance with my proposals will be made dependent, not on a unilateral German petition or on German measures of force, but rather, on the one hand, on a free vote under no outside influence and, on the other, to a very wide degree on German–Czech agreement on matters of detail to be reached subsequently. Not only the exact definition of the territories in which the plebiscite is to take place, but the execution of the plebiscite and the delimitation of the frontier to be made on the basis of its result are, in accordance with my proposals, to be made independently of any unilateral decision by Germany. Moreover, all other details are to be reserved for agreement on the part of a German–Czech Commission....

It is clear from my Memorandum that the German occupation would only extend to the given line, and that the final delimitation of the frontier would take place in accordance with the procedure which I have already described. The Prague Government has no right to doubt that the German military measures would stop within these limits. If, nevertheless, it desires such a doubt to be taken into account the British and, if necessary, also the French Government can guarantee the quick fulfillment of my proposal. I can, moreover, only refer to my speech yesterday, in which I clearly declared that I regret the idea of any attack on Czechoslovak territory, and that under the condition which I laid down I am even ready to give a formal guarantee for the remainder of Czechoslovakia....

I must assume that the Government in Prague is only using a proposal for the occupation by German troops in order, by distorting the meaning and object of my proposal, to mobilize those forces in other countries, in particular in England and France, from which they hope to receive unreserved support for their aim and thus to achieve the possibility of a general warlike conflagration. I must leave it to your judgment whether,

> in view of these facts, you consider that you should continue your effort, for which I should like to take this opportunity of once more thanking you, to spoil such manoeuvres and bring the Government in Prague to reason at the very last hour.[86]

Also that day, Chamberlain addressed the British people in a poignant radio broadcast. His heartfelt dedication to the cause of peace was striking:

> How horrible, fantastic, incredible, it is that we should be digging trenches and trying on gas-masks here because of a quarrel in a far-away country between people of whom we know nothing!... I would not hesitate to pay even a third visit to Germany, if I thought it would do any good.... I am myself a man of peace to the depths of my soul. Armed conflict between nations is a nightmare to me; but if I were convinced that any nation had made up its mind to dominate the world by fear of its force, I should feel that it must be resisted. Under such a domination, life for people who believe in liberty would not be worth living: but war is a fearful thing, and we must be very clear, before we embark on it, that it is really the great issues that are at stake.[87]

Chamberlain's speech resonated with all Britons insightful enough to discern that the crisis concerned not merely the fate of a small, distant nation in the heart of Europe, but the future of all freedom-loving peoples. Later that night, after his memorable and stirring broadcast, Chamberlain wrote another letter to Hitler:

> ... I feel certain that you can get all essentials without war and without delay. I am ready to come to Berlin myself at once to discuss arrangements for transfers with you and representatives of the Czech Government, together with representatives of France and Italy, if you desire. I feel convinced that we can reach agreement in a week.
>
> However much you distrust the Prague Government's intentions, you cannot doubt the power of the British and French Governments to see that the promises are carried out fully and carefully and forthwith.
>
> As you know, I have stated publicly that we are prepared to undertake that they shall be so carried out.
>
> I cannot believe that you will take the responsibility of starting a world war which may end civilization for the sake of a few days' delay in settling this long-standing problem.[88]

So intent on averting a general war was Chamberlain that he also sent Mussolini a brief note. It was essentially a repetition of his entreaty to Hitler:

> I have today addressed a last appeal to Herr Hitler to abstain from force to settle the Sudeten problem, which I feel sure can be settled by a short discussion, and will give him the essential territory, population, and protection for both Sudetens and Czechs during the transfer.
>
> I have offered myself to go at once to Berlin to discuss arrangements with German and Czech representatives and, if the Chancellor desires, representatives also of Italy and France.
>
> I trust Your Excellency will inform the German Chancellor that you are willing to be represented and urge him to agree to my proposal which will keep all our peoples out of war.
>
> I have already guaranteed that Czech promises should be carried out and feel confident full agreement could be reached in a week.[89]

On 26 and 27 September, there was an exchange of telegrams between Franklin Roosevelt and Hitler 'in the interest of the maintenance of peace'. In Roosevelt's second communication, sent at 10 p.m. on the 27th, he entreated the Führer to remain open to a diplomatic solution in order to prevent an outbreak of hostilities in Europe. Roosevelt was of the view that the issues of contention between Germany and Czechoslovakia should be worked out without resorting to arms. The American President called attention to the fact that present tensions could, if exacerbated, escalate into a European-wide conflagration. He therefore suggested that a major conference should be held at once to resolve the crisis, under the following conditions: one, that the conference be held in a neutral nation; and two, that all nations with a vested interest participate. Roosevelt wrapped up his urgent appeal to Hitler with these eloquent words:

> Allow me to state my unqualified conviction that history, and the souls of every man, woman, and child whose lives will be lost in the threatened war, will hold us and all of us accountable should we omit any appeal for its prevention.
>
> The Government of the United States has no political involvements in Europe, and will assume no obligations in the conduct of the present negotiations. Yet in our own right we recognize our responsibilities as a part of a world of neighbours.
>
> The conscience and the impelling desire of the people of my country demand that the voice of their Government be raised again and yet again to avert and to avoid war.[90]

Although Roosevelt could not have expected it, let alone foreseen it, a peace conference along the lines he had proposed was to take place in less than two days, although not in a neutral country nor with all affected parties included—most notably Czechoslovakia and, to a lesser degree, the Soviet Union.

André François-Poncet, the French Ambassador to Germany, met with Hitler at the Chancellery on 28 September. He was there to present new proposals on behalf of the French Government. The interview began at 11:15 a.m. and took place in Hitler's office, with Ribbentrop present. François-Poncet started by earnestly remonstrating with Hitler:

> You deceive yourself, Chancellor, if you believe you can confine the conflict to Czechoslovakia. If you attack that country, you will set all Europe ablaze. You are naturally confident of winning the war, just as we believe that we can defeat you. But why should you take that risk when your essential demands can be met without war?[91]

François-Poncet had with him a map of Czechoslovakia which outlined the specific sections the French Government was willing to grant to Germany. The map had been prepared by the French General Staff, and Hitler found it most satisfactory. While François-Poncet was engaged with Hitler, Bernardo Attolico, the Italian Ambassador, hurried into the Chancellery. Flushed and perspiring heavily, he insisted on seeing Hitler immediately. Due to the apparent urgency of Attolico's purpose, Hitler agreed to take a moment to consult privately with the Italian diplomat. In a state of tremulous agitation, Attolico informed Hitler that he had a critical message to deliver to him from Mussolini personally: the British Government had requested for Mussolini to mediate the Sudeten matter! Mediation was not exactly what Hitler had in mind, so Attolico continued:

> The Duce informs you that whatever you decide, Führer, Fascist Italy stands behind you.[92]

Attolico pointed out to Hitler that Mussolini felt it would be best for the Führer to 'accept the British proposal' and to 'refrain from mobilization'. Hitler held Mussolini's opinion in high regard, and after mulling it over he agreed to a quadruplicate conference with himself, Mussolini, Chamberlain, and Daladier as the primaries. To Attolico's immense satisfaction, Hitler instructed him to inform Mussolini that he had decided to accept the offer. Daladier was also in favour of the proposal. The venue for the historic event was fixed for Munich, the birthplace of National Socialism, on 29 September.

That afternoon Hitler's deadline of 2 p.m. expired. Refusing to be bullied, the Czech Government declared, as it had on before on 25 September, that it rejected Hitler's Godesberg terms. Alarmed at this latest development, the French Government promptly ordered a partial mobilization of 600,000 soldiers. The British Government also reacted by mobilizing the Royal Navy and auxiliary aerial forces. However, the German Army did not invade as Hitler had threatened it would because of the planned summit conference in Munich. There was still hope.

At 4:20 p.m., while Chamberlain was recounting his various 'efforts, negotiations, and journeys' to the House of Commons, Sir John Simon handed him a document. It read:

> Herr Hitler accepts your proposals [for a four-Power conference]. He will be glad to meet you at Munich tomorrow, together with M. Daladier and Signor Mussolini.[93]

The Munich Peace Conference was an exclusive affair. Delegates of the Soviet Government were not invited, and at Hitler's insistence Czechs representatives were specifically excluded. Instead, the Czechs were notified on the night of 28 September that a conference between the 'Big Four' would be held the next day in Munich, where the Anglo–French democracies and their Axis counterparts would settle the ongoing Sudeten–Czech dispute once and for all. The conference was held at the Führerhaus and started shortly after midday, at 12:30 p.m. Schmidt once more served as chief interpreter. The talks were conducted informally and were congenial in nature. With Mussolini 'mediating', Chamberlain and Daladier finally acquiesced, and Hitler got his way. The Munich Agreement (see Appendix H) was ratified at 1:35 a.m. on 30 September. Its terms were nearly the same as the Godesberg Memorandum, with a few insignificant concessions on Hitler's part.

The German occupation of the Sudetenland was scheduled to take place over a ten-day period, beginning 1 October. The Sudetenland was divided into zones, and the occupation was to unfold in phases: Zone I (southern Bohemia) on 1–2 October; Zone II (northern Bohemia) on 2–3 October; Zone III (the largest and westernmost of the four zones) on 3, 4, and 5 October; and Zone IV (northern Moravia) on 6–7 October. The occupation of remaining Sudeten territory containing a Germanic majority was to be completed by 10 October. The Czechoslovak Government was to ensure that Czech forces had evacuated the occupied areas by this date, and was responsible to see to it that 'existing installations' were left intact. The exact demarcations of the Sudetenland's borders were to be determined by a plebiscite. They were to be adjusted to reflect the realities of the Sudetenland's ethnogeographic makeup. The plebiscite was to be overseen by an international commission of German, British, French, Italian, and Czech representatives. They were to assure the integrity of the voting process.

After the conference, the British and French informed the Czechs of the decisions reached by the 'Big Four' and urged the Czechs to fulfill them without delay. The Czechs were told in no uncertain terms that they could either stand alone (i.e. without Anglo–French assistance) against the overwhelming might of the Wehrmacht, or they could defer to the settlement provisions decided by the four Major Powers on their behalf. Recognizing the futility of offering resistance to the Nazis all by themselves, the Czechs succumbed. General Syrový informed the nation over the radio that in the interest of European peace and the continued existence of the nation, the Czech Government was yielding to international pressure and would, per the terms of the Munich Agreement, surrender the westernmost territories of Bohemia populated predominantly by ethnic Germans to the more powerful German Reich. The Czech war hero declared:

> Citizens and Soldiers!… I must tell you frankly, as my conscience as the responsible head of the Army commands me to do, that the [German] power which has now set itself against us compels us to recognize its superior force and to act accordingly.
>
> My highest aim, like that of every one of you, is to preserve the life of the nation. We have received this duty from the hands of our fathers, who lived a harder life than ours, because they were not free. And we must fulfill this mission not only with love in our hearts, but also with lucid reason. In this fateful hour our task is to weigh everything, to see everything, and to recognize clearly what road leads to this highest aim of ours. As a soldier, I declare to you, with a full sense of my responsibility: it is the road of peace. It is the road of peace because we shall enter on our new life with undiminished national strength and with the consciousness that we are more nationally compact and therefore a stronger State.…
>
> The four European Great Powers met in Munich and decided to call upon us to accept our new frontiers which take from us the German districts of our State. We had the choice between a desperate and hopeless defence, which would have meant the sacrifice not only of an entire population of our adult men, but also of women and children, and the acceptance of conditions which, in view of the fact that they were imposed under pressure and without fighting, are unparalleled in history for ruthlessness. We wanted to make a contribution to peace, and we would have made it willingly, but not in the way in which we were constrained to do it.
>
> But we were deserted, and we stood alone.
>
> All the States of Europe, including our neighbours to the North and South, are under arms. We are in a certain sense a fortress beleaguered by forces which are far more powerful than ours.

> Deeply moved by our situation, all our leaders, together with the Army and the President of the Republic, have considered all the possibilities which remained to us. They came to the conclusion that if we had to choose between a reduction of our territory and the death of our nation, it was our sacred duty to preserve the life of our people, so that we might emerge from this time of terror unweakened and so that we might not have to abandon our confidence that our nation will recover itself, as it has so often done in the past.[94]

After Syrový's broadcast, General Ludvík Krejči issued a proclamation to the Czech Army:

> Soldiers! The Government of the Czechoslovak Republic has been obliged, under the pressure of world events, to agree to the cession of certain territories of our State to our neighbour the Reich. The Army too associates itself with the deep mourning of the nation at the mutilation of the inheritance of our forebears. If we soldiers have up to now been the protection and the pride of the nation, we must continue to be so in the sad days through which we are now living. Western Europe, including our allies, categorically demands this sacrifice of us so that a world war may be averted.
>
> By the oath which we have taken, we have promised the President of the Republic and its Government absolute obedience in all circumstances. Fate has now called upon us to perform our duty in the most painful circumstances. We are soldiers, and must always be ready to suppress our feelings and to be guided solely and exclusively by cool reason. Cool reason had to be the guide, too, of our Commander-in-Chief, the President of the Republic, the Prime Minister, and all the representatives of our State, who, in view of their heavy responsibility, could not allow unnecessary losses, so as not to weaken our State still more. At the head of our State are persons who are among the most prominent of its founders and creators. They have always had our complete confidence, and will have it in the future, for we are convinced that they have done everything which lay within human power.

Krejči concluded by enjoining Czech soldiers to dutifully defend the remainder of the truncated Czechoslovak nation:

> A true soldier must also be able to endure ill-success. Great and genuine heroism can also manifest itself in this way. Our Army has not been beaten, and has kept its good name wholly untarnished. It must keep it so in the future too. The Republic will still need us, and will require our

> whole powers. Let us therefore keep cool heads, and close our ranks. We shall keep our oath to the last letter. A manly word is harder than rock. By its preparedness, the Army has even today saved the nation from a worse danger. We are firmly convinced that our nation will emerge happily out of the present difficult period. We soldiers will do everything in our power to promote this end. And so our Government and our nation will at all times find us ready for any sacrifice.[95]

With the Munich Agreement finalized, General Jodl jotted down in his diary:

> The Pact of Munich is signed. Czechoslovakia as a power is out. Four zones as set forth will be occupied between the 2nd and 7th of October. The remaining part of mainly German character will be occupied by the 10th of October. The genius of the Führer and his determination not to shun even a World War have again won victory without the use of force. The hope remains that the incredulous, the weak and the doubtful people have been converted and will remain that way.[96]

Chamberlain spent the night at Munich's Regina Palace Hotel, and on the morning of 30 September, he met with Hitler for a confidential talk at the latter's luxury apartment at Prinzregentenplatz 16. It was their final meeting. Chamberlain presented to Hitler the draft of an Anglo–German Declaration. The text consisted of a pledge by the British and German peoples to renounce warfare forevermore and to resolve future disputes peacefully, through diplomacy:

> We, the German Führer and Reich Chancellor, and the British Prime Minister, have had a further meeting today and are agreed in recognizing that the question of Anglo–German relations is of the first importance for the two countries and for Europe.
>
> We regard the Agreement signed last night, and the Anglo–German Naval Agreement, as symbolic of the desire of our two peoples never to go to war with one another again.
>
> We are resolved that the method of consultation shall be the method adopted to deal with any other questions that may concern our two countries, and we are determined to continue our efforts to remove possible sources of difference, and thus to contribute to assure the peace of Europe.[97]

Hitler perused the document and signed it without hesitation; Chamberlain followed suit. The well-intentioned but naïve British statesman seemed to be under the misguided impression he had brought peace to Europe for the next quarter-century. In fact, the Anglo–German Declaration was merely a worthless scrap of paper. Satisfied, Chamberlain flew back to England with his prized note. At Heston Airport that evening, Chamberlain announced before an expectant crowd of press representatives and prominent Englishmen:

> I want to say that the settlement of the Czechoslovakian problem, which has now been achieved is, in my view only the prelude to a larger settlement in which all Europe may find peace. This morning I had another talk with the German Chancellor, Herr Hitler. Here is the paper which bears his name upon it, as well as mine.[98]

Chamberlain raised the document and displayed it to the crowd, turning left and right, then solemnly read aloud the text. When he finished he was loudly cheered; the refrain 'Hip, hip, hooray!' was repeated several times. Thereupon Chamberlain, 'the man of the hour', was driven to Buckingham Palace to report to King George VI the success of his third diplomatic journey to Germany. Despite heavy rain, ecstatic Britons were packed all along the route to Buckingham Palace, obstructing Chamberlain's car. As a result, the drive took nearly two hours. After dusk, the King and Queen, along with Chamberlain and his wife, stepped out onto the front balcony to receive the plaudits of the immense crowd gathered below. Weary from his travels and the intense pressure of ongoing summit negotiations with a difficult autocrat, Chamberlain retired to his official government residence at 10 Downing Street. From a second-story window, he once again brandished the Anglo–German Agreement and proclaimed to the jubilant Londoners amassed outside:

> My good friends, this is the second time[10*] in our history that peace with honour has returned to Downing Street from Germany. I believe it is peace in our time. We thank you from the bottom of our hearts. Now I recommend you all to go home and sleep quietly in your beds.[99]

In England, the atmosphere of unease dissipated and despite the glaring fact that Czechoslovakia had been sold down the river, there was much appreciation for Chamberlain's diplomatic achievement. The fact that the conference had in actuality been a fiasco for the cause of democracy was grasped by only a small minority. The Germans too were grateful

10 * The first being the occasion of Benjamin Disraeli's return to Britain after the Congress of Berlin of 1878.

that Europe's politicians had averted a general war—they had cheered Chamberlain in the streets of Munich—but there was something more. Their nationalistic fervour had been aroused to fever pitch, for no one could deny that Nazi Germany was now Continental Europe's most dynamic Power. The Reich could hold her own not only with small fry, but *vis-à-vis* Britain and France as well. Moreover, it was undeniable that Germany's victory at Munich and all that went with it had been Hitler's work. He had proven to collaborators and adversaries alike that his political instincts had, apparently, been correct all along. Hitler's skeptical generals were taken aback; perhaps it was they who should defer to the Führer's judgment and not *vice-versa*. And throughout Europe, Anglo–French irresoluteness had been exposed for all to see. But although the Western Powers had handed the Sudetenland to Hitler on a silver platter, Hitler was nonetheless dissatisfied. He had been relishing the notion of the mighty Wehrmacht making short shrift of Czech forces and of himself grandly entering Prague as a conqueror.

While on trial at Nuremberg after the war, Keitel was questioned by the Czech representative, Colonel Eger, about what Germany would have done had the British and French backed Czechoslovakia and not succumbed to Hitler's demands:

> EGER: Would the Reich have attacked Czechoslovakia in 1938 if the Western Powers had stood by Prague?
>
> KEITEL: Certainly not. We were not strong enough militarily. The object of Munich was to get Russia out of Europe, to gain time, and to complete the German armaments.[100]

The Germans were not the only ones to take advantage of Czechoslovakia in her hour of distress. The Polish Government saw their chance to profit by Czechoslovakia's dismemberment, and they took it. On 30 September, the Czech Government received an ultimatum demanding the immediate cession of the industrial Teschen District, adjacent to the Polish border. Czech forces were to be evacuated at once. The Czechs were given until noon on 1 October to agree. Beneš tried to stall by requesting British and French intervention, but eventually acquiesced. Fifteen minutes before the expiration of the ultimatum, the Czech Government notified Kazimierz Papée, the Polish Ambassador in Prague, that it had accepted Poland's terms. The Polish Army promptly moved into Teschen on 2 October. Afterwards it was perceived by all concerned that Poland had sprung on a prostrate Czechoslovakia like a jackal. As for the Poles, they were of the opinion that the ethnic Polish inhabitants of the predominantly Polish Teschen District were entitled to the same right of self-determination as were the Germans of the Sudeten region.

Unlike most of the British people and their politicians, Winston Churchill was one who did not share Chamberlain's enthusiasm for the Munich Agreement. Churchill was so appalled at the way events had unfolded at Munich that he said bitterly to the House of Commons on 5 October:

> I will begin by saying what everybody would like to ignore or forget but which must nevertheless be stated, namely, that we have sustained a total and unmitigated defeat, and that France has suffered even more than we have. The utmost my right honourable friend the Prime Minister has been able to secure by all his immense exertions, by all the great efforts and mobilization which took place in this country, and by all the anguish and strain through which we have passed in this country, the utmost he has been able to gain for Czechoslovakia in the matters which were in dispute has been that the German dictator, instead of snatching the victuals from the table, has been content to have them served to him course by course....

Churchill compared the Sudetenland negotiations conducted throughout the second half of September to an armed robbery:

> We really must not waste time after all this long debate upon the difference between the positions reached at Berchtesgaden [15 September], at Godesberg [22–23 September], and at Munich [29–30 September]. They can be very simply epitomized, if the House will permit me to vary the metaphor. £1 was demanded at the pistol's point. When it was given, £2 were demanded at the pistol's point. Finally, the [German] dictator consented to take £1 17*s.* 6*d.* and the rest in promises of good will for the future.[101]

Churchill spoke mournfully over the bleak fate of the Czechoslovak nation:

> All is over. Silent, mournful, abandoned, broken, Czechoslovakia recedes into the darkness. She has suffered in every respect by her association with the Western democracies and with the League of Nations, of which she has always been an obedient servant. She has suffered in particular from her association with France, under whose guidance and policy she has been actuated for so long....
>
> We in this country, as in other liberal and democratic countries, have a perfect right to exalt the principle of self-determination, but it comes ill out of the mouths of those in totalitarian States who deny even the smallest element of toleration to every section and creed within their bounds. But, however you put it, this particular block of land, this mass

> of human beings to be handed over, has never expressed the desire to go into the Nazi rule. I do not believe that even now, if their opinion could be asked, they would exercise such an opinion.
>
> What is the remaining position of Czechoslovakia? Not only are they politically mutilated, but, economically and financially, they are in complete confusion. Their banking, their railway arrangements, are severed and broken, their industries are curtailed, and the movement of their population is most cruel....
>
> I venture to think that in future the Czechoslovak State cannot be maintained as an independent entity. I think you will find that in a period of time which may be measured by years, but may be measured only by months, Czechoslovakia will be engulfed in the Nazi régime. Perhaps they may join it in despair or in revenge. At any rate, that story is over and told.[102]

Churchill's prediction would be borne out in a little over five months' time. But unfortunately, at the time of Munich, his perspicacious words went largely unheeded.

On 1 October at noon, German forces began their occupation of Zone I of the Sudetenland. Reichenberg (today Liberec) became its capital. Also on the first of the month, after returning from Munich to Berlin, Hitler ratified a new decree for the administration of the Sudetenland. The Sudeten German territories were to be administered by a *Reichskommissar* (Reich Commissar) 'directly subordinate' to Hitler, once the interim authority presently held by Army chief Brauchitsch was 'withdrawn'. Not surprisingly, Hitler selected his Sudeten underling Henlein for this post. Two days later, Hitler entered the Bohemian town of Eger to address its overwhelmingly German population:

> Through me the whole German people greets you.... This greeting is also a vow: never shall this land in the future be torn from the Reich! Over this Greater German Reich lies for protection the German shield, and guarding it the German sword. You yourselves are a part of this protection. From henceforth like all other Germans you will have to bear your part of the burden. For it is the pride of us all that every son of Germany takes his share not only in the joys of Germany but also in our duties, and if necessary in our sacrifices.
>
> For you the nation was ready to draw the sword. You will be just as ready to do so if ever German soil or German people is threatened....
>
> Now begin your march which leads into the great German future. In this hour we wish to render thanks to the Almighty that He has guarded us on our path in the past, and we would implore Him that in the future, too, he would go with us and prosper our way.[103]

On 4 October, Hitler delivered a brief speech in the town of Carlsbad. From a theatre balcony, before a vast crowd, he proclaimed:

> It was a hard decision which brought me to this place. Behind this decision stood the will, if necessary, to call force to my aid in order to make you free. We wish to be only the happier and the more thankful that this last and gravest appeal was not necessary to procure for us our rights....
>
> I did not know how or by what way I should one day come here. But that I would stand here one day, that I knew! If I now stand before you here, it is not only you who have to thank me, but I would also thank you for your loyalty, your affection, and your readiness for sacrifice.[104]

Beneš resigned as Czechoslovakia's second president on 5 October. He could see the writing on the wall, and he had no illusions. He knew perfectly well that the rest of the Czech lands would be subsumed by the Reich in short order. That day, Beneš delivered his farewell broadcast to the nation. In his peroration he exhorted his Czech compatriots to remain resolute and undivided:

> I conclude with an expression of my genuine conviction and my profound belief in the enduring strength and firmness of our people; in its energy, persistence, and endurance, and above all in its faith in the ideals of humanity, freedom, law, and justice, for which it has so often fought and suffered, and in the name of which it has always been victorious. I too have fought for them. And I shall remain true to them. I am not leaving the ship in time of storm. But I believe at this moment such a sacrifice is a political necessity, though it does not mean that I forget my duty to continue to work as a citizen and a patriot.
>
> I wish that all of you, and the [Czechoslovak] Republic and the nation, may soon see better days, and that they may grow and bloom again as a glorious branch of the human race and as one of the noblest and finest of European peoples. May all of you remain sound, united, and brave.[105]

To avoid Nazi persecution, Beneš left for England[11*] on 22 October. He was succeeded on 30 November by the elderly Dr. Emil Hácha, a lawyer. The latter was unflatteringly described by Churchill after the war as a 'nonentity'.[106]

---

11 * In London, Beneš later established a Czechoslovak government-in-exile, the 'Provisional Government of Czechoslovakia'. It was officially recognized by Britain as of 18 July 1941. A strongly anti-Nazi body, its primary aims were to undo the terms of the Munich Agreement, to liberate Bohemia–Moravia from German dominion (following its unlawful incorporation into Greater Germany as a protectorate in mid-March 1939), and to restore Czechoslovakia to her pre-Munich frontiers.

Also on 5 October, Hitler spoke at the Berlin Sportpalast. He again took the opportunity to thank Mussolini for his contribution to the Munich Agreement, and 'the two other great statesmen [Chamberlain and Daladier] who at the last minute recognized the historical hour, declared themselves ready to give their support to the solution of one of Europe's most burning problems and who thereby made it possible for me, too, to offer the hand towards an understanding'. But he was 'above all' most proud of the German people, who had 'in these long months never deserted me'. As for the Sudeten situation, he anticipated 'that in a few days the problem of the Sudeten Germans will be finally solved. By 10 October we shall have occupied all the areas which belong to us. Thus one of Europe's most serious crises will be ended, and all of us, not only in Germany but those far beyond our borders, will then in this year for the first time really rejoice ...' Hitler also described his personal time in the Sudetenland over the past few days:

> I have had just had my first sight of these [Sudeten] areas and what moved me so profoundly was two impressions. First: I have often known the jubilation and the enthusiasm of joy, but here for the first time I have seen hundreds of thousands shedding tears of joy. And secondly I saw appalling distress. When in England a Duff Cooper or a Mr. Eden say that injustice has been done to the Czechs, then these men should just for once see what in reality has happened there. How can one so pervert the truth! I have seen here whole villages undernourished, whole towns reduced to ruin.

Hitler concluded with a reference to the historic significance of 1938, the momentous year Germany had restored herself to her rightful place on the European stage:

> In the history of our people the year 1938 will be a great, incomparable, proud year.... Later historians will show that the German nation found its way back again to the position of an honourable great nation—that our history has once more become a worthy history....[107]

Following the Munich Conference, Prague gave Slovakia and Ruthenia a certain degree of political independence (as of 7 October and 11 October respectively). But the partition of Czechoslovakia was far from over. Like the Germans, the Hungarians also had considerable territorial demands to make of Czechoslovakia. The corollary was that on 2 November, per the First Vienna Award, the Axis nations jointly granted to Hungary large sections of southern Slovakia (approximately one-third) and southern Carpathian Rus. The inhabitants of these areas were mostly Magyar.

On 9 October, Hitler gave a speech at Saarbrücken in which he rebuked anti-appeasement politicians Churchill, Cooper, and Eden for their anti-German militancy:

> Opposite us are [foreign] statesmen who—that, we must believe of them—also want peace. However, they govern in countries whose internal construction makes it possible for them at any time to be supplanted by others who do not aim at peace. These others are there. In England, it merely is necessary that instead of Chamberlain, a Duff Cooper or an Eden or a Churchill come into power. We know that the aim of these men would be to start war.[108]

Also in October, Keitel was briefly installed as the Sudetenland's military governor. He served in this capacity until 20 October. On 18 October Hitler drafted a letter, which was dispatched from Berchtesgaden to Army chief Brauchitsch in Berlin on 19 October. The letter informed Brauchitsch of an intended change in administration over the Sudeten Germans:

> The occupation of the Sudeten German territory has been completed, the operation being carried out by sections of the Army, the Air Forces, the Police, the military S.S. (S.S.-Verfügungstruppe), the S.S. and S.A.
>
> Placed under protection of the [German] Armed Forces, 3½ millions of German compatriots have returned to the Reich once and for all. The Civil Administration is taking over charge of them on 21 October 1938. Simultaneously I relieve you of your right to exercise executive power, while acknowledging the understanding co-operation of all departments.
>
> Along with our Sudeten German compatriots, the entire German *Volk* express their gratitude to those who participated in the liberation of the Sudetenland.
>
> Adolf Hitler[109]

In accordance with Hitler's decree of 1 October, Henlein became Reich Commissar of the Sudeten district on 21 October. He held this post until 1 May 1939. From then on he ruled as Reich Governor. Behind the scenes, on 21 October—just three weeks following his victory at Munich—Hitler issued a top secret directive to his generals for the occupation of Bohemia and Moravia by means of a swift and unexpected incursion:

> The future tasks of the Wehrmacht and the preparations for the conduct of war resulting from these tasks will be laid down by me in a later directive.

Until this directive comes into force, the Wehrmacht must at all times be prepared for the following eventualities:

1. Securing of the frontiers of the German Reich and protection against surprise air attacks.

2. Liquidation of the remainder of the Czech State.

3. The occupation of the Memelland....

Liquidation of the Remainder of the Czech State

It must be possible to smash at any time the remainder of the Czech State, should it pursue an anti-German policy.

The preparations to be made by the Wehrmacht for this eventuality will be considerably less in extent than those for Operation 'Green'; on the other hand, as planned mobilization measures will have to be dispensed with, they must guarantee a continuous and considerably higher state of preparedness. The organization, order of battle, and degree of preparedness of the units earmarked for that purpose are to be prearranged in peace time for a surprise assault so that Czechoslovakia herself will be deprived of all possibility of organized resistance. The aim is the speedy occupation of Bohemia and Moravia and the cutting off of Slovakia. The preparations must be so made that the defence of the western frontier [*Grenzsicherung West*] can be carried out simultaneously.

The following are the individual tasks of the Army and Air Force:

A. *Army*

The units stationed near the Czech frontier and certain motorized formations are to be detailed for surprise attack. Their number will be determined by the forces left to Czechoslovakia; quick and decisive success must be assured. The deployment and preparations for the attack must be worked out. Forces not required are to be kept in readiness in such a manner that they either can be used for securing the frontier or can follow up the attacking army.

B. *Air Force*

The rapid advance of our Army is to be assured by the early elimination of the Czech Air Force.

> For this purpose the rapid move of the formations near the frontier from their peace stations is to be prepared. Whether even stronger forces will be required for this purpose can only be seen from the development of the military and political situation in Czechoslovakia.
>
> In addition, the simultaneous deployment of the remainder of the offensive forces against the West must be prepared.[110]

The directive bore Hitler's signature and was disseminated to the chiefs of the Army, Luftwaffe, and Navy. On 17 December, a 'supplement' by General Keitel was appended to Hitler's directive of 21 October:

> With reference to the 'liquidation of the Rump Czech State', the Führer has given the following orders:
>
> The case is to be prepared on the assumption that no appreciable resistance is to be expected.
>
> Outwardly it must be quite clear that it is only a peaceful action and not a warlike undertaking.
>
> The action must therefore be carried out *only* with the peacetime Wehrmacht, without reinforcement by mobilization. The necessary mobility, in particular safeguarding the transport of the most vital supplies, must be achieved by transfers within formations.
>
> Likewise, the army units detailed to march in must not as a general rule leave their stations until the night before the crossing of the frontier and must not, as previously planned, deploy on the frontier. Administrative transport required beforehand must be kept to a minimum and must as far as possible be camouflaged. Any necessary movements of individual units—especially of motorized formations—to training areas near the frontier require the approval of the Führer.
>
> The Air Force is to act on corresponding lines.
>
> For the same reasons the exercise of executive power by the Commander-in-Chief of the Army is envisaged only for the newly occupied territory and only for a short period.[111]

On 4 December, elections were held for forty-one seats in the new Reichsgau Sudetenland. The ballot read:

> Do you acknowledge our leader Adolf Hitler, the liberator of the Sudetenland, and do you give your vote to the election proposal of the National Socialist German Workers' Party?

As usual, the electorate could vote either 'Yes' or 'No'. The National Socialists received 98.8 per cent of the vote.[112] The remainder, consisting of some 30,000 votes (1.2 per cent), were either negative, blank, or invalid. Afterwards many German Sudeteners hastened to join the N.S.D.A.P. Over 500,000 former members of the S.d.P. (which had been dissolved a month earlier, on 5 November) were accepted into the ranks. This figure was over one-sixth of the Sudetenland's German population. The Sudetenland was therefore one of Greater Germany's most thoroughly Nazified districts.

The post-Munich period was particularly stressful for all concerned. Lord Halifax learned that Hitler was contemplating still greater conquests. It was possible, and even likely, that in 1939 Germany would direct her aggression westwards. In early November, Chamberlain rationalized to the House of Commons the official post-Munich transfer of Slovakian and Carpathian territory to Hungary, with a reference to the statesmen who had formulated the Versailles Treaty:

> What we are doing now is witnessing the readjustment of frontiers laid down in the Treaty of Versailles. I do not know whether the people who were responsible for those frontiers thought they would remain permanently as they were laid down. I doubt very much whether they did. They probably expected that from time to time the frontiers would have to be adjusted. It is impossible to conceive that those people would be such supermen as to be able to see what would be the right frontiers for all time. The question is not whether those frontiers should be readjusted from time to time, but whether they should be readjusted by negotiation and discussion or be readjusted by war.[113]

On 17 November, Churchill sharply criticized Chamberlain's appeasement policy. He wrote:

> The Prime Minister is persuaded that Herr Hitler seeks no further territorial expansion upon the Continent of Europe; that the mastering and absorption of the Republic of Czechoslovakia has satiated the appetite of the German Nazi régime. It may be that he wishes to induce the Conservative Party to return to Germany the mandated territories in British possession, or what is judged to be their full equivalent. He believes that this act of restoration will bring about prolonged good and secure relations between Great Britain and Germany. He believes further that these good relations can be achieved without weakening in any way the fundamental ties of self-preservation which bind us to the French Republic, which ties, it is common ground between us all, must be preserved. Mr. Chamberlain is convinced that all this will lead to general agreement, to the appeasement of the discontented Powers, and to a lasting peace.

> But all lies in the regions of hope and speculation. A whole set of contrary possibilities must be held in mind. He [Hitler] may ask us to submit to things which we cannot endure; he may be forced to ask us to submit to things which we cannot endure. Or again, the other side in this difficult negotiation may not act in the same spirit of good will and good faith as animates the Prime Minister. What we have to give, what we are made to give, may cost us dear, but it may not be enough. It may involve great injury and humbling to the British Empire, but it may not stay or even divert for more than a few months, if that, the march of events upon the Continent. By this time next year we shall know whether the Prime Minister's view of Herr Hitler and the German Nazi Party is right or wrong. By this time next year we shall know whether the policy of appeasement has appeased, or whether it has only stimulated a more ferocious appetite.[114]

Instead of cultivating a spirit of peace and stabilizing relations between the Western democracies and the Axis nations, the Munich Agreement had the opposite effect. All four signatories of the Munich Agreement were busily rearming and increasing the strength of their armed forces. As for the Russians, they were resentful for having been excluded from the Munich Conference. Their exclusion deprived them from having a voice in the negotiations to which—not least in part due to the Czecho–Soviet Mutual Assistance Pact of 1935—they had felt entitled. They regarded the whole affair as a debacle, a failure of collective security. Molotov gave a critical and accurate assessment of the Munich Agreement in his address to the Supreme Soviet on 6 November:

> The Fascist and so-called democratic Powers of Europe came together at Munich and the victory over Czechoslovakia was complete.... The bargain between the Fascist governments and the governments of the so-called democratic countries, far from lessening the danger of the outbreak of the second imperialist war, has on the contrary added fuel to the flames. At such a moment we cannot expect the second imperialist war to cease or be extinguished. On the contrary, the danger of its breaking out at new points and expanding its scope is obvious.

Molotov added that the U.S.S.R., with its resolute foreign policy and military preparedness, was the only nation truly capable of acting for the maintenance of peace:

> Only the Soviet State, strong in its foreign policy, ready for any test from the outside, only our State is able to pursue a consistent policy of

> peace, firm in the defence of its frontiers and of the interests of socialism. Anyone who wants to be convinced of the strength and power of our forces is welcome to try.[115]

After the loss of the Sudetenland, the new Prague Government did all it could to curry favour with Hitler. One of the decisive actions it took along these lines was to outlaw Czechoslovakia's Communist Party, headed by General Secretary Klement Gottwald, in October 1938. Czechoslovakia's new leaders walked on eggshells, hoping they would do nothing that might incur Hitler's wrath.

At 7:05 p.m. on 12 January, a telegram from Czech Foreign Minister František Chvalkovský—in office since 4 October—was transmitted by the Chargé d'Affaires in Czechoslovakia to the German Foreign Ministry. Chvalkovský gave the following servile assurance:

> In the present tense international situation, the Czechoslovak Government is anxious to assure the Reich Government that it adheres unswervingly to the policy ... of close political co-operation with the Reich. The Prague Government will endeavour to prove its loyalty and good will by far-reaching fulfillment of Germany's wishes, for example, in the manner of armament deliveries, German military transports, etc.[116]

Nine days later, Hitler received Chvalkovský in Berlin for a one-hour discussion. The meeting began at 5 p.m. Chvalkovský ingratiatingly began by reiterating that he had upheld the 'promise [of 14 October 1938] made to the Führer'; namely, that his sole aim was to enable their two countries to 'live together on friendly terms'. Hitler rejoined by saying that 'from the very beginning developments in Czechoslovakia had drifted toward a catastrophe' which had only 'been halted through Germany's moderation'. It was the Reich's 'National Socialist principles' that kept her from 'annexing foreign nationalities'. The Axis alliance, including Hungary and to a certain extent Poland as well, was 'invincible.' In geographic and economic considerations, Hitler declared, 'Czechoslovakia's destiny was interwoven with that of Germany.' It would therefore behoove Czechoslovakia to conform accordingly. Hitler warned Chvalkovský that Czechoslovakia would only survive on one condition: that she 'live together with Germany on the closest terms'. Meanwhile, Czechoslovakia would be permitted 'her own individual ethic existence'. Hitler enumerated the crucial steps Czechoslovakia should take forthwith: 'to eliminate' at once any Beneš tendencies in the Czechoslovak Press and elsewhere and to 'reduce the [Czech] Army to reasonable proportions'. Any armed aggression towards Germany, Hitler threatened, would lead to 'the annihilation of Czechoslovakia'. Finally, Hitler added that Czechoslovakia's Jewish elements 'were still poisoning the nation'. Chvalkovský hastily promised Hitler that Czechoslovakia 'would set about solving the Jewish question'.[117] The one-sided conference made it plain that Czechoslovakia's continued existence hung by the slenderest of threads.

On 10 February, Hitler summoned his generals for a secret meeting in which he clarified that his politics and diplomacy from 1933 to 1938—withdrawal from the League of Nations, rearmament, the remilitarization of the Rhineland, the *Anschluss*, the annexation of the Sudetenland—all had been preliminary steps of his ultimate aim: to embark on a war of conquest in Eastern Europe to settle the long-standing issue of German living space:

> The year 1938 with all its events is only a consistent continuation of decisions which originated in 1933. It is not as if 1938 would, let us say, represent a special action that had previously gone unnoticed. On the contrary, all the individual decisions that had been taken since 1933 are not the result of immediate considerations, but rather the implementation of an existing plan, only perhaps not exactly in keeping with precise dates. It was, for example, not clear to me in 1933 when we would leave the League of Nations. But that this had to be the first step to rebuilding Germany was clear, and that we should pick the first suitable moment was also clear. The next step then became national rearmament, and that had been planned from the beginning without the agreement of any foreign powers, only the pace could not be quite exactly, shall we say, assessed. It was also clear that after a certain development, after a certain time of this rearmament, Germany, at great risk, would have to proclaim to the rest of the world that she was free to rearm. The moment of this step was naturally not foreseeable. It finally became clear that any further steps would result in the remilitarization of the Rhineland. Here again the date was actually planned for a year later; I didn't think of carrying this out until 1937. Conditions at the time made it appear sensible to take this step earlier in 1936. It was also quite clear that in order to strengthen Germany's political and especially military position, it was necessary to solve the Austrian and Czechoslovakian problem. In the beginning I wasn't quite sure whether both problems had to be or could be tackled at the same time, or whether to take on Czechoslovakia first or Austria first. There was no doubt that these problems had to be solved. So all these decisions, therefore, were not just ideas that were realized on the spur of the moment, but were the result of long-range plans, which I was determined to realize the moment I believed the general conditions were suitable.[118]

As established by Hitler's directive of 21 October (to say nothing of his earlier revelations at the Hossbach Conference and his directive of 30 May 1938), Hitler was plotting to seize the Czech lands. His anti-Czech feelings notwithstanding, he intended to incorporate Bohemia and Moravia into Germany as a protectorate. But the first step was to undermine Czechoslovakia by fomenting civil unrest within her own borders. This would be done by playing up the numerous issues of contention between the Czech and Slovak peoples, and fanning the flames of Slovak nationalism. As Hitler was perfectly aware, the Slovaks had been pushing for total autonomy since Czechoslovakia's inception two decades earlier.

On 12 February, Hitler met with Dr. Vojtech Tuka in Berlin to discuss the prospect of Slovakian secession from the Czechoslovak Republic. The talk lasted seventy-five minutes. Tuka was a Slovak extremist and a member of the far-right Slovak People's Party. In October 1928 Tuka had been convicted of treason by the Czech Government. He was conditionally released in 1937, although his prison term only had the effect of intensifying his anti-Czech feelings. Tuka stated to Hitler that 'he and his fellow-combatants were determined to follow the wishes of the Slovak people and to create an independent Slovakia'. He asked Hitler for his protection against Czech oppression and also against 'Hungarian and Polish [territorial] aspirations' which the Führer could deter with a mere utterance. Tuka added that he was prepared 'to give his life for his ideals' and he ended his appeal to Hitler with the following supplication: 'I lay the destiny of my people in your hands, my Führer; my people await their complete liberation by you.' Hitler replied to Tuka that 'until quite recently he had had no idea of the Slovak urge for independence ... Up to six months ago he had been under the impression that Slovakia desired a reunion with Hungary.' He informed Tuka that 'He could guarantee an independent Slovakia at any time, even today.' These were precisely the words Tuka wished to hear, and he was much heartened. For him, he declared, this day had been 'the greatest of his life'.[119]

Hitler was willing to permit the existence of an independent Slovakia so long its domestic and foreign activities remained consonant with those of Nazi Germany. Plus, Hitler knew perfectly well that the establishment of a fully autonomous Slovakian nation-state would greatly weaken the Czechoslovak Republic.

On 6 March, the situation escalated. In both Slovakia and Ruthenia, nationalist elements agitating for complete autonomy had become so unmanageable as to seriously imperil Czechoslovakia's internal stability. Consequently, Czech President Hácha discharged the Slovakian and Ruthenian Governments. He also ordered the arrest of Jozef Tiso, the head of the Slovak People's Party, along with key party members Tuka and Ferdinand Ďurčanský. Czech Army troops were sent into Slovakia to restore order and over two hundred Slovak nationalists were locked up, including Tuka. On 9 March, Hácha declared a new Slovak Government headed by Jozef Sivák, but two days later replaced this government with yet another one, this time with Karol Sidor in charge. Sidor received three Nazi politicians on 12 March: Arthur Seyss-Inquart, Governor of Austria; Josef Bürckel, Gauleiter of Vienna; and Wilhelm Keppler, the Reich Commissioner in Slovakia. They handed him a pre-prepared telegram to be forwarded directly to Hitler. It contained a written declaration of independence for Slovakia, including the names of the Slovak ministers who were to form its new government. However, Sidor was unwilling to take part in this shady scheme and rejected it. Rebuffed by Sidor, the German Government decided instead to deal with Tiso.

On 13 March, Hitler summoned Tiso and Ďurčanský to Berlin. He received them at the Reich Chancellery, in his study, at 6:40 p.m. The Führer was accompanied by Ribbentrop, his two senior generals Keitel and Brauchitsch, and several ministers. Hitler wasted no time:

> Czechoslovakia owed it only to Germany that she had not been mutilated further. With the greatest self-control Germany had renounced the language enclaves situated on her frontiers, only in order to ensure normal living space for Czechoslovakia. No thanks had been received for this. No Czech in Germany had lost his employment. On the contrary, countless Czechs had been accepted by us. No hair of their heads had been harmed; neither had they been insulted or attacked. On the Czech side the picture was a completely different one. The most stringent measures of dismissal had been practised on Germans. Thousands had become unemployed. Everywhere Germans were being provoked in some way, or there was discrimination against them. The Germans were under constant supervision so that their position was worse than before the September crisis. This development was not in keeping with the agreements.... Central Europe was a definite compact economic unit which could live only if it were completely at peace. It needed a *détente*. Geographically this was already demonstrated by the fact that Bohemia and Moravia were surrounded by Germany, and Germany could never tolerate a centre of unrest in her own sphere.
>
> During recent weeks conditions had become intolerable. The old Beneš spirit had come to life again. The Czech people were being incited to resist. Conditions were uncertain and disturbed.... Germany could no longer tolerate these conditions. Also the *Volksdeutsche* there were rebelling, because they could not see why they should be worse off today than previously.
>
> We solved the Czech problem once in accordance with our general outlook [*Weltauffassung*]. But, if this solution did not lead to success, we were resolved to carry it to its conclusion completely without regard to this ideological basis.

Hitler advised the Slovak dignitaries that he had antagonized the Hungarians by not permitting them to annex all of Slovakia outright. He explained that he had done so because he knew of the Slovak peoples' desire for independence. Next, Hitler pressured Tiso to declare Slovakia an independent state. Germany would back the fledgling new nation. Hitler also bluntly stated that if Tiso refused, 'he would leave the fate of Slovakia to events for which he was no longer responsible'. In other words, he would abandon Slovakia to Hungary and Poland.[12*] Ribbentrop then introduced a fictional telegram intended to soften up the Slovak politicians. The spurious document was read aloud; it warned of Hungarian troops advancing towards the Slovakian frontier. Hitler stated to Tiso that in view of the precarious situation, an immediate decision was called for. Under duress, Tiso tried to delay. To Hitler he replied that 'he could make no definite statement at once, let alone give a decision' but he would consult with Ďurčanský privately and 'calmly' consider his options. However, Tiso promised Hitler that he and Ďurčanský would 'prove themselves worthy of the Führer's benevolence and interest in their country'.[120] Tiso quickly succumbed to Hitler's coercion. A pronouncement declaring Slovakian independence was drafted and Tiso was instructed to relay it to his Slovak deputies for affirmation. The following day the Slovak Parliament convened in Bratislava. The first order of business was to accept Karol Sidor's resignation. Next, to the deputies present, Tiso related the particulars of his meeting with Hitler the previous day. He then put forth the question: 'Do you agree with the declaration of an independent Slovak State?'[121]

A debate followed. Several deputies were reluctant to accept Tiso's proposal. Among the concerns raised were the dimensions of the new autonomous Slovak nation—it would be less than half the size of Czechoslovakia, plus it would contain a substantial Hungarian population. Thereupon Franz Karmasin, an ethnic German minority leader, interjected that if they dragged their feet in declaring Slovakia an independent state, Slovakia would end up being partitioned between Nazi Germany and Hungary. In light of Karmasin's undeniable point, that afternoon all fifty-seven deputies voted in favour of Slovakian independence. The First Slovak Republic was thus born, aligned with Nazi Germany—although not as an equal, but as a client state. Tiso was designated President of the new Slovak State. To add legitimacy to the whole scheme, Tiso dispatched a phony telegram previously prepared by the Germans in Berlin. The telegram formally requested Hitler to assume a protective role over the new Slovak republic:

---

12 * Ever since the Czechoslovak–Polish War in late January 1919 over Czech Silesia, the Poles had wanted returned to them Spiš, an historic district in northern Slovakia.

In the name of the legal Slovak Government I have the honour to inform Your Excellency that the sovereign Slovak nation has today thrown off the intolerable Czech yoke and, in accordance with the wishes of the overwhelming majority of the population, the independence of our state has been proclaimed. Independent Slovakia is determined to live in peace and friendship with all her neighbours. In the early stages of her development, however, the young State requires strong protection. In the name of the people and of the Government of the new Slovakia, I request Your Excellency, as the Führer of the great German Reich, which under your rule has always supported freedom and the self-determination of peoples, to take over the guarantee for the existence of our State and to take immediately all necessary measures for the protection of its frontiers.

Minister President of Independent Slovakia[122]

Hitler granted the request on 16 March, stating in his reply to Tiso that he would 'take over the protection of the Slovak State'.[123] A week later, a protection treaty 'extended by the German Reich to the State of Slovakia' was concluded. It specified that 'the undersigned representatives of the two governments'—Ribbentrop for Germany, Tiso, Tuka, and Ďurčanský for Slovakia—had consented to the following terms:

Article 1. The German Reich undertakes to protect the political independence of the State of Slovakia and the integrity of its territory.

Article 2. For the purpose of making effective the protection undertaken by the German Reich, the German armed forces shall have the right, at all times, to construct military installations and to keep them garrisoned in the strength they deem necessary, in an area delimited on its western side by the frontiers of the State of Slovakia, and on its eastern side by a line formed by the eastern rims of the Lower Carpathians, the White Carpathians, and the Javornik Mountains....

Article 3. The Government of Slovakia will organize its military forces in close agreement with the German Armed Forces.

Article 4. In accordance with the relationship of protection agreed upon, the Government of Slovakia will at all times conduct its foreign affairs in close agreement with the German Government.

Article 5. This treaty shall become effective as of the date of its signature and shall be valid for a period of twenty-five years....[124]

That same day, 23 March, a 'Confidential Protocol Concerning Economic and Financial Collaboration between the German Reich and the State of Slovakia' was also enacted. It was not to be made public until the signatories agreed to make it so. It delineated the co-operation between Nazi Germany and the Slovak State in such areas as agriculture, forestry, natural resources, industrial production, communication, and transportation. It also stipulated that Slovakia would introduce its own currency, 'create a Slovak National Bank as a central mint', and that Germany would support Slovakia in this endeavour and 'in the development and execution of the foreign exchange policy'.[125]

Carpathian Ruthenia, Czechoslovakia's easternmost province, noted with envy Slovakia's new 'independent' status. Ruthenia likewise sought to be master of her own destiny, and in the pursuit of self-determination boldly declared her independence on 15 March. A telegram sent by Ruthenian Prime Minister Dr. Augustin Vološin from Sighet to the German Foreign Ministry—received at 4 p.m.—urgently requested protection against Hungarian armed aggression:

> We proclaim the independence of the Carpatho–Ukraine, and we request the protection of the German Reich. At the same time we inform you that Hungarian troops crossed our frontiers near Mukačevo at 6 a.m. today. We ask for measures against the Hungarians and protection and help against the Czechs, who are resorting to force.[126]

An hour later, Berlin sent a brief 'most urgent' response, informing the Carpatho–Ukrainian Government that with regard to the 'Hungarian troops having advanced against Carpatho–Ukraine on a broad front, the German Government advises it to offer no resistance. As matters stand, the German Government regrets that it is not in a position to assume the protectorate.'[127]

Meanwhile Vološin, of Ukrainian descent, became president of the new 'Republic of Carpatho–Ukraine' (as it had been called since 22 November 1938). But Ruthenia's independence was destined to be extremely short-lived. The very next day Hungarian forces, which were already on the march, invaded the tiny new nation and annexed it. Hitler was not interested in Ruthenia's plight and he permitted the Hungarians to satisfy their territorial claim. Ineffectual Ruthenian opposition ceased on 18 March, and Vološin's brief tenure as president—three days—was over.

It was now time to settle accounts with Czechoslovakia once and for all. On 14 March German newspapers once again—as during the Sudeten crisis—began printing outrageous tales of government-sponsored mistreatment of German minorities. Spurious accounts of vicious assaults and cruel murders at the hands of local Czech citizens and police throughout 'Czechia' were propagated. This smear campaign was intended to fill the German masses with a righteous indignation that would make the impending seizure of Bohemia–Moravia more palatable to them.

That day Hitler summoned Czech President Emil Hácha to Berlin. Like Schuschnigg a year earlier, Hitler intended to hector the elderly Czech statesman into submission. Hácha's train arrived at Anhalt Station at 10:40 in the evening. He was accompanied by Chvalkovský. The Czech dignitaries were courteously received in a manner befitting their high status—they were met by an honour guard—then withdrew to the Adlon Hotel. After being deliberately kept waiting to prolong their anxiety and to reduce their powers of resistance, at a quarter-past one on the morning of 15 March, Hácha and Chvalkovský were ushered into Hitler's study at the Chancellery. But unlike the meeting with Schuschnigg thirteen months ago, this time the Führer was not alone. Also present was an intimidating assortment of top Nazis: Göring, Ribbentrop, Keitel, State Minister Otto Meissner, and State Secretaries Ernst von Weizsäcker and Dr. Otto Dietrich. Chief interpreter Schmidt performed the necessary translations, as usual.

The meeting started with a nauseating exhibition of Hácha attempting to curry favour with Hitler. Hácha protested that he 'had never mixed in politics' nor did he have any 'connections with politicians'. As for his predecessors, he had only encountered Masaryk once annually 'at the judges' dinner' and Beneš 'even less often'. Hácha added that the Czechoslovakian régime 'was alien to him', so much so that 'he had asked himself whether it was fortunate for Czechoslovakia to be an independent State at all'. Hácha was certain that 'the destiny of Czechoslovakia lay in the Führer's hands'. As for the Slovaks, 'he was not shedding any tears' over their secession, for they were 'inclined more towards the Magyars', whereas the Czechs were 'more akin' to the Germans. He believed that the Czechs and Slovaks 'could not live together' and he asserted that '80 per cent of the population' held the same view as he. But the greatest concern to Hácha was 'the fate of his people'. Hácha contended that the Czechs 'had the right to wish to live a national life' and that the Führer would surely understand this. Lastly, Hácha reasoned that it was unfair to blame Czechoslovakia because proponents of the 'Beneš system' still lurked about. The truth was (so the memorandum summarizing the meeting recorded Hácha as saying) that the old Beneš régime only found favour 'in journalistic circles' and that his new post-Munich Government was taking every conceivable measure to suppress these agitators.

In response to Hácha's supplications, Hitler listed a series of Czech transgressions: the Czechs' anti-German 'attitude', the Franco–Czech mutual assistance pact targeting Germany, the 'heavy political liability' of the Czech Army, the 'protests from the minorities' who continued to be relentlessly maltreated. Hitler pointed out that he had made it absolutely clear at the time of the Sudeten crisis that 'if the Beneš tendencies did not disappear completely' then Czechoslovakia itself would be eliminated once and for all. To his regret, 'the new [post-Munich] régime had not succeeded in making the old one disappear psychologically; he saw this in the press, in propaganda by word of mouth, in the dismissal of Germans, and in many [other] acts ...' Unfortunately, Hitler explained, the Czech Government had proven itself unreliable and untrustworthy. Although he was personally convinced that both Hácha and Chvalkovský were acting in good faith, he was skeptical 'as to the Government's chance of prevailing upon the [Czech] population as a whole'. And now, the 'die was cast'. Hitler broke the news to Hácha and Chvalkovský that in order to restabilize Central Europe, on 12 March 'he had given the order for invasion by the German troops and for the incorporation of Czechoslovakia into the German Reich'. At 6 a.m. that morning the German Army would penetrate into Bohemia–Moravia from every direction; the Luftwaffe would seize the Czech aerodromes. This revelation shocked the Czech leaders to their core. (Schmidt was able to later recollect that 'Hácha and Chvalkovský sat as though turned to stone. Only their eyes showed that they were alive.')

Hitler continued; he foresaw two possible outcomes. If the German occupation were opposed by the Czechs, then 'resistance would be broken by brute force with all available means'. On the other hand, if 'the entry of the German troops would take place satisfactorily', he would permit the Czech people a 'national life ... autonomy, and a certain measure of national liberty'. Should there be bloodshed, however, the resultant hatred would push the German people over the edge. Under such circumstances the Reich would be able to grant the Czechs 'no concessions'. But perhaps Hácha's visit would bring about a peaceable solution, one that would gain the Czechs more than 'anything she could ever have hoped for in the old Austrian Empire'. Hitler maintained that his only goal was 'to provide the necessary security for the German people'.

Meanwhile, time was fleeting. In just a few hours the German Army would cross the Czech frontier. To intimidate the Czechs further and reinforce the futility of offering resistance, Hitler mentioned to them that 'for every Czech battalion there was a German division'. Thereupon Hitler advised Hácha 'to withdraw with Chvalkovský and discuss what was to be done'. Hácha hastily replied that 'the position was quite clear and that resistance was folly'. Nevertheless, Hácha was stymied. Exactly what could he do, he asked, with just four hours remaining, to prevent his proud countrymen from opposing the Germans? Hitler responded that Hácha's best course of action would be to 'consult with his companions' and to 'get in touch with his Prague offices' by telephone. Hácha was to instruct his War Minister to order Czech forces not to hinder German troops. As for the Wehrmacht, 'the military machine was now already in motion [and] could not be stopped'.[128]

At 2:15 a.m. Hitler abruptly ended the talk. Hácha and Chvalkovský were led out of the room and left to the tender mercies of Göring and Ribbentrop, who gave them no quarter. The pair harassed the Czechs relentlessly, pursuing them about like predators honing in on their prey, all the while pressuring them to sign away the Czech lands. At that point Hácha and Chvalkovský found their nerve. They retorted that they were unwilling to sanction the demotion of their nation to a second-rate German dominion. If they did, the Czech people would condemn them for all time for such a gross betrayal. Göring brutally informed them that unless they signed, he would order his Luftwaffe to Prague and in the span of a couple of hours half the city would be a smoldering heap. In truth, this was an imposture, for Prague had some 40,000 ethnic Germans whom the Nazis would not have been willing to sacrifice in a reckless bombing campaign. And militarily, reducing Prague to ruins would not have yielded any advantage.

Nevertheless, the strain of these threats took their toll on Hácha; he fainted. Too late it occurred to the Nazi leaders that they may have overplayed their hand. Should the feeble Hácha die in their midst, then—as the interpreter Schmidt declared—'the whole world will say tomorrow that he was murdered at the Chancellery'.[129] But the Nazis had anticipated a development of this sort. Hitler's personal physician Dr. Theodor Morell was immediately summoned. The quack doctor revived the elderly president with an injection of stimulants. Once technicians managed to re-establish a telephone connection with Prague (the line was down), Hácha was pressured into relaying orders to the Czech Army not to impede the German occupation of Bohemia–Moravia.

After a 'final consultation' in Hitler's study, at 3:55 a.m. a joint declaration 'by the German and Czechoslovak Governments' was signed in duplicate by Hitler, Ribbentrop, Hácha, and Chvalkovský. Along with its two accompanying enclosures, it was the same as a text prepared the previous day by the Foreign Ministry:

> The Führer and Reich Chancellor today received in Berlin, at their own request, the President of the Czecho–Slovak State, Dr. Hácha, and the Czecho–Slovak Foreign Minister, Dr. Chvalkovský, in the presence of Herr von Ribbentrop, the Foreign Minister of the Reich.
>
> At this meeting the serious situation which had arisen within the previous territory of Czecho–Slovakia, owing to the events of recent weeks, was subjected to a completely open examination.

> The conviction was unanimously expressed on both sides that the object of all their efforts must be to assure quiet, order and peace in this part of Central Europe.
>
> The President of the Czecho–Slovak State declared that, in order to serve this end and to reach a final pacification, he confidently placed the fate of the Czech people and of their country in the hands of the Führer of the German Reich.
>
> The Führer accepted this declaration and expressed his decision to assure the Czech people, under the protection of the German Reich, the autonomous development of their national life in accordance with their special characteristics.[130]

An hour later, at 5 a.m., Prague radio broadcast a cautionary message by President Hácha urging compliance with the occupying forces:

> The German Army, infantry, and aircraft, will begin occupation of territory of the [Czechoslovak] Republic at 6 a.m. Their advance must nowhere be resisted. The slightest resistance will cause most unforeseen consequences and lead to intervention becoming utterly brutal. All commanders must obey the orders of the occupying army. Various units of the Czech Army are being disarmed. Military and civil airplanes must remain in airdromes; none must attempt to take [to] the air. Prague will be occupied at 6:30 a.m.[131]

In his capacity as Supreme Commander-in-Chief, Hitler issued the following order to the German Armed Forces:

> Czechoslovakia is in dissolution. In Bohemia and Moravia terror against German fellow-countrymen reigns. From 15 March 1939 onward formations of the German Army and Air Force will enter Czech territory in order to safeguard lives and property of all inhabitants of the country.
>
> I expect every German soldier to consider himself not as an enemy of the inhabitants of the territory to be occupied, but only as an instrument for carrying out the German Reich Government's decision to restore a satisfactory order in that territory. But should resistance be offered anywhere, it will immediately be crushed with all means.
>
> For the rest, remember that you set foot on Czech soil as representatives of Greater Germany.[132]

At precisely 6 a.m., the invasion of the Czech lands—*Unternehmen Südost* (Operation Southeast)—began. The vanguard of the German Army crossed over into Bohemia–Moravia, encountering no Czech resistance.

Despite sub-zero temperatures and a severe blizzard, Army units entered Prague by midmorning. Czech citizens wept openly in the streets; some shook their fists in impotent rage; a few hurled snowballs at the hated German occupiers. The hostile reception prompted Nazi authorities to order a curfew for 8 p.m. Cinemas, restaurants, and coffeehouses were shut down. Hitler did not enter Prague at the forefront of his soldiers, as might have been expected of a conquering warlord. He travelled from Berlin to the Sudetenland by special train, then transferred to his armoured Mercedes to complete the journey. He traversed the Czech frontier at Liboch and by the time he reached Prague, the city was dark. Hitler stayed overnight at the ancient Hradschin Castle, residence and centre of power of bygone Bohemian rulers. A *hakenkreuz* flag fluttered from its tower. Henlein and Bürckel were appointed civil administrators for Bohemia and Moravia respectively, and General Eccard von Gablenz was given the post of military governor of Prague.

To the German *Volk*, Hitler proclaimed his decision to render aid to 'terrorized' ethnic Germans, to disarm the Czech Army, and to restore order in Bohemia–Moravia:

> To the German People:
>
> Only a few months ago Germany was compelled to protect her fellow-countrymen living in well-defined settlements against the unbearable Czechoslovakian terror régime; and during the last weeks the same thing has happened on an ever-increasing scale. This is bound to create an intolerable state of affairs within an area inhabited by citizens of so many nationalities.
>
> These national groups, to counteract the renewed attacks against their freedom and life, have now broken away from the Prague Government. Czechoslovakia has ceased to exist.
>
> Since Sunday at many places wild excesses have broken out, amongst the victims of which are again many Germans. Hourly the number of oppressed and persecuted people crying for help is increasing. From areas thickly populated by German-speaking inhabitants, which last autumn Czechoslovakia was allowed by German generosity to retain, refugees robbed of their personal belongings are streaming into the Reich.
>
> Continuation of such a state of affairs would lead to the destruction of every vestige of order in an area in which Germany is vitally interested, particularly as for over 1,000 years it formed a part of the German Reich.
>
> In order definitely to remove this menace to peace and to create the conditions for a necessary new order in this living space, I have today resolved to allow German troops to March into Bohemia and Moravia.

> They will disarm the terror gangs and the Czechoslovakian forces supporting them, and protect the lives of all who are menaced. Thus they will lay the foundations for introducing a fundamental re-ordering of affairs which will be in accordance with the 1,000 year-old history and will satisfy the practical needs of the German and Czech peoples.[133]

The British took no decisive action to rectify this egregious breach of the Munich Agreement, nor did the French. Chamberlain's justification to the House of Commons for not coming to Czechoslovakia's aid was that Britain was no longer obligated to do. His distorted reasoning was that since Slovakia had declared its independence the previous day (14 March), Czechoslovakia as a country had technically ceased to exist and was therefore at the present time (15 March) no longer entitled to British support!

On 16 March at Hradschin Castle, Hitler signed a decree (see Appendix I) inaugurating the newly-created Protectorate of Bohemia and Moravia. The preamble described the centuries-old German roots of Bohemia–Moravia and how the artificial creation of the Czechoslovak State disrupted the stability of Central Europe, failed to take into account the needs of the racial minorities dwelling there, and endangered the security of Germany. This was a state of affairs which the Reich was no longer prepared to condone:

> For ten centuries the Bohemian–Moravian lands belonged to the living space of the German people. Force and lack of understanding arbitrarily tore them from their old historical surroundings and finally created a source of permanent unrest by incorporating them within the artificial edifice of Czecho–Slovakia. From year to year the danger that a new, appalling menace to European peace would emanate, as had happened once before in the past, from this living space, increased.
>
> For the Czecho–Slovak State, and those in power there, had not succeeded in properly organizing the existence side by side of the national groups arbitrarily united within its boundaries and had thereby failed to awaken the interest of all concerned in the maintenance of their common State. It has thereby proved its inmost incapacity to exist and has for this reason now also fallen into actual dissolution.
>
> The German Reich, however, cannot tolerate permanent disturbances in these territories that are so all-important to its own peace and security and also so important to the general well-being and universal peace. Sooner or later the Reich, as the Power most interested and affected, by history and geographical position, would have to suffer the most serious consequences.

> Self-preservation, therefore, requires that the German Reich should be determined to intervene decisively in favour of the restoration of a basis for a reasonable Central European order and should take the requisite measures. For it has already proved in the course of its historical past of a thousand years that it alone, thanks to its greatness and to the qualities of the German people, can be called upon to solve these tasks.

Hitler added that he was 'Filled with the earnest desire to serve the true interests of the people domiciled in this living space, to guarantee the individual national life of the German and of the Czech peoples, [and] to benefit peace and the social welfare of all' ... The third article of the decree specified that the Protectorate would remain 'autonomous and self-administering' and would 'exercise its sovereign rights within the scope of the protectorate in consonance with the political, military, and economic importance to the Reich'.[134]

Czechoslovakia was no more. The Czech lands were 'placed under the protection' of the German Reich. Per the 'Reich Citizenship Law of 1935' those of German race were to be granted German nationality. Non-Germans were to be nationals of the 'Protectorate of Bohemia and Moravia'. The new protectorate was to be governed by a *Reichsprotektor* (Reich Protector) chosen by Hitler. The first was the ex-diplomat Neurath, who began his reign as Hitler's personal representative on 21 March 1939. Karl Hermann Frank, the S.d.P. ex-deputy leader, was named the protectorate's Secretary of State.

On 17 March, the British and French Ambassadors to Germany—Nevile Henderson and Robert Coulondre respectively—received letters in which they were charged by their Foreign Affairs Ministers (Lord Halifax for Britain, and Georges Bonnet for France) to officially protest the annexation of Bohemia–Moravia to the Reich Government, which was, of course, in direct contravention of the provisions of the Munich Agreement. In the British letter, Halifax directed Henderson to advise the German Government that the British Government 'cannot but regard the events of the past few days as a complete repudiation of the Munich Agreement and a denial of the spirit in which the negotiators of that agreement bound themselves to co-operate for a peaceful settlement'. The letter further stated that the British Government was also taking this opportunity to 'protest against the changes effected in Czecho–Slovakia by German military action, which are, in their view, devoid of any basis of legality'.[135] In the French letter, Bonnet instructed Coulondre to inform the German Foreign Minister [Ribbentrop] of the following:

> The Government of the [French] Republic consider in fact that, in face of the action directed by the German Government against Czechoslovakia,

> they are confronted with a flagrant violation of the letter and the spirit of the agreements signed at Munich on 29 September 1938.

Bonnet added that Coulondre was also to advise Ribbentrop that the French Government 'cannot recognize, under these conditions, the legality of the new situation created in Czechoslovakia by the action of the German Reich'.[136]

Like the British and French Governments, the Soviet leadership was also disturbed by the fate of Czechoslovakia. Foreign Minister Maxim Litvinov proposed a Six-Power Conference. This initiative, made on behalf of the Soviet Government on 21 March—and notwithstanding the fact that the Russians had been excluded from the talks at Munich—would have included Britain, France, the U.S.S.R., Poland, Romania, and Turkey. But Chamberlain was extremely wary of the Russians, whom he considered ineffectual, cynically opportunistic, and duplicitous. On 26 March, he penned a letter to a relative:

> I must confess to the most profound distrust of Russia. I have no belief whatever in her ability to maintain an effective offensive, even if she wanted to. And I distrust her motives, which seem to me to have little connection with our ideas of liberty, and to be concerned only with getting everyone else by the ears. Moreover, she is both hated and suspected by many of the smaller states, notably by Poland, Romania, and Finland.[137]

Accordingly, Litvinov's proposal for a conference was discounted.

For Britain and France, the German annexation of the Czech lands was the last straw. It signified a critical juncture in European international relations. No longer would the democratic nations permit Hitler to achieve significant territorial gains with relative ease, without bloodshed. With the exception of the acquisition of Memelland (today the Klaipėda Region) a week after the seizure of the Czech provinces, Germany would thereafter encounter resistance backed by force of arms. For the first time, Hitler had imposed hegemony over a non-Germanic people. No longer could Hitler posit the argument that his policy of expansionism was justified in that he was only bringing racial comrades *Heim ins Reich* (Home to the Reich). For the Czechs were not *Volksdeutsche* (ethnic Germans) but a foreign people. And to the democratic nations, it was obvious that their policy of appeasement had proven wholly ineffectual. To their dismay, the British were left with no alternative but to ready themselves for war.

Two days after the Wehrmacht marched into Bohemia–Moravia, Chamberlain spoke in Birmingham. To justify himself to his detractors, particularly those who condemned the seemingly endless concessions made by the British Government to Hitler, Chamberlain stated:

> It has been suggested that this occupation of Czechoslovakia was the direct consequence of the visit which I paid to Germany last autumn, and that, since the result of these events has been to tear up the settlement that was arrived at at Munich, that proves that the whole circumstances of those visits were wrong. It is said that, as this was the personal policy of the Prime Minister, the blame for the fate of Czechoslovakia must rest upon his shoulders. That is an entirely unwarrantable conclusion. The facts as they are today cannot change the facts as they were last September. If I was right then, I am still right now. Then there are some people who say: 'We considered you were wrong in September, and now we have been proved to be right....'
>
> When I decided to go to Germany I never expected that I was going to escape criticism.... I went there first and foremost because, in what appeared to be an almost desperate situation, that seemed to me to offer the only chance of averting a European war.

Chamberlain further defended himself:

> And I might remind you that, when it was first announced that I was going, not a voice was raised in criticism. Everyone applauded that effort. It was only later, when it appeared that the results of the final settlement fell short of the expectations of some who did not fully appreciate the facts—it was only then that the attack began, and even then it was not the visit, it was the terms of settlement that were disapproved.

Hitler's two-faced nature had by this time become evident to Chamberlain. With deep indignation, the Prime Minister railed at the injustice done to the Czechs:

> Who can fail to feel his heart go out in sympathy to the proud and brave people who have so suddenly been subjected to this invasion, whose liberties are curtailed, whose national independence has gone? What has become of this declaration of 'No further territorial ambition?' What has become of the assurance 'We don't want Czechs in the Reich?' What regard had been paid here to that principle of self-determination on which Herr Hitler argued so vehemently with me at Berchtesgaden when he was asking for the severance of Sudetenland from Czechoslovakia and its inclusion in the German Reich?

Here Chamberlain expressed his misgivings about Germany's future intentions, concerns which he believed were now on everyone's mind. He asked:

> Is this the end of an old adventure, or is it the beginning of a new? Is this the last attack upon a small State, or is it to be followed by others? Is this, in fact, a step in the direction of an attempt to dominate the world by force?

If the latter were true, Chamberlain made it plain that England would stand firm. In his peroration he stated:

> I do not believe there is anyone who will question my sincerity when I say there is hardly anything I would not sacrifice for peace. But there is one thing that I must except, and that is the liberty that we have enjoyed for hundreds of years, and which we will never surrender....
>
> I feel bound to repeat that ... no greater mistake could be made than to suppose that, because it believes war to be a senseless and cruel thing, this nation has so lost its fibre that it will not take part to the utmost of its power in resisting such a challenge if it were ever made.... I am convinced that I have not merely the support of my fellow-countrymen and countrywomen, but also the approval of the whole British Empire and of all other nations who value peace.[138]

The age of appeasement was over.

Hitler next turned his attention to the Memelland (Memel Territory), a small patch of Lithuanian territory bordering northern East Prussia and containing a significant German population. Its ethnic breakdown according to a 1925 census (language being the criteria used) revealed the following results from a total of 141,000 inhabitants: Lithuanian—74,500 (52.8 per cent); German—61,300 (43.5 per cent); Jews—2,500 (1.8 per cent); and Other—2,700 (1.9 per cent).[139] In 1919, Germany had been obliged to relinquish the Memelland (then a part of East Prussia) per the Versailles Treaty, Section X, Article 99:

> Germany renounces in favour of the Principal Allied and Associated Powers all rights and title over the territories included between the Baltic, the north eastern frontier of East Prussia as defined in Article 28 of Part II (Boundaries of Germany) of the present Treaty and the former frontier between Germany and Russia.
>
> Germany undertakes to accept the settlement made by the Principal Allied and Associated Powers in regard to these territories, particularly in so far as concerns the nationality of the inhabitants.[140]

This disposition did not last, for on 9 January 1923, Lithuanian militia forces occupied the Memelland. Ten days later, the Lithuanian Government claimed it. The annexation was ratified on 8 May 1924 per the Memel Convention by Lithuanian negotiators and representatives of the Entente Powers (Britain, France, Italy, and Japan). Henceforth the Memelland became a self-governing district with its own Diet and Directorate.

Hitler decided that March 1939 was the time to reverse this 'aberration' and reintegrate the Memelland back into Germany. This had been a top priority for Hitler before which only the Sudetenland took precedence. In accordance with Hitler's wishes, on 20 March, Ribbentrop gave Juozas Urbšys, his opposite number in Lithuania, a verbal ultimatum for the immediate cession of the Memelland to the Reich. During the forty-minute meeting Ribbentrop made it abundantly clear to Urbšys that if the *Seimas* (Lithuanian Parliament) refused to agree, the Reich was prepared to settle the matter by force. A small Baltic nation, Lithuania was militarily incapable of resisting the Wehrmacht. The following day Urbšys returned to Kaunas to relay the terms of the German ultimatum to his government. Unfortunately for the Lithuanian Government, the Western Powers—while sympathetic—were unwilling to intervene on their behalf. The Lithuanians were therefore faced with no alternative other than to accept the German *Diktat*, fervently hoping that the Nazis would not escalate their demands over time as they had done with Czechoslovakia.

Hitler set sail on the evening of 22 March from the Pomeranian city of Swinemünde aboard the *Panzerschiff* (armoured ship) *Deutschland*. His destination was Memel, in the Middle Ages a Teutonic stronghold and in 1939 a seaport of some 47,000 people. Meanwhile, Ribbentrop and Urbšys were busy in Berlin drafting a treaty for the restoration of the Memelland to Germany and any related issues stemming therefrom. It was signed on 23 March at 1 a.m. by three plenipotentiaries—Ribbentrop for Germany, Urbšys and Škirpa for Lithuania—and backdated to the previous day:

> Article 1: The Memel Territory, which was severed from Germany by the Treaty of Versailles, shall be reunited with the German Reich as of this date.
>
> Article 2: The Memel Territory shall be evacuated at once by the Lithuanian military and police forces. The Lithuanian Government will see to it that upon evacuation the Territory is left in good order....
>
> Article 3: In order to meet Lithuania's economic needs, a free-port zone shall be established in Memel for Lithuania....
>
> Article 4: In confirmation of their resolution to ensure the development of friendly relations between Germany and Lithuania, both parties pledge themselves to refrain from using force against each other and not to support the use of force directed against either of them by third parties.
>
> Article 5: The present treaty shall come into force upon signature....[141]

In high spirits, at 1:30 a.m. Ribbentrop fired off a dispatch to Hitler:

> MY FÜHRER: I report the signing of the treaty with Lithuania reuniting the Memel Territory with the Reich. Lithuania will complete military evacuation of the Memel Territory by 7 a.m. on 23 March.
>
> RIBBENTROP[142]

While still aboard the *Deutschland*, Hitler signed 'The Law concerning the Reunion of the Memelland with the German Reich'. Its articles reincorporated the Memelland into the Reich; restored German citizenship to the Memelland's inhabitants who had lost it in 1924, providing they were presently domiciled in either Germany or the Memelland; introduced into the Memelland 'the whole body' of German and Prussian law effective 1 May; and stipulated that the Reich Interior Minister was in charge of the 'Central Office for the Reunion of the Memelland' and was empowered to issue corresponding legislation.[143]

That morning, with Luftwaffe planes streaking by overhead in formation, German Army troops occupied the Memelland. Himmler and his S.S. had entered Memel the previous day to purge the city of unreliable elements ahead of the Führer's pending arrival. The *Deutschland*, along with a contingent of escort ships, finally reached Memel at 9:30 a.m. After debarking in the early afternoon, Hitler conducted an inspection of Memel German security police. He was then chauffeured to Memel's Theatre Square. Waiting for him was Dr. Ernst Neumann, the Memel German leader.[13*] Neumann accompanied Hitler to the rostrum on stage. In recognition of Neumann's services, Hitler pinned the prestigious *Goldenes Parteiabzeichen* (Golden Party Badge) to his topcoat. To the Memel Germans gathered in the Theatre Square, Hitler delivered an unusually brief (for him) speech:

> Memel Germans! Fellow citizens!
>
> In the name of the entire German people I greet you today and am happy to receive you into our Greater German Reich. I thereby lead you back into that home which you have not forgotten and which has never forgotten you ... You had been left in the lurch at one time by a Germany that surrendered to disgrace and ignominy. Now, however, you have returned into a mighty new Germany that again knows the unshakable conceptions of honour, that does not want to and will not entrust its fate to strangers, but that is ready and determined to master its own fate and to give it form even if another world does not like it.

13 * Hitler had met with Neumann on 17 December 1938 and had then assured Neumann of his intention to annex the Memelland into the Reich in either March or April 1939.[144]

> For this new Germany today more than 80,000,000 Germans stand sponsor.
>
> You will now flow into this great stream of our national life, of our labour, our faith, our hopes and, if necessary, also our sacrifices. You will understand this better than other Germans who have the good fortune of being permitted to live in the heart of our great Reich. You are the frontier of the country and you will feel what it means not to be forsaken but to know that behind you is a powerful Reich, a consolidated nation.
>
> Just as you were the sufferers from German impotence and disunion, so also were other Germans. From dire need and suffering, however, there has now sprung up for us a new community spirit. Let it be our will and our determination that it shall never again break asunder and let it be our oath that no other power on earth shall ever break or bend it.[145]

Less than a fortnight later, a 'marginal note' was appended to 'The Law concerning the Reunion of the Memel Territory with the Reich'. It stated that as of 3 April, the Memelland had been integrated into the *Regierungsbezirk* (government district) of Gumbinnen, East Prussia by Überleitungskommissar (Transfer Commissioner) Erich Koch.

The Memelland was Nazi Germany's final bloodless territorial gain before the outbreak of war.

PART III

# Preparations for War

From the early years of the Nazi régime to the summer of 1939, the Third Reich's foreign policy—characterized by ever-increasing boldness and lack of scruple—had set the German nation on a direct path to war. Almost immediately it became obvious that Hitler would resume his campaign of intimidation and coercion, this time against the Poles. Meanwhile, the Czech affair had made a grave impression on the British and French democratic leaders. The scales had finally fallen from their eyes. No longer could they, or would they, rely on Hitler's disingenuous assurances. Hitler proceeded warily, taking his measure of the Western Powers' resolve. He had long been preparing for a conflict. An entry from Ciano's diary dated 28 October, less than a month after Munich, revealed that the German leadership was intent on war. Ciano recorded the comments made by Ribbentrop to him and Mussolini at a meeting in Rome:

> The Führer is convinced that we must inevitably count on a war with the Western democracies in the course of a few years, perhaps three or four ... The Czech crisis has shown our power! We have the advantage of the initiative and are masters of the situation. We cannot be attacked. The military situation is excellent: as from September [1939] we could face a war with the great democracies.[1]

Still, Hitler preferred that war, when it came, remained a limited German–Polish skirmish. He did not want a major war spanning the entire European Continent, if it could be avoided. But in the autumn of 1938, the time was not yet ripe to strike. It was only later, after Hitler had encountered uncompromising resistance from the Poles in diplomatic talks, that he decided to eliminate Poland through conquest. Up to this point, the Reich had maintained cordial relations with its eastern Slavic neighbour. As far back as November 1933, Hitler had confided to Józef Lipski, Poland's Ambassador to Germany from 1934 to 1939:

> Poland is an outpost against Asia.[2]

By this Hitler meant that Poland stood as a bulwark against Asiatic Bolshevism which threatened to engulf Europe, and Poland's extermination by the latter would be disastrous for the European nations who would thereafter find themselves sharing a frontier with Asiatics. Thus, the German–Polish Non-Aggression Pact of 1934, which had undeniably ameliorated German–Polish relations, had been at least *partially* well-intentioned.

Since Poland's leaders were staunchly anti-Communist, Poland—in Hitler's eyes—might conceivably be a useful partner to Germany in the eventual clash versus the U.S.S.R. Moreover, the Poland of the 1930s was authoritarian, reactionary, repressive, and anti-Semitic—all political traits shared by Nazi Germany. The Reich strove to maintain friendly ongoing diplomatic relations with Poland. Göring flew to Krakow to attend the funeral of Józef Piłsudski[14*] on 15 May 1935. And throughout the late 1930s, Göring travelled to Warsaw on multiple occasions: a brief trip on 19 February 1936; for a formal meeting with high-ranking Polish officials on 16 February 1937; and again in February 1938 to dispel rumours of intended German aggression towards Poland.

In his Reichstag speech of 20 February 1938, Hitler reviewed how satisfactorily German–Polish relations had improved over the past five years as a result of the bona fide good will of both the German and Polish Governments, prior to which the two nations had harboured strong sentiments of resentment:

> In the fifth year following the first great foreign political agreement of the Reich, it fills us with sincere gratification to be able to state that in our relations with the State with which we had had perhaps the greatest differences, not only has there been a *détente*, but in the course of these years there has been a constant improvement in relations.... This good work, which was regarded with suspicion by so many at the time, has stood the test, and I may say that, since the League of Nations finally gave up its continual attempts to unsettle Danzig and appointed a man of great personal attainments as the new Commissioner, the most dangerous spot from the point of view of European peace has entirely lost

14 * The late Marshal Piłsudski, First Marshal of Poland, was a patriot and statesman who had served as Chief of State, Prime Minister, General Inspector of the Armed Forces, and Minister of Military Affairs. He is today recognized as the embodiment of Polish independence.

> its menacing character. The Polish State respects the national conditions by this State, and both the city of Danzig and Germany respect Polish rights. And so the way to a friendly understanding has been successfully paved, an understanding which, beginning with Danzig, has today, in spite of the attempts of certain mischief-makers, succeeded in finally taking the poison out of the relations between Germany and Poland and transforming them into a sincere, friendly co-operation.
>
> Relying on her friendships, Germany will not leave a stone unturned to save that ideal which provides the foundation for the task which is ahead of us—peace.[3]

After an alliance lasting nearly five years, German–Polish relations soured in late 1938, not long after the Sudeten affair. The issue of contention this time was the *Freie Stadt Danzig* (Free City of Danzig; today Gdańsk), a major port city with a 1939 population of 420,000. Ethnically it was predominantly German—over 95 per cent. The rest were chiefly Poles and Kashubians. Like the Rhineland, the Saar Basin, Alsace–Lorraine, Austria, Czechoslovakia, Poland, East Prussia, and the Memelland, the disposition of Danzig was dealt with by the Versailles Treaty. Article 102 stipulated: 'The Principal Allied and Associated Powers undertake to establish the town of Danzig ... as a Free City. It will be placed under the protection of the League of Nations.'[4] And Article 104 provided that 'a Treaty between the Polish Government and the Free City of Danzig' would accord to Poland the following rights and privileges:

> (1) To effect the inclusion of the Free City of Danzig within the Polish Customs frontiers, and to establish a free area in the port;
>
> (2) To ensure to Poland without any restriction the free use and service of all waterways, docks, basins, wharves and other works within the territory of the Free City necessary for Polish imports and exports;
>
> (3) To ensure to Poland the control and administration of the Vistula and of the whole railway system within the Free City, except such street and other railways as serve primarily the needs of the Free City, and of postal, telegraphic and telephonic communication between Poland and the port of Danzig;
>
> (4) To ensure to Poland the right to develop and improve the waterways, docks, basins, wharves, railways and other works and means of communication mentioned in this Article, as well as to lease or purchase through appropriate processes such land and other property as may be necessary for these purposes;

(5) To provide against any discrimination within the Free City of Danzig to the detriment of citizens of Poland and other persons of Polish origin or speech;

(6) To provide that the Polish Government shall undertake the conduct of the foreign relations of the Free City of Danzig as well as the diplomatic protection of citizens of that city when abroad.[5]

In 1930, Albert Forster—then not yet thirty—was appointed the Nazi District Leader of Danzig. Forster was a virulently anti-Polish extremist who later advocated the extermination of the Poles 'starting from the cradle'. In the Danzig Volkstag (Parliament) elections held on 28 May 1933, the National Socialists won an additional twenty-six seats, up from twelve in 1930 to thirty-eight. They received 107,331 votes out of 214,128 valid ballots cast. This narrow majority (50.12 per cent) enabled them to dominate the Danzig Senate in June; Hitler's old crony, Hermann Rauschning, became *Senatspräsident* (Senate President) on the 20th. Rauschning became disaffected with the Nazis, and after his resignation, was succeeded by Arthur Greiser on 23 November 1934. Like Forster, his nominal superior, Greiser also intensely hated the Poles. As of 1936, the Danzig Senate was predominantly membered by Nazi Danzigers.

On 24 October 1938, Ribbentrop received Józef Lipski, the Polish Ambassador to Germany, at the Grand Hotel in Berchtesgaden. During the friendly meeting, which took place over a three-hour luncheon, Ribbentrop made two major proposals. The first was for the restoration of Danzig to Germany, and the second was for an extraterritorial roadway and railway that would cross Pomorze (Polish Pomerania, also known as the 'Corridor') to East Prussia. According to Lipski's notes of the conversation:

> ... Herr von Ribbentrop put forward ... a proposal for a basic settlement of issues between Poland and Germany which, as he expressed himself, would remove the causes of future strife. This included the reunion of Danzig with the Reich, while Poland would be assured of retaining railway and economic facilities there. Poland would agree to the building of an extraterritorial superhighway and railway line across Pomerania.[6]

In return, Ribbentrop offered 'the possibility of an extension of the Polish–German agreement by twenty-five years' plus 'a guarantee of Polish–German frontiers'. Ribbentrop also alluded to the prospect of 'future co-operation between the two countries', specifically with regard to 'joint action in colonial matters, the emigration of Jews from Poland,

and a joint policy towards Russia on the basis of the Anti-Comintern Pact'. Lastly, Ribbentrop requested that Lipski 'communicate his suggestions to Minister Beck. He [Ribbentrop] would like to discuss these matters with him with the Ambassador's participation.' But in the end, Lipski pointed out to Ribbentrop that he 'could see no possibility of an agreement involving the reunion of the Free City [of Danzig] with the Reich'.[7] Lipski did agree, however, to pass on Ribbentrop's proposals to Polish Foreign Minister Józef Beck in Warsaw.

The sudden broaching of the Danzig issue was a major red flag to the Polish Government. The reasons for this were twofold. First, back on 5 November 1937, Hitler had explained to Lipski his position concerning Danzig in three unequivocal points:

1. In the legal-political situation of Danzig no changes will occur;

2. The rights of the Polish population in Danzig have to be respected; [and]

3. Poland's rights in Danzig will not be violated.

To this Hitler had added that 'the agreement [of 26 January 1934] concluded by him with Poland will be respected, and this applies also to Danzig'. All Hitler wanted, he had said, was for 'the German population in Danzig to adopt a system of rule most suitable for the Germans'. Lipski also recorded Hitler's statement, uttered twice, that '*Danzig ist mit Polen verbunden*' ('Poland is connected to Danzig').[8] Second, in a ninety-minute conversation on 14 January 1938, Hitler had again repeated (this time to Beck, in Lipski's presence) that 'Poland's rights in Danzig will not be infringed upon, and that, moreover, the legal status of the Free City will remain unaltered'. As far as Hitler was concerned, 'Polish–German relations were of essential and decisive importance ...' His only wish, he repeated, was 'that the local German population could adopt a form of government which would suit it best, and which as a result would contribute to the maintenance of peace'. These assurances, Hitler declared, were 'binding'.[9]

But the German Government was now reneging on its promises.

On 19 November, Lipski again consulted with Ribbentrop at the Foreign Ministry in Berlin, and read aloud to him Beck's written response to his (Ribbentrop's) proposals of 24 October. It stated that 'any tendency to incorporate the Free City [of Danzig] into the Reich must inevitably lead to conflict, not of a local character only, but one also jeopardizing Polish–German relations in their entirety'. Lipski also quoted to Ribbentrop the late Marshal Piłsudski's strong view 'that the Danzig question would constitute a criterion for evaluating Germany's relations to Poland'.[10]

Greatly displeased by Polish obduracy, on 24 November Hitler issued a top secret order titled 'The First Supplement to the Instruction Dated the 21st of October 1938'. This confidential document was sent to all three branches of the Wehrmacht and was signed by General Keitel. It read in part:

> The Führer has ordered: Apart from the three contingencies mentioned in the instructions of that date of 21 October 1938, preparations are also to be made to enable the Free State of Danzig to be occupied by German troops by surprise.
>
> The preparations will be made on the following basis: Condition is a *quasi-revolutionary* occupation of Danzig, exploiting a politically favourable situation, *not a war against Poland.*[11]

In the post-Munich *milieu*, the German and French Governments sought to bring about a *rapprochement* between them. Accordingly, on 6 December, the German and French Foreign Ministers—Ribbentrop and Bonnet respectively—signed the German–French Declaration in Paris. Its purpose was, in Ribbentrop's words, for France and Germany 'to put an end to their centuries-old boundary dispute, and, in reciprocally recognizing their frontiers, to clear the way for a mutual recognition of and consideration for their vital national interests'. Ribbentrop continued: 'As partners with full equality of rights, two great nations declare themselves ready, after serious differences in the past [The Franco–Prussian War of 1871 and the First World War], to establish good neighbourly relations for the future. With this declaration of their intentions, they express the conviction that there does not exist between them any real difference of vital importance, such as might justify a serious conflict.' The Declaration consisted of three articles and it came into effect immediately:

> 1. The German Government and the French Government fully share the conviction that peaceful and neighbourly relations between Germany and France constitute one of the most essential elements for the consolidation of the situation in Europe and the maintenance of general peace. The two Governments will in consequence use all their efforts to ensure the development in this direction of the relations between their countries.
>
> 2. The two Governments recognize that between the two countries there is no territorial question outstanding and they solemnly recognize as final the frontiers between their two countries as they now exist.
>
> 3. The two Governments are resolved, while leaving unaffected their particular relations with other Powers, to remain in contact with

> regard to all questions concerning their two countries, and mutually to consult, should the later evolution of those questions lead to international difficulties.[12]

The day before the German–French Declaration was signed, Ribbentrop gave an interview to a representative of the *Paris-Soir*, a daily French newspaper with a circulation of two million-plus:

> Many Frenchmen should know that for a long time I have been seeking and working for an understanding with France. No one was more pleased than I when the Führer, after the National Socialists' assumption of power, took the view that a *rapprochement* with France was the primary condition for the appeasement of Europe. The German people gladly followed him, for they have nothing against the French, just as the French people, whom I think I know well, have nothing against the Germans.
>
> The great respect felt by the German combatants for the French combatants was born of the War. This respect is a favourable soil for all understanding and for this reason during the last few years no one has worked harder for a *rapprochement* between our two nations than the former combatants.
>
> I am sure that there are no vital questions between France and Germany that cannot be settled in an amicable manner. France has friends just as Germany has. Why should it not be possible to build a bridge between these friends in order to find a basis which can only be of advantage to all countries concerned?...[13]

Early in the New Year, on 5 January, Foreign Minister Beck was received at the Berghof by Hitler. On this occasion, Hitler comported himself agreeably. When the subject of the talks turned to German–Polish relations, Hitler advised that 'since 1934 there had been no change in the German attitude towards Poland'. However, in order to reach a conclusive resolution of the issues outstanding between them, it would be necessary 'not to confine oneself to the rather negative agreement of 1934, but ... to bring the individual problems to a definite settlement by treaty'. Hitler explained that from the German standpoint, the final issues 'in direct German–Polish relations' to be redressed were Danzig and the Polish Corridor. 'It was necessary', Hitler continued, 'to depart from old patterns here and seek solutions along entirely new lines.' What he had in mind was an arrangement whereby 'Danzig would come into the German community politically but remain with Poland economically'. Hitler declared:

> Danzig is German, will always remain German, and will sooner or later become part of Germany.

But he promised Beck that the Polish Government would not be confronted with a *fait accompli* in Danzig as had faced the European community with the remilitarization of the Rhineland in 1936 and the annexation of Austria in 1938. In connection with the Corridor, Hitler acknowledged 'that it was of course completely absurd to want to deprive Poland of her outlet to the sea'. However, it was likewise necessary for the Reich to have a route intersecting the Polish Corridor to East Prussia. '[B]y using entirely new methods of solution', Hitler added diplomatically, 'one could perhaps do justice to the interests of both [the German and Polish nations].' In this way Poland would gain 'the great advantage of having her frontier with Germany, including the Corridor, secured by treaty', one which would 'supplement' the German–Polish Non-Aggression Pact of 1934.

Beck was very skeptical of Hitler's proposals. 'The Danzig question', as far as he was concerned, 'seemed extremely difficult.' The primary obstacle was Polish public opinion, which he had to take into consideration, for the Poles strongly opposed even the prospect of ceding Danzig to the Reich. He was not referring to mere 'coffee-house opposition', which he had thoroughly ignored for the past seven years (and kept his position in spite of it), but 'the real opinion of the people'. Under the circumstances, he wished to give the matter further consideration. Beck ended by remarking 'that Poland would, as heretofore, remain true to the line followed since 1934'.[14]

The following day, Beck met with Ribbentrop in Munich for a ninety-minute conversation. To Ribbentrop, Beck averred that Poland endeavoured to maintain harmonious relations with the Reich. However, he was concerned that the Nazis in Danzig 'had used the tactics of little *faits accomplis*' to the detriment of Poland's rights in the Free City. Beck foresaw two possible scenarios that would compel the Polish Government to directly intervene:

1. The League of Nations might disinterest itself in the Danzig question and withdraw its High Commissioner. Germany and Poland would then have to deal with the question themselves;

2. The above-mentioned tactics of *faits accomplis* would force Poland to take a stand.

Regarding the Danzig problem, 'he had already racked his brains to find a solution, thus far without success'. Finally, Beck emphasized the point that 'in the minds of the whole Polish people Danzig represented a touchstone of German–Polish relations and that it would be very difficult to change this in any manner'.[15] To the Polish people, the subject of Danzig was an extremely touchy one; they saw Danzig as a symbol, regardless of its value.

In mid-March 1939, the Poles were confronted with the destruction of the Czechoslovak Republic. The German seizure of Bohemia–Moravia and the establishment of an 'autonomous' Slovak State (in reality a client state of the Reich) did not bode well, to say the least. But unlike the democratic politicians of the West, the Polish leaders showed far greater resolve in refusing the German Government's demands. They remained firm.

On 21 March, Lipski again spoke with Ribbentrop, who had summoned him 'in order to discuss Polish–German relations in their entirety'. This time the conversation was far more strained than their previous talks in the autumn of 1938. Ribbentrop griped about the Polish Press and 'the Warsaw students' [anti-German] demonstrations during Count Ciano's visit'. In turn, Lipski informed Ribbentrop of the Polish Government's dissatisfaction with Germany's recent annexation of the Czech lands, not to mention her backing of the new Slovak State, a measure which the Poles felt had been taken against them. Lipski wrote:

> I stated [to Ribbentrop] that now, during the settlement of the Czechoslovakian question, there was no understanding whatever between us [the Poles and Germans]. The Czech issue was already hard enough for the Polish public to swallow, for, despite our disputes with the Czechs, they were after all a Slav people. But in regard to Slovakia, the position was far worse. I emphasized our community of race, language, and religion, and mentioned the help we had given in their achievement of independence. I pointed out our long frontier with Slovakia. I indicated that the Polish man in the street could not understand why the Reich had assumed the protection of Slovakia, that protection being directed against Poland. I said emphatically that this question was a serious blow to our relations.

After pausing momentarily to consider Lipski's words, Ribbentrop advised him to return to Warsaw and discuss the matter with Beck as soon as possible, 'lest the Chancellor [Hitler] should come to the conclusion that Poland was rejecting all his offers'. Lastly, Lipski inquired if Ribbentrop could share some details of his talks with Urbšys, the Lithuanian Foreign Minister. Ribbentrop evaded the question with an ambiguous reply: he stated that he and Urbšys 'had discussed the Memel question, which called for a solution'.[16] Little did Lipski realize that this so-called 'solution'—namely, the German annexation of the Memelland—would be effected in the space of the next forty-eight hours.

In an early-morning telegram to the German Foreign Ministry dated 24 March, Germany's Ambassador to Poland, Hans-Adolf von Moltke, recorded the following observation in connection with the reincorporation of the Memel Territory into Germany the day before:

> Agitation among the Polish population has increased considerably since the return of Memel to the Reich. The main reason for this is that it is generally feared that now it will be the turn of Danzig and the Corridor.

Moltke reported that the Polish Under State Secretary had mentioned to him that the *fait accompli* in the Memelland had been a 'very unpleasant surprise'. Moltke also noted that the Polish Government, by 'the call-up of reservists', wished 'to make it known abroad, but particularly at home, that Poland will not submit to any interference with her vital interests'.[17]

At 11 a.m. on 25 March, Abwehr chief Wilhelm Canaris urgently telephoned Deputy Director Otto C. A. von Bismarck of the German Foreign Office to notify him of 'Polish mobilization measures'. Bismarck documented the particulars of Canaris' call in a memorandum:

> 1. Some 4,000 troops are concentrated at Danzig.
>
> 2. The troops of a garrison previously stationed in the southern part of the Corridor have been transferred to the immediate vicinity of the Danzig frontier.
>
> 3. Poland has mobilized three age-groups.
>
> All these measures concern only the northern part of Poland; in the other districts of the country there is nothing to report militarily.
>
> General Keitel does not believe in any aggressive intentions on the part of the Poles, neither, therefore, does he believe that Poland wishes rather to forestall us by a military occupation of Danzig, but attributes these measures to the generally noticeable nervousness of the Poles. In the General Staff, on the other hand, the tendency is to take a somewhat more serious view of the situation.[18]

Later that day, Army chief Brauchitsch jotted down the contents of a lengthy discussion with Hitler. The day before the Führer had sailed back from Memel to Swinemünde and thence to Berlin by special train:

> The Führer *does not* wish to solve the Danzig question by force ... He does not wish to drive Poland into the arms of Britain by this. A possible military occupation of Danzig could be contemplated only if ... the Polish Government could not justify voluntary cession of Danzig to their own people and ... a *fait accompli* would make a solution easier for them.

Brauchitsch also set down Hitler's general views regarding Poland:

> For the present the Führer does not intend to solve the Polish question. However, it should now be worked upon. A solution in the near future would have to be based on especially favourable political conditions. In such a case Poland would have to be so beaten down that, during the next few decades, she need not be taken into account as a political factor.

And as for the Ukraine, Brauchitsch recorded:

> The Führer does *not* wish to enter the Ukraine.

However, it was possible in the future that 'a Ukrainian State might be established'. Brauchitsch further believed it possible that Hitler might, at an opportune moment, renounce his treaty with Slovakia and 'use Slovakia as a political bargaining counter between himself, Poland, and Hungary'. Meanwhile, Brauchitsch noted, Hungary was 'to be kept in check'.[19]

Hitler also found the time to send a congratulatory telegram to Mussolini on the eve of the twentieth anniversary of the Fascist Movement:

> On the twentieth anniversary of the foundation of the Fascist fighting units I think of you in hearty and true friendship as the victorious creator of a proud new Italy.
>
> Filled with the same ideals, the German people stand shoulder to shoulder with the battle-proved Italian nation in defence against all hateful and incomprehensible attempts to restrict the justified will for living of our peoples and to shake the peace of the world.[20]

Next day Ribbentrop had another conversation with Lipski in Berlin, which began at 12:30 p.m. Ribbentrop brought to Lipski's attention the reports of 'Polish troop concentrations' around Danzig, and warned Lipski that 'a violation of the sovereignty of Danzig territory by Polish troops would be regarded by Germany in the same way as a violation of the Reich frontiers'. To this Lipski 'energetically denied that Poland had any military intentions toward Danzig'. On the contrary, Lipski explained, 'The troop movements undertaken by Poland merely represented precautionary measures.'[21] After all, the Germans had just snatched Bohemia–Moravia and the Memelland; who was to say that Danzig and the Polish Corridor were not next on their list? Under the circumstances, the Polish Government had reasonable grounds for concern, and were entitled to protect their interests whether it pleased the Germans or not.

*Above left:* The historic first meeting of the dictators. Reich Chancellor Adolf Hitler and Italian Prime Minister Benito Mussolini at the Venice-Lido airfield. 14 June 1934. Hitler mistakenly believed the meeting was to be a quiet and private discussion, and was embarrassed to have arrived in a suit and ill-fitting raincoat when Mussolini greeted him dressed in full military uniform in front of 200 journalists. (*Alfred Eisenstaedt*)

*Above right:* Hitler strolling alongside Mussolini in Italy, 15 June 1934. Relations were strained between the two politicians on this occasion with the two clashing on the matter of Austria. (*United States Holocaust Memorial Museum*)

*Below:* Italian officers salute Hitler and Mussolini, shortly after the Führer's arrival on his first visit to Italy, 14 June 1934. (*Instituto Nazionale Luce*)

On taking over the palace of the Reich president, on 12 September 1934 Hitler received foreign diplomats accredited to Berlin. Here he is in conversation with the French Ambassador, André François-Poncet. (*United States Holocaust Memorial Museum*)

The British delegation in Berlin. Hitler in conversation with Foreign Secretary Sir John Simon, 25 March 1935. (*United States Holocaust Memorial Museum*)

*Above left:* The funeral ceremony of Polish Marshal Józef Piłsudski. Hitler is seated in the centre, in front of the catafalque, 18 May 1935. (*National Digital Archives, Poland*)

*Above right:* Hitler and former British Prime Minister David Lloyd George at Hitler's mountain home, the Berghof at Berchtesgaden, 4 September 1936. (*United States Holocaust Memorial Museum*)

*Below:* Hitler and Polish Foreign Minister Colonel Józef Beck at the Polish Embassy in Berlin, 4 July 1935. (*United States Holocaust Memorial Museum*)

*Above left:* An early Hitler encounter in Count Galleazzo Ciano's career as Italian Foreign Minister meeting at Hitler's mountain home, the Berghof at Berchtesgaden, 24 October 1936. (*Fonthill Archive*)

*Above right:* Chancellor Kurt Schuschnigg at an Austrian Fatherland Front rally in Vienna, probably the proclamation of Chancellor Schuschnigg as Front führer on 10 October 1936. (*Fonthill Archive*)

*Below:* Count Bernardo Attolico (1880–1942), Italian ambassador to Berlin, 1935–40 and Konstantin von Neurath (1873–1956), Minister of Foreign Affairs, during von Neurath's visit to Rome, 3 May 1937. (*Fonthill Archive*)

*Above left:* The Axis leaders in front of the Heerstrasse Bahnhof during Mussolini's state visit to Germany. 27 September 1937. (*United States Holocaust Memorial Museum*)

*Above right:* Berliners gather around a sign advertising the dictators' scheduled speeches at the Maifeld on the evening of 28 September 1937. (*United States Holocaust Memorial Museum*)

*Right:* Hitler in dialogue with pro-Nazi Viennese politician Arthur Seyss-Inquart. On the far left: Reinhard Heydrich, Chief of the Security Police, 15 March 1938. (*United States Holocaust Memorial Museum*)

*Above:* Hitler addressing tens of thousands of Austrians in Vienna's Heldenplatz following the *Anschluss*, 15 March 1938. (*Bundesarchiv*)

*Below left:* Hitler's Reichstag deputies applauding their Führer for the reunification of Austria with the Reich, 18 March 1938. (*United States Holocaust Memorial Museum*)

*Below right:* The Führer and the Duce in Florence, Italy, 9 May 1938. (*National Digital Archives, Poland*)

*Right:* The dictators at Rome during the Führer's state visit to Italy, 4 May 1938. (*National Digital Archives, Poland*)

*Below:* Hitler with Mussolini at Naples aboard the RM *Conte di Cavour*, 5 May 1938. (*Instituto Nazionale Luce*)

*Above:* Adolf Hitler greets Neville Chamberlain at the Berghof, 15 September 1938. 69-year-old Chamberlain had left Croydon at dawn, taken a seven-hour flight to Munich and after a short car journey had a three hour train journey to Berchtesgaden. (*Fonthill Archive*)

*Below:* The tea party. *From left to right*: Chamberlain, Hitler, Paul Schmidt (1899–1970), Hitler's interpreter, and Nevile Henderson (1882–1942), British Ambassador to Berlin. After tea, Hitler and Chamberlain retired to Hitler's study. There Hitler began his harangue. Chamberlain interrupted to say, 'If the Führer is determined to settle this matter by force without waiting even for a discussion between ourselves, why did he let me come? I have wasted my time.' Hitler was shocked—no German would dare to make an interruption. He calmed down. (*Fonthill Archive*)

Henderson in animated conversation with Ribbentrop at the Grand Hotel at Berchtesgaden, 15 September 1938. German State Secretary Dr Otto Meissner, Sir Horace Wilson and Neville Chamberlain are in the background. At the urging of Henderson, Ribbentrop was left out of the meeting between Chamberlain and Hitler. This exclusion so irritated Ribbentrop that the next morning he refused to give Schmidt's notes on the conference. Chamberlain was forced to rely on his memory. (*Fonthill Archive*)

Neville Chamberlain, Joachim von Ribbentrop, and George Ward Price (1886–1961) of the *Daily Mail*, at Lake Chiemsee, 16 September 1938 with Nevile Henderson, in background. (*Fonthill Archive*)

Chamberlain walks with von Ribbentrop as he leaves for home after the Berchtesgaden meeting, 16 September 1938. On the left is Alexander von Dörnberg, (1901–1983). Dörnberg was head of the Protocol Department of the German Foreign Office from 1938 to 1945. (*Fonthill Archive*)

*Above:* Neville Chamberlain and Hitler at Godesberg, their second encounter, 22 September 1938. In the centre, between the heads of government is chief interpreter Paul Schmidt. (*Bundesarchiv*)

*Below:* Hitler and Chamberlain at Godesberg, 22 September 1938. The negotiations between the statesmen concerned the Sudeten crisis. (*National Digital Archives, Poland*)

*Above:* Luftwaffe chief Hermann Göring, Italian Foreign Minister Galeazzo Ciano, Hitler, and Mussolini on their way to the Munich Conference, 29 September 1938. (*Brazilian National Archives*)

*Below left:* Hitler and Chamberlain greeting each other warmly at Munich, 29 September 1938. (*United States Holocaust Memorial Museum*)

*Below right:* The Prime Minister and Reich Chancellor shaking hands at Munich, 29 September 1938. (*Brazilian National Archives*)

The 'Big Four' at Munich. *From left to right*: Chamberlain, Daladier, Hitler, and Mussolini. On the far right: Ciano, 29/30 September 1938. (*Bundesarchiv*)

Hitler signing the Munich Agreement. Behind the Führer, Göring and Mussolini are engaged in a lively discussion. 29/30 September 1938. (*Bundesarchiv*)

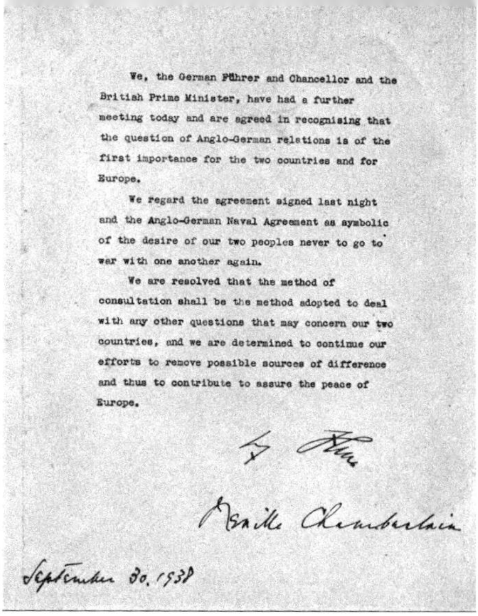

We, the German Führer and Chancellor and the British Prime Minister, have had a further meeting today and are agreed in recognising that the question of Anglo-German relations is of the first importance for the two countries and for Europe.

We regard the agreement signed last night and the Anglo-German Naval Agreement as symbolic of the desire of our two peoples never to go to war with one another again.

We are resolved that the method of consultation shall be the method adopted to deal with any other questions that may concern our two countries, and we are determined to continue our efforts to remove possible sources of difference and thus to contribute to assure the peace of Europe.

Neville Chamberlain

September 30, 1938

*Above left:* Mussolini and Hitler leaving the Führerbau, Munich, 30 September 1938. (*National Digital Archives, Poland*)

*Above right:* English text of the Anglo-German Declaration signed by Chamberlain and Hitler on the morning of 30 September 1938. (*Imperial War Museum*)

*Below left:* Propaganda poster featuring Hitler and Sudeten leader Konrad Henlein urging a pro-vote for the Sudeten election of 4 December 1938. (*United States Holocaust Memorial Museum*)

*Below right:* Hitler in Prague, gazing downwards from the Hradčany Castle following the annexation of Bohemia–Moravia into the Reich as a protectorate, 16 March 1939. (*National Digital Archives, Poland*)

*Above:* Hitler entering Memel the day following its annexation into Germany; 23 March 1939. (*United States Holocaust Memorial Museum, No. 20351*)

*Below left:* German Foreign Minister Joachim von Ribbentrop, calendar portrait, May 1939. (*United States Holocaust Memorial Museum*)

*Below right:* Soviet dictator Josef Stalin and Ribbentrop at the Kremlin, Moscow, 23 August 1939. (*Bundesarchiv*)

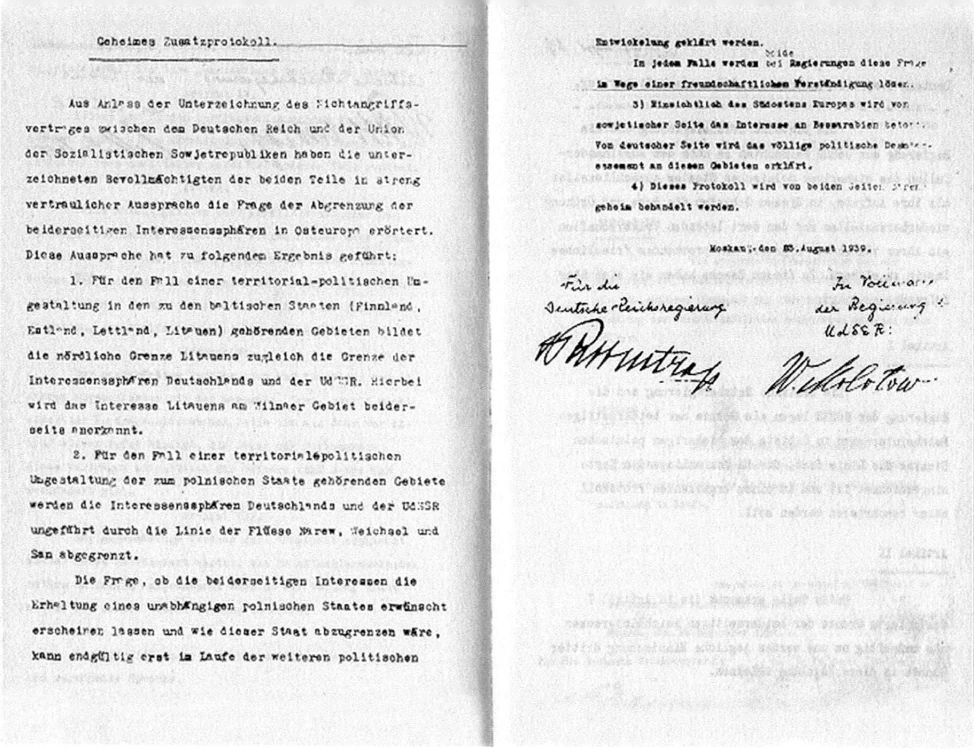

Geheimes Zusatzprotokoll.

Aus Anlass der Unterzeichnung des Nichtangriffsvertrages zwischen dem Deutschen Reich und der Union der Sozialistischen Sowjetrepubliken haben die unterzeichneten Bevollmächtigten der beiden Teile in streng vertraulicher Aussprache die Frage der Abgrenzung der beiderseitigen Interessensphären in Osteuropa erörtert. Diese Aussprache hat zu folgendem Ergebnis geführt:

1. Für den Fall einer territorial-politischen Umgestaltung in den zu den baltischen Staaten (Finnland, Estland, Lettland, Litauen) gehörenden Gebieten bildet die nördliche Grenze Litauens zugleich die Grenze der Interessensphären Deutschlands und der UdSSR. Hierbei wird das Interesse Litauens am Wilnaer Gebiet beiderseits anerkannt.

2. Für den Fall einer territorial-politischen Umgestaltung der zum polnischen Staate gehörenden Gebiete werden die Interessensphären Deutschlands und der UdSSR ungefähr durch die Linie der Flüsse Narew, Weichsel und San abgegrenzt.

Die Frage, ob die beiderseitigen Interessen die Erhaltung eines unabhängigen polnischen Staates erwünscht erscheinen lassen und wie dieser Staat abzugrenzen wäre, kann endgültig erst im Laufe der weiteren politischen Entwickelung geklärt werden.

In jedem Falle werden beide Regierungen diese Frage im Wege einer freundschaftlichen Verständigung lösen.

3) Hinsichtlich des Südostens Europas wird von sowjetischer Seite das Interesse an Bessarabien betont. Von deutscher Seite wird das völlige politische Desinteressement an diesen Gebieten erklärt.

4) Dieses Protokoll wird von beiden Seiten streng geheim behandelt werden.

Moskau, den 23. August 1939.

Für die Deutsche Reichsregierung

In Vollmacht der Regierung der UdSSR:

*Above:* German text of the Nazi-Soviet Pact's Secret Additional Protocol. (*Internet Archive*)

*Below:* Newspaper cartoon satirizing the cynical partnership between Nazi Germany and the Soviet Union: 'Wonder How Long the Honeymoon Will Last?' (*The Washington Star*)

*Above:* Hitler at the Eastern front saluting German troops advancing into Poland, 15 September 1939. (*National Digital Archives, Poland*)

*Left:* Hitler and Göring at Oksywie, Gdynia, during the Polish campaign, 21 September 1939. (*National Digital Archives, Poland*)

German–Polish negotiations continued in Warsaw on 28 March, when Beck summoned Moltke to convey his formal reply to Ribbentrop's warning of 26 March (to Lipski) against a potential Polish *coup* in Danzig. Beck emphatically stated that 'if an attempt should be made by Germany to alter the status of the Free City unilaterally [i.e. without Polish consent], Poland would regard this as a *casus belli*. The same applied if such an attempt were to be made by the [Nazi-controlled] Danzig Senate.' This led to the following heated exchange:

> THE GERMAN AMBASSADOR: You want to negotiate at the point of the bayonet!
>
> COLONEL BECK: That is your own method.[22]

Hitler's intention to refrain from using force to settle outstanding territorial claims with Poland abruptly changed on 31 March, when Chamberlain gave a verbal assurance of unilateral military assistance to Poland in case of an attack by another country.[15*] Chamberlain declared to the House of Commons:

> In order to make perfectly clear the position of His Majesty's Government ... in the event of any action which clearly threatened Polish independence, and which the Polish Government accordingly considered it vital to resist with their national forces, His Majesty's Government would feel themselves bound at once to lend the Polish Government all support in their power. They have given the Polish Government an assurance to this effect.
>
> I may add that the French Government have authorized me to make it plain that they stand in the same position in this matter as do His Majesty's Government.[23]

Six days later, a joint communiqué was issued by both the British and Polish Governments:

> The conversations with M. Beck have covered a wide field and shown that the two Governments are in complete agreement upon certain general principles.
>
> It was agreed that the two countries were prepared to enter into an agreement of a permanent and reciprocal character to replace the present

15 * Later (in July) the British Government added to its pledge of military assistance of 31 March 1939 to include Danzig.

> temporary and unilateral assurance given by His Majesty's Government to the Polish Government. Pending the completion of the permanent agreement, M. Beck gave His Majesty's Government an assurance that the Polish Government would consider themselves under an obligation to render assistance to His Majesty's Government under the same conditions as those contained in the temporary assurance already given by His Majesty's Government to Poland.
>
> Like the temporary assurance, the permanent agreement would not be directed against any other country but would be designed to assure Great Britain and Poland of mutual assistance in the event of any threat, direct or indirect, to the independence of either. It was recognized that certain matters, including a more precise definition of the various ways in which the necessity for such assistance might arise, would require further examination before the permanent agreement could be completed.
>
> It was understood that the arrangements above mentioned should not preclude either Government from making agreements with other countries in the general interest of the consolidation of peace.[24]

When the news of Chamberlain's assurance to Poland of 31 March reached him, Hitler was apoplectic with rage. Canaris, who was present, recalled that Hitler struck the table with his fists and ranted, 'I'll cook them a stew they'll choke on!'[25] In reply, the very next day Hitler delivered an aggressive speech at the Municipal Hall Square in Wilhelmshaven, a harbour city along the North Sea coast. The harangue was directed chiefly against the British:

> The German people was created by Providence, not in order to obey a law which suits Englishmen or Frenchmen, but to stand up for its vital right[s]. That is what we are there for!...
>
> If an English statesman today believes that all problems can and must be solved by frank discussion and negotiations, then I would like to say to this statesman: an opportunity to do so existed for fifteen years before our time! If the world today says that one must divide the nations into virtuous and non-virtuous categories—and that the English and French belong in the first place to the virtuous nations and the Germans and Italians to the non-virtuous—then we can only answer: the decision as to whether a nation is virtuous or not virtuous can hardly be made by a mortal human being, and should be left to God!
>
> Perhaps this same British statesman will reply: God has already delivered judgment, for he has given to the virtuous nations one-quarter of the globe and has taken away everything from the non-virtuous! In answer to that, one may be permitted to ask: by what means have the

virtuous nations acquired this quarter of the globe? And the answer must be, they have not been virtuous methods!

For 300 years this England has acted only as an unvirtuous nation, and now in old age she is beginning to talk about virtue. It was thus possible that during the British non-virtuous period 46 million Englishmen have conquered almost a quarter of the world, while 80 million Germans, on account of their virtue, have to exist at the rate of 140 to the square kilometre.

Yes, twenty years ago the question of virtue was not yet quite clear in the minds of British statesmen, in so far as it touched conceptions of property. At that time it was still thought to be compatible with virtue simply to take away from another people the colonies which it had acquired by contract or by purchase because one had the power to do so....

If a British statesman today demands that every problem concerning vital German interests should first be discussed with England, then I could make precisely the same claim and demand that every British problem must first be discussed with us. Admittedly, this Englishman would answer: Palestine is none of your business! But, just as Germany has no business in Palestine, so has England no business in the German *Lebensraum*! And if the problem is claimed to be a question of general rights, then I can only agree to this opinion if it were regarded as universal and obligatory. One says we had no right to do this or that. I would like to ask a counter-question: what right—just to quote only one example—has England to shoot down Arabs in Palestine, only because they are standing up for their home? Who gives England the right to do so?

We at any rate have not slaughtered thousands in Central Europe, but have solved our problems in a peaceful and orderly manner! There is one thing, however, that I must say: the German people of today, the German Reich of the present time, are not willing to sacrifice interests, and they are also not willing to stand up to rising dangers without taking action! When the Allies at one time changed the map of Europe with no consideration for expediency, justice, tradition or even common sense, we did not have the power to prevent them from doing so. But if they expect the Germany of the present day patiently to allow vassal States, whose only duty consists in their being set to work against Germany, to carry on as they like until the day comes when their services are to be actively employed, then they are confounding present-day Germany with the Germany of pre-war days. Those who declare that they are prepared to pull chestnuts out of the fire for these Great Powers must also expect to burn their fingers in the course of the process.[26]

Behind the scenes, Hitler issued to his military chiefs a new directive for the conquest of Poland, '*Fall Weiss*' ('Case White'). It was titled 'Directive for the Uniform Preparation of War by the Armed Forces, 1939–40'. A covering letter dated 3 April and signed by General Keitel specified:

> The Führer has added the following Directives to Case White:
>
> 1. Preparations must be made in such a way that the operation can be carried out at any time from [the] 1st of September 1939 onwards.
>
> 2. The High Command of the Armed Forces has been directed to draw up a precise timetable for Case White and to arrange by conferences the synchronized timings between the three branches of the Armed Forces.
>
> 3. The plans for the branches of the Armed Forces and the details of the timetable must be submitted to the O.K.W. by the 1st of May.[27]

Drafted by Hitler, Case White outlined in detail the tasks of the political leadership and the objectives of the Army, Navy, and Air Force for crushing Poland in the event the Poles chose to abandon their pro-German stance (which Hitler had already perceived they had done) and the situation deteriorated into war. It was distributed on 11 April:

> 1. *Political Requirements and Aims.* German relations with Poland continue to be based on the principle of avoiding any quarrels. Should Poland, however, change her policy towards Germany, a final settlement might become necessary, notwithstanding the [non-aggression] pact in effect with Poland.
>
> The aim then will be to destroy Polish military strength, and create in the East a situation which satisfies the requirements of national defence. The Free State of Danzig will be proclaimed a part of the Reich territory at the outbreak of the conflict, at the latest.
>
> The political leadership considers it its task in this case to isolate Poland if possible, that is to say, to limit the war to Poland only.
>
> The development of increasing internal crises in France and the resulting British cautiousness might produce such a situation in the not too distant future.
>
> Intervention by Russia so far as she would be able to do this cannot be expected to be of any use for Poland, because this would imply Poland's destruction by Bolshevism.
>
> The attitudes of the Baltic States will be determined wholly by German military exigencies.

> On the German side, Hungary cannot be considered a certain German ally. Italy's attitude is determined by the Berlin–Rome Axis.
>
> 2. *Military Conclusions*. The great objectives in the building up of the German Armed Forces will continue to be determined by the antagonism of the Western Democracies. '*Fall Weiss*' ['Case White'] constitutes only a precautionary complement to these preparations. It is not to be looked upon in any way, however, as the necessary prerequisite for a military settlement with the Western opponents.
>
> The isolation of Poland will be more easily maintained, even after the beginning of operations, if we succeed in starting the war with heavy, sudden blows and in gaining rapid successes.
>
> The entire situation will require, however, that precautions be taken to safeguard the Western boundary and the German North Sea coast, as well as the air over them.[28]

It was around this time that Mussolini, envious of Germany's recent territorial gains, decided to emulate his Axis partner and reap the benefits due a conqueror. And so, on the morning of 7 April, Italian forces invaded Albania. The Balkan nation was defeated in six days and incorporated into the Italian Empire as a protectorate. Albania's Emperor, King Zog I—who had served as Albania's Prime Minister from 1922 to 1924 and as President from 1925 to 1928—fled to England, in exile. It was Italy's intention that Albania be used as a base for future attacks in Southeastern Europe, particularly against Greece.

After Italy's invasion of Albania, to the British it seemed possible, and even likely, that additional Axis incursions in the Balkan region might ensue. As a precaution, on 13 April Chamberlain offered (as with Poland a fortnight earlier) further pledges of military assistance, this time to Greece and Romania. The British Government had also commenced 'active negotiations with Turkey'. These talks resulted, on 12 May, 'to an exchange of public declarations' in which the British and Turkish Governments pledged to 'conclude a definitive long-term agreement of a reciprocal character'. Meanwhile, 'in the event of an act of aggression leading to war in the Mediterranean area they would be prepared to co-operate effectively and to lend each other all aid and assistance in their power'.[29] A Franco–Turkish agreement along these lines was also concluded later, on 23 June. As for Turkey, her motivation was to dissuade the Axis Powers from perpetrating any further acts of aggression in the Balkan region.

These promises by Britain to render military aid signalled a major change in British foreign policy. Chamberlain had at last accepted that Hitler was insatiable, and that the continual granting of concessions would only result in new and greater demands by the Nazi régime. The only language Hitler understood was the use of force, and only force of equal or greater potency could contain him. The Führer had long sought to reach an agreement with England that would enable him to establish his conception of an immense, sprawling Germanic empire in Eastern Europe. Britain could oblige him by refraining from meddling in continental affairs and instead, as a maritime power, tend to her many colonies abroad. And as recently as 30 January, in his annual anniversary speech to the Reichstag, Hitler maintained that the Germans had no intention of encroaching on British interests:

> I have stated over and over again and again that there is no German, and, above all, no National Socialist, who even in his most secret thoughts has the intention of causing the British Empire any kind of difficulty. From England, too, the voices of men who think reasonably and calmly express a similar attitude with regard to Germany. It would be a blessing for the whole world if mutual confidence and co-operation could be established between our two peoples.[30]

Hitler had occasionally indicated to his military chiefs that the Western Powers would not interfere with his designs in the East. This was not the case at all, but nevertheless a few of them were taken in. They held the notion that their Führer had arranged *vis-à-vis* the democracies to be given free rein to counter the Communist threat as he saw fit.

On 13 April, Daladier made the following declaration to the French Press in connection with Britain's recent guarantee of military support to Poland:

> The French Government ... derives great satisfaction from the conclusion of the reciprocal undertakings between Great Britain and Poland, who have decided to give each other mutual support in defence of their independence in the event of either being threatened directly or indirectly.
>
> The Franco–Polish alliance is, moreover, confirmed in the same spirit by the French Government and the Polish Government. France and Poland guarantee each other immediate and direct aid against any threat direct or indirect, which might aim a blow at their vital interests.[31]

On 19 April, Hitler conferred with Grigore Gafencu, the Romanian Foreign Minister, at the Reich Chancellery. Gafencu was a shrewd diplomat with a doctorate in law. He spoke first, touching upon the recent economic pact between Germany and Romania signed in Bucharest on

23 March. He then turned to the subject of collective security among the European nations. When it was his turn, Hitler spoke of the Anglo–French guarantee given six days earlier to Romania in the aftermath of the rapid Italian conquest of Albania (from 7 to 12 April). The Western Powers had pledged to offer military assistance should either of the Axis Powers embark on further campaigns in Southeastern Europe. Hitler declared:

> The Anglo–French guarantees [given to Poland on 31 March, and extended to Greece and Romania on 13 April] will be of no use to you. But I shall not take exception to them. I know your weakness for France. My attitude would be quite different were you to take part, alongside the Soviets, in this vast plan of encirclement which the government in London is preparing. Such a plan endangers the existence of the Reich, and we are determined to defend ourselves by every means.

Hitler railed at the Anglo–Polish defence agreement of 31 March. He interpreted this assurance of military assistance to mean that after five years of friendly German–Polish relations, Poland had switched sides from Germany to England. Hitler ominously forecast that this sudden turnabout in policy might spell disaster for the Poles, in spite of his good will towards them:

> The fault of [Polish Foreign Minister] M. Beck is that he has turned to London. I shall never understand the change that has come over Poland's attitude. It is a change which may prove fatal to it. Beck's arguments are of no value. His story about reassurance does not hold water. The Anglo–Polish engagement is in flagrant contradiction of the agreement which I concluded earlier with Marshal Piłsudski. In case of a conflict between the Reich and any other power, a conflict in which England would be led to participate, Poland is pledged to take up a position against Germany. I am told in reply that I approved the existence of the Franco–Polish Agreement. That has nothing to do with the case. In 1934 I took note of the Polish engagements then existing, but I do not accept a subsequent enlargement of these engagements. In the conditions created by these new engagements, I should never have signed my agreement with Poland! There you have the reason why I no longer attach any importance to it.
>
> Nevertheless, I had the best of intentions towards Piłsudski's Poland. I respected its frontiers and all the absurd provisions of Versailles. I prevented the German Press from protesting against the scandalous way in which the German minorities were treated....
>
> In all circumstances, I have shown the Polish people my understanding and friendship.

He explained to Gafencu the recent offer he had made to the Polish Government regarding the re-unification of Danzig with the Reich, plus an extraterritorial link to East Prussia, in return for an official guarantee of Poland's frontiers and the relinquishment of any territorial claims by the Reich for a quarter-century:

> Only recently, I made Poland an offer that will abide in the annals of history as an act of incredible generosity. If Poland had understood it, it might have helped us to resolve all matters outstanding between us—and which in any event cannot remain as they are. I offered Poland an understanding regarding the German city of Danzig. This city, in conformity with its express will, must be reunited with the Reich. Nothing, absolutely nothing, can stop that. In exchange, I proposed that Danzig should remain economically bound to Poland. I have always recognized that this city was the prolongation of Poland's economic territory. I also asked for an extraterritorial right of passage to Danzig and East Prussia. In addition, I was ready to recognize formally all Poland's frontiers; and I was prepared to promise to not raise any political or territorial claims against Poland for twenty-five years. Still further, I was disposed to place the new Slovakian State under the protection of a tripartite régime—German–Magyar–Polish. Such a collaboration could assure peace in Central Europe for years to come. That is the extraordinary offer which Poland refused. I assure you that Poland certainly will not soon see another. M. Beck has joined up with the Western Powers. He has settled his own fate.

Hitler promised that he would resolve the Danzig situation speedily—but this time, without regard to Poland's wishes:

> I do not know what will follow, but one thing is certain: the solution that will be reached will no longer consider Poland's interests in the same way. As for the Danzig affair, it must be settled with the utmost dispatch—and it will be, whatever political schemes M. Beck may have!

Hitler made reference to the seizure of Bohemia, the plight of the Sudeteners, and the recent dissolution of Czechoslovak State:

> I intend to extend the German Reich to its natural limits, and no more. If I have occupied Bohemia, it is not for the pleasure of making conquests but to prevent the continuance, within the German living space, of an alien, hostile wedge driven into the body of the Reich....

> I never wanted to annex the Czechs, I assure you. My sole thought was to liberate the four million [Sudeten] Germans who found themselves in an intolerable situation in Bohemia....
>
> Why should this solution [the dismemberment of Czechoslovakia] be in opposition to the Munich Agreements? What could these agreements accomplish against a decay which was in the nature of things? And by what right did England claim to intervene in order to prevent the normal, natural evolution of the situation in Central Europe?

Hitler inveighed against the British Government for refusing to give Germany *carte blanche* in Central and Eastern Europe. He accused the British of continually trying to obstruct Germany at every turn:

> The English are determined not to understand. Instead of coming to an agreement with us, as I have so often proposed to them, they insist on blocking our path and seeking a quarrel with us. They do not admit our political power. They stand in the way of our economic development. They seek allies against us everywhere. They undermine our influence and raise illusory barriers against us; they maintain a campaign of hatred and prepare a general war, the responsibility for which they already seek to put on us. With what do they reproach us? We only want what is our due. We want our colonies, which we need; they are essential to our economic life, to our sense of strength and honour. We wish England, whose empire we respect, to respect in turn our own sphere of interest, and the space without which we cannot live.

He also raised the grim prospect of war with England. Such a conflict would utterly devastate Europe, leaving it in shambles:

> Oh, well, if England wants war, it will have it. It won't be so easy a war as it thinks, nor one on the old pattern. England will no longer have the whole world at its side. At least half the world is with us. And it will be a war of destruction beyond belief. Besides, how can England think of a modern war when she cannot mount two divisions on any front?
>
> As for us our misfortunes have been of use. We shall fight with other arms than those of 1914. We shall fight ruthlessly, to the end, with no consideration. We have never been as strong as we are now. To the invincibility of our armies must be added the genius of our technicians, engineers, and chemists. We shall astound the world with our methods and inventions. So on what do they rely to hold us in check? Their air force? They may perhaps succeed in bombarding a few towns, but how can they measure up to us? Our air force leads the world, and no enemy town will be left standing!

Finally, Hitler pointed out that the sole beneficiary of a general war between Germany and the Western Powers would be Stalin:

> But, after all, why this unimaginable massacre? In the end victor or vanquished, we shall all be buried in the same ruins; and the only one who will profit is that man in Moscow [Stalin].
>
> And to think that it is I—I who am accused in Germany of being an impenitent admirer of the British Empire, I who have so often tried to establish a lasting understanding between the Reich and England—an understanding which today I still consider necessary to the defence of European civilization—to think that it is I who must envisage such a conflict! And this entirely on account of the incomprehension and blind obduracy of the leaders of Great Britain![32]

In his 1940 book, *Failure of a Mission*, Nevile Henderson recalled a memorable conversation with Göring in 1937. The crux of the *tête-à-tête* was that Germany and Britain should come to terms. Specifically, Göring proposed that the Reich would acknowledge and respect the British Empire's naval supremacy and promise to render assistance should the circumstances arise, and in return Britain would allow the Reich unrestricted freedom to act on the Continent and promise not to obstruct her territorial ambitions. Henderson wrote:

> I had had one long political talk with Göring. Very shrewd and astute … his mind was simple and dealt only with essentials. His idea of an understanding between Great Britain and Germany was an agreement limited to two clauses.
>
> In the first, Germany would recognize the supreme position of Great Britain overseas, and undertake to put all her resources at the disposal of the British Empire in case of need.
>
> By the second, Great Britain would recognize the predominant continental position of Germany in Europe, and undertake to do nothing to hinder her legitimate expansion.
>
> It was the theory of the free hand for Germany in Central and Eastern Europe … Its very simplicity made it the more plausible, but it left out of all account not only the national conscience and international idealism of the Western democracies, but also the methods and exaggerated pretentions of Nazism.

Perhaps with a more moderate German Government, this proposal could have been entertained. But after the brazen seizure of Bohemia–Moravia, contrary to the terms of the Munich Agreement, this was impossible. Henderson had written further to this effect:

> With a Germany prepared to admit the equality of rights of others, and to solve problems by negotiation instead of by force, a gentleman's agreement on such lines would have had much to recommend it. Any attempt to achieve it was bound to fail as long as the Nazi régime of Hitler persisted in employing outside Germany the same methods which it had used to secure its position within Germany. In the name of the Führer and the Party it had crushed out all individual personality and freedom within the boundaries of the Reich, and in the name of the superiority of German culture and of the transcendental rights of Germans over all other races it was preparing to destroy the national liberty and freedom of its weaker neighbours outside those boundaries.[33]

The British Government could no longer afford to trust Hitler. His double-crossing tactics over time proved that he could not be counted on to adhere to any agreement he had made. And even if an Anglo–German alliance had materialized in 1939, it would not have prevented Hitler from launching an all-out attack on Britain or her possessions in the years to come.

On 28 April, Hitler addressed the Reichstag in a two-hour speech. He reiterated—for the umpteenth time—his desire to reach an understanding with the British, but complained that Britain's leaders had decided to take an uncompromising, adversarial position against Germany in the belief that an armed conflict was unavoidable:

> ... During the whole of my political activity I have always expounded the idea of close friendship and collaboration between Germany and England.... This desire for Anglo–German friendship and co-operation conforms not merely to sentiments which results from the racial origins of our two people but also to my realization of the importance for the whole of mankind of the existence of the British Empire....
>
> I regard it as impossible to achieve lasting friendship between the German and Anglo–Saxon peoples if the other side does not recognize that there are German as well as British interests, that not only is preservation of the British Empire the meaning and purpose of the lives of Britishers, but also that for Germans freedom and preservation of the German Reich is their life and purpose....
>
> Now, if England cannot understand our point of view, thinking, perchance, that she may look upon Germany as a vassal State, then our love and friendly feelings have indeed been wasted on England....
>
> I have heard the statement of the British Prime Minister to the effect that he is not able to put any trust in German assurances. Under the circumstances, I consider it a matter of course that we no longer wish or

> expect him or the British people to bear the burden of a situation which is only conceivable in an atmosphere of mutual confidence.
>
> When Germany became National Socialist and thus paved the way for her national resurrection in pursuance of my unswerving policy of friendship with England, of my own accord I made the proposal for voluntary restriction of German naval armaments. That restriction was, however, based on one condition; namely, the will and conviction that war between England and Germany would never again be possible. This wish, this conviction, is alive in me today.
>
> I am now, however, compelled to state that the policy of England is both unofficially and officially leaving no doubt about the fact that such a conviction is no longer shared in London and that, on the contrary, opinion prevails there that no matter in what conflict Germany should some day be entangled, Great Britain would always have to take her stand against Germany. Thus war against Germany is taken for granted in that country.

Hitler stated that the sole demand he had placed upon England was the return of the Reich's colonies, of which Germany had been stripped per the Versailles Treaty. But he maintained that the issue of colonies was not one which would lead to war between them:

> ... the only claim I have ever made and shall continue to make on England is that for [the] return of our colonies. But I always made it very clear that this would never become a cause of military conflict. I have always held that the English, to whom these colonies are of no value, would one day understand the German situation and would then value German friendship higher than the possession of territories which, while yielding no real profit whatever to them, are of vital importance to Germany.
>
> Apart from this, however, I have never advanced a claim which might in any way have interfered with British interests or have become a danger to the [British] Empire and thus have meant any damage to England. I have always kept within the limit of such demands as are intimately connected with Germany's living space, and thus the eternal property of the German nation.

Hitler also chose to repudiate the Anglo–German Naval Agreement due to the present anti-German stance taken by the British Government and Press:

> Since England today, by press and officially, upholds the view that Germany should be opposed under all circumstances and confirms this policy of encirclement known to us, the basis for the [Anglo–German] Naval Treaty has been removed. I have therefore resolved to send today a communication to this effect [see Appendix J] to the British Government.

As for the Poles, they too had rebuffed him. He had extended a most generous offer to the Polish Government, and all he had asked from them were two items: one, that Danzig be returned 'as a Free State into the framework of the German Reich'; and two, that Germany be granted 'a route through the Corridor and a railway line at her own disposal possessing the same extra-territorial status for Germany as the Corridor itself has for Poland'. Hitler explained that in exchange for these reasonable concessions, Germany was prepared:

> (1) To recognize all Polish economic rights in Danzig.
>
> (2) To ensure for Poland a free harbour in Danzig of any size desired which would have completely free access to the sea.
>
> (3) To accept at the same time the present boundaries between Germany and Poland and to regard them as ultimate.
>
> (4) To conclude a twenty-five-year non-aggression treaty with Poland, the treaty, therefore, which would extend far beyond the duration of my own life; and
>
> (5) To guarantee the independence of the Slovak State by Germany, Poland and Hungary jointly—which means, in practice, renunciation of any unilateral German hegemony in this territory.

However, the Polish Government had refused his territorial demands. This Hitler found unfathomable, but according to him, that was not the most egregious aspect of it:

> The Polish Government has rejected my one and only offer ...
>
> I have regretted greatly this incomprehensible attitude of the Polish Government, but that alone is not the decisive fact; the worst is that now Poland, like Czechoslovakia a year ago, believes, under pressure of a lying international campaign, that it must call up troops although Germany on her part has not called up a single man and had not thought of proceeding in any way against Poland.

Hitler also repudiated the German–Polish Non-Aggression Pact of 1934 on the basis of the recent guarantees of mutual assistance extended by Britain to Poland and *vice-versa*:

> An intention to attack on the part of Germany, which was merely invented by the international Press, led as you know, to a so-called guarantee offer and

> to the obligation on the part of the Polish Government for mutual assistance which would also, under certain circumstances, compel Poland to take military action against Germany in the event of conflict between Germany and any other Power and in which England, in her turn, would be involved.
>
> This obligation is contradictory to the agreement which I made with Marshal Piłsudski some time ago …
>
> Therefore I look upon the agreement which Marshal Piłsudski and I at one time concluded as having been unilaterally infringed by Poland and thereby no longer in existence![34]

That same day the German Government sent official notice to the Polish Government that they considered the recent Anglo–Polish mutual assistance agreement to have 'arbitrarily and unilaterally' rendered the German–Polish Non-Aggression Pact of 1934 'null and void'. Two reasons were given: first, that the Polish Government had failed to resolve the issue of Danzig to the German Government's satisfaction; and second, that the Polish Government had accepted from Britain a pledge of military assistance in the event of foreign aggression, directed against the Reich:

> (1) The Polish Government did not avail themselves of the opportunity offered to them by the German Government for a just settlement of the Danzig question, for the final safeguarding of Poland's frontiers with the Reich, and thereby for a permanent strengthening of the friendly neighbourly relations between the two countries. The Polish Government even rejected German proposals made with this object.
>
> (2) At the same time the Polish Government accepted, with regard to another State, political obligations which are not compatible either with the spirit, the meaning or the text of the German–Polish Declaration of the 26th January, 1934.[35]

In his speech Hitler also took the time to acknowledge President Roosevelt's well-intentioned personal letter dated 14 April.[16*] Hitler

16 * In the letter, Roosevelt—who had been disturbed by the recent German occupation of Bohemia–Moravia and the Italian invasion of Albania—had commented on the 'constant fear' of many millions of people worldwide of 'a new war or even a series of wars'. He had then asked the German dictator to 'give assurance that your armed forces will not attack or invade the territory or possessions of the following independent nations: Finland, Estonia, Latvia, Lithuania, Sweden, Norway, Denmark, The Netherlands, Belgium, Great Britain and Ireland, France, Portugal, Spain, Switzerland, Liechtenstein, Luxembourg, Poland, Hungary, Romania, Yugoslavia, Russia, Bulgaria, Greece, Turkey, Iraq, the Arabias, Syria, Palestine, Egypt, and Iran.' He had also requested that Hitler agree to a 'minimum period of assured non-aggression' of at least ten years, twenty-five if possible. Finally, he had advised Hitler that he was sending a similar letter 'to the Chief of the Italian Government'.[36]

responded to Roosevelt's sincere message in a condescending manner intended to ridicule him. He answered each of the American President's specific concerns in turn with mocking rebuttals that reduced the Reichstag deputies present to helpless laughter. His peroration was a sarcastic rejoinder in which he emphasized the difficulties he had surmounted in order to restore Germany to her rightful place in the world since 1933, and Roosevelt's comparatively less difficult undertaking:

> Mr. Roosevelt! I fully understand that the vastness of your nation and the immense wealth of your country allow you to feel responsible for the history of the whole world and for the history of all nations. I, sir, am placed in a much more modest and smaller sphere. You have 130,000,00 people on 9,500,000 square kilometres.
>
> You possess a country with enormous riches in all mineral resources, fertile enough to feed a half-billion people and to provide them with all necessities.
>
> I once took over a State which was faced by complete ruin, thanks to its trust in the promises of the rest of the world and to the bad régime of democratic governments. In this State there are roughly 140 people to each square kilometre—not 15, as in America. The fertility of our country cannot be compared with that of yours.
>
> We lack numerous minerals which nature has placed at your disposal in unlimited quantities.
>
> Billions of German savings accumulated in gold and foreign exchange during many years of peace were squeezed out of us and taken from us. We lost our colonies. In 1933 I had in my country 7,000,000 unemployed, a few million workers on half-time, millions of peasants sinking into poverty, destroyed trade, ruined commerce; in short, general chaos.
>
> Since then, Mr. Roosevelt, I have only been able to fulfill one simple task. I cannot feel myself responsible for the fate of the world, as this world took no interest in the pitiful state of my own people.
>
> I have regarded myself as called upon by Providence to serve my own people alone and to deliver them from their frightful misery.

Hitler enumerated his many accomplishments and achievements since becoming Chancellor in 1933:

> Consequently, during the past six and one-half years, I have lived day and night for the single task of awakening the powers of my people, in view of our desertion by the whole of the rest of the world, of developing these powers to the utmost and of utilizing them for the salvation of our community.

> I have conquered chaos in Germany, re-established order, and enormously increased production in all branches of our national economy, by strenuous efforts produced substitutes for numerous materials which we lack, smoothed the way for new inventions, developed traffic, caused mighty roads to be built and canals to be dug, called into being gigantic new factories and at the same time endeavoured to further the education and culture of our people.
>
> I have succeeded in finding useful work once more for the whole of 7,000,000 unemployed, who so appeal to the hearts of us all, in keeping the German peasant on his soil in spite of all difficulties, and in saving the land itself for him, in once more bringing German trade to a peak and in assisting traffic to the utmost.
>
> As precaution against the threats of another world war, not only have I united the German people politically, but I have also re-armed them; I have also endeavoured to destroy sheet by sheet that Treaty which in its 448 articles contains the vilest oppression which peoples and human beings have ever been expected to put up with.
>
> I have brought back to the Reich provinces stolen from us in 1919; I have led back to their native country millions of Germans who were torn away from us and were in misery; I have re-established the historic unity of German living space and, Mr. Roosevelt, I have endeavoured to attain all this without spilling blood and without bringing to my people, and consequently to others, the misery of war.
>
> I, who twenty-one years ago was an unknown worker and soldier of my people, have attained this, Mr. Roosevelt, by my own energy, and can, therefore, in the face of history, claim a place among those men who have done the utmost which can be fairly and justly demanded from a single individual.

In contrast, Hitler pointed out how Roosevelt's obstacles when he first entered into office (also in 1933) were much easier to surmount than his own, due to America's vast size, affluence, and abundant natural resources:

> You, Mr. Roosevelt, have a much easier task in comparison. You became President of the United States in 1933 when I became Chancellor of the Reich. In other words, from the very outset you stepped to the head of one of the largest and wealthiest States in the world.
>
> You have the good fortune to have to feed scarcely fifteen people per square kilometre in your country. You have at your disposal the most unlimited mineral resources in the world. As a result of the large area covered by your country and the fertility of your fields, you are enabled to insure for each individual American ten times the amount of

> commodities possible in Germany. Nature has in any case enabled you to do this.
>
> In spite of the fact that the population of your country is scarcely one-third greater than the number of inhabitants in Greater Germany, you possess more than fifteen times as much living space. Conditions prevailing in your country are on such a large scale that you can find time and leisure to give your attention to universal problems. Consequently, the world is undoubtedly so small for you that you perhaps believe that your intervention and action can be effective anywhere.
>
> In this sense, therefore, your concerns and suggestions cover a much larger and wider area than mine, because my world, Mr. Roosevelt, in which Providence has placed me and for which I am therefore obliged to work, is unfortunately much smaller, although for me it is more precious than anything else, for it is limited to my people!
>
> I believe, however, that this is the way in which I can be of the most service to that for which we are all concerned, namely, the justice, well-being, progress and peace of the whole human community.[37]

A few days later there was an unexpected development in the Soviet arena. Moscow revealed in an official bulletin on 3 May that 'M. Litvinov had been released from the office of Foreign Commissar at his request and that his duties would be assumed by the Premier, M. Molotov'.[38] Having held the top diplomatic post of the Soviet régime since 1930, Maxim Litvinov had been a strong proponent of collective security. He had long striven to establish an anti-Fascist front together with the Western Powers, and so his termination seemingly suggested that the Soviet Government might now be prepared to entertain the possibility of an alliance with Germany.

It was later revealed in a communication from Warsaw that Litvinov had stepped down from his post following a stormy disagreement with Kliment Voroshilov, a Soviet Marshal and the U.S.S.R.'s Defence Commissar. The latter had asserted that the Red Army would not come to Poland's defence in the event of hostilities, and on behalf of the Russian General Staff denounced 'excessively far-reaching military obligations'.[39] Furthermore, the Nazi leadership had been averse to dealing with the Soviet Government on account of Litvinov's Jewish ethnicity. With his removal and replacement by Molotov, a non-Jew, this serious handicap (as the Nazis perceived it) was no longer a barrier to the opening of negotiations. The following day, 4 May, the German Chargé d'Affaires noted that Litvinov's abrupt termination 'appears to be the result of a spontaneous decision by Stalin'. A Soviet broadcast declared that Molotov would continue his predecessor's policy of collective security with the West. Thus Molotov, 'the most intimate friend and closest collaborator of Stalin', took over as Commissar for Foreign Affairs. This appointment would ensure that Soviet foreign policy would continue 'strictly in accordance with Stalin's ideas'.[40]

After the debacle of Munich, the Soviets regarded the British and French with disdain. They were certain that the Western democracies would not lift a finger to defend themselves until war was brought to their doorstep, and believed even then that their contribution would be of limited value. Thus, the Soviet leadership deemed it necessary to take matters into their own hands. They could no longer rely on the weak-willed British and French to stand firm, and perhaps now was the time to partner up with a stronger, more resilient Power. Molotov, for one, had for some time been receptive to potential dealings with the Hitlerite régime. Henceforth the Reich Government discontinued their venomous anti-Soviet propaganda, and instead directed their invective against the 'decadent and corrupt' Western democracies headed by smug plutocrats.

After the war, Churchill gave an incisive description of the new Soviet Foreign Minister:

> Vyacheslav Molotov was a man of outstanding ability and cold-blooded ruthlessness. He had survived the fearful hazards and ordeals to which all the Bolshevik leaders had been subjected in the years of triumphant revolution. He had lived and thrived in a society where ever-varying intrigue was accompanied by the constant menace of personal liquidation. His cannonball head, black moustache, and comprehending eyes, his slab face, his verbal adroitness and imperturbable demeanour, were appropriate manifestations of his qualities and skill. He was above all men fitted to be the agent and instrument of the policy of an incalculable machine.... I have never seen a human being who more perfectly represented the modern conception of a robot.[41]

In a speech before the Polish Parliament on 5 May, Beck rejected the Reich's claims on Danzig. He underscored the fact that unlike the British and French, the Polish Government did not follow a policy of appeasement and would not succumb to Hitler's bullying tactics. The Poles were of a stronger mettle. He ended his speech with these noble words:

> Peace is a valuable and desirable thing. Our generation, which has shed its blood in several wars, surely deserves a period of peace. But peace, like almost anything else in this world, has its price, high but definable. We in Poland [unlike the Anglo–French democracies] do not recognize the conception of 'peace at any price'. There is only one thing in the life of men, nations and States which is without price, and that is honour.[42]

Ribbentrop travelled to Milan for a meeting with Ciano on 6 May. There, Ciano spoke frankly. He advised Ribbentrop that Fascist Italy was not prepared for a European war and that it would be three years before she would be. Ribbentrop acknowledged Ciano's open admission and, lying shamelessly, assured him that the Führer was not presently contemplating launching a war. Nevertheless, on 22 May—'in the XVII year of the Fascist Era'—Germany and Italy concluded in Berlin a pact of military assistance. This was despite the fact that Mussolini had grave doubts about Italy being drawn into a major European conflict for which she was ill-prepared. The pact's full name was the 'Pact of Friendship and Alliance between Germany and Italy', also known as the *Stahlpakt* (Pact of Steel; see Appendix K). Its original title was the 'Pact of Blood', but this was rejected, for Mussolini felt that such a sinister appellation was too ominous for the Italian masses. The signatories were Foreign Ministers Ribbentrop and Ciano. The latter believed, correctly, that a general war would be the ruin of Italy. But Mussolini entered into the deal for reasons of prestige. He thought that an official military partnership with the redoubtable Germany, which had by then become a powerhouse, would increase Italy's standing throughout Europe. The preamble boldly stated:

> Firmly bound together through the inner unity of their ideologies and the comprehensive solidarity of their interests, the German and the Italian people are determined also in future to stand side by side and to strive with united effort for the securing of their *Lebensraum* and the maintenance of peace.
>
> In this way, prescribed for them by history, Germany and Italy wish, in a world of unrest and disintegration, to carry out the assignment of making safe the foundations of European culture.

The pact's third article provided that in the event one of the Axis partners became 'involved in military complications' with a hostile third party, the other would 'immediately step to its side as an ally and will support it with all its military might on land, at sea, and in the air'. Also, in the pact's fourth article, Germany and Italy pledged to 'further intensify their co-operation in the military sphere and in the sphere of war economy'. Lastly, the pact was to take effect 'immediately upon its signing' and its 'period of validity' was fixed 'at ten years'.[43]

Eight days later Mussolini set down in writing his 'thoughts about the present [political] condition and its probably future developments'. According to Mussolini, 'war between the plutocratic and therefore selfishly conservative nations [Britain and France] and the densely populated and poor nations [Germany and Italy] is inevitable'. And due to 'the strategic positions attained in Bohemia [by Germany] and Albania [by Italy], the Axis Powers have in their hands a basic factor for success'. However, as Mussolini had pointed out in a memorandum to Ribbentrop, Italy required 'a preparatory period which may extend to the end of 1942'. He added: 'The two European Axis Powers need a peace time of at least three years. Only after 1943', Mussolini noted, 'can a war have the greatest prospects of success,' and he gave many reasons for this:

a. For the military organization of Libya and Albania; also for the pacification of Ethiopia; from which latter region an army of half a million must be created.

b. To complete the building and rebuilding of six capital ships already started.

c. To rejuvenate completely our medium and larger calibre artillery.

d. For further development of our autarkic plans by which any attempt at blockade by the satiated democracies must be foiled.

e. To carry out the world exposition in 1942 by which not only the activity of the Fascist régime for 20 years will be documented, but also reserves of foreign exchange can be obtained.

f. To complete the return of Italians from France, which poses a very serious military and *moral* question.

g. To complete the shifting of many war industries from the Po Plains to Southern Italy, which has already been started.

h. To deepen further the relationships not only of the governments of the Axis Powers but also of the two nations. For this purpose a relaxation of the tension in the relationships between the Catholic churches and National Socialism would undoubtedly be useful, as is also very much desired by the Vatican.

Mussolini also recognized the necessity for the Axis Powers to make themselves autarkic before embarking on a war of conquest, because he 'expected that the triangle London–Paris–Moscow will try everything during peace times to harm the Axis Powers especially in economic and moral spheres'. As for the war in Western Europe, for Italy it 'would take the character of a predominantly air and sea war'. Fortunately, the recent occupation of Albania had rendered the situation at sea far more manageable, since the Adriatic Sea, which separated the Italian Peninsula from the Balkan Peninsula, 'has become a continental lake which can be closed hermetically'. Mussolini envisaged that the war could 'become dynamic only against the East and the Southeast'. As for 'Poland and other guaranteed states', they would have to fend for themselves and would 'probably be paralyzed before they can get any real help, even from neighbouring Russia'. The democratic Powers, Mussolini believed, were readying themselves for 'a war of exhaustion'. Therefore, it had to be assumed that the Axis Powers would 'get nothing more from the rest of the world'. In Mussolini's estimation, Italy's military priorities were to 'take the whole Danube and Balkan area immediately after the first hours of the war. One cannot be satisfied with declarations of neutrality but must occupy the territories and use them for procurement of necessary food and industrial war supplies. By this lightning-like operation which is to be carried out decisively, not only the "guaranteed states", like Greece, Romania, and Turkey, would be out of the fight, but one would also protect one's back. In this game we count—like in a chess game—on two favourable "pawns": Hungary and Bulgaria.' And finally, Mussolini noted that Italy's contribution to 'the [Axis] war plan' would consist of 'more people than means' whereas Germany would provide 'more means than people'.[44]

It is noteworthy that Mussolini's cynical and ruthless notions—the pre-emptive invasion of non-belligerent countries to seize their foodstuffs and to take advantage of their armaments potential; the talk of a 'lightning-like' operation in order to secure the Axis from behind; and the use of medium-sized, pro-Axis nations as expendable tools, or 'pawns'—all mirrored Hitler's own way of thinking. With the exception of the timetable (i.e. 1939 vs. 1943) the Führer and the Duce were on the same page.

Just several months earlier, on 4 February 1939, Mussolini had summarized Italy's foreign policy to the Fascist Grand Council in a report. He explained:

> … states are more or less independent according to their maritime position. In other words, states that possess coasts on the oceans or have free access to the oceans are independent. States that cannot communicate freely with the oceans and are enclosed in inland seas are semi-independent. States that are absolutely continental and have outlets neither on the oceans nor on inland seas are not independent. Italy belongs to the second category of states. It is bathed by a landlocked sea that communicates with the oceans through the Suez Canal, an artificial link easily blocked even by improvised methods, and through the straits of Gibraltar, dominated by the cannons of Great Britain.

> Italy therefore does not have free connection with the oceans. Italy is therefore in truth a prisoner of the Mediterranean, and the more populous and prosperous Italy becomes, the more its imprisonment will gall.
>
> The bars of this prison are Corsica, Tunisia, Malta, Cyprus. The sentinels of this prison are Gibraltar and Suez. Corsica is a pistol pointed at the heart of Italy; Tunisia at Sicily; while Malta and Cyprus constitute a threat to all our positions in the eastern and western Mediterranean. Greece, Turkey and Egypt have been ready to form a chain with Great Britain and complete the politico-military encirclement of Italy. [Therefore] Greece, Turkey and Egypt must be considered virtual enemies of Italy and of its expansion. From this situation, whose geographical rigour leaps to one's eyes and which tormented, even before our régime, those men who saw beyond considerations of momentary political expediency, one can draw the following conclusions:
>
> 1. The task of Italian policy, which cannot have and does not have continental objectives of a European territorial nature except Albania, is to first of all break the bars of the prison.
>
> 2. Once the bars are broken, Italian policy can have only one watchword—to march to the ocean.
>
> Which ocean? The Indian Ocean, joining Libya with Ethiopia through the Sudan or the Atlantic, through French North Africa.
>
> In either case, we will find ourselves confronted with Anglo–French opposition....[45]

The day after the Pact of Steel was signed, top brass assembled at the Reich Chancellery to hear Hitler elaborate on his secret plans to crush Poland. Among the fourteen principals in attendance were Göring, Keitel, and Grand Admiral Raeder. Minutes of the meeting were taken by Lieutenant-Colonel Schmundt. Hitler explained:

> The Pole is not a fresh enemy. Poland will always be on the side of our adversaries. In spite of treaties of friendship Poland has always been bent on exploiting every opportunity against us.
>
> It is not Danzig that is at stake. For us it is a matter of expanding our living space in the East and ... also solving the problem of the Baltic States....
>
> The problem 'Poland' cannot be dissociated from the showdown with the West. Poland's internal solidarity against Bolshevism is doubtful. Therefore Poland is also a doubtful barrier against Russia.

> Success in war in the West with a rapid decision is questionable and so is Poland's attitude.
>
> The Polish régime will not stand up to Russian pressure. Poland sees danger in a German victory over the West and will try to deprive us of victory.
>
> There is therefore no question of sparing Poland and we are left with the decision:
>
> *To attack Poland at the first suitable opportunity.*
>
> We cannot expect a repetition of Czechia. There will be war. Our task is to isolate Poland. Success in isolating her will be decisive....
>
> It must not come to a simultaneous showdown with the West (France and England).
>
> If it is not definitely certain that a German–Polish conflict will not lead to war with the West then the fight must be primarily against England and France.
>
> *Thesis*: Conflict with Poland—beginning with an attack on Poland—will only be successful if the West keeps out of the ring.
>
> If that is not possible it is better to fall upon the West and finish off Poland at the same time.

Poland's destruction, however, was only a preview to the main event: the battle royale with Britain. For it was Britain, and not Poland, that stood in the way of German supremacy on the Continent. A blockade of the English Isles by U-boats would starve the English population and, at the same time, the Luftwaffe would bombard vital English targets. These air attacks would be launched from bases on conquered French territory. England would be compelled to surrender or sue for peace. France, on the other hand, would be defeated by the German Army. German land forces would circumvent the Maginot Line by avoiding it altogether. They would proceed through the neutral and vulnerable Low Countries, and then swoop upwards in the direction of the English seaports. Any British Army soldiers on French soil would be netted by this manoeuvre. But in spite of his absolute confidence in a final German victory, Hitler could not deny that the British were tenacious foes with tremendous resources, and he openly admitted this:

> *England* is the motive force driving against Germany. Her strength lies in the following:
>
> (1) The Briton himself is proud, brave, tough, dogged and a gifted organizer. He knows how to exploit every new development. He has the love of adventure and the courage of the Nordic race....

> (2) England is a World Power in herself. Constant for three hundred years. Increased by alliances. This power is to be regarded as embracing the whole world not only physically but also psychologically.
> Add to this immeasurable wealth and the solvency that goes with it.
>
> (3) Geopolitical security and protection by a strong sea power and valiant air force.

Britain was formidable, but not invulnerable. Hitler noted that Luftwaffe attacks alone on England would not be sufficient to defeat her; the decisive factor would be the elimination of the Royal Navy from the equation:

> Luftwaffe attacks on England herself will not force her to capitulate … But if the Fleet is annihilated instant capitulation results.

It was Hitler's intention to inflict upon Britain a mortal wound that would cripple the Royal Navy and knock the Royal Air Force from the skies, all at one stroke:

> (1) *The aim* must be to deal the enemy at the start a smashing blow or *the* smashing blow. Here right or wrong, or treaties, play no part.
> This is only possible if we do not 'slide' into a war with England on account of Poland.
>
> (2) *Preparations* must be made for a *long war as well as* for a surprise *attack* and every possible intervention by England on the Continent must be smashed.

How was this to be achieved? Hitler divulged his strategy:

> The Army must occupy the positions important for the Fleet and the Luftwaffe. If we succeed in occupying and securing Holland and Belgium, as well as beating France, the basis for a successful war against England has been created.
> The Luftwaffe can then closely blockade England from western France and the Fleet undertake the wider blockade with submarines.

The ultimate goal was 'to force England to her knees'. Hitler wrapped up his discourse with a final enjoinder to his audience—the need for secrecy, even from his partners:

> *Secrecy* is the decisive prerequisite for success. Our objects must be kept secret from both Italy and Japan.[46]

Hitler was committed to war. He had no reservations. Poland would be annihilated, and Germany would snatch territory in Eastern Europe to solve the issue of *Lebensraum*. Any interference in his plans by the Anglo–French democracies and he would be forced to eliminate each of them in turn. Of the two, England was the primary opponent; France was an ancillary threat. In the long run, it was imperative that the Greater German Reich dominate the Continent, once and for all. But for the moment, the goal was to limit the conflict to Poland. Throughout the summer, the German Army prepared itself for war. A deadline of 20 August was set. Hitler foresaw two possibilities: the democratic Powers would either renege on their obligations to Poland and leave her to Germany to deal with as the latter saw fit; or they would take action on Poland's behalf in the event of German aggression, but it would just be a lukewarm, token gesture which they would abandon once Poland was no more. And practically speaking, only if the Western Powers were in league with the Soviets would they be able to aid Poland adequately and immediately in the event of German aggression. Only the U.S.S.R., which shared a frontier with Poland, was in a position to *directly* intervene at once. Thus, if the German Government could ensure that the Soviet Union would remain inactive during a German–Polish war, the value of the Anglo–French pledges of military assistance to Poland would be greatly diminished, if not negated altogether.

In an effort to induce the Poles to give in to German demands, the Reich Government continued its campaign of undue influence. Nazi Danzigers agitated, brought in weapons, constructed barricades, and readied themselves for an imminent conflict. All the while, Goebbels' propaganda machine trumpeted for international consumption that it would be folly to go to war over Danzig. Also, the Reich Government cultivated friendly diplomatic relations with other pro-Axis nations in Central Europe and the Balkans—Hungary, Bulgaria, and Yugoslavia—to deter them from allying themselves with Poland. On 7 June, Germany concluded non-aggression pacts with Estonia, Latvia, and Lithuania in Berlin. Each pact was fixed to last for a decade. Their collective purpose was to block the Soviets from penetrating into the Baltic region and encircling the Reich thereby. Such an arrangement would leave the Germans free to conduct their intended campaign against the Poles without unwanted interference.

Meanwhile, German operational plans were being formed. A top secret enclosure outlining the objectives of *Fall Weiss* (Case White) was prepared by Blaskowitz, Commander-in-Chief of Army Group 3. Dated 14 June, it read:

Aims of Operation *Fall Weiss*

> 1. *a.* The operation, in order to forestall an orderly Polish mobilization and concentration, is to be opened by surprise with forces which are for the most part armoured and motorized, placed on alert in the neighbourhood of the border. The initial superiority over the Polish frontier-guards and surprise that can be expected with certainty are to be maintained by quickly bringing up other parts of the [German] Army as well to counteract the marching up of the Polish Army.
>
> *Accordingly all units have to keep the initiative against the foe by quick acting and ruthless attacks.*
>
> *b.* If the development of the political situation should show that a surprise at the beginning of the war is out of question, because of well advanced defence preparations on the part of the Polish Army, the Commander-in-Chief of the [German] Army will order the opening of the hostilities only after the assembling of sufficient additional forces. The basis of all preparations will be to surprise the enemy.
>
> Case b—is to be prepared in theory by the High Command only so that necessary changes can be quickly carried out.[47]

In a patriotic speech before 100,000 Poles at the Polish port city of Gdynia on 29 June, Polish President Ignacy Mościcki touched on the vital importance of Danzig, Gdynia, and the Corridor for Poland's national existence and prosperity, for these three entities provided essential access to the Baltic Sea:

> Danzig has been connected with Poland for centuries. It is the desire of Poland to remain connected with Danzig for all time to come. My government desires that there shall be co-operation between Danzig and Gdynia in the interests of peaceful trade. Through these two ports three-quarters of Poland's export trade is handled.

Mościcki movingly described the 'inseparable union' between Poland and her 'maritime province of Pomorze':

> Every inch of Polish soil is equally dear to us. Of the territory which goes to make up this entity, Pomorze and the seacoast are basic elements. Upon them our political and economic independence depends. They are valued above price, above the air and above the sun, to our existence as a state.

Mościcki proclaimed that the Polish Corridor would 'be defended at all costs'. His words were interpreted 'as a direct challenge' to Hitler that any German aggression against the Corridor would trigger a war:

> Consciousness of this value exists in the hearts and minds of every Pole. The greater adversities encountered and the more inimical become external circumstances [i.e. Nazi coercion], the firmer is our determination and readiness to make even the greatest sacrifices so that Poland's outlet to the sea can be made to endure for all time.[48]

What were Chamberlain's views on the Danzig crisis? On 10 July, Chamberlain shared his thoughts on Danzig with the House of Commons:

> Racially Danzig is, almost wholly, a German city; but the prosperity of its inhabitants depends to a very large extent upon Polish trade. The Vistula is Poland's only waterway to the Baltic, and the port at its mouth is therefore of vital strategic and economic importance to her. Another Power established in Danzig could, if it so desired, block Poland's access to the sea and so exert an economic and military stranglehold upon her. Those who were responsible for framing the present statute of the Free City were fully conscious of these facts, and did their best to make provision accordingly. Moreover, there is no question of any oppression of the German population in Danzig. On the contrary, the administration of the Free City is in German hands, and the only restrictions imposed upon it are not of a kind to curtail the liberties of its citizens. The present settlement, though it may be capable of improvement, cannot in itself be regarded as basically unjust or illogical. The maintenance of the *status quo* had in fact been guaranteed by the German Chancellor himself up to 1944 by the ten-year Treaty which he had concluded with Marshal Piłsudski.[49]

Both Britain and Germany began to vie for an alliance with the U.S.S.R. In April, the British had first tentatively contacted the Soviets; negotiations commenced in mid-June. The British Government had, somewhat belatedly, devised a strategy aimed at curbing German aggression by way of collective security—this time with the Russians. Meanwhile, the Reich Government also endeavoured to broker a deal with Russia, their most loathed foe. This was an attempt by the Germans to ensure that the forthcoming war against the Poles would remain localized. The irony, of course, was that Nazi Germany and Soviet Russia were ideological opposites, and that Hitler eventually intended to launch a war of extermination against the very nation with which he now sought a partnership.

Naturally, the Soviet Government was extremely distrustful of all 'imperialist' nations that cringed to the almighty dollar, whether ruled by democrats, plutocrats, or Fascist demagogues. The dismal track record to date of the British and French in stemming the tide of German expansionism—the Munich fiasco was a case in point—led the Soviet leadership to regard the democratic Powers as all but useless. From the Soviets' perspective, therefore, to align themselves with the British and French was a dubious prospect. The Soviets wished, ideally, for Nazi Germany and the democratic Powers to become enmeshed in a destructive conflict that would remove them both from the equation, thereby leaving the spoils to them. This was not unlike the cynical outlook of certain Anglo–French politicians who welcomed the prospect of a Nazi–Soviet clash, one which would knock out both totalitarian States as threats to democracy in one fell swoop. However, to oppose the powerful German Reich singlehandedly would be devastating. To best confront, contain, and eradicate Hitlerism, a coalition of the Major European Powers—namely, Britain, France, and the U.S.S.R.—was necessary. Unfortunately, the Western Allies and the Soviets in particular would suffer tremendous losses throughout the Second World War on account of their failure to ally themselves against the Nazi menace in time.

Anglo–French–Soviet negotiations in Moscow progressed slowly and did not bear much fruit. Nevertheless, not a few anticipated that a worthwhile agreement would eventually be reached. The British Press even went so far as to report that Britain and Russia had come to terms and that a pact was sure to follow. Such a claim was not only premature but inaccurate.

Although Hitler had inveighed unremittingly against the evils of Communism for the past two decades, there were certain German traditionalist elements who were not averse to a German–Russian alliance. From 1922 to 1933 there had been a period of collaboration between the German Reichswehr and the Soviet Red Army. Germans troops had received flight training in Russia. In exchange, the Soviets had requested and were given technical instruction. For Germany, a non-aggression pact with the U.S.S.R. had the potential to yield great dividends. In the upcoming Polish campaign, the Reich could proceed untrammelled in the East against the hated Polish 'bastard of Versailles'. Over the summer, economic negotiations were initiated. These culminated in the German–Soviet Credit Agreement of 19 August and paved the way to the Nazi–Soviet Pact of 23 August.

At the start of July, the intensifying German–Polish tensions over Danzig prompted the French Government to let the German Government know exactly where it stood. On 1 July, French Foreign Minister Bonnet communicated a grave warning to Johannes von Welczeck, the German Ambassador to France:

> I … regard it as my duty to state definitely that any action, whatever its form, which would tend to modify the *status quo* in Danzig, and so provoke armed resistance by Poland, would bring the Franco–Polish Agreement into play and oblige France to give immediate assistance to Poland.[50]

On 13 July, Ribbentrop replied to Bonnet's note of 1 July:

> On 1 July you handed to Count von Welczeck a note personally intended for me, which obliges me now to make known to you, clearly and in a manner free from any misunderstanding, the attitude of the German Government with regard to Franco–German relations in general, and the question of Danzig in particular.
>
> On 6 December 1938 … I expressly pointed out that Eastern Europe constituted a sphere of German interests, and, contrary to what is stated in your note, you then stressed on your part, that, in France's attitude with regard to the problems of Eastern Europe, a radical change had taken place since the Munich Conference.

Ribbentrop had three crucial points to make: the first concerned unwanted French interference in Germany's Eastern European interests; the second concerned the Reich's unwillingness to tolerate Polish provocations or any Polish encroachment on Danzig; and the third concerned the French policy of backing Poland militarily in the event of a German–Polish conflict:

> (1) Germany, just as it has never interfered in France's vital interests, must reject, once for all and categorically, any interference by France in its spheres of vital interest. Germany's relations with its Eastern neighbours, whatever form they assume, in no way affect French interests; they are a matter which only concerns German policy. Accordingly the Government of the Reich does not find itself in a position to discuss with the French Government questions concerning German–Polish relations, or to recognize its right to exercise any influence upon questions dealing with the future settlement of the destiny of the German city of Danzig.
>
> (2) … The Polish Government has replied to the Führer's historic and unique offer, aiming at the settlement of the question of Danzig and at a definitive consolidation of German–Polish relations, by threats of war which can only be described as strange. At the present moment

> it is impossible to say whether the Polish Government will depart from this peculiar position and return to reason. But, as long as it maintains the unreasonable attitude which it has taken up one can only say that any violation of Danzig soil by Poland, or any Polish provocation incompatible with the prestige of the German Reich, would meet in reply with an immediate march by the Germans and the total destruction of the Polish Army.
>
> (3) The statement ... contained in the final sentence of your note [of 1 July], would, if taken literally, mean that France recognizes Poland's right to oppose by arms any departure in any respect from the *status quo* in Danzig, and that, if Germany declines to tolerate that violence should thus be done to German interests, France will attack Germany. If such was in fact the purpose of French policy, I would beg you to consider that such threats could only further strengthen the Führer in his resolve to ensure the safeguarding of German interests by all the means at his disposal. The Führer has always desired Franco–German understanding and described as madness a fresh war between the two countries, which are no longer separated by any conflict of vital interests.

Ribbentrop cautioned Bonnet that the Reich would be prepared if France attacked, and that she would be held responsible for it by both her own countrymen and the nations of the world:

> But, if we have reached a point where the French Government wants war, it will find Germany ready at any moment. It would then be the French Government alone which would have to bear before its people and before the world the responsibility for such a war.[51]

Eight days later, Bonnet wrote a personal letter to Ribbentrop in response to his message of 13 July. He clarified that what transpired in Eastern Europe was important to the French Government, both prior to the German–French Declaration and thereafter. He asserted that the downturn in German–Polish relations in March was no fault of France, and that France would continue to avoid interfering in the relations of her neighbours, provided that neither 'the general international situation' nor peace itself was menaced:

> There is one point which I am anxious to make absolutely clear. At no moment either before or after the declaration of 6 December, has it been possible for the German Government to think that France had decided to disinterest herself in the East of Europe....

> In the month of March relations between Germany and Poland became strained, and that fact brought about a new situation.
>
> France bears no responsibility for the development of these relations between Berlin and Warsaw. She has in fact always refrained—and will continue to refrain—from any interference in matters bearing upon the special relationships of the two neighbouring countries, and not affecting in any way the general international situation and the maintenance of peace.

Finally, Bonnet reiterated his desire for cordial Franco–German relations, but he upheld the stance he had taken in his note of 1 July, and he rejected the German view that France would bear the responsibility for a Franco–German war should France be compelled to fulfill her treaty obligations to Poland:

> I desire, as you do, the continued maintenance of friendly relations between France and Germany. It is for that reason that, in my communication of 1 July, whose validity is maintained with all its implications, I made a point of reminding you ... of the position of the French Government in respect of Poland, particularly in relation to the situation at Danzig.
>
> France is eagerly desirous of peace. No one can doubt that fact. Moreover, no one can doubt the determination of the French Government to fulfill its obligations. But I cannot permit it to be said that our country would be in any way responsible for war because it remained true to its pledged word.[52]

That summer, an unexpected letter dated 23 July from no less a personage than the venerable Mohandas Karamchand Gandhi, the East Indian activist, was sent to Hitler. Gandhi's lifelong aim (which was achieved in 1947) was to secure Indian independence from British colonial rule through a policy of non-violent resistance. Like his Western counterparts, Gandhi also wished to make his own personal appeal to Hitler in the name of peace:

> Friends have been urging me to write to you for the sake of humanity. But I have resisted their request, because of the feeling that any letter from me would be an impertinence. Something tells me that I must make my appeal for whatever it may be worth. It is quite clear that you are today the one person in the world who can prevent a war which may reduce humanity to the savage state. Must you pay that price for an object however worthy it may appear to you to be? Will you listen to the appeal of one who has deliberately shunned the method of war not

> without considerable success? Anyway I anticipate your forgiveness, if I have erred in writing to you.[53]

The letter never reached Hitler, for the British authorities in India intercepted it *en route*. Nevertheless, such a letter would naturally have been in vain, despite Gandhi's obvious sincerity. A feeble supplication from an Asiatic pacifist would inevitably have been discounted by Hitler. The Führer would have felt deep disdain for the mild, even timidly-phrased message, for he was impressed by force and brutality, not weakness.

On 24 July, Hungarian Prime Minister Pál Teleki sent Hitler two letters. The first was ambiguous and verbose. It stated that 'in the event of a general conflict Hungary will make her policy conform to the policy of the Axis; this we have also previously proved to be our endeavour. Nor can there be any doubt that alignment with this policy can in no way prejudice our national sovereignty, embodied in our constitution, or set obstacles to the accomplishment of our national aspirations.' What Teleki meant by all this was that in the event of a German–Polish war, Hungary—while 'guided by a profound confidence in the moral and material strength of the Berlin–Rome Axis'—would *not* join in at Germany's side.[54] In his second letter, Teleki clarified what he had meant to convey. He wrote: 'In order to prevent any possible misinterpretation of my letter of 24 July, I have the honour to repeat also to Your Excellency that ... Hungary could not, on moral grounds, be in a position to take armed action against Poland.'[55] Duplicates of both letters were also sent to Mussolini. These notifications greatly displeased the German Government, and in a 100-minute meeting in Berlin on 8 August, Hungarian Foreign Affairs Minister István Csáky advised Hitler that the German Government could regard the two letters of 24 July, which had been so ill-received, 'as not having been written'.[56]

Also on 24 July, Ribbentrop and Ambassador Attolico gathered at Fuschl, Austria. Attolico informed Ribbentrop of Mussolini's attitude concerning a possible outbreak of war, the gist of which was summed up in a 'personal memorandum'. It consisted of three essential points:

1. If the Führer had decided to go to war, Mussolini would also be prepared to do so at any time.

2. If ... the present moment was not the most favourable for a war, then ... something would have to be done to prevent war breaking out not on the initiative of the Axis....

3. ... it was essential that the initiative for the maintenance of peace should rest with the Führer and the Duce.

In connection with the third point, Mussolini also suggested a special summit conference on the Brenner to take place on 4 August. The purpose of the conference would be to 'disrupt the unity of the [Anglo–French] front opposing us, both between the States and the different peoples'. Mussolini felt that 'a meeting between him and the Führer on the German–Italian frontier would cause such a sensation that it would be impossible for such a conference not to produce positive results'. Other nations, too, could participate. However, these would be strictly limited to specific European Powers—Britain, France, Germany, Italy, Poland, and Spain. Intercontinental and non-European Powers—the U.S.S.R., Japan, and America respectively—would be excluded. But Ribbentrop disagreed with the idea for a conference. In his opinion, 'any peace initiative by the Axis would be interpreted as a sign of weakness'. Nevertheless, Ribbentrop promised to communicate Mussolini's proposal for a conference to Hitler, who would make the final decision.[57]

On 3 August, at Ribbentrop's insistence, Friedrich-Werner von der Schulenburg, the German Ambassador to the U.S.S.R., conferred with Molotov regarding a possible political arrangement. The meeting took place in the evening and lasted seventy-five minutes. To his satisfaction, Schulenburg observed that 'Molotov abandoned his habitual reserve and appeared unusually open'. Schulenburg 'explained how ... we [the German Government] contemplated the normalization and improvement of our relations with the Soviet Union'. He reiterated to Molotov the German Government's proposals 'to safeguard all Soviet interests' in Eastern Poland and the Baltic region, to which Molotov appeared somewhat receptive:

> I thereupon again stressed the fact that there were no differences between us in foreign policy and mentioned German readiness to adopt such an attitude in the Baltic States, if occasion arose, as would guard vital Soviet interests in the Baltic Sea....
>
> On the Polish question I stated that we upheld our well-known demands on Poland [for Danzig and the Polish Corridor] but strove for a peaceful situation. If, on the other hand, a different solution [i.e. war] were forced on us, we were prepared to protect all Soviet interests [in Poland] and come to an understanding with the Soviet Government on this matter.

Although Molotov 'showed evident interest' in the German proposals, he nonetheless maintained an equivocal attitude. Schulenburg was of the opinion that although 'the Soviet Government are ... increasingly prepared for improvement in German–Soviet relations ... the old mistrust of Germany persists.' Schulenburg also felt that the Soviet Government was 'at present determined to conclude an agreement with Britain and France, if they fulfill all Soviet wishes'. However, Schulenburg noted, the Soviet Government's 'mistrust of Britain is also great'.[58]

Molotov was understandably wary of German intentions. Still, he was cognizant of two facts: for the Germans, speed was of the essence; and more importantly, here was a golden opportunity for the Soviet Government to conclude a very profitable agreement. And so the Soviet Government continued their double-dealing. Such duplicity, however, could not go on indefinitely. Eventually, the Soviets would have to pick a side, for better or for worse—the Western Powers or Nazi Germany.

In early August, a customs dispute arose in Danzig. Intending to crack down on the smuggling of weapons into the Free City from East Prussia, the Poles heightened border security with extra customs personnel. In turn, the Danzig Customs Office presented the Polish Customs Inspectors with notice that as of seven o'clock on the morning of 6 August, they would refuse to submit to the latter's lawful authority. Consequently, Foreign Minister Beck sharply cautioned the Senate that it could not defy the binding provisions of the Versailles Treaty and pointed out that the Reich Government (which was obviously pulling the strings) did not call the shots on Danzig's behalf. On 4 August, matters came to a head. The Polish Government issued an ultimatum to the Danzig Senate, which was received the next day by Senate President Greiser. The document was signed by the Polish General Commissioner in Danzig, Marian Chodacki:

> I have learned that the local Danzig Customs Authorities at the frontier posts between the Free City of Danzig and East Prussia have approached the Polish Customs Inspectors with a statement ... that the Danzig administrative authorities intend, from 7 a.m. on 6 August, to resist a certain section of the Polish Inspectors in the performance of their control functions, which functions arise out of the rights of the Polish Government on the Customs frontier....
>
> I do not doubt that you, Mr. President of the Senate, have no doubts that such an infringement of the fundamental rights of Poland would under no pretext be tolerated by the Polish Government.
>
> I await your answer assuring me that you have issued orders which cancel the action of your subordinates, at the latest by 6 p.m. on 5 August.
>
> In view of the fact that the above-mentioned action has taken place at a number of frontier posts, I am compelled to warn you, Mr. President of the Senate, that all Polish Customs Inspectors have received the order to carry out their duties in uniform and with arms on 6 August 1939 and the following days at all points on the frontier which they

regard as necessary for the control. All attempts to hamper them in the performance of their duties, all attacks or intervention by the [Danzig] police authorities will be regarded as acts of violence against officials of the Polish State during the performance of their duties.

Should the above-mentioned abuses take place the Polish Government will retaliate without delay against the Free City, and the responsibility for this will fall exclusively on the Senate of the Free City.

I hope to receive a satisfactory explanation by the time stated.

CHODACKI
Diplomatic Representative of the Polish Republic[59]

On 6 August, Polish Marshal Edward Śmigły-Rydz attended the anniversary celebration of the Piłsudski Legions' entry into the Great War twenty-five years earlier. Before an enormous crowd of some 150,000 people, Śmigły-Rydz declared that 'violence inflicted by force must be resisted by force'. He alluded to Britain and France when he remarked that it was, for him, a 'pleasant duty to record with the deep understanding and appreciation of a soldier that Poland has sincere friends among other nations, nations who understand the real meaning of things and who have defined their attitude towards us'. Śmigły-Rydz addressed the gathering of patriotic Poles in explicit terms:

> Danzig has been linked to Poland for centuries. It constitutes the lungs of our economic life.
>
> Poland has defined its position plainly and unequivocally. It is not we who started the Danzig affair. It is not we who have withdrawn from our obligations. Our actions in Danzig will conform with the actions of the other party.

Thereupon the assembled Poles roared enthusiastically, 'Danzig is Polish. Danzig must remain Polish.' When the tumultuous shouts abated, Śmigły-Rydz resumed his speech:

> The fighting principles of Piłsudski are the readiness of every Polish soldier to die for the independence of the fatherland and are inscribed in the blood of the nation.
>
> These principles constitute our sub-soil and we will give up none of them. We appreciate peace as other nations do but there is no force that can convince us that there exists any law which for some mean to take, and for others to give. We have no aggressive intentions against anyone whatever. There can be no doubt of that.

> But we will repel any attempt, direct or indirect, to damage our interests, our rights, or the dignity of our State.[60]

On 7 August, Greiser responded to Chodacki's ultimatum. He denied the allegation that the Danzig Customs Office had intended to obstruct the duties of Polish Customs Inspectors and, as Lipski put it, 'took exception to the attitude adopted in the matter by the Polish Government':

> ... I must express to you my astonishment that you have taken a completely unauthenticated rumour as an occasion to send the Danzig Government a short term ultimatum from the Polish Government ...
>
> According to the inquiries made by me ... it is established ... that no authority, and particularly no office of the State Customs Office of the Free City of Danzig, has issued an order stating that the Danzig administrative authorities must, from 6 August at 7 a.m., resist a certain section of the Polish Customs Inspectors in the performance of their control functions.

Greiser indignantly concluded:

> The Danzig Government protest most strongly against the reprisals which the Polish Government threaten, and which they regard as an unwarrantable threat, the consequences of which will fall only upon the Polish Government.[61]

Also that day, Gauleiter Forster was ordered to Berlin where an enraged Hitler informed him that his patience with the insolent Poles was exhausted.

On 9 August, State Secretary Weizsäcker read aloud the text of an 'oral communication' to the Polish Chargé d'Affaires, Prince Zdzisław Lubomirski. It stated that the Polish Government's hardball tactics, if repeated, might erode German–Polish relations further, and that if this occurred, Poland would be at fault:

> The Reich Government find themselves obliged to point out to the Polish Government that a repetition of such demands in the form of an ultimatum to the Free City of Danzig and threat of reprisals would lead to an aggravation of German–Polish relations, for the consequences of which responsibility would fall exclusively on the Polish Government and for which the Reich Government must now at this stage disclaim all responsibility.[62]

The Polish Government sharply replied the next day that they would continue, as before, to protect 'the rights and interests which Poland enjoys in Danzig' as they saw fit. 'Any interventions by the Reich Government to the detriment of these rights and interests' would be considered 'an act of aggression.'[63] Shortly thereafter, Beck proposed a compromise: Poland would agree to relinquish control of Danzig customs to the Reich. In Berlin, this paltry offer (as it was perceived) was taken as an insult, and on the morning of 19 August, Weizsäcker dispatched a communication to Ribbentrop on behalf of Edmund Veesenmayer, Ribbentrop's Special Representative in Danzig. Received at the Foreign Ministry 10:20 a.m., it read:

> Gauleiter Forster intends to raise his demands ... to cover about fifty Polish Customs officials and their immediate withdrawal. If the Poles again give way, then it is proposed to increase the demands still further, so as to make agreement impossible.

The brief token reply—drafted by Weizsäcker for Ribbentrop's approval and intended for Veesenmayer—stated:

> I agree with your views on the conduct of negotiations on the Customs officials controversy. Negotiations must, however, be conducted in such a way, and pressure on Poland in other respects be so applied, that the responsibility for a breakdown of the negotiations and for all consequences falls on Poland.[64]

On 11 August, Carl Burckhardt flew to Salzburg and then motored up to Berchtesgaden for an audience with Hitler. A Swiss, Burckhardt was the League of Nations' High Commissioner for Danzig. He had served in this post since February 1937. The private interview had been arranged for them to talk over 'the Danzig question in its relationship to the general European situation', which was steadily worsening. It commenced at 4 p.m. and lasted two and a half hours. After touching on the recent customs dispute and Chodacki's ultimatum to Greiser a week earlier, Hitler gave Burckhardt a dire warning:

> If the slightest thing was attempted by the Poles, he would fall upon them like lightning with all the powerful arms at his disposal, of which the Poles had not the slightest idea.

Burckhardt responded that that such a course of action 'would lead to a general conflict', to which Hitler countered by saying that 'if he had to make war he would rather to it today than tomorrow, that he would not conduct it like the Germany of William II, who had always had scruples about the full use of every weapon, and that he would fight without mercy up to the extreme limit'. Hitler was also certain that he could count on his Italian and Japanese partners. (He was sorely mistaken, as it would turn out.) Hitler further declared that he could defend the Western front 'with about sixty divisions and the [West Wall] fortifications'. Meanwhile, the remainder of the German Army would be let loose in Poland; in three weeks' time the Poles would be defeated. 'The general tendency', Hitler explained, 'was to try and impress him with the rearmament figures of the foreign air forces.' He continued:

> I am the specialist on rearmament, not the others. Their air forces may be summed up as follows: England has 135,000 men in her air force, France has 75,000, but I have 600,000 in time of peace and a million in time of war. My air-raid protection is the best in the world, as it proved in Spain.

As for the Russians, Hitler claimed that 'the Germans knew them better than others'. He noted that 'hundreds of his officers had served in the Russian armies'. He therefore knew that they 'had no offensive power'. Hitler next discussed the German harvests of the past two years and the Reich's need for 'wheat and timber'. Under no circumstances, Hitler declared, would he permit the Germans 'to be dragged down into want and famine as it had endured between 1914 and 1920'. When Burckhardt commented that Britain and France 'would certainly be ready to settle this problem by negotiation', Hitler inquired: if this was so, why had they 'stirred up the Poles?' On the contrary, Burckhardt said, the democratic Powers were 'exercising a moderating influence on Warsaw'. Hitler told Burckhardt of the reasonable offer he had made to the Poles in March after he had neutralized 'the danger of war constituted by Czechoslovakia on his southeastern flank'. He wanted to settle two other questions; namely, Memel and Danzig, but on each occasion the British and French opposed him. Hitler continued:

> We are not acting as we did in Czechoslovakia. There, an acute danger had to be removed; the solution was a passable one and has proved more satisfactory than was usually believed abroad. Calm reigned in Bohemia and Moravia. In Bohemia, the peasants and workers were content with their lot, as they always were when they were offered simplified solutions. All the difficulties [Hitler claimed] came from the intellectuals.

Hitler complimented Czech war *matériel*, the 'quality of the Czech officials, and their orderly methods'. The Czechs were certainly 'different', i.e. superior to the Poles. Considering how technically substandard the Polish

Army was, the Polish Government's repeated refusals to come to terms filled the German leadership with 'much surprise'. But the Danzig issue had to be settled; this was crucial. 'If the Poles left Danzig alone', Hitler promised, he would desist from 'any interference in the Free City', but only if the ethnic German population 'ceased to be molested in Poland.'[65] Hitler also divulged to Burckhardt his plan to eventually attack Soviet Russia. This was one of the most revelatory comments Hitler had ever made to a neutral foreigner before the outbreak of war:

> Everything I undertake is directed against the Russians; if the West is too stupid and blind to grasp this, then I shall be compelled to come to an agreement with the Russians, beat the West, and then after their defeat turn against the Soviet Union with all my forces.[66]

Burckhardt neglected to report this shocking statement by Hitler at his meeting two days later with British and French diplomats Roger Makins and Pierre Arnal in Basel, Switzerland. By Burckhardt's own admission, the utterance had made such a fantastic impression on him that it seemed, after the fact, like a 'hallucination'.

Also on 11 August, Ribbentrop received Ciano at his Fuschl estate, near Salzburg. The long discussion between the two foreign ministers was marked by coldness, tension, and distrust. Ribbentrop informed Ciano in no uncertain terms that Germany planned to attack Poland in the near future. Ciano recalled:

> While we were waiting to be seated at the dinner table, Ribbentrop informed me of the decision that the storm must break, as he would have talked with me of a minor, administrative measure. 'Well, Ribbentrop', I asked, 'what do you want? The Corridor or Danzig?' 'Not that any more', he said, gazing at me with his cold expressionless eyes, 'we want war!'

But at his post-war trial at Nuremberg, on 1 April 1946, Ribbentrop denied that he had made this statement. He explained to the court:

> I told Count Ciano that Hitler was resolved to settle the Polish problem by any means; Hitler ordered me to tell Ciano this. It is simply preposterous to affirm that I said 'we want war', for one does not say such things even to one's best and most faithful ally—certainly not to Count Ciano.[67]

The news that the Germans were intent on war was most unwelcome to Ciano, but not entirely unexpected, considering the downturn in

German–Polish relations over Danzig and the Corridor. What concerned Ciano were the ramifications of an all-out war, for Italy was contractually bound to render military aid to Germany per the Pact of Steel. Ciano was categorically opposed to Italian participation in a German–Polish conflict because, as he had set down in his diary the previous day (10 August), it would be 'impossible to localize it, and a general war would be disastrous for everybody'. On the 11th he noted, to his dismay, that the militant Germans were dead set on attacking. Ribbentrop was confident that the British would not involve themselves, and he attributed this belief (erroneous, as it turned out) to his so-called 'psychological knowledge' of the English. As far as Ciano was concerned, the Germans were 'possessed by the demon of destruction'.

On 12 August, Ciano travelled with Ribbentrop to the Berghof, where he discussed with Hitler the Germans' aggressive designs *vis-á-vis* Poland. Hitler assured him repeatedly that 'he would localize the conflict with Poland' and that 'the great war must be fought while he and the Duce are still young ...' After their first meeting, Ciano wrote in his diary that 'there is no longer anything that can be done. He [Hitler] has decided to strike, and strike he will.' Ciano had hoped that he would be able to dissuade Hitler from his chosen course, but to no avail. The Führer remained 'implacable in his decision'. Ciano spoke with Hitler again on 13 August. The second conversation was briefer, but to Ciano, more revealing. Nevertheless, after the talks were over, Ciano's revulsion with the Nazis was evidenced by his latest diary entry:

> I return to Rome completely disgusted with the Germans, with their leader, with their way of doing things. They have betrayed us and lied to us. Now they are dragging us into an adventure which we have not wanted and which might compromise the [Fascist] régime and the country as a whole. The Italian people will boil over with horror when they know about the aggression against Poland ... I don't know whether to wish Italy a victory or Germany a defeat.

After returning to Rome, Ciano made a full report to Mussolini and shared with him his 'judgment of the situation'. Mussolini initially agreed, but in the end the prospect of getting 'his part of the booty in Croatia and Dalmatia' convinced him to throw in his lot with Hitler.[68]

In his war journal, Franz Halder, Chief of the Army General Staff, recorded the contents of a meeting with Hitler at Obersalzberg on 14 August. 'Poland', Hitler stated confidently, 'will be polished off in six or eight weeks.' Hitler declared that there were only two potential antagonists other than Poland that Germany need reckon with: Britain and France. Hitler spoke a great deal of Britain and shared his view that the British would not wage war due to the heavy cost involved in taking part in a protracted conflict. Why would Britain not fight? Because 'England only stands to lose'. Hitler explained:

> *England*, unlike in 1914, will not allow herself to blunder into a war lasting for years. Talk of England wanting a long war [is] discounted. No Government will make a long war their primary aim. England, knowing war, is well aware that she stands to lose in a war, and that even a victorious war would not make up for the cost of such a war. Such is the fate of rich countries. England is overburdened with responsibilities because of the excessive size of her empire. She has no leaders of real calibre. ('The men I got to know in Munich are not the kind that start a new World War.') Moreover, the other side is well aware that it has to deal with a different Germany from 1914 (Socialism, Church). (What should England fight for? You don't get yourself killed for an ally.) Not even England has the money nowadays to fight a world war. She can get nothing on credit.

Hitler casually brushed France aside. 'France', said Hitler, 'resembles a weak man trying to carry machine-guns, heavy guns, etc., on his back.' Above all, France was 'not directly interested in waging a war'. And what about the Soviet Union? In Hitler's estimation:

> *Russia* has no intention of pulling England's chestnuts out of the fire and will keep out of war. A lost war is as dangerous for Stalin as a victorious army. His interests at most extend to the Baltic States [Estonia, Latvia, and Lithuania].

As for Scandinavia and the Low Countries, they would all remain neutral. Not even the Balkan States, Hitler posited, could be of any help to the democratic Powers. And in the final analysis, there was nothing the British or French could do in time to save Poland:

> *What military measures can France and Britain undertake?* Drive against West Wall unlikely. A northwards swing through Belgium and Holland will not bring speedy victory. None of this would help the Poles. Blockade works slowly and provokes dangerous counter measures.

Axis partners, collaborators, and sympathizers could be described as follows:

> *Hungary* requires no mention....
>
> *Italy* is not interested in a major conflict, but would welcome certain adjustments. A victory of the democratic nations would be the end of Italy....

> *Spain* will look with disfavour upon any victory of the democratic nations. Democracies would introduce a monarchy and dependence on the Western Powers.

Hitler concluded that Britain would most certainly stay out of the war:

> English and French General Staffs take a very sober view of the prospects of an armed conflict and advise against it.
>
> Further evidence that no determined action is expected on the part of England may above all be inferred from Poland's attitude. Poland would be even more cocky if she knew she could depend on England. England has strongly remonstrated with Poland over the latest Polish Notes and is continuously putting on the brakes. Tapped telephone conversations in Poland! Even now England is putting out feelers to find out how the Führer envisages developments after Poland has been disposed of.
>
> All this supports the convictions that while England may talk big, even recall her ambassador, perhaps put a complete embargo on trade, she is sure not to resort to armed intervention in the [German–Polish] conflict.[69]

On 18 August, Ambassador Herbert von Dirksen transmitted to Weizsäcker an insightful memorandum concerning 'Britain's Probable Attitude in the Event of a German–Polish Conflict' to be passed on to Ribbentrop. Dirksen observed:

> 1. It must be stated, as a general preliminary observation, that Great Britain has not pledged herself in advance one hundred per cent to support Poland in *any* conflict. This would be contrary to the British mentality, which always wants to leave a possible loophole. Hence the stipulation that, for Britain a *casus foederis* would arise only if Poland's independence were threatened. This assures a certain amount of elasticity. It is also asserted, but has not yet been proved, that Poland has pledged herself to obtain Britain's consent before taking up arms. This would mean that Britain would have a free hand should Poland declare war on her own accord.
>
> Small though the likelihood is that Britain would *automatically* become involved in a German–Polish conflict over Danzig or the Corridor, it would be a mistake to accept the way the question has been posed in the article by the French politician [Marcel] Déat, '*Pourquoi mourrir pour Danzig*' ['*Why Die for Danzig*'], and apply it to Britain. To pose such a question would be to ignore the essence of the problem. Britain is not vitally interested in the fate of Danzig, but she is vitally interested in proving that she honours her political promissory notes.

Dirksen envisaged four distinct scenarios and objectively assessed the likely British response:

(a) Danzig—by Senate decree or by plebiscite—announces its return to the Reich. Poland does not retaliate with military action. There is no fighting, or at most only local skirmishes. In this case Britain would hold aloof.

(b) If Poland replied to a 'return to the Reich' resolution by the Senate with military invasion, and declared that the *casus foederis* had arisen, Britain, in conformity with Chamberlain's and Halifax's repeated declarations, would render Poland military assistance.

(c) If the Polish side should stage an act of provocation—such as the shelling of a German village by a Polish battery commander run amok, or the bombing of German villages by a Polish airman—it would be of decisive importance in the determination of Britain's attitude, first, that the facts of the case should be made clear beyond doubt to the peoples of the world, and secondly, that British public opinion should have time to form a clear judgment of the facts and to convince itself that Poland alone was to blame. Otherwise, there would be the danger that, owing to the prejudice against Germany, Britain would side with Poland and, should military action ensue, respond to Poland's appeal for help.

(d) Should Germany, from military considerations of any kind—e.g. in order to forestall a Polish attack believed to be imminent—feel herself forced to take military action against Poland, the fact would have to be reckoned with that Britain would come to Poland's aid. It is also unlikely that Britain would remain neutral if, in such a war with Germany, Poland were very soon defeated. Here, too, Britain would make her decision, not out of regard for Poland's weal or woe, but from considerations of safeguarding her world position.

Dirksen concluded his analysis by noting the numerous factors influencing the British Government's position regarding Poland. These included the treacherous nature of Eastern European politics, the virulence of the Polish Press, the troubled co-existence of the Poles and Russians, the pending outcome of Anglo–Soviet discussions presently underway, the lack of clarity in Anglo–German relations, and the resolve of the British to disprove the ever-increasing perception that Britain was complacent and feeble:

> The British attitude towards Poland and the complex of German–Polish problems, as set out above, is not a constant factor, invariable for all times. In spite of its outward rigidity, the Anglo–Polish alliance is inwardly subject to constant change. This has already been demonstrated in the few months of its existence. The more deeply Britain is drawn into the devious paths of Eastern [European] politics, the more she becomes the prey to doubt and misgiving. Poland's insatiable need of money has already led to a partial failure of the financial negotiations. The insolent tone of the Polish Press, although carefully hushed up in the British Press, meets with disapproval in high quarters. Poland's military strength proves, on closer examination, to be dubious. It is gradually being recognized that the exceptional difficulties of Russo–Polish relations lessen the value of Poland as an ally. Britain's Eastern policy is still in a state of flux, if only because of the continuing negotiations with the Soviet Union. The fact that, on the British side, relations with Germany are not regarded as definitely clarified, contributes to this. The British determination to refute the growing opinion that Britain is decadent, unreliable and weak must be regarded as a constant factor in Britain's general attitude. It is precisely in her attitude towards Poland that Great Britain will continue, for the time being, to be guided by these considerations.[70]

During the first few weeks of August there were exchanged a flurry of 'most urgent' telegrams between Ribbentrop and Schulenburg. On 14 August, Ribbentrop directed Schulenburg to request a reception by Molotov, and to inform him of the following:

> 1. … differing philosophies [i.e. National Socialism and Communism] do not prohibit a reasonable relationship between the two States [Germany and the U.S.S.R.], and the restoration of new, friendly co-operation. The period of opposition in foreign policy could therefore be brought to an end once and for all and the way opened to a new future for both countries.
>
> 2. There exist no real conflicts of interest between Germany and Russia. The living spaces of Germany and Russia touch each other, but in their natural requirements they do not overlap. Thus there is lacking all cause for an aggressive attitude on the part of one country against the other. Germany has no aggressive intentions against the U.S.S.R.…
>
> 4. It is true that Germany and Soviet Russia, as a result of years of ideological opposition, today face each other distrustfully. A great deal of accumulated rubble will have to be cleared away. It must be

said, however, that even during this period the natural sympathy of the Germans for the Russians never disappeared. The policy of both States can be built anew on that basis.

5. The Reich Government and the Soviet Government must ... take into account that the capitalistic Western democracies are the implacable enemies of both National Socialist Germany and Soviet Russia. They are today trying again, by the conclusion of a military alliance, to drive Russia into war against Germany....

6. The crisis which has been produced in German–Polish relations by English policy, as well as English agitation for war and the attempts at an [Anglo–Polish] alliance which are bound up with that policy, make a speedy clarification of German–Russian relations necessary....

As we have been informed, the Soviet Government also feel the desire for a clarification of German–Russian relations. Since ... this clarification can be achieved only slowly through the usual diplomatic channels, I [Ribbentrop] am prepared to make a short visit to Moscow in order, in the name of the Führer, to set forth the Führer's views to M. Stalin.[71]

Next day at 8 p.m. Schulenburg met with Molotov and communicated the above spiel to him.

In his telegram sent to Schulenburg at the German Embassy in the Soviet Union on 16 August, Ribbentrop proposed to fly to Moscow 'at any time after Friday, 18 August' with plenary powers to negotiate an 'undenounceable' non-aggression pact with the Soviet Union of twenty-five years' duration. Germany would further 'guarantee the Baltic States jointly with the Soviet Union'.[72] Molotov stalled, insisting that 'detailed preparation' was necessary before the Soviet Government could receive the Reich Foreign Minister.[73]

In order to accelerate the negotiations, Hitler personally intervened by drafting a telegram of his own, addressed to Stalin. Dated 20 August, the telegram requested that due to the intense friction at present between Germany and Poland, Ribbentrop be permitted to fly to Moscow to finalize the non-aggression pact as soon as possible, preferably on 22 August, but no later than 23 August. Ribbentrop told Schulenburg that the Führer wanted him to personally hand his (Hitler's) telegram to Molotov. It read:

M. Stalin, Moscow.

1. I sincerely welcome the signing of the new German–Soviet Commercial Agreement [the Credit Agreement between the German Reich and the

U.S.S.R., signed on 20 August at 2 a.m. and backdated to the 19th] as the first step in the re-shaping of German–Soviet relations.

2. The conclusion of a non-aggression pact with the Soviet Union means to me the establishment of German policy for a long time. Germany thereby resumes a political course that was beneficial to both States during by-gone centuries. The Government of the Reich are therefore resolved in such a case to accept all the consequences of such a far-reaching change.

3. I accept the draft of the non-aggression pact that your Foreign Minister, M. Molotov, handed over, but consider it urgently necessary to clarify the questions connected with it as soon as possible.

4. The substance of the supplementary protocol desired by the Government of the Soviet Union can, I am convinced, be clarified in the shortest time possible if a responsible German statesman can come to Moscow himself to negotiate. Otherwise the Government of the Reich are not clear as to how the supplementary protocol could be cleared up and settled in a short time.

5. The tension between Germany and Poland has become intolerable. The Polish demeanour towards a great Power is such that a crisis may arise any day. German is at any rate determined, in the face of this presumption, from now on to look after the interests of the Reich with all the means at her disposal.

6. In my opinion, it is desirable, in view of the intentions of the two States to enter into a new relationship to each other, not to lose any time. I therefore again propose that you receive my Foreign Minister [Ribbentrop] on Tuesday, 22 August, but at the latest on Wednesday, 23 August. The Reich Foreign Minister has the fullest powers to draw up and sign the non-aggression pact as well as the protocol. A longer stay by the Foreign Minister in Moscow than one to two days at most is impossible in view of the international situation. I should be glad to receive your early answer.

Adolf Hitler[74]

For the Soviets, there were three obvious benefits in concluding a pact with the Germans: 1. When war broke out between Germany and Poland—which was obviously just a matter of time—the Soviets could remain inactive, or they could enter the conflict on Germany's side at their convenience; 2. They could extract a great deal from the Germans in negotiations, due to Hitler's critical need for Soviet co-operation (Germany could not invade Poland and, if need be, take on the Western Powers as well, if Soviet benevolence could not be assured); and 3. Territory acquired by the Soviet Union in Eastern Poland would add an extra buffer between Germany and the U.S.S.R., should hostilities between them materialize in the future.

At 5 p.m. on 21 August, Molotov presented Schulenburg with Stalin's courteous reply to Hitler's telegram, the gist of which was that the Soviet Government had agreed to confer with Ribbentrop at the Kremlin on 23 August. Schulenburg transmitted the text verbatim to the German Foreign Ministry that evening:

> To the Chancellor of the German Reich, Herr A. Hitler.
>
> I thank you for the letter. I hope that the German–Soviet Non-Aggression Pact will bring about a decided turn for the better in the political relations between our countries.
>
> The peoples of our countries need peaceful relations with each other. The assent of the German Government to the conclusion of a non-aggression pact provides the foundation for eliminating the political tension and for the establishment of peace and collaboration between our countries.
>
> The Soviet Government have instructed me to inform you that they agree to Herr von Ribbentrop's arriving in Moscow on 23 August.
>
> J. Stalin[75]

On the morning of 22 August, Hitler delivered a secret speech to the heads of the Army, Navy, and Luftwaffe at Obersalzberg. He assessed the international political situation and emphasized his preference for war sooner rather than later. He spoke arrogantly, and not a few of his audience must have perceived that their Supreme Commander was a megalomaniac, albeit a cunning and perceptive one:

> It was clear to me that a conflict with Poland had to come sooner or later. I had already made this decision in the spring, but I thought that I would first turn against the West in a few years, and only after that against the East. But the sequence of these things cannot be fixed. Nor should one close one's eyes to threatening situations. I wanted first of all to establish a tolerable relationship with Poland in order to fight

first against the West. But this plan, which appealed to me, could not be executed, as fundamental points had changed. It became clear to me that, in the event of a conflict with the West, Poland would attack us. Poland is striving for access to the sea. The further development appeared after the occupation of the Memel Territory and it became clear to me that in certain circumstances a conflict with Poland might come at an inopportune moment. I give as reasons for this conclusion:

1. First of all two personal factors:

My own personality and that of Mussolini.

Essentially all depends on me, on my existence, because of my political talents. Furthermore, the fact that probably no one will ever again have the confidence of the whole German people as I have. There will probably never again in the future be a man with more authority than I have. My existence is therefore a factor of great value. But I can be eliminated at any time by a criminal or a lunatic.

The second personal factor is the Duce. His existence is also decisive. If anything happens to him, Italy's loyalty to the alliance will no longer be certain. The Italian Court is fundamentally opposed to the Duce. Above all, the Court regards the expansion of the [Italian] Empire as an encumbrance. The Duce is the man with the strongest nerves in Italy.

The third personal factor in our favour is Franco. We can ask only for benevolent neutrality from Spain. But this depends on Franco's personality. He guarantees a certain uniformity and stability in the present system in Spain. We must accept the fact that Spain does not as yet have a Fascist party with our internal unity.

The other side presents a negative picture as far as authoritative persons are concerned. There is no outstanding personality in England and France....

We have nothing to lose; we have everything to gain.... Our opponents will be risking a great deal and can gain only a little. Britain's stake in a war is inconceivably great. Our enemies have leaders who are below the average. No personalities. No masters, no men of action.

Besides the personal factors, the political situation is favourable for us: in the Mediterranean, rivalry between Italy, France, and England; in the Far East, tension between Japan and England; in the Middle East, tension which causes alarm in the Mohammedan world.

The English Empire did not emerge stronger from the last war. Nothing was achieved from the maritime point of view. Strife between England and Ireland. The Union of South Africa has become more independent. Concessions have had to be made to India. England is in the utmost peril. Unhealthy industrialization. A British statesman can only view the future with concern.

> France's position has also deteriorated, above all in the Mediterranean.
> Further factors in our favour are these:
> Since Albania, there has been a balance of power in the Balkans. Yugoslavia is infected with the fatal germ of decay because of her internal situation.
> Romania has not grown stronger. She is open to attack and vulnerable. She is threatened by Hungary and Bulgaria. Since Kemal's death, Turkey has been ruled by petty minds, unsteady, weak men.
> All these favourable circumstances will no longer prevail in two or three years' time. No one knows how much longer I shall live. Therefore, better a conflict now.[76]

Hitler also accentuated the fact that the war in Poland would be genocidal in nature. The idea to perpetrate mass murder against certain targeted groups had long been in his mind. Hitler intended to put into practice a policy of wholesale racial extermination, and he made this abundantly clear to Brauchitsch and other commanding generals with one of the cruellest utterances of his career:

> Our strength is in our quickness and our brutality. Ghengis Khan had millions of women and children killed ... History sees only in him a great state builder. What weak Western European civilization thinks about me does not matter. I have given the order and will have everyone shot, who utters even one word of criticism that the aim of the war is not to attain certain lines, but consists in the physical destruction of the opponent. Thus for the time being I have sent to the East only my 'Death's Head Units' with the order to kill without pity or mercy all men, women, and children of Polish race or language. Only in such a way will we win the vital space that we need. Who still talks nowadays of the extermination of the Armenians?[77]

That afternoon, Hitler addressed his military chiefs a second time. From his words it was evident that he was not encumbered by personal scruples or traditional notions of military honour or fair play. The ends would justify the means, no matter how they were to be attained. In the final analysis, Poland had to be crushed, and Germany's future had to be assured. This was all that counted and Hitler wanted to instill this precept into his generals:

> Even if war breaks out in the West, the destruction of Poland remains the priority....
> I shall give a propagandist reason for starting the war, no matter whether it is plausible or not. The victor will not be asked afterwards

> whether he told the truth or not. When starting and waging a war it is not right that matters, but victory.
>
> Close your hearts to pity. Act brutally. Eighty million people must obtain what is their right. Their existence must be made secure. The stronger man is right. The greatest harshness....
>
> First requirement: Advance up to the Vistula and the Narew. Our technical superiority will shatter the nerves of the Poles. Every newly formed active Polish force is to be destroyed again immediately....
>
> The wholesale destruction of Poland is the military objective.[78]

The Nazi–Soviet Non-Aggression Pact was set to be finalized the following day, 23 August. Accordingly, Hitler ordered the campaign against Poland to commence at daybreak on Saturday, 26 August. This was known as 'Day Y', according to General Halder's diary.

At 9 p.m. on 22 August, Ambassador Henderson received instructions from his government to ask for an audience with Hitler in order to deliver a private letter by Chamberlain. With the Nazi–Soviet Non-Aggression Pact in the works, Hitler did not particularly want to deal with a British diplomat just then, but he reluctantly agreed to see him. Thus on 23 August, Henderson flew from Berlin to Salzburg, then motored up to the Berghof for his interview with Hitler, which began soon after 1 p.m. The first round of talks lasted forty-five minutes.

Chamberlain's letter informed Hitler of the decision reached by the British Cabinet the previous afternoon. It explicitly stated that no matter what the Nazi–Soviet Pact's articles might contain, it would have no bearing on Britain's pledge of military assistance to Poland should she be attacked by Germany. Chamberlain wrote:

> ... the announcement of a German–Soviet Agreement is taken in some quarters in Berlin to indicate that intervention by Great Britain on behalf of Poland is no longer a contingency that need to be reckoned with. No greater mistake could be made. Whatever may prove to be the nature of the German–Soviet Agreement, it cannot alter Great Britain's obligation to Poland, which His Majesty's Government ... are determined to fulfill.

Chamberlain hastened to add that the British Government 'are resolved and prepared to employ without delay all the forces at their command ... war between our two peoples would be the greatest calamity that could occur.'[79] The letter, the translated text of which Hitler claimed to already have in his possession, incensed him, and during his conversation with Henderson he was agitated. He railed angrily against the Poles and the British. He advised Henderson that he had given notice to the Polish

Government that 'any further persecution of the Germans in Poland would immediately entail action by the Reich'. It had been brought to his attention, Hitler said, that Chamberlain had ordered 'increased military preparations' in Britain, while Germany had restricted her preparations to 'purely defensive measures'. Hitler warned:

> If I should hear of further measures of this sort being taken by England today or tomorrow, I shall immediately order general mobilization in Germany.

Hitler blamed Britain for creating a 'poisoned atmosphere'. But for England, he was convinced, he would certainly have settled the 'Danzig problem' peacefully by now. It was England who was at fault. Moreover, Hitler accused, 'hundreds of thousands of *Volksdeutsche*' in Poland were subjected to mistreatment, locked up in Polish concentration camps, and cast out of their homes. He had extended to the Poles a perfectly acceptable offer (regarding Danzig) which the Anglo–French democracies had interfered with. The case in point was the British guarantee of military assistance to Poland, which, directly aimed at Germany, had emboldened the Poles and made them unamenable to reasonable and moderate German proposals. Hitler vowed that if the Poles made even 'the slightest attempt' to take action 'against Germans or Danzig', he would step in at once. But when Hitler declared that if the Western Powers were to mobilize their armed forces the Reich would do likewise, Henderson indignantly interjected:

> HENDERSON: Is that a threat?
>
> HITLER: No, a protective measure!

Hitler informed Henderson that he believed the Western Powers sought to destroy Germany. For this reason he had ordered the construction of the nearly 400-mile Siegfried Line along the western German frontier, opposite France, Luxembourg, Belgium, and the Netherlands, at a staggering cost of nine billion marks. 'Should it come to war', Hitler predicted, 'it would be a war of life and death.' Throughout the talks Henderson interposed with remarks and protestations of his own: that mobilization by Germany would make war 'inevitable'; that Germany's offer to Poland had been an ultimatum; that the 'change in British opinion' had occurred only after the seizure of Bohemia–Moravia on 15 March; that 'according to Clausewitz, war always brought surprises'; that the British were only averse to the 'principle of force' and not the Germans themselves.

The subject of negotiations with Soviet Russia was then raised. Henderson stated that he had never been in favour of an Anglo–French–Russian Pact. The Russians were merely playing for time. They wanted 'to be rid of Chamberlain' and then 'to profit from a war'. As far as he was concerned, Henderson said, it was better that Germany had concluded a pact with Russia, and not England. Hitler replied that the Nazi–Soviet Pact would be a long-lasting one. Henderson pointed out that 'the Russians always made difficulties', to which Hitler answered, 'I must judge by deeds in this matter.' Thereupon Hitler broke off the meeting to compose a written response to Chamberlain's letter. When the conversation resumed at 5 p.m. that afternoon, Hitler was less agitated. He did not, however, mince his words. After assuring Henderson that he did not consider him to be one of Germany's enemies—unlike British War Minister Leslie Hore-Belisha, for instance—Hitler lamented that 'his relationship with England had been a series of disappointments'. And now, as Hitler saw it, the situation was such:

> He was now 50, therefore if war had to come, it was better that it should come now than when he was 55 or even 60 years old. There could only be understanding or war between England and Germany. England would do well to realize that as a front-line soldier he knew what war was and would utilize every means available. It was surely quite clear to everyone that the World War would not have been lost if he had been Chancellor at the time.

Hitler pressed on. 'At the next instance of Polish provocation, I shall act. The questions of Danzig and the Corridor will be settled one way or another.' Henderson indicated that 'England and Germany were equals and had equal rights'. If this was so, Hitler countered, England 'ought not to intervene against Germany if she were clearly safeguarding her rights'. Lastly, Hitler let Henderson know that the text of his reply to Chamberlain would be given in London the next day by Ambassador Dirksen.[80]

In his written response to Chamberlain's letter, which he permitted Henderson to peruse, Hitler enumerated his grievances against the Poles. These included the issuance of ultimata by the Polish Government to Danzig, the ongoing 'terrorism' of the 1.5 million ethnic Germans residing in Poland, the multiple violations of Poland's 'legal obligations' towards Danzig, the 'strangulation' of Danzig's economy by a 'customs blockade', etc. In answer to Britain's promise to stand by Poland, Hitler gave Chamberlain a grim warning:

> Germany, if attacked by England, will be found prepared and determined.

Hitler repeated his threats of German mobilization, which were identical to those he had made to Henderson:

> The Government of the German Reich have received information to the effect that the British Government intend to carry out measures of mobilization which ... are clearly directed against Germany alone. This appears to be true of France as well. Since Germany has never had the intention of taking military measures, other than those of a defensive character, against either England or France, and ... has never intended, and does not in the future intend, to attack England or France, it follows that this announcement ... can only refer to a proposed act of menace directed against the Reich.
>
> *I therefore inform Your Excellency that, in the event of these military announcements being carried into effect, I shall order immediate mobilization of the German forces.*

Hitler ended his letter with a plea for Anglo–German friendship:

> I have all my life fought for German–English friendship; the attitude adopted by British diplomacy—at any rate up to the present—has, however, convinced me of the futility of such an attempt. Should there be any change in this respect in the future, nobody could be happier than I.[81]

In Danzig, District Leader Forster convoked a session of the Senate in which a vote was held to reunite Danzig with the Reich. This was, of course, a highly provocative step to take, considering the present heightened state of German–Polish antagonism. There was another order of business: Forster took over the presidency, becoming *Staatspräsident* (State President) of Danzig. He thereby supplanted his long-time nemesis, Greiser. Spurred on by Berlin, Forster continued to push for Danzig's annexation into the Reich, adding fuel to the fire of German–Polish tensions.

Meanwhile, Ribbentrop had reached Moscow at noon on 23 August vested with complete authority to conclude a non-aggression pact with the Soviet Union. The day before, Hitler had written and signed a short note to this effect:

> *Full Powers*
> *To the Reich Foreign Minister,*
> *Herr Joachim von Ribbentrop*
>
> I hereby grant full power to negotiate, in the name of the German Reich with authorized representatives of the Government of the Union of

> Soviet Socialist Republics, regarding a non-aggression treaty, as well as all related questions, and if occasion arises, to sign both the non-aggression treaty and other agreements resulting from the negotiations, with the proviso that this treaty and these agreements shall enter into force as soon as they are signed.
>
> ADOLF HITLER
> RIBBENTROP
> OBERSALZBERG, 22 August 1939[82]

At the Kremlin, Ribbentrop consulted with both Molotov and Stalin. Throughout the course of their talks, they touched on relations with Japan, Italy, Turkey, France, and the Anti-Comintern Pact itself, an understandably sticky subject. Ribbentrop downplayed the Anti-Comintern Pact, explaining that it was chiefly directed against the Western Powers, not Russia, and telling Stalin of a recent joke 'going the rounds' among Berliners that 'Stalin will yet join the Anti-Comintern Pact himself'. They also discussed England's shortcomings. Ribbentrop maintained that 'England was weak and wanted to let others fight for her presumptuous claim to world domination'. Stalin agreed wholeheartedly and reflected:

> The British Army was weak; nor was the British Navy as important as it had formerly been. England's air arm was being increased, to be sure, but there was a lack of pilots. If England dominated the world in spite of this, that was due to the stupidity of the other countries that always let themselves be bluffed. It was ridiculous, for example, that a few hundred Englishmen should dominate India.

They discussed the advantages of a German–Soviet alliance, and that afternoon, Ribbentrop succeeded in convincing his Soviet interlocutors that a deal with the Reich was preferable to one with the Anglo–French democracies. In the evening Ribbentrop returned for a social get-together with Stalin. Ironically, Ribbentrop and Stalin got along like bosom buddies. (Ribbentrop later related to Hitler that he had felt as though he had been in the presence of old Nazi Party comrades, and not hated Bolsheviks.) To everyone's surprise, Stalin unexpectedly proposed a toast to Hitler. 'I know how much the German nation loves its Führer; I should therefore like to drink to his health.' In this spirit of camaraderie, enhanced by strong liquor, further toasts were exchanged. Stalin and Molotov drank to the new pact and to the 'new era of German–Russian relations'. Ribbentrop toasted the Soviet Government and drank 'to a favourable development of relations between Germany and the Soviet Union'. Later that evening, Ribbentrop and Molotov affixed their signatures to the Nazi–Soviet Non-Aggression Pact (see Appendix L), while Stalin looked on, beaming broadly. Before taking his leave, Stalin delivered a few parting words to Ribbentrop. He solemnly stated, 'The Soviet Government take the new Pact very seriously' and he pledged to Ribbentrop 'on his word of honour that the Soviet Union would not betray its partner.'[83]

The first part of the Nazi–Soviet Non-Aggression Pact was revealed to the public. Its articles provided that each nation pledged not to wage war against the other, nor to assist a hostile third party in the event that one of them was attacked by it. Any disagreements between the two nations would be resolved through friendly discussion or arbitration. It was to be a decade-long pact. But in addition to the Nazi–Soviet Pact's preamble and its first seven clauses, the agreement contained a 'Secret Additional Protocol'. Unlike the first portion, it was not publicized. The world only learned of it after Germany's defeat in 1945, when the private documents in the voluminous German archives were discovered by the victorious Allies. Behind the scenes, Eastern Europe was cynically divided by Germany and the Soviet Union into respective spheres of influence. Poland was to be split in two between the Reich and the U.S.S.R. Lithuania fell into the German sphere,[17*] while Finland, Estonia, and Latvia fell into the Soviet sphere:

> 1. In the event of a territorial and political rearrangement in the areas belonging to the Baltic States (Finland, Estonia, Latvia, Lithuania), the northern boundary of Lithuania shall represent the boundary of the spheres of influence of Germany and the U.S.S.R. In this connection the interest of Lithuania in the Vilna area is recognized by each Party.
> 2. In the event of a territorial and political rearrangement of the areas belonging to the Polish State the spheres of influence of Germany and the U.S.S.R. shall be bounded approximately by the line of the rivers Narew, Vistula, and San.

Whether an 'independent Polish State' would be permitted to exist was to be decided only 'in the course of further political developments'. Any questions which might arise afterwards were to be resolved 'by means of a friendly agreement' by both Governments. In the third clause of the secret protocols, the Soviets had one further claim to make:

> 3. With regard to Southeastern Europe attention is called by the Soviet side to its interest in Bessarabia [formerly a Romanian province].

---

17 * Five weeks later, per the Secret Additional Protocol to the German–Soviet Boundary and Friendship Treaty dated 28 September 1939—signed again by Ribbentrop and Molotov—the Germans would grant the Soviets Lithuania as well.

In turn, the Germans declared their 'complete political disinterestedness in these areas'. And lastly, both the Germans and Soviets were to treat the protocols as 'strictly secret'.[84] Before flying back to the Reich to report to Hitler, Ribbentrop made a statement 'to the D.N.B. [German News Agency] representative in Moscow' on the newly-concluded pact:

> Formerly Germany and Russia always fared badly when they were enemies, but well when they were friends. Yesterday [it was now after midnight on 24 August] was a fateful day for both nations. The Führer and Stalin have decided on friendship. The Non-Aggression Pact and Consultation Pact which M. Molotov and I signed yesterday evening is a firm and unshakable foundation on which both States will build and come into close co-operation. This is perhaps one of the most significant turning points in the history of two peoples. An attempt was made [by the Western Powers] to encircle Germany and Russia and from that very encirclement the German–Russian understanding has now emerged.[85]

The Western Powers were dismayed by the Nazi–Soviet Pact, for not only was it a blatant rejection to their own overtures, they knew Hitler would be emboldened by it. As for the secret articles, what was important was the fact was that Germany and the U.S.S.R. now saw eye to eye. In a German–Polish clash, the U.S.S.R. would sit on the sidelines while Germany crushed Poland at her convenience. It showed that both Hitler and Stalin were willing to compromise their ideological principles for the sake of political expedience.

The alliance of National Socialist Germany with the hated Soviets was a bolt from the blue to the entire world. But in Germany itself, this 180-degree turnabout in foreign policy met with the disapproval of the majority of Germans, who interpreted it more as an opportunistic betrayal of political principles than a diplomatic achievement. To the ordinary German man in the street, a dalliance with the Bolsheviks was unfathomable, especially after all of Hitler's violent anti-Communist rhetoric. Nevertheless, when the news broke it was sensational.

Two and a half years earlier, on the fourth anniversary of his appointment to the Chancellorship, Hitler had spoken out against the Bolshevist doctrine to his Reichstag deputies in the strongest possible terms. He vehemently thundered that 'for us it [Bolshevism] is a pestilence against which we have had to struggle at the cost of much bloodshed ... It is not suitable that National Socialist Germans should ever hope to protect Bolshevism or that we should ever accept help from a Bolshevist State.' And in *Mein Kampf*, Hitler had scathingly written:

> Never forget that the [Bolshevist] rulers of present-day [Soviet] Russia are common blood-stained criminals; that they are the scum of humanity which, favoured by circumstances, overran a great state in a tragic hour, slaughtered and wiped out thousands of her leading intellectuals in wild blood lust, and now for almost ten years have been carrying on the most cruel and tyrannical régime of all time.[86]

But in his Reichstag speech of 1 September 1939, Hitler defended and rationalized the Nazi–Soviet Pact to his deputies:

> I am happy particularly to be able to tell you of one event. You know that Russia and Germany are governed by two different doctrines. There was only one question that had to be cleared up. Germany has no intention of exporting its doctrine. Given the fact that Soviet Russia has no intention of exporting its doctrine to Germany, I no longer see any reason why we should still oppose one another. On both sides we are clear on that. Any struggle between our people would only be of advantage to others. We have, therefore, resolved to conclude a pact which rules out forever any use of violence between us. It imposes the obligation on us to consult together in certain European questions. It makes possible for us economic co-operation, and above all it assures that the powers of both these powerful States are not wasted against one another. Every attempt of the West to bring about any change in this will fail.
>
> At the same time I should like here to declare that this political decision means a tremendous departure for the future, and that it is a final one. Russia and Germany fought against one another in the World War. That shall not and will not happen a second time.[87]

The diplomatic chess-move Ribbentrop had managed to pull off exceeded both his own and Hitler's expectations. Yet Hitler was not entirely satisfied with the overall situation, for the British pro-Polish stance remained as firm as ever. This was confirmed by Chamberlain's assertive speech of 24 August in the House of Commons, in which he maintained that England's commitments to Poland would be upheld. Chamberlain's emphatic words made a strong impression on Hitler, particularly those which specified that the Nazi–Soviet Pact would not, contrary to the German Government's belief, deter the British from aiding the Poles in the event of German aggression:

> ... in Berlin and Moscow it was announced [on 22 August] that negotiations had been taking place, and were likely soon to be concluded, for a non-aggression pact between the two countries. I do not attempt to conceal from the House that that announcement came to the [British]

> Government as a surprise, and a surprise of a very unpleasant character. For some time past there had been rumours about an impending change in the relations between Germany and the Soviet Union, but no inkling of that change had been conveyed either to us or to the French Government by the Soviet Government....
>
> In Berlin the announcement was hailed, with extraordinary cynicism, as a great diplomatic victory which removed any danger of war [for the Germans], since we and France would no longer be likely to fulfill our obligations to Poland....
>
> I therefore made it plain [to the German Government] ... that if the case should arise His Majesty's Government were resolved and prepared to employ without delay all the forces at their command [in Poland's defence]....
>
> On numerous occasions I have stated my conviction that war between our two countries, admitted on all sides to be the greatest calamity that could occur, is not desired either by our own people or the German people....
>
> We do not think of asking Germany to sacrifice her national interests, but we cannot agree that [Germany's] national interests can only be secured by the shedding of blood or the destruction of the independence of other States.[88]

By this point Hitler was unshakably resolved to utterly destroy Poland. Nevertheless, he still entertained the mistaken notion that he might be able to convince the democratic Powers to disinterest themselves in the fate of Poland and his designs in Eastern Europe.

And what were Stalin's views? Did he deem the German–Soviet Pact of August 1939 to have been a wise undertaking, or did he consider it a mistake? When Hitler's armies—over three million men along a battlefront over one thousand miles long—eventually attacked the U.S.S.R. without a declaration of war on 22 June 1941, Stalin had this to say in a broadcast to the peoples of the Soviet Union eleven days later:

> It may be asked: How could the Soviet Government have consented to conclude a non-aggression pact with such treacherous fiends as Hitler and Ribbentrop? Was not this an error on the part of the Soviet Government? Of course not!
>
> Non-aggression pacts are pacts of peace between two states. It was such a pact that Germany proposed to us in 1939. Could the Soviet Government have declined such a proposal? I think that not a single peace-loving state could decline a peace treaty with a neighbouring state even though the latter was headed by such fiends and cannibals as Hitler and Ribbentrop.

> But that, of course, only on one indispensable condition—namely, that this peace treaty does not infringe either directly or indirectly on the territorial integrity, independence and honour of the peace-loving state.
>
> As is well known, the non-aggression pact between Germany and the U.S.S.R. is precisely such a pact.
>
> What did we gain by concluding a non-aggression pact with Germany? We secured for our country peace for a year and a half and the opportunity of preparing its forces to repulse Fascist Germany should she risk an attack on our country despite the pact.
>
> This was a definite advantage for us and a disadvantage for Fascist Germany.
>
> What has Fascist Germany gained and what has she lost by treacherously tearing up the pact and attacking the U.S.S.R.?
>
> She gained a certain advantageous position for her troops for a short period, but she has lost politically by exposing herself in the eyes of the entire world as a bloodthirsty aggressor.
>
> There can be no doubt that this short-lived military gain for Germany is only an episode, while the tremendous political gain of the U.S.S.R. is a serious and lasting factor that is bound to form the basis for development of decisive military successes of the Red Army in the war with Fascist Germany.[89]

President Roosevelt sent Hitler a letter on 24 August urging a resolution of German–Polish differences by diplomacy, but Hitler—contemptuous of that 'gangster' Roosevelt—did not deem it worthy of a reply. Roosevelt wrote that 'because of my confident belief that the cause of world peace—which is the cause of humanity itself—rises above all other considerations I am again addressing myself to you, with the hope that the war which impends and the consequent disaster to all peoples may yet be averted'. Roosevelt suggested three possible means for Germany and Poland to settle their differences: direct negotiation, impartial arbitration, and conciliation. He added that in order for any of the above three methods to be successful, it was imperative that the 'independence and territorial integrity' of either country could not be compromised by the other. Roosevelt concluded with these noble words:

> The people of the United States are as one in their opposition to policies of military conquest and domination. They are as one in rejecting the thesis that any ruler or any people possess the right to achieve their ends or objectives through the taking of action which will plunge countless of millions into war, and which will bring distress and suffering to every nation of the world, belligerent and neutral, when such ends and

> objectives, so far as they are just and reasonable, can be satisfied through the processes of peaceful negotiation or by resort to judicial arbitration.
>
> I appeal to you in the name of the people of the United States, and I believe in the name of peace-loving men and women everywhere, to agree to a solution of the controversies existing between your Government and that of Poland through the adoption of one of the [three] alternative methods I have proposed.[90]

In a second letter sent the following day, Roosevelt added:

> Countless human lives can yet be saved and hope may still be restored that the nations of the modern world may even now construct the foundation for a peaceful and happier relationship, if you [Hitler] and the Government of the German Reich will agree to the pacific means of settlement accepted by the Government of Poland. All the world prays that Germany, too, will accept.[91]

Like the first, this sincere imploration was also ignored.

On the morning of 25 August, Birger Dahlerus, a Swedish industrialist, civil engineer, and friend of Field Marshal Göring, departed for England at the latter's request as a go-between to advise Halifax that the Reich still wished to come to terms with the British Government. However, when Dahlerus saw Halifax early that evening, Halifax told him that conventional 'official channels were open' to the German Government and 'that he did not think his [Dahlerus'] services would be required any longer'.[92]

Before midday Hitler sent a letter to Mussolini containing his justification for the Nazi–Soviet Pact, which to Mussolini—on the surface at least—must have seemed outrageous. It was personally delivered to him at 3:20 p.m. by Hans Georg von Mackensen, the German Ambassador to Italy. Hitler gave the reason he had not kept Mussolini 'informed in detail' of the 'German–Russian conversations'. It was because not even he could have anticipated that the talks would progress so swiftly and so successfully:

> DUCE:
>
> For some time Germany and Russia have been engaged in an exchange of views concerning a reshaping of their mutual political relations.
>
> The necessity of achieving results in this direction was increased by:
>
> 1. The general situation of world politics in so far as this is decisive for the Axis Powers.

2. The constant procrastination of the Japanese Cabinet over taking a definite attitude. Japan had agreed to an alliance against Russia, which in the prevailing circumstances would have only a *secondary* interest for Germany, and, in my opinion, for Italy also. She had not, however, agreed to an equally definite obligation against England, and this, from the standpoint not only of Germany but also of Italy, would have been one of the decisive factors. Months ago the military party had asserted that it would be able to induce the Japanese Government in a short time to take up a definite attitude towards England too, but this had not been realized in practice.

3. Germany's relations with Poland, through no fault of the Reich, but largely as a result of England's interference, have been unsatisfactory since the spring, and in recent weeks simply intolerable. The reports about the persecution of the Germans in this area are not invented press reports but represent only a fraction of the terrible truth. Poland's throttling of Danzig by a Customs policy which for weeks past has led to a complete paralysis of all trade, will destroy the [Free] City if continued even for a short time.

> These reasons led me to hasten the conclusion of the German–Russian conversations. I have not yet informed you in detail, Duce, since I had no idea of the possible extent of these conversations, or any assurance of the possibility of their success.

The Nazi–Soviet Pact and the resultant 'new situation in world politics', Hitler boasted to Mussolini, had to be considered 'the greatest possible gain for the Axis'. He characterized it as 'the most extensive non-aggression pact in existence'. The pact was unconditional and contained the proviso that Germany and Soviet Russia would consult 'on all questions' concerning both parties. Moreover, the Axis nations no longer needed to concern themselves with a potential attack against them by Romania, and there was also the possibility that Turkey would reconsider her pro-British stance (Anglo–Turkish declarations were signed on 12 May and a mutual assistance pact was concluded in Ankara on 19 October):

> The readiness on the part of the Kremlin to reshape its relations with Germany, which became apparent after the departure of Litvinov, has become ever stronger in the last few weeks and has now made it possible for me, after a preliminary clarification, to send my Foreign Minister to Moscow for the conclusion of a treaty which is the most extensive non-aggression pact in existence and the text of which has been made public. The

> pact is unconditional and includes also the obligation for consultation on all questions affecting Russia and Germany. Over and above that, however, I must tell you, Duce, that, through the agreements, the most benevolent attitude by Russia in case of any conflict is assured, and above all, *that the possibility of intervention by Romania in such a conflict no longer exists!*
>
> Even Turkey in these circumstances can only proceed to revise her previous position. But I repeat once more, *that Romania is no longer in a position to take part in any conflict against the Axis!* I believe I may say to you, Duce, that through the negotiations with Soviet Russia a completely new situation in world politics has been produced which must be regarded as the greatest possible gain for the Axis.

However, Hitler's chief preoccupation was to advise Mussolini that the outbreak of a German–Polish war was fast approaching due to Polish excesses. (Hitler felt it unnecessary to request Italian assistance, since the Pact of Steel specified that Italy was obliged to immediately join the conflict at Germany's side in any case):

> As to the situation on the German–Polish frontier, I can only inform Your Excellency that for weeks we have been standing by for action; that, keeping pace with Polish mobilization, German preparations have naturally also gone forward; and that in case of intolerable events in Poland I will act immediately. The assertion of the Polish Government that they are not responsible for the inhuman activities, for the numerous frontier incidents (last night alone there were twenty-one Polish frontier violations), and for firing on German civil aircraft—which had already received orders to fly to East Prussia over the sea in order to avoid incidents—merely shows that the Polish Government are no longer in control of the soldiery which they have themselves stirred up. Since yesterday Danzig has been blockaded by Polish troops, a situation unendurable in itself. In these circumstances no one can say what the next hour may bring. I can only assure you that there is a definite limit beyond which I can in no circumstances retreat.

Lastly, Hitler assured Mussolini that if the circumstances were reversed, his loyalty to Italy would be unshakable:

> In conclusion I can assure you, Duce, that in a similar situation I should have complete understanding for Italy and that in any such case you could be sure of my attitude from the outset.
>
> ADOLF HITLER[93]

At 1:30 p.m. Henderson arrived at the Reich Chancellery for another audience with Hitler. The Führer told Henderson that he wished to reach an understanding with England that would 'be as decisive as the move as regards Russia which had led to the recent [Nazi–Soviet] agreement'. In other words, Hitler wanted to make a deal with England that would permit Germany to settle accounts with Poland without British interference, just as Germany had done with the U.S.S.R. on the 23rd. Hitler scoffed at the preposterous British notion that Germany sought world conquest. After all, one only had to look at the figures; they spoke for themselves:

> The British Empire embraced 40 million square kilometres, Russia 19 million square kilometres, America 9.5 million square kilometres, whereas Germany embraced less than 600,000 square kilometres.

Considering these sobering statistics, was it not the British who sought to dominate the world? Next, Hitler imparted three points to Henderson: first, Germany could no longer countenance Polish provocation; second, Germany was resolved to put an end to the 'Macedonian conditions' in the East for the sake of 'European peace'; and third, the issue of Danzig and the Polish Corridor had to be settled. Furthermore, Hitler asserted, the non-aggression pact between Germany and the Soviet Union was 'unconditional' and permanent; the two nations were committed to 'never again take up arms against each other'. This arrangement would also make the Reich economically self-sufficient in the event of a lengthy war.

Thereupon Hitler extended his final offer: he was 'ready to conclude agreements with England which ... would not only guarantee the existence of the British Empire in all circumstances as far as Germany is concerned, but also if necessary an assurance to the British Empire of German assistance regardless of where such assistance would be necessary'. In exchange, Hitler insisted on the ensuing terms; namely, that: Germany's 'colonial demands', which were 'limited' and open to 'peaceful' negotiation, be granted (there was no hurry); Germany's 'obligations towards Italy' remain intact; and Britain recognize the 'irrevocable determination of Germany never again to enter into conflict with Russia'. Moreover, Hitler was willing to consider 'a reasonable limitation of armaments which would correspond to the new political situation' and which would be financially feasible. Hitler reiterated that he was 'not interested in Western [European] problems'. He was not seeking 'a frontier modification in the West' and he gave his assurance that the 'Western fortifications' built at a staggering cost of billions 'were the final Reich frontier on the West'. Lastly, Hitler noted that should the British Government be amenable to his proposals, it would be 'a blessing' for both sides. However, if they were not accepted, it would mean war.[94]

His duty done, Henderson returned to England to pass on Hitler's offer to Chamberlain.

After his interview with Henderson, Hitler saw Ambassador Coulondre at 5:30 p.m. He reiterated to Coulondre (as he had said to Henderson) that the Reich could tolerate no further 'Polish provocation'. He added that he would not take offensive action against France. However, should France attack the Reich, he would wage war against her relentlessly. After this grave warning, Coulondre had a few words of his own to share with Hitler. Coulondre informed Hitler on his 'word of honour as a soldier' that if Germany attacked Poland, then France would come to her aid 'with all the forces at her command'. To this Hitler passed the buck. He deflected with these words:

> It is very painful for me to think I might have to fight your country, but the decision does not rest with me. Please tell this to M. Daladier.[95]

Late that afternoon two unexpected developments occurred which, for Hitler, were catastrophal. The first shock was the signing of the Anglo–Polish Mutual Assistance Pact in London at 5:35 p.m. by Lord Halifax and Edward Raczyńsky, the Polish Ambassador to England. The pact was intended for a five-year duration and officially turned Chamberlain's one-sided pledge of military assistance to Poland of 31 March into a bilateral agreement:

> Agreement of Mutual Assistance between the United Kingdom and Poland
>
> The Government of the United Kingdom of Great Britain and Northern Ireland and the Polish Government:
>
> Desiring to place on a permanent basis the collaboration between their respective countries resulting from the assurances of mutual assistance of a defensive character which they have already exchanged:
>
> Have resolved to conclude an Agreement for that purpose and ... have agreed on the following provisions:
>
> ARTICLE 1
>
> Should one of the Contracting Parties become engaged in hostilities with a European Power in consequence of aggression by the latter against that Contracting Party, the other Contracting Party will at once give the Contracting Party engaged in hostilities all the support and assistance in its power.[96]

The second setback for Hitler was a cautious letter from Mussolini which reached him at approximately 6 p.m., roughly around the time he learned of the Anglo–Polish pact. In the opening points, Mussolini shared his opinion of the German–Russian pact and assessed the political advantages derived therefrom:

> FÜHRER:
>
> I am replying to your letter which has just been delivered to me by Ambassador von Mackensen.
>
> 1. Concerning the agreement with Russia, I approve of it completely. His Excellency Göring will tell you that in the discussions which I had with him since last April, I affirmed that a *rapprochement* between Germany and Russia was necessary to prevent encirclement by the democracies.
>
> 2. I consider it useful to try to avoid a break or a cooling off in relations with Japan, since that would result in a *rapprochement* between Japan and the democratic States. I have telegraphed to Tokyo to this effect and it appears that, the first surprise having been overcome, a better spirit prevails in public opinion there.
>
> 3. The Moscow treaty blockades Romania and may alter the position of Turkey, who has accepted the English loans but has not yet signed the treaty of alliance. A new attitude on the part of Turkey would upset all the strategic plans of the French and English in the Eastern Mediterranean.
>
> 4. Concerning Poland, I have complete understanding for the German position and for the fact that such a tense situation cannot continue indefinitely.

Then Mussolini came to the crux of the matter. In tactful language, Mussolini informed Hitler that in the event of war with the Anglo–French democracies, Italy would not, at this time, be able to enter the war on Germany's side due to a lack of preparedness on the part of the Italian Armed Forces:

> 5. As for the *practical* attitude of Italy, in case of a military action, my point of view is as follows:

> If Germany attacks Poland and the conflict remains localized, Italy will afford Germany every form of political and economic assistance which is requested of her.
>
> If Poland attacks and her allies [Britain and France] open a counter attack against Germany, I inform you in advance that it will be opportune for me not to take the *initiative* in military operations in view of the *present* state of Italian war preparations, of which we have repeatedly and in good time informed you, Führer, and Herr von Ribbentrop.
>
> Our intervention can, nevertheless, take place at once if Germany delivers to us immediately the military supplies and the raw materials to resist the attack which the French and English would predominantly direct against us.
>
> At our meetings, the war was envisaged for after 1942, and by that time I would have been ready on land, on sea, and in the air, according to the plans which had been concerted.
>
> I am furthermore of the opinion that the purely military measures which have already been taken, and other measures to be taken later, will immobilize, in Europe and Africa, considerable French and British forces.
>
> I consider it my bounden duty as a loyal friend to tell you the whole truth and inform you beforehand about the real situation. Not to do so might have unpleasant consequences for us all. This is my view, and since within a short time I must summon the highest governmental bodies, I beg of you to let me know yours.
>
> MUSSOLINI[97]

Taken aback by both the new Anglo–Polish pact and Mussolini's eleventh hour defection, Hitler had to pause and reassess the political situation. In a flash, the whole European state of affairs had been radically altered. Of these two major reversals, however, it was the Anglo–Polish mutual assistance agreement which weighed more heavily on Hitler than the fact that his Axis partner had weaseled out of his binding commitment. Hitler summoned General Keitel before him and ordered that the attack on Poland, set for 26 August at 4:30 a.m., was to be cancelled immediately. Considerable efforts were made by frantic officers to recall German Army units, which had already begun to advance to the Polish border for the imminent invasion. According to the German Naval Register, the attack on Poland (Case White), which was already in its early stages, was to be halted at 22:30 hours due to 'changed political conditions'.

Thoroughly vexed by Mussolini's backpedalling, Hitler responded to his Italian ally's last message with a short communication. It was transmitted by Ribbentrop to Mackensen at 7:40 p.m. and brought to Mussolini at half-past nine. Hitler asked Mussolini which particular 'implements of war and raw materials' Italy would need, and when, in order to be able to militarily assist the Reich in case of a general war:

> DUCE:
>
> You have informed me that you can enter a major European conflict only if Germany supplies you at once with implements of war and raw materials in order to resist the attack which the French and British would launch predominantly against you. I would ask you to inform me what implements of war and raw materials you require and within what time, so that I may be in a position to judge whether and to what extent I can fulfill your demands for implements of war and raw materials.
>
> Furthermore, I thank you heartily for Italy's military measures, of which I have been acquainted in the meantime and which I already regard as a great relief.
>
> ADOLF HITLER[98]

On 25 August, the Dominion of Canada began a partial mobilization of its armed forces in anticipation of war. That night, at precisely 8:37 p.m., Prime Minister Mackenzie King sent a personal telegram to Hitler. He had already submitted 'a similar appeal to Rome' for Mussolini's consideration. As can be seen, the dispatch of grave telegrams urging restraint and conciliation during this last week of peace was not yet over:

> To Herr Hitler, Reichsführer, from W. L. M. King, Prime Minister of Canada.
>
> The people of Canada are of one mind that there is no international problem which cannot be settled by conference and negotiation. They equally believe that force is not a substitute for reason, and that an appeal to force as a means of adjusting international differences defeats rather than furthers the ends of justice. They are prepared to join their authority and power to that of their fellow nations in the British Commonwealth in seeking a just and equitable settlement of the great problems with which the nations are faced.
>
> On behalf of the Canadian people, but equally in the interests of the whole of humanity, I join with those from other countries and Powers who have appealed to you in the firm hope that your great power and [authority] will be used to prevent the impending catastrophe by having recourse to every possible peaceful means to effect the solution of the momentous issues of this period of transition and change in world affairs.
>
> W. L. Mackenzie King.[99]

To the German Consul General in Ottawa, Dr. Erich Windels, King stated that Canada's entire Cabinet, in total accord with public sentiment, 'was unanimously resolved to enter immediately into a war in which France and Britain were involved'. King's telegram was received the next morning at the Foreign Ministry at 7:50 a.m., and when it was brought to Hitler's attention, he must have dismissed it as impertinent and inconsequential. After all, Hitler must have thought, of what business were the affairs of Central and Eastern Europe to a sparsely-populated, distant British dominion?

On 26 August, Mussolini's latest letter to Hitler was communicated to Berlin by telephone at 12:10 p.m. Approximately an hour later it was in Hitler's hands, delivered by Ambassador Attolico with alacrity. As seen below, Mussolini's requirements for Italian participation in a general war were tremendous to the point of being absurd. In total, Mussolini insisted on 16 million tons of coal, steel, petroleum, and timber, plus another million tons or so of other supplies. Ciano wryly recorded in his diary that the list was 'enough to kill a bull—if a bull could read it'. And on top of everything else, these excessive demands had to be met forthwith. 'All material', Attolico informed Hitler (on his own initiative and without Mussolini's authorization), 'must be in Italy *before* the beginning of hostilities':

> FÜHRER:
>
> I called a meeting this morning of the Chiefs of the General Staff of the Army, the Navy, and the Air Force, at which Minister Ciano and the Minister of Communications were also present, and this is the minimum required by the Italian Armed Forces to sustain a war lasting *twelve months* apart from what we have already:
>
> Coal for gas and metallurgy—6 million tons; Steel—2 million tons; Petroleum—7 million tons; Timber—1 million tons; Copper—150,000 tons; Sodium Nitrate—220,000 tons; Potassium Salts—70,000 tons; Colophony—25,000 tons; Rubber—22,000 tons; Methylbenzol—18,000 tons; Turpentine—6,000 tons; Lead—10,000 tons; Tin—7,000 tons; Nickel—5,000 tons; Molybdenum—600 tons; Tungsten—600 tons; Zirconium—20 tons; Titanium—400 tons....
>
> Apart from all the raw materials which are mentioned above, you are aware that all our war industries are situated in the Turin–Genoa–Milan–Savona quadrilateral and along the shores of the Tyrrhenian Sea, that is half an hour's flight from Corsica. The immediate dispatch of 150 90 mm. batteries and the appropriate ammunition is necessary for the protection of these industrial plants, the destruction of which could literally paralyze our war effort....

> It is my duty to tell you that unless I am certain of receiving these supplies, the sacrifices I should call on the Italian people to make ... could well be in vain and could compromise your cause along with my own.[100]

Hitler swiftly composed a reply to Mussolini's letter, which the latter received shortly after 5 p.m. In meticulous detail Hitler explained to Mussolini which provisions Germany would be able to fulfill and when. Germany was prepared to provide the requisite iron, coal, and lumber in full. Thirty 4-gun anti-aircraft batteries could be contributed without delay, another thirty after the end of the Polish campaign, and another thirty within a year's time. As for the other items, they could either be supplied in part or not at all. However, Hitler regarded the 'immediate delivery of all the material before the outbreak of war ... as impossible ... purely for reasons of organization and for technical reasons'. Instead, he asked Mussolini to undermine the Western Powers with propaganda and to distract them with spectacles of Italian martial might (which would naturally have the effect of giving the Anglo–French democracies an exaggerated impression of Italian strength). Lastly, Hitler shared his confident opinion that Germany, due the Nazi–Soviet Pact and her overall military supremacy, could withstand any Anglo–French assault:

> In these circumstances, Duce, I understand your position, and would only ask you to try to achieve the pinning down of Anglo–French forces by active propaganda and suitable military demonstrations such as you have already proposed to me. As neither France nor Britain can achieve any decisive successes in the West, and as Germany, as a result of the Agreement with Russia, will have all her forces free in the East after the defeat of Poland, and as air supremacy is undoubtedly on our side, I do not shrink from solving the Eastern question even at the risk of complications in the West.[101]

That afternoon Hitler received Coulondre at the Reich Chancellery. Coulondre had brought with him a telegram from Daladier, which was a response to Hitler's heated comments of the previous day. Daladier assured Hitler of his pacific intentions towards the Reich, but warned that should Germany attack Poland, France was determined to honour her commitments to Poland:

> You cannot doubt my sentiments towards Germany, nor France's peaceful sentiments towards your nation. No Frenchman has ever done more than I have to strengthen between our two peoples not merely

> peace, but a sincere co-operation in their own interest as well as in that of Europe and the world.
>
> Unless you attribute to the French people a conception of national honour less high than that which I myself recognize in the German people, you cannot doubt, either, that France will be true to her solemn promises to other nations, such as Poland …

Daladier urged Hitler to make a final diplomatic attempt to come to an agreement with Poland 'in connection with the Danzig questions' to preserve the peace. This could be done without compromising German integrity. He, the French Prime Minister, would do everything in his power to help bring this about:

> In so serious an hour I sincerely believe that no man endowed with human feelings could understand that a war of destruction should be allowed to break out without a last attempt at a pacific adjustment between Germany and Poland. Your will for peace may be exercised in all confidence in this direction without the slightest derogation from your sense of German honour. As for myself, the Head of the French Government, concerned only for harmony between the French people and the German people and, on the other hand, united to Poland by bonds of friendship and by their pledged word, I am ready to make all the efforts that an honest man can make in order to ensure the success of this attempt.

Daladier ended his letter on a personal note, addressing Hitler man to man. As a non-commissioned officer on the Western Front in the Great War (and later a lieutenant and captain), he too knew the carnage of war firsthand, and he warned that the end result would be a lose-lose scenario for both Germany and France:

> Like myself, you were a soldier in the last war. You realize, as I do, how a people's memory retains for ever a horror and condemnation of the disasters of war, whatever may be the result. The conception which I have been able to form of your eminent role as leader of the German people, to guide them along the paths of peace towards the full accomplishment of their mission in the common work of civilization, prompts me to ask you for a reply to this proposal. If the blood of France and that of Germany flows again, as it did twenty-five years ago, in a longer and even more murderous war, each of the two peoples will fight with confidence in its own victory, but the most certain victors will be the forces of destruction and barbarism.[102]

In the early evening Mussolini drafted yet another letter, which was telephoned in at 6:42 p.m. and rushed to Hitler at the Reich Chancellery. Mussolini first corrected Attolico's error and clarified that 'except for the anti-aircraft batteries', all the material he had requested 'was to be delivered in the course of 12 months', not immediately. Then, without beating around the bush, Mussolini confessed that after participating in two wars—in Spain and Ethiopia—Italy was seriously weakened and consequently would not be equal to the task of contending with the Western Powers in a general war. He expressed his regret at not being able to contribute to the imminent conflict at this time. Finally, Mussolini wrote that he personally preferred a diplomatic solution to the differences between the Germans and Poles, to war:

> FÜHRER:
>
> I believe that the misunderstanding into which Attolico involuntarily fell was cleared up immediately, in accordance with my instructions. That which I asked of you, except for the anti-aircraft batteries, was to be delivered in the course of twelve months. But even though the misunderstanding has been cleared up, it is evident that it is impossible for you to assist me materially in filling the large gaps which the wars in Ethiopia and Spain have made in Italian armaments.
>
> I will therefore adopt the attitude which you advise, at least during the initial phase of the conflict, thereby immobilizing the maximum Franco–British forces, as is already happening, while I shall speed up military preparations to the utmost possible extent.
>
> I leave you to imagine my state of mind in finding myself compelled by forces beyond my control not to afford you real solidarity at the moment of action.
>
> And it is also for this reason that I venture to insist anew, and not at all from considerations of a pacifist character foreign to my nature, but by reason of the interests of our two peoples and our two régimes, on the opportunity for a political solution, which I regard as still possible and such a one as will give full moral and material satisfaction to Germany.
>
> MUSSOLINI[103]

That evening Hitler wrote another letter to Mussolini. Sent by telegram shortly after midnight, it was delivered to the Duce at 9 a.m. Hitler had seemingly accepted that his Fascist ally would not throw in his lot at Germany's side in the forthcoming war. Hitler conveyed to Mussolini his understanding of the latter's decision to remain inactive under the circumstances (although privately it must have vexed him greatly), and expressed an optimistic outlook for the future:

DUCE:

I have received your communication on your final attitude. I respect the reasons and motives which led you to take this decision. In certain circumstances it can nevertheless work out well. In my opinion, however, the prerequisite is that, at least until the outbreak of the struggle, the world should have no idea of the attitude Italy intends to adopt. I therefore cordially request you to support my struggle psychologically with your press or by other means. I would also ask you, Duce, if you possibly can, by demonstrative military measures, at least to compel Britain and France to tie down certain of their forces, or at all events to leave them in uncertainty. But Duce, the most important thing is this: If, as I have said, it should come to a major war, the issue in the East will be decided before the two Western Powers can score a success. Then, this winter, at latest in the spring, I shall attack in the West with forces which will be at least equal to those of France and Britain. The blockade will have little effect, particularly because of the new circumstances prevailing in the East, and also thanks to my preparations for autarky. Its danger will not increase but diminish with the duration of the war. I must now ask a great favour of you, Duce. In this difficult struggle you and your people can best help me by sending me Italian workers, both for industrial and agricultural purposes. Should you later be compelled to intervene by the course of events, or find yourself after all in a position to do so, then the reinforced autarky of the Reich would be of the greatest importance to you too. In specially commending this request of mine to your generosity, I thank you for all the efforts you have made for our common cause.

ADOLF HITLER[104]

Arriving back in Berlin at 6:20 p.m., Dahlerus, Göring's informal envoy, got together with Göring to convey to him the details of a written message from Lord Halifax.[18*] It was aboard Göring's special train, speeding its way to the Luftwaffe base at Oranienburg some twenty miles from Berlin, that Dahlerus informed Göring of the specifics of Halifax's letter. In his memorandum dated 27 August, Dahlerus reported that Halifax's

18 * While in London earlier that day, after a long-distance talk with Göring, Dahlerus had consulted with Halifax at 11 a.m. He had convinced Halifax to pen a general note to Göring, who would hopefully 'use all his influence' as Hitler's number two man 'to induce a calmer atmosphere' in Germany. The correspondence contained an expression of the British Government's 'desire to find a satisfactory solution of the questions now causing anxiety' and highlighted that it was now 'vital to avoid further inflammation of the dangers in the local situation by continuance of frontier and minority incidents on either side'. Several days' time were requested in order to reach a peaceful solution.[105]

letter had 'moved him [Göring] very deeply'.[106] Evidently the Luftwaffe chief perceived its contents to be very significant, because he decided to bring it to Hitler's attention straightaway, in person.

At Göring's prompting, he and Dahlerus got off the train 'at the next station' and Dahlerus 'followed him in a car to Berlin'. The lights were out at the Reich Chancellery when they arrived at midnight. Göring was informed by a colonel that Hitler had already retired for the evening, and Dahlerus returned to his hotel, the Esplanade. However, Göring was adamant and had Hitler awakened. They spoke privately, and the Führer was sufficiently impressed. At 12:15 a.m. Dahlerus was collected from his hotel by two officers, driven to the Chancellery, and ushered into Hitler's presence. But Hitler completely disregarded Halifax's note, which Göring had considered so crucial, and proceeded instead to regale Dahlerus with a twenty-minute spiel on the difficulties he had faced since becoming Chancellor and his efforts in attempting to broker an agreement with England. During a momentary lull in Hitler's monologue, Dahlerus mentioned his days in Britain 'as a workman, as an engineer, and as a manager of industrial enterprises' and that he 'knew the English people well'. This interjection caught Hitler's attention at once, and he 'asked many questions about England and the English people'.[107]

Thereupon Hitler became agitated and he launched into a lengthy exposition on the technical superiority of each branch of the Reich's armed forces. When Hitler finally finished, Dahlerus replied that despite Germany's martial might, the Great War had clearly proven that the Allies were more powerful. The British Isles were the bedrock of the British Empire and were largely impervious to attack. To attempt to conquer them with a fleet only a fraction of the strength of the Royal Navy would be foolhardy. These words did not sit well with Hitler, and Dahlerus recounted the following outrageous scene:

> Hitler listened without interrupting me. I spoke slowly and quietly to avoid irritating him unnecessarily, since his mental equilibrium was patently unstable. He seemed to ponder what I said, but then suddenly got up, and becoming very excited and nervous, walked up and down saying, as though to himself, that Germany was irresistible and could defeat her adversaries by means of a rapid war. Suddenly he stopped in the middle of the room and stood there staring. His voice was blurred and his behaviour that of a completely abnormal person. He spoke in staccato phrases, and it was clear that his thoughts were concentrated on the tasks which awaited him in case of war.
>
> 'If there should be war, then I shall build U-boats, build U-boats, U-boats, U-boats, U-boats.' His voice became more indistinct and

> finally one could not follow him at all. Then he pulled himself together, raised his voice as though addressing a large audience and shrieked: 'I shall build airplanes, build airplanes, airplanes, airplanes, and I shall annihilate my enemies.' He seemed more like a phantom from a story book than a real person. I stared at him in amazement and turned to see how Göring was reacting, but he did not turn a hair.

When Hitler regained control of himself, there ensued this remarkable exchange:

> HITLER: Herr Dahlerus, you who know England so well, can you give me any reason for my perpetual failure to come to an agreement with her?
>
> DAHLERUS: Your Excellency, with my comprehensive knowledge of the English people, their mentality, and their attitude towards Germany, I must definitely assure you that I am absolutely convinced that these difficulties are founded on a lack of confidence in you personally and in your government.
>
> HITLER [dramatically clasping a hand to his chest]: Idiots! Have I ever told a lie in my life?[108]

At this point, Dahlerus requested further specific details of Hitler's previous proposals to Henderson. Göring obliged him by removing a page from an atlas and demarcating with a red pencil the territory which the German Government sought. After a further talk, it was ultimately decided that Dahlerus would return to England with another proposal consisting of six points for Chamberlain and Halifax. However, Göring refused to provide Dahlerus with a written copy, so Dahlerus had to memorize them:

1. Germany wanted an agreement or an alliance with England.

2. England was to help Germany in the annexation of Danzig and the Corridor [except a harbour reserved for Polish use. Poland would also receive a corridor to Gdynia, Gdynia itself, and sufficient adjacent territory].

3. Germany gave the assurance that it would guarantee Poland's boundaries.

4. An agreement should be reached on Germany's colonies [i.e. Germany's former colonies would be returned to her, or she would be commensurately compensated instead].

5. Adequate guarantees should be given for the treatment of German minorities.

6. Germany gave its word to defend the British Empire with the German Wehrmacht wherever it should be attacked.[109]

At 8 a.m. on 27 August, with the six-point German proposal uppermost on his mind, Dahlerus set off for London to confer with Chamberlain, Halifax, and Wilson at 10 Downing Street. They received him in the early afternoon. Dahlerus disclosed the six-point proposal to the British politicians. This proposal, which was about as fair an offer as the German Government was ever likely to make, was nonetheless rejected by the British after some deliberation. They believed that the Polish Government might possibly consent to cede Danzig to the Reich, so long as certain Polish rights to the Free City remained in force. But the British felt that the Poles would never relinquish the Polish Corridor and that they would go to war over it if necessary:

> The Prime Minister [Chamberlain] had told Dahlerus that if these were the German terms [the return of Danzig and the Polish Corridor to the Reich] he could see no prospect of a settlement, and that the Poles would rather fight than surrender the Corridor: he thought that the maximum the Poles could concede would be Danzig, subject to the retention of special Polish rights, and extra-territorial roads for Germany across the Corridor, subject to international guarantees.[110]

The upshot was that Dahlerus would meet with Hitler in Berlin and present him with a preliminary, informal response to his six-point proposal. He would then contact the British Government to inform them how the Führer had taken it. This was to be done before Henderson brought Hitler the official British memorandum on the evening of the 28th. The unofficial British stance, which Halifax imparted to Dahlerus, consisted of three items:

> *i*. Solemn assurance of desire for good understanding between G. and Gt.B. Not a single member of the Govt. who thinks different. *ii*. Gt.B. bound to honour her obligations to Poland. *iii*. German–Polish differences must be settled peacefully.[111]

In his post-war testimony at Nuremberg, Dahlerus gave his account of the unofficial British position:

> Naturally, Point 6, the offer to defend the British Empire, was rejected. Similarly, they did not want to have any discussion on the colonies as long as Germany was not demobilized. With regard to the Polish boundaries, they wanted these boundaries to be guaranteed by the five great powers: Russia, Germany, England, France, and Italy.
>
> Concerning the Corridor, they proposed that negotiations with Poland be undertaken immediately.
>
> With reference to the first point, England was willing in principle to come to an agreement with Germany.[112]

Hitler was preoccupied for much of the 27th preparing a lengthy reply to Daladier's earnest letter of the day before. He noted that the restoration of the Saarland to Germany, now accomplished, had put an end to the age-old Franco–German antagonism. The bitter feelings of the German *Volk* for the valorous French people, which had lasted for generations, were no more:

> I understand the misgivings which you express. I, too, have never overlooked the high obligations laid on those who are in charge of the fate of peoples. As an old front-line soldier, I know, as you do, the horrors of war. This conviction and this knowledge have led me, too, to strive honourably to remove all subjects of dispute between our two peoples. I assured the French nation quite openly of one thing, that the condition for this was the return of the Saar Territory. When this had been returned, I at once solemnly affirmed my renunciation of any further claims whatsoever which might affect France. The German people have approved this attitude of mine. As you were able to convince yourself on your last visit here, conscious of their own attitude, they did not and do not feel any ill-will, much less hatred, for their erstwhile gallant foe.

In addition, with the construction of the West Wall, Germany's border in the West was set for all time. Alsace and Lorraine, the ex-German provinces, had been renounced permanently. There was therefore no cause for any conflict to presently exist between the Germans and French:

> The construction of the great fortifications in the West, which swallowed and continues to swallow many thousands of millions, represents for Germany both a deed of acceptance and a delimitation of the final Reich frontier. The German nation has thus renounced two provinces [Alsace–Lorraine], which once were part of the old German Reich, which were conquered later at much cost in bloodshed and which, finally, were defended at still greater cost in bloodshed.... I had thought that by this

> renunciation and by this attitude I had eliminated every conceivable subject of dispute between our two peoples which might have led to a repetition of the tragedy of 1914–1918.

Hitler appealed to Daladier's sense of honour, asking the French statesman to put himself in his unenviable position with regard to the loss of German territory in Eastern Europe due to the Versailles Treaty:

> ... Your Excellency must always grant me this: Revision had to come. The Versailles Dictate was intolerable. No Frenchman of honour, certainly not you yourself, Monsieur Daladier, would, in a like situation, have acted other than I did.... May I now ask, Monsieur Daladier, how you, as a Frenchman, would act if, as a result of the unfortunate outcome of a gallant struggle, one of your provinces were cut off by a corridor occupied by a foreign Power, a great city—let us say Marseilles—were prevented from professing allegiance to France, and the Frenchmen living in precisely this region were persecuted, beaten, ill-treated, even bestially murdered? You are a Frenchman, Monsieur Daladier, so I know how you would act. I am a German, Monsieur Daladier. Do not doubt my sense of honour or my consciousness of my duty to act in just the same way.

Hitler reasoned that in the final analysis, Germany could not abandon her *Volksgenossen* in Danzig, nor tolerate their mistreatment by the Poles, and Danzig and the Polish Corridor had to be restored to the Reich:

> ... I only ask you to understand that it is impossible for a nation of honour to renounce nearly two million people and see them being ill-treated on its own frontiers. I have therefore put forward a clear demand: Danzig and the Corridor must come back to Germany. The Macedonian conditions on our Eastern frontier must be removed. I can see no way of inducing Poland to adopt a peaceful solution as, under the protection of her [Anglo–French] guarantees, she now feels unassailable. I would, however, despair of an honourable future for my people if, in such circumstances, we were not determined to solve the problem one way or another.[113]

Mussolini composed another short message to Hitler, which was called in at 4:30 p.m. Ambassador Mackensen received it the following day. Mussolini assured Hitler that the Western Powers would not learn of Italy's military stance (i.e. non-participation). In a spurious show of strength, Italy had amassed numerous divisions along her border with

France. This ploy would keep a substantial amount of Anglo–French forces preoccupied and unsure of Italian intentions:

> The world does not and will not know before the outbreak of hostilities what the attitude of Italy is, and will learn instead that Italy has concentrated her forces towards the frontiers of the great democracies. On the French frontiers I have actually concentrated seventeen divisions, plus twenty-seven Alpini battalions, plus the frontier guards. Two new divisions are proceeding to Libya—a weak point in our strategic dispositions—and these will bring up the number of metropolitan divisions to six, plus four of Libyan Arabs. These measures are more than a demonstration; they will leave the French and British in a state of uncertainty, and will confront them with a disposition of forces at least equal to theirs.

The use of mass media and propaganda, Mussolini averred, would be used to impress upon the Anglo–French democracies the unshakable unity between Fascist Italy and Nazi Germany:

> All that can be done from the psychological point of view to underline Italian–German solidarity will be intensified by press, radio, cinema and through propaganda.

Mussolini also informed Hitler that he was ready to dispatch to the Reich 'the greatest possible number of workers for your industries and agriculture' and expressed his desire to 'keep in closest contact' with Hitler 'in order to coordinate the action' of both Axis nations.[114]

That evening, Dahlerus returned to Berlin at 11 p.m. and met with Göring to deliver to him the informal British response to the German six points, which Göring found unfavourable. Nevertheless, Göring conveyed the British reply to Hitler at once, albeit reluctantly (Göring hated to be the bearer of negative news to the Führer), and telephoned Dahlerus after 1 a.m. to inform him that Hitler would agree to it if Ambassador Henderson's official offer matched it.

At 10:30 p.m. on 28 August, Henderson again consulted with Hitler at the Reich Chancellery. Ribbentrop was also present at the interview. There, Henderson gave Hitler a memorandum from the British Government containing eight points. It was a reply to Hitler's offer of 25 August, given to Henderson, in which Hitler had proposed an arrangement with Britain much along the lines of the Nazi–Soviet Pact. In that deal the Führer had been prepared 'to pledge himself personally' for the British Empire's 'continued existence' and 'to commit the power of the German Reich for this'. Hitler perused the document, whereupon Henderson expatiated on each individual point 'without adding anything essentially new to the contents'.[115] The eight points were:

1. The British Government reciprocated the German Government's 'desire' to reach 'a complete and lasting understanding';

2. The British Government would be 'fully prepared' to enter into discussions for a 'general understanding' with the German Government 'if the differences between Germany and Poland' were resolved peaceably;

3. The British Government agreed that first and foremost Germany and Poland had to settle their differences; this was a necessary precondition to any Anglo–German agreement which might ensue. Again the British Government underscored the fact that: (a) they were obligated to assist Poland; (b) they intended to do so; and (c) under no circumstances could the British Government consent to a German–Polish settlement that violated Poland's independence.

4. The British Government held the view that among the terms agreed upon by German and Poland should be included 'the safeguarding of Poland's essential interests', which Hitler had himself acknowledged in his two-hour speech of 28 April. It was also necessary for the German Government to accept the stipulation that any German–Polish settlement 'would be guaranteed by other Powers'—in other words, it would be an 'international guarantee'. Thereafter, the British Government would be ready to enter into negotiations with the German Government for a 'wider and more complete understanding' between them.

5. The British Government were in accord with Hitler that the maltreatment of ethnic German minorities in Poland was one of the most serious aggravating factors in present German–Polish relations. Violent 'frontier incidents' and 'inflammatory propaganda' were also 'a constant danger to peace'. Therefore it was critical that these excesses 'be promptly and rigidly suppressed'. Reports of such occurrences that were unsubstantiated should be stifled to prevent needless antagonism.

6. Its military obligations to Poland notwithstanding, the British Government was willing to use its not inconsiderable influence to help bring about an amicable settlement between the Germans and Poles.

7. The British Government felt it 'unnecessary' to emphasize the benefits of a peaceful resolution to one involving the use of force. Once the German and Polish Governments reached a satisfactory agreement by non-violent means, it would be possible to 'transition' from rearmament to 'peaceful trade' in accordance with Hitler's earlier reference to 'a limitation of armaments'.

8. The British Government were of the opinion that a 'just settlement' of the German–Polish conflict might lead to 'world peace'. But should Germany and Poland go to war, it would eliminate any possibility of an Anglo–German friendship and instead trigger a war between them. Such a conflict might even be global in scale, which would be a disaster of the greatest magnitude.[116]

Henderson then repeated the British Government's original position, which had not changed. It was not Britain's intention to 'destroy Germany'. Germany was entitled to her 'vital rights'. But the British Government had entered into a mutual assistance pact with Poland; it had guaranteed to help preserve the independence of Poland with its word of honour, and this covenant could not be broken. The English, especially Chamberlain, were keen to arrive at a mutually beneficial arrangement with Germany. But Germany, on her part, had to settle her differences with Poland peaceably, and this was not negotiable. Hitler countered that he had initially been very willing to resolve the Danzig matter with the Polish Government diplomatically. But the 'provocative and insolent' Poles, buttressed by English promises of military aid (first on 31 March and most recently on 25 August), were not amenable to reason. Hitler alleged that repressive actions against ethnic German minorities in Poland were taking place on a daily basis, that these atrocities were growing in viciousness and scale, and that 'all this was a matter of indifference to Britain'.

Henderson took umbrage at this comment, which he interpreted as being directed at himself. He shot back that ever since assuming the Ambassadorship in Berlin two years earlier, he had made every conceivable effort 'to prevent war and bloodshed'. It was the Führer, Henderson, asserted, who would now decide 'between war and peace'. To Henderson's last rejoinder, Hitler retorted that 'this was not a correct picture of the situation'. As he saw it, he had two options: he could either uphold the rights of his *Volk*, or sacrifice them in the course of obtaining an Anglo–German alliance. As Führer of the Greater German Reich, his allegiance was to his *Volk*; they were his first priority, and he could not forsake them. Germany was Continental Europe's most dynamic Power and could not be held to the same standard as Poland, which—as far as Hitler was concerned—was a lesser nation. Germany would not allow herself to be put in a position, where, as during the Sudeten crisis, England was to choose between friendship with Germany or Czechoslovakia. Before the meeting's end, Hitler again expounded on his ongoing attempts to establish a profitable alliance with Britain. This had been one of his chief political aims for nearly two decades, as evidenced by his manifesto. But Britain had rejected his overtures repeatedly over the years. Consequently, he had been left with no alternative but to enter into a partnership with the U.S.S.R., even though this was contrary to his 'original intentions'. But in spite of all, Hitler affirmed that he still sought an understanding with Britain, and he 'expressed the sincere hope' that Britain would not fail to seize this final opportunity to join forces with the Reich.[117]

In a subsequent report (dated 30 August) by Dahlerus to Chamberlain about his meeting with Göring on 29 August at 10:30 a.m., Dahlerus noted Göring's statement that the eight-point British note of 28 August 'had caused satisfaction and that Hitler was starting at midday to draft a reply to His Majesty's Government'.[118] On that occasion, Göring had gripped his hand, shaken it vigorously, and joyously proclaimed, 'We shall have peace; peace is assured!'[119] Dahlerus also noted Göring's further statement, made at 6:30 p.m., that Hitler's reply 'was so clear that it was not necessary to communicate with His Majesty's Government in regard to its wording'.[120]

Mussolini penned another letter to Hitler, which was conveyed by telephone to Mackensen in Berlin at 4:40 p.m. Mussolini raised the subject of Henderson's eight-point proposal of the day before, with which he was familiar on account of a recent conversation between Ribbentrop and Attolico. Mussolini stated that in his view, the British proposals of 28 August were satisfactory and would grant to Germany that which she sought, without the need to resort to arms. He opined that to accept the proposals would not detract in the slightest from Germany's prior notable accomplishments, and he ended the letter with yet another obsequious assurance of his loyalty to Hitler:

> FÜHRER:
>
> Ambassador Attolico informs me that he has learned from von Ribbentrop that you will today be studying the [eight-point] British Note, with which I am acquainted, and will be making your decisions. As a true friend of yourself and the German people I wish to tell you that in my opinion the British proposals contain the prerequisites and factors for reaching a solution favourable to Germany in all the problems which concern her. With this solution the rhythm of your splendid

achievements will not be disturbed and you will add a fresh indisputable success to those you have already obtained. You are aware that at this difficult moment the guiding principles of my actions have been defined in agreement with you. Please regard my appeal therefore as another proof of my constant solidarity.

MUSSOLINI[121]

That evening, Hitler gave his response to the British Government's eight-point note of 28 August in the form of a memorandum to Henderson.[19*] Ribbentrop was again present at the meeting, which began at 7:15 p.m. Hitler began by reiterating once again the German Government's desire for 'German–British understanding, co-operation, and friendship'. He was also pleased with the sentiments expressed in this regard by the British Government in their eight-point note, especially those pertaining to an amelioration and extension of Anglo–German relations. However, an understanding of this kind would be impossible if it could only be brought about by 'a renunciation of vital German interests', for this would encroach 'upon the national dignity and honour' of the German *Volk*. Hitler took cognizance of the fact that the British Government believed the precondition for a German–British understanding was 'the removal of German–Polish tension'. Next, Hitler recapitulated the unreceptive and hostile attitude of the Polish Government. Hitler complained that the Polish Government had spurned the Reich's modest proposals, taken unwarranted 'military measures', and infringed upon Danzig with threatening ultimata and the imposition of a restrictive customs policy. Moreover, Hitler alleged, the Polish Government was guilty of the oppression of *Volksdeutsche* in Poland, including their murder in large numbers and their expulsion under the harshest and most unjust circumstances.

For Germany, Hitler asserted, this was intolerable. The Reich could not sit idly by and permit such an egregious 'condition of affairs' to continue unchecked. What the German Government sought were Danzig and the Polish Corridor, plus a solid assurance that the rights of ethnic Germans under Polish rule would be respected. Unfortunately, contrary to the British Government's way of thinking, these legitimate demands, Hitler claimed, could not be obtained through diplomacy. The obstinate Poles had proven this by their brusque and senseless rejection of reasonable

19 * Afterwards, in a telegram to Halifax received in London at 10:25 p.m., Henderson described Hitler that evening as having been 'far less reasonable than yesterday'. Henderson noted the reason for this as being a 'Press announcement ... that five more Germans had been killed in Poland and news of Polish mobilization'.[122]

German proposals and by their military measures. Hitler summarized the British Government's position, which—as he saw it—was twofold: first, that any possibility of an armed conflict between Germany and Poland 'be eliminated as quickly as possible by direct negotiation'; and second, that Poland's independence should be assured 'in the economic and political spheres by means of international guarantees'. To the likelihood of fulfilling these two items, the German Government was 'skeptical'. That being said, the German Government was willing 'to enter into direct negotiations' per the British Government's wishes. This act of good will by the Reich Government should serve to prove to the British Government Germany's genuine desire for a permanent Anglo–German collaboration. However, due to the recently concluded Nazi–Soviet Pact, any 'territorial rearrangement in Poland' could not be guaranteed by Germany without the express input and sanction of the U.S.S.R., whose interests had to be taken into consideration.

Hitler ended the memorandum with a mendacious pronouncement: he averred that Germany had never entertained the notion of 'attacking Poland's vital interests or questioning the existence of an independent Polish State'. The German Government therefore, in line with Britain's prerequisites for an Anglo–German alliance, consented to receive in Berlin 'a Polish emissary with full powers'. This plenipotentiary was expected to arrive the very next day, 30 August, and Hitler advised that Germany's proposals to the Polish emissary would be drafted at once and made available to the British Government 'if possible ... before the arrival of the Polish negotiator'.[123]

Henderson perused the memorandum without saying a word. Hitler and Ribbentrop waited patiently, their eyes on him. But once Henderson reached the paragraph which stipulated that 'the German Government counted upon the arrival in Berlin of a Polish emissary with full powers on Wednesday, 30th August,' he observed 'that this phrase sounded very much like an ultimatum ("*hatte den Klang eines Ultimatums*")'. Henderson recognized it at once for what it was: 'a case of the "dictate" and "memorandum" of Godesberg over again'. Both Hitler and Ribbentrop 'strenuously and heatedly' denied this allegation. Hitler explicated that 'this sentence merely emphasized the urgency of the moment, not only on account of the risk of incidents when two mobilized armies were standing opposite one another but also when Germans were being massacred in Poland'.[124]

Hitler's latest proposal was an especially underhanded ploy, for it was obvious that a lone Polish plenipotentiary at the Reich Chancellery, surrounded by Nazi leaders, might conceivably find himself browbeaten into submission like Schuschnigg in Vienna and Hácha in Prague. This time around, however, the British Government did not take the bait.

In his report to Halifax, which was received in London the next day at 4:20 a.m., Henderson recalled Hitler's bitter accusation at this point: that he (Henderson) and the British Government 'did not care a row of pins whether Germans were slaughtered in Poland or not'. This offensive remark was too much for Henderson, who felt that it impugned both his own and British honour, and he roared at Hitler that he 'would not listen to such language from him or anybody'.[125] The rest of the conversation between them, Henderson wrote, 'was of a somewhat stormy character'. Hitler concluded with a tirade on his sincere efforts 'to win Britain's friendship, of his respect for the British Empire, and of his liking for Englishmen generally'. Henderson noted that Hitler simply could not understand why Nazism was 'repugnant' to the British conception of 'individual and national freedom and liberty'. He added:

> He [Hitler] failed to realize ... why he should not be allowed a free hand in Central and Eastern Europe to subjugate smaller and, as he regards them, inferior peoples to superior German rule and culture. He believed he could buy British acquiescence in his own extensive schemes by offers of alliance with, and guarantees for, the British Empire. Such preliminary acquiescence was indispensable to the success of his ambitions, and he worked unceasingly to secure it. His great mistake was his complete failure to understand the British sense of morality, humanity, and freedom.

When Henderson departed the Reich Chancellery that evening, he was 'filled with the gloomiest forebodings'. Henderson recalled that when he had objected to the deadline of little more than one day for the arrival of a Polish negotiator, Hitler had replied that his generals 'were pressing for a decision' to be made at once:

> 'My soldiers', he said, 'are asking me "Yes" or "No".' His army and his air force were ready to strike and had been since 25th August. They were telling him that one week had already been lost, and that they could not afford to lose another, lest the rainy season in Poland be added to their enemies.[126]

At 11:30 p.m. Dahlerus again conferred with Göring, this time at the latter's residence. Göring had just returned from a discussion with Hitler and had a copy of the German reply (the memorandum given to Henderson earlier that evening) in his possession. Dahlerus inquired of Göring why the German Government had expressed its 'reluctance' to negotiate with the Poles. Göring explained that the German Government only wanted to highlight the fact that 'they were not optimistic as to a successful result'. Thereupon Göring, while relating a recent incident 'in which five Germans had been shot [by the Poles] while trying to cross a river', became very worked up. He railed against the Poles and told Dahlerus 'that if it had not been for the receipt of the British reply [the eight-point British Note of 28 August] there would have been war that morning'. But Göring soon composed himself and informed Dahlerus of Hitler's latest terms: first and foremost, the cession of Danzig to the Reich. This was non-negotiable. As to the Polish Corridor, a plebiscite would be held to determine its fate. If the results were a Polish majority, Germany would agree to settle for an intersecting route across it. Should there be a German majority, the Reich would agree to grant the Poles two corridors, 'one to Gdynia and one to Danzig'. The vote would be held along the lines of the Saar plebiscite of 1935.[127] Acceding to Göring's request, Dahlerus undertook to return to London straightaway to convey to the British Government that Hitler still sought a peaceful understanding with England, and that he had already begun drafting a new proposal for the Polish Government.

Also on the 29th, Beck ordered the mobilization of the Polish Armed Forces, but the British and French Governments persuaded him to rescind the order, and it was stopped. On 30 August, Marshal Śmigły-Rydz declared that Polish forces had mobilized. Once again the order was cancelled due to French intervention. Even at this late date the French Government thought a diplomatic solution might yet be possible. Little did they know that the bulk of Hitler's armies were already assembled at the Polish frontier, fully prepared for war.

At 2 a.m. on 30 August, Halifax wired to Henderson a terse note concerning the German proposal of the previous day:

> We shall give careful consideration to the German Government's reply, but it is of course unreasonable to expect that we can produce a Polish representative in Berlin today and the German Government must not expect this.
>
> It might be well for you at once to let this be known in proper quarters through appropriate channels.[128]

Also that morning, Hitler saw Albert Forster in Berlin, who had been summoned from Danzig to receive specific directions on the particulars of issuing new legislation for the incorporation of Danzig into Germany. (It will be remembered that District Leader Forster had illegally—i.e. contrary to the Constitution—taken over as State President of Danzig on 23 August.)

A telegram intended for Halifax was received in London at 10 a.m. from Howard Kennard, the British Ambassador to Poland. Kennard's outlook was pessimistic. He did not believe that the Polish Government would be inclined to dispatch Beck or another delegate to Berlin for negotiations with the Nazis. It would be best, Kennard felt, for any such talks to be held not in Germany or Poland but instead a neutral nation, or perhaps Italy. In Kennard's opinion, the chances for a German–Polish settlement were nil, particularly since the Poles could now count on Anglo–French military support and they refused to be coerced as the Austrians, Czechs, and Lithuanians had been:

1. I feel sure that it would be impossible to induce the Polish Government to send Colonel Beck or any other representative immediately to Berlin to discuss a settlement on the basis proposed by Herr Hitler. They would certainly sooner fight and perish rather than submit to such humiliation especially after the examples of Czechoslovakia, Lithuania, and Austria.

2. I would suggest that if negotiations are to be between equals it is essential that they should take place in some neutral country or even possibly in Italy, and that the basis for any negotiations should be some compromise between the clearly defined limits of the March proposals on the German side and *status quo* on the Polish side.

3. Considering that the Polish Government, standing alone and when they were largely unprepared for war, refused the March terms it would surely be impossible for them to agree to proposals which appear to go beyond the March terms now that they have Great Britain as their ally, France has confirmed her support, and world public opinion is clearly in favour of direct negotiations on equal terms and is behind Poland's resistance to a dictated settlement.[129]

Dahlerus had returned to London early that morning for a consultation with Chamberlain, Halifax, and Wilson, which began at 10:30 a.m. But Dahlerus soon learned that as far as the three Englishmen were concerned, neither Hitler nor Göring could be taken at their word. Both had proven time and time again to be expert dissimulators (although it may be said that Göring's efforts to preserve European peace appeared, on the surface at least, to be well-intentioned). Furthermore, the British trio were under the impression that Hitler intended to attack Poland shortly and would not be deterred. To their credit, the British politicians had not put any stock in Hitler's totally unreasonable proposal for a Polish negotiator to arrive in Berlin before midnight on 30 August.

From London, at 12:30 p.m., Dahlerus made a long-distance telephone call to Göring, who informed him that Hitler was in the process of 'drafting his proposals'. He could not be certain, Göring explained, but he believed the Führer would propose a plebiscite. As for the ethnic German minorities in Poland, Göring indicated that Hitler would propose that they 'should have the right to be evacuated if they so desire'; those who opted to stay 'should be released from military service and ... treated as Germans'. The same conditions would apply to the Poles in the Reich. Dahlerus then recommended to Göring that Hitler's new proposals be transmitted through Ambassador Lipski rather than have a Polish representative come to Berlin. Dahlerus noted that Göring seemed receptive to this suggestion. As to whether the proposals would be ready that evening, Göring declared that 'the Führer's on it'. In a second telephone call to Göring, the latter advised Dahlerus that Hitler's proposals were being drafted in the form of a *Diskussionsgrundlage* (Basis for discussion) and not a *Diktat*. However, Göring emphasized, the new proposals would have to be retrieved from Berlin by a Polish emissary as previously stipulated, and this condition was non-negotiable.[130] Thus little, if anything, had been achieved by Dahlerus in London this time around, and he flew back to Germany that night.

Halifax sent Henderson a further quick message at 2:45 p.m. in connection with the German proposal of 29 August. Henderson was instructed to advise Ribbentrop of the following:

> We are considering the German Note with all urgency and shall send an official reply later ...
>
> We are representing at Warsaw how vital it is to reinforce all instructions for the avoidance of frontier incidents and I would beg you to confirm similar instructions on the German side.
>
> I welcome the evidence in the exchanges of views which are taking place of that desire for Anglo–German understanding ...[131]

At 6:30 p.m. Henderson dispatched a telegram to Halifax in which he expressed his twofold view on why the Polish Government was unwilling to accept Hitler's proposals (conveyed through Ribbentrop) of March. These reasons were the German disposition of Slovakia and Memel, of which the Polish Government disapproved, and also the fact that the German Government's proposals regarding Danzig and the Corridor were peremptory in tone. He also stated his belief that a long-lasting peace between Germany and Poland would only materialize once Danzig was returned to the Reich, a connecting highway and railway line across the Polish Corridor linking Germany and East Prussia was established, and the *Volksdeutsche* in Poland were transferred to Germany. Lukewarm concessions or diplomatic half-measures would only prolong and exacerbate German–Polish tensions. Lastly, Henderson strongly recommended that at this point Poland agree to the German Government's recent offer of direct negotiation to settle the crisis:

> My conviction is that [the] Polish Government refused Herr Hitler's March demands less in view of their intrinsic merit than (*a*) because Germany double-crossed them over Slovakia and Memel, and (*b*) because they were put in [the] form of [an] ultimatum....
>
> If there is to be any genuine peace in future between Poland and her powerful neighbour, grievances of [the] latter which are not of Herr Hitler's making but national must be eliminated. In my opinion, in order to achieve this end [the] City of Danzig as distinct from [the] port must revert to Germany; there must be direct and extra-territorial communication between [the] Reich and East Prussia; and [the] German minority in Poland must be got rid of by means of some exchange of population. On no other basis can there ever be [a] genuine and lasting peace between the two countries. No diplomatic compromise has a hope of surviving indefinitely....
>
> In the meantime I can only urge once more [the] importance of Poland accepting at once [the] proposal for direct negotiation and thereby putting herself right in the eyes of the world.[132]

By evening the British Government had finished reviewing the German proposal of 29 August. At 6:50 p.m. Halifax sent Henderson a telegram about the German condition that a Polish plenipotentiary authorized to negotiate make himself available in Berlin. Not surprisingly, Halifax informed Henderson that the British Government 'cannot advise the Polish Government to comply with this procedure which is wholly unreasonable' and asked Henderson to 'suggest to the German Government that they adopt the normal procedure ... of inviting the Polish Ambassador to call and handing proposals to him for transmission to Warsaw and inviting suggestions as to the conduct of negotiations'.[133]

Henderson called on Ribbentrop at midnight on 30–31 August to relay to him the response of the British Government—a nine-point document—to the German proposal by Hitler of 29 August:

1. The British Government expressed their appreciation for the German Government's 'desire for an Anglo–German understanding'.

2. The British Government reiterated that they too sought to ameliorate German–British relations. However, under no circumstances could they permit the violation of Poland's independence in order to achieve this. Both German and Polish interests had to be preserved, for they were 'not incompatible'.

3. The British Government recognized that the German Government had agreed to initiate direct negotiations with the Polish Government.

4. The British Government took notice of the German Government's acceptance of the provision that any German–Polish resolution would be upheld by an international guarantee. The Powers involved—presumably the U.S.S.R. would be one of them—would be determined pending further discussion.

5. The British Government acknowledged the German Government's acceptance of Britain as a backer of Poland's sovereignty.

6. The British Government recognized that the German Government was in the process of preparing further proposals for a German–Polish settlement. These new proposals would be, of course, carefully evaluated to ensure their conformity with the British Government's requirements.

7. The British Government would advise the Polish Government immediately of the German Government's response, as time was of the essence.

8. The British Government was as concerned as Hitler about the fact that the German and Polish armies, both mobilized, presently stood 'face to face'. Owing to the gravity of the situation, the British Government therefore recommended that both Governments agree to refrain from any 'aggressive military movements' while they deliberated.

9. Lastly, the British Government urged that in the meantime 'a temporary *modus vivendi* might be arranged for Danzig' in order to minimize the possibility of further clashes likely to exacerbate German–Polish tensions.[134]

Henderson next proposed to take up the nine-point note with Hitler personally, but Ribbentrop declined the offer; he advised Henderson that he himself would do so. Henderson then brought up disturbing reports 'circulating to the effect that the Germans in Poland were committing acts of sabotage which would justify the strongest counter measures on the part of the Polish Government'. Ribbentrop leaped to his feet and angrily yelled that these were lies—'Polish propaganda'—which apparently had 'not failed in its effect on the British Government'. It was the Poles, Ribbentrop shouted, who had been murdering ethnic Germans; there were no fewer (he claimed) than two hundred such cases.

Thereupon Henderson too arose to confront Ribbentrop, and the meeting deteriorated into a tempestuous shouting match in which both diplomats took aggressive stances, glowered venomously at each other, and hurled furious exchanges.[135]

To Schmidt, the official interpreter, the confrontation was 'the stormiest I have ever experienced during my twenty-three years as interpreter'.[136] But eventually the two officials calmed themselves and they sat back down. Henderson asked Ribbentrop if the latest German proposals for the Polish Government were ready. If they were, he would be pleased to receive them. To this, Ribbentrop made two comments. The first was that 'so far British mediation had produced only one definite result, namely, Polish general mobilization'; and the second was that 'Germany had expected a Polish representative to arrive today [30 August]'. Ribbentrop added that the time limit given had not been an ultimatum to the Poles, 'but, as the Führer had already explained the day before, a practical proposal dictated by the requirements of present circumstances'. It was now past midnight, Ribbentrop complained, and 'Germany has heard nothing from the Poles'. Therefore, the German proposals had expired. Nevertheless, for Henderson's benefit and to establish for the record Germany's genuine desire for peace, he would disclose its contents.[137] Ribbentrop then read aloud the articles of the sixteen-point proposal for a German–Polish settlement (see Appendix M). It was, in contrast to Hitler's prior demands, surprisingly moderate and not unfair. Danzig was to be incorporated into the Reich; Poland would retain the Kashubian port city of Gdynia; the Polish Corridor would either be ceded to Germany or remain a part of Poland, depending on the result of a plebiscite to be held not 'before a period of twelve months has elapsed'; an 'extraterritorial road and railway connection' across the Polish Corridor would be granted to whichever country lost the plebiscite; if the Polish Corridor reverted back to Germany, the Reich Government would 'arrange ... an exchange of population'; and both nations would 'mutually agree to safeguard' the rights of German minorities in Poland and Polish minorities in Germany respectively.[138] However, Ribbentrop deliberately read the sixteen-point proposal so quickly and so brusquely—in German—that Henderson found his 'jabber of words' (as he later put it) almost entirely incomprehensible. And when Henderson requested the text of the sixteen-point proposal, Ribbentrop turned him down outright. In his memoirs, Henderson recalled the offensive manner in which Ribbentrop had presented the sixteen-point proposal to him:

> ... he [Ribbentrop] produced a lengthy document which he read out to me in German or rather gabbled through to me as fast as he could,

> in a tone of the utmost scorn and annoyance. Of the sixteen articles in it I was able to gather the gist of six or seven, but it would have been quite impossible to guarantee even the comparative accuracy of these without a careful study of the text itself. Herr von Ribbentrop, who always mistook rudeness for strength, refused categorically; threw the document with a contemptuous gesture on the table; and said that it was now out of date since no Polish emissary had arrived at Berlin by midnight.[139]

Henderson then made an observation regarding Ribbentrop's declaration that the failure of a Polish delegate to reach Berlin by midnight on the 30th invalidated the sixteen-point proposal: he pointed out that this would seemingly indicate that the deadline given was indeed an ultimatum. Ribbentrop once more emphatically denied this interpretation and cited Hitler's explanation of 29 August that speed was crucial since 'two mobilized armies were facing each other within firing range' and an impulsive act at the frontier by either side might inadvertently provoke a bloody clash. Finally, Henderson suggested that Ribbentrop receive Lipski and give him the sixteen-point proposal for the Polish Government's consideration, but Ribbentrop rejected this option out of hand. The Führer, Ribbentrop stated, would decide the matter.[140]

At 12:30 a.m. on 31 August, Dahlerus arrived at Luftwaffe headquarters. He had just flown in from London a half-hour ago. Göring advised Dahlerus that Ribbentrop, on Hitler's instructions, had disclosed to Henderson the terms of a sixteen-point proposal, which Göring characterized as 'fair and workable'. This was good news to Dahlerus, but when he telephoned the British Embassy for confirmation, to his dismay he was informed of how Ribbentrop had jabbered the contents of the proposal so quickly as to make them almost entirely incomprehensible to Henderson. Dahlerus expressed to Göring his disapproval of the Ambassador of the British Empire being subjected to such high-handed and discourteous treatment. Under the circumstances, Dahlerus recommended to Göring that he himself be permitted to remit the sixteen-point proposal to the British Government. Göring soon agreed after giving the matter due consideration, although he was taking a great chance by doing so, for Hitler had given strict orders that the sixteen-point proposal not be publicized.

Dahlerus arrived at the British Embassy at 10 a.m. with the sixteen-point proposal for Henderson's perusal. In turn, Henderson sent Dahlerus to Lipski with the document. But Lipski was taken aback, for Dahlerus was totally unknown to him. Dahlerus strongly recommended that Lipski return to see Göring at once and agree to Hitler's sixteen-point proposal. This suggestion irked Lipski. Weary from intense diplomatic pressure by both the British and Germans, Lipski asked Dahlerus to go into the next room and have a secretary take down the sixteen-point proposal. However, despite the fact that Henderson himself endorsed the sixteen-point proposal (the British Ambassador considered it not entirely unreasonable), Lipski did not intend to heed Dahlerus' advice. Lipski could not have in any case, since the Polish Government had not granted him such powers.[141]

When Attolico called on Ribbentrop at 5 p.m., he relayed to Ribbentrop Mussolini's latest request: that Hitler agree to see Lipski purely as a diplomatic gesture in order to prevent an irreparable rift in German–Polish relations. Ribbentrop then described to Attolico the circumstances surrounding the German Government's sixteen-point proposal. He laid special emphasis on how Hitler had waited all day yesterday, to no avail, for the timely arrival of a Polish plenipotentiary. He also assured Attolico that he would pass on Mussolini's request to Hitler straightaway. And when Attolico inquired about the sixteen-point proposal to the Poles, Ribbentrop promised him that a copy would be made available to him shortly.[142]

In accordance with British wishes—Henderson had been pressuring him to negotiate with the German Government—Lipski paid another visit to Ribbentrop. After being kept waiting for hours (he had requested the meeting at 1 p.m.), he was finally received at 6:30 p.m. Lipski advised that the Polish Government were willing to consider further negotiations. He read aloud to Ribbentrop a prepared note to this effect:

> During the past night the Polish Government were informed by the Government of Great Britain of the exchange of views with the German Government regarding the possibility of direct conversations between the Reich Government and the Polish Government.
>
> The Polish Government are favourably considering the suggestions of the Government of Great Britain and will make them a formal reply on the subject within the next few hours.

Next, Ribbentrop inquired whether Lipski was 'empowered to negotiate' in connection with the German sixteen-point proposal, and complained how 'The Führer had waited throughout the whole day [of 30 August] ...' but no Polish emissary had come. Lipski emphatically stated that he was not authorized to do so. He told Ribbentrop that he had only been tasked with relaying to him the Polish Government's message. This he had done, and he gave Ribbentrop a copy of it. When Ribbentrop again inquired 'as to the possibility of Lipski being empowered to negotiate' on behalf of the Polish Government, Lipski once more replied 'that he had no plenary powers for any negotiations', whereupon he was curtly given the brush-off.[143]

Two hours after he had seen Ribbentrop, Attolico was granted an audience with Hitler, who gave him two documents—one containing the text of the sixteen-point proposal he had asked Ribbentrop for, and the other a press bulletin. Hitler noted that due to the Polish Government's intransigence (i.e. their failure to dispatch a plenipotentiary to Berlin the previous day), the deadline for the Poles to accept the sixteen-point proposal had lapsed. Therefore, Hitler reasoned, it was evident that the British efforts to mediate between the German and Polish Governments had come to naught. Attolico thereupon raised the subject of Mussolini's offer of 25 August to act as a mediator between the Germans and Poles. At that time, Attolico reminded Hitler, the British had recently made a proposal, and he (Hitler) had first wanted to give it his consideration. But now that Hitler deemed the British proposals to have been futile, Attolico inquired of Hitler if he would be willing to take advantage of Mussolini's offer to mediate. To this Hitler replied that 'we must first await the course of events'. He was unwilling, he said, to tolerate any further indignities by the Polish Government, nor did he wish to unduly inconvenience Mussolini. Hitler was certain that the Polish Government would reject any mediatory contributions by Mussolini in any case, and when Attolico inquired 'as to whether everything was now at an end', Hitler answered 'in the affirmative'.[144]

There yet remained one final matter to be attended to: the orchestration of a major false-flag operation to justify offensive operations in Poland. Hitler had decided that it would be necessary to convince the public, at home and abroad alike, that responsibility for the outbreak of war rested with Poland. S.S. chief Himmler, his deputy Heydrich, and Gestapo chief Heinrich Müller had concocted a sinister plan to this end. Three weeks earlier, on 10 August, Heydrich had sent for S.S. Sturmbannführer (Major) Alfred Naujocks, a thug with an engineering background. Naujocks was a trusted subordinate in charge of a sub-department of the Ausland-S.D. Heydrich had tasked him with a special mission: he was to lead a small unit of S.D. men to stage a phony attack on the German radio station at Gleiwitz, a town at the German–Polish frontier some fifteen miles from Kattowitz. At 4 p.m. on 31 August, Heydrich officially confirmed to Naujocks that the operation, code-named 'Himmler', was on. At approximately 8 p.m. Naujocks and his abettors launched their 'attack'. Outfitted in Polish Army uniforms prepared by the Abwehr, they stormed their way into the German radio station, shoving aside the few on-duty technicians. One of Naujock's agents who was fluent in Polish seized the emergency transmitter and shouted, 'Attention. This is Gliwice. The broadcasting station is in Poland hands.' He then broadcast a provocative speech inciting the Silesian Poles to rise up and revolt against the Hitlerites.

To add credibility to the charade, Dachau camp inmates—cynically referred to as '*Konserve*' ('Canned Goods')—were given lethal injections and their corpses left strewn about. Their features were mutilated and they were riddled with bullets to make it appear as though they were Polish insurgents killed in combat. Afterwards German newsmen were brought to the site to see with their own eyes 'evidence' of 'Polish' criminality. The report of the Chief Constable at Gleiwitz gave the following 'official' version of events:

> Towards 8 p.m. the German Broadcasting Station at Gleiwitz was attacked by a troop of Polish insurgents and temporarily occupied. The insurgents were driven off by German frontier police officers. One of the insurgents was fatally injured.[145]

Radio Cologne announced that the Polish attackers at Gleiwitz were being repulsed by German policemen. The attackers were, German radiomen claimed, 'Polish irregular formations'. The word soon spread. The British Broadcasting Corporation aired a notification of their own, echoing the German newsflashes and noting that some of the 'Poles' had been fatally shot.

Although there were numerous simulated pre-war attacks perpetrated by the Nazis, the most prominent was the incident at Gleiwitz. Another significant 'attack' was executed by Abwehr operatives at the Jabłonków Pass, and others were carried out against the German customs houses at Geyersdorf, Hruschau, Hoflinden, Neukrug, and Pfalzdorf. Collectively they gave the impression of coordinated Polish aggression against the Reich which Hitler could then use as a pretext for 'retaliating' against Poland. In his post-war deposition at Nuremberg on 20 November 1945, Naujocks explained his role in the faked Gleiwitz radio station attack:

> 2. On or about 10 August 1939, the chief of the Sipo [Security Police] and S.D., Heydrich, personally ordered me to simulate an attack on the radio station near Gleiwitz near the Polish border and to make it appear that the attacking force consisted of Poles. Heydrich said, 'Practical proof is needed for these attacks of the Poles for the foreign press as well as for German propaganda purposes.' I was directed to go to Gleiwitz with five or six other S.D. men and wait there until I received a code word from Heydrich indicating that the attack should take place. My instructions were to seize the radio station and to hold it long enough to permit a Polish-speaking German who would be put at my disposal to broadcast a speech in Polish. Heydrich told me that this speech should state that the time had come for conflict between Germans and Poles and that Poles should get together and smash

down any Germans from whom they met resistance. Heydrich also told me at this time that he expected an attack on Poland by Germany in a few days.

3. I went to Gleiwitz and waited there a fortnight. Then I requested permission of Heydrich to return to Berlin but was told to say in Gleiwitz. Between the 25th and 31st of August I went to see Heinrich Müller, head of the Gestapo, who was then nearby at Oppeln. In my presence Müller discussed with a man named Mehlhorn plans for another border incident, in which it should be made to appear that Polish soldiers were attacking German troops.... Germans in the approximate strength of a company were to be used. Müller stated that he had 12 or 13 condemned criminals who were to be dressed in Polish uniforms and left dead on the ground at the scene of the incident to show that they had been killed while attacking. For this purpose they were to be given fatal injections by a doctor employed by Heydrich. Then they were also to be given gunshot wounds. After the assault, members of the press and other persons were to be taken to the spot of the incident. A police report was subsequently to be prepared.

4. Müller told me that he had an order from Heydrich to make one of those criminals available to me for the action at Gleiwitz. The code name by which he referred to these criminals was 'Canned Goods'.

5. The incident at Gleiwitz in which I participated was carried out on the evening preceding the German attack on Poland.... At noon on the 31st of August I received by telephone from Heydrich the code word for the attack which was to take place at 8 o'clock that evening. Heydrich said, 'In order to carry out this attack, report to Müller for "Canned Goods".' I did this ...

6. We seized the radio station as ordered, broadcast a speech of three to four minutes over an emergency transmitter, fired some pistol shots and left.[146]

In an official German communiqué, the Reich Government saw fit to inform the German public by radio of the sixteen-point proposal and of the circumstances surrounding it. The introductory words of the radiocast, aired at 9 p.m., heaped the blame onto the Polish Government:

> In spite of their skepticism regarding the willingness of the Polish Government to reach any agreement, the German Government ...

declared themselves prepared in the interests of peace to accept British intermediation or suggestions. Taking into account all the circumstances prevailing at the moment they considered it necessary to point out in their reply that, if the danger of catastrophe is to be avoided at all, quick and immediate action is indispensable. The German Government have therefore declared themselves willing to receive a delegate appointed by the Polish Government by the evening of 30 August 1939, provided that this delegate should be invested with full power not only to take part in discussions but to negotiate and to make a final decision....

Instead of a declaration regarding the arrival of an authorized Polish representative of the German Government, in reply to their readiness to negotiate, received firstly the news of the Polish mobilization ...

Under these circumstances the German Government considered that they had every right to expect that, at least subsequently to this, the nomination of a Polish delegate would immediately take place. It was clearly too much to expect of the German Government that they should continue not only to reiterate their willingness to enter upon such negotiations, but even to sit and wait and allow themselves to be put off by the Polish side with feeble subterfuges and empty declarations.

In the meantime a *démarche* by the Polish Ambassador [Lipski] has again shown that not even he is authorized to enter upon any discussion whatsoever, much less to negotiate.

Thus the Führer and the German Government have now waited for two days in vain for the arrival of an authorized Polish delegate.

Under these circumstances the German Government cannot but regard their proposals as having been once more virtually rejected, although they are of the opinion that in the form in which they were also communicated to the British Government, they were formulated in a spirit of more than good will and fairness, and could have been accepted.[147]

The radiocast was intended as internal propaganda for the German masses to assure them that their Führer was a reasonable, moderate statesman—and not a warmonger—who had given the obdurate Polish Government every opportunity to reach an understanding with Germany. Hitler's own words, spoken in confidence (but overheard by interpreter Schmidt), bear this out:

I needed an alibi, especially with the German people, to show that I had done everything to maintain peace.[148]

The problems of Danzig, the Polish Corridor, and the maltreatment of ethnic German minorities in Poland were now going to be 'solved' by force. The start of the German invasion of Poland was less than eight hours away, and the clock was ticking.

Not surprisingly, the Polish Government rejected Germany's sixteen-point proposal out of hand and at 11 p.m. countered with a sharp rebuttal. They stated that the German radiocast made the Reich's plans to subjugate Europe plain for all to see and demonstrated how correct they had been to order the mobilization of their armed forces in anticipation of a German attack:

> Words can now no longer veil the aggressive plans of the new Huns. Germany is aiming at the domination of Europe and is cancelling the rights of nations with as yet unprecedented cynicism. This impudent [sixteen-point] proposal shows clearly how necessary were the military orders given by the Polish Government.[149]

In any event, at this late stage the wheels were already in motion and could not be stopped. There would be not be another cancellation or postponement as had taken place six days ago, for at 12:30 p.m. Hitler issued his first war directive (see Appendix N). Hostilities were to commence the next morning, at dawn:

> Directive No. 1 for the Conduct of the War.
>
> 1. Now that all the *political possibilities* of disposing by peaceful means of a situation on the Eastern Frontier which is intolerable for Germany *are exhausted*, I have determined on a *solution by force*.
>
> 2. The *attack on Poland* is to be carried out in accordance with the preparations made for '*Fall Weiss*' ...
>
> Allotment of tasks and the operational target remain unchanged.
> Date of attack—1 September 1939
> Time of attack—04:45
> This time also applies to the operation at Gdynia, Bay of Danzig, and the Dirschau Bridge.

Hitler specified that German forces were not to attack the Anglo–French democracies first. He intended for the Allies to bear the blame for starting a war in the West. Minor border infractions by the Allies were to be repelled in the immediate vicinity where they occurred. The neutrality of the Low Countries and Switzerland was not to be violated (yet), and German troops were forbidden to cross Germany's western frontier without his permission:

> 3. In the West it is important that the responsibility for the opening of hostilities should rest unequivocally with England and France. At first purely local action should be taken against insignificant frontier violations. The neutrality assured by us to Holland, Belgium, Luxembourg and Switzerland should be scrupulously observed.
>
> The German *land* frontier in the West is not to be crossed at any point without my express consent.

Should the Allies attack Germany, the Wehrmacht in the West was to ensure, by taking the appropriate defensive measures, that the Polish campaign not be impeded in any way. The infliction of casualties and destruction of the enemy's *matériel* was to be carried out to the greatest extent possible. The decision to take the offensive, however, lay with Hitler:

> 4. If *England and France open hostilities* against Germany, the task of those sections of the Armed Forces which are operating in the West is to uphold, while conserving their strength as far as possible, those conditions necessary for the successful conclusion of the operations against Poland. Within the scope of this duty, damage should be done to enemy forces and their economic sources of supply as far as resources allow. In any case I reserve to myself the order to commence *attack* operations.[150]

At sunrise on 1 September, Hitler's armies attacked Poland from three sides simultaneously: north, west, and south. The 3rd Army attacked from East Prussia; the 4th Army attacked from Pomerania; and the 8th, 10th, and 14th Armies attacked from German Silesia. Also, the Bernolák Army Group, composed of three Slovak infantry divisions, attacked from Slovakia.[20*] The German invaders fought their way to Warsaw, their main target. They advanced quickly. Over the course of the next few weeks, the mechanized German Army swiftly encircled and eliminated all Polish opposition up to the Vistula River. Beyond this natural boundary was Eastern Poland, which was invaded and occupied on 17 September by the Red Army. All the while, the Luftwaffe destroyed key targets from above. Open cities were bombarded relentlessly, without regard for civilian lives. Fleeing refugees were strafed at will. The Polish Air Force was mostly destroyed in the opening days of the invasion before it even

---

20 * Slovakia was the only pro-Axis nation to participate in the German invasion of Poland. In July 1939, the Slovaks had agreed to join in the invasion, plus permit German forces to use Slovakia as an assembly point beforehand.

had the opportunity to take to the skies. Polish cavalry fought bravely, but were easily repelled by technically and numerically superior land forces. After courageous but futile resistance, Warsaw finally surrendered on 27 September. The Western Powers did not render aid to Poland. Both England and France were unwilling to launch aerial attacks against the Reich for fear of retaliation. The French Army, commanded by Army chief Maurice Gamelin, saw fit to quietly stand guard at the Maginot Line and monitor the German troops stationed along the German–French border.[151]

The *Polenfeldzug* (Polish campaign) was the brainchild of General Halder. General Brauchitsch was in overall command of the operation. The Germans employed the military tactic of *Blitzkrieg* (lightning war), which proved to be devastatingly effective. An early proponent of the *Blitzkrieg* concept was *Panzer* (tank) General Heinz Guderian, to whom it is largely attributed. In general terms, *Blitzkrieg* consisted of a swift, penetrating attack by armoured tanks, backed by air support, that was intended to overwhelm, surround, and destroy the enemy before they could recover.

On 1 September, Hitler issued an official proclamation to the German Army, replete with the usual fabrications:

> The Polish State has refused the peaceful settlement of relations which I desired, and has appealed to arms. Germans in Poland are persecuted with bloody terror and driven from their houses. A series of violations of the frontier, intolerable to a great Power, prove that Poland is no longer willing to respect the frontier of the Reich.
>
> In order to put an end to this lunacy, I have no other choice than to meet force with force from now on. The German Army will fight the battle for the honour and the vital rights of reborn Germany with hard determination. I expect that every soldier, mindful of the great traditions of eternal German soldiery, will ever remain conscious that he is a representative of the National Socialist Greater Germany. Long live our people and our Reich![152]

At 10 a.m. Hitler appeared before the Reichstag to deliver his first wartime address. As was customary, he began by recapitulating the iniquities of the Versailles Treaty unjustly imposed upon the vanquished Germans in 1919 before moving on to the breakdown in German–Polish relations. Naturally, Hitler explained, this estrangement between them was entirely the fault of stiff-necked, senseless Polish statesmen who had refused his moderate proposals. Furthermore, Hitler complained, instead of reasonably settling the matters of Danzig and the Corridor, the Polish Government had opted to respond initially with mobilization, and then 'with increased terror and pressure against our German compatriots and with a slow strangling of the Free City of Danzig—economically, politically, and in recent weeks by military and transport means'. To these Polish 'methods of oppression' and 'atrocities', a 'great Power' such as Germany could no longer stand idly by, Hitler asserted. He would now 'speak to Poland in the same language that Poland for months past has used towards us'. He continued:

> I am determined to solve 1. the Danzig question; 2. the question of the Corridor; and 3. to see to it that a change is made in the relationship between Germany and Poland that shall ensure a peaceful co-existence. In this I am resolved to continue to fight until either the present Polish Government is willing to bring about this change or until another Polish Government is ready to do so. I am resolved to remove from the German frontiers the element of uncertainty, the everlasting atmosphere of conditions resembling civil war. I will see to it that in the East there is, on the frontier, a peace precisely similar to that on our other frontiers.

Hitler then told the lie that Polish troops had wrongfully attacked the Reich and that Germany was defending herself. He threatened to use the same underhanded methods as the enemy, if necessary—even poison gas:

> This night for the first time Polish regular soldiers fired on our own territory. Since 5:45 a.m. [actually 4:45 a.m.] we have been returning the fire, and from now on bombs will be met with bombs. Whoever fights with poison gas will be fought with poison gas. Whoever departs from the rules of humane warfare can only expect that we shall do the same. I will continue this struggle, no matter against whom, until the safety of the Reich and its rights are secured.

Germany had been rearming for the past six years, Hitler declared, with billions spent for that express purpose. In his estimation, the greatly expanded Wehrmacht was ready; it had his utmost confidence. He also promised he would not subject the German people to any burdens that he himself had not been prepared to endure during his service from 1914–18. This new war would be an all-or-nothing struggle, with no holds barred, and would end in either a total German victory or in his death:

> For six years now I have been working on the building up of the German defences. Over 90 milliards have in that time been spent on the building up of these defence forces. They are now the best equipped and are above all comparison with what they were in 1914. My trust in them is unshakable. When I called up these forces and when I now ask sacrifices of the German people and if necessary every sacrifice, then I have a right

> to do so, for I also am today absolutely ready, just as we were formerly, to make every personal sacrifice.
>
> I am asking of no German man more than I myself was ready throughout four years at any time to do. There will be no hardships for Germans to which I myself will not submit. My whole life henceforth belongs more than ever to my people. I am from now on just the first soldier of the German Reich. I have once more put on that coat that was the most sacred and dear to me. I will not take it off again until victory is secured, or I will not survive the outcome.

Next, Hitler nominated his successors. He announced that if he perished during the course of the war, Göring was to succeed him as Führer. If Göring fell, then Hess was to take his place. In such circumstances, both men in turn were to be rendered the same unconditional allegiance as himself. Thereafter, if worst came to worst, Hitler said, the Senate (although no such Senate existed) would nominate from among them a deserving replacement:

> Should anything happen to me in the struggle then my first successor is Party Comrade Göring; should anything happen to Party Comrade Göring my next successor is Party Comrade Hess.
>
> You would then be under obligation to give to them as Führer the same blind loyalty and obedience as to myself. Should anything happen to Party Comrade Hess, then by law the Senate will be called, and will choose from its midst the most worthy—that is to say the bravest—successor.

But above all, Germany would never capitulate. Hitler vowed that the ignominious events of November 1918—namely, the betrayal by the *Novemberverbrecher* (November Criminals) who had signed the Armistice—would never reoccur:

> As a National Socialist and as [a] German soldier I enter upon this struggle with a stout heart. My whole life has been nothing but one long struggle for my people, for its restoration, and for Germany. There was only one watchword for that struggle: faith in this people. One word I have never learned: that is, surrender.
>
> If, however, anyone thinks that we are facing a hard time, I should ask him to remember that once a Prussian King [Frederick the Great], with a ridiculously small State [the Kingdom of Prussia], opposed a stronger coalition [Austria, France, Russia, Saxony, and Sweden], and in three wars finally came out successful because that State had that stout heart

> that we need in these times. I would, therefore, like to assure all the world that a November 1918 will never be repeated in German history.[153]

Earlier that morning, Gauleiter Forster—at Hitler's behest—had introduced a 'constitutional law concerning the reunion of the Free City of Danzig with the German Reich from 1 September [1939]'. This law consisted of four articles, and at 5 a.m. it was sent to Hitler in Berlin by telegram:

> The constitutional law concerning the reunion of the Free City of Danzig with the German Reich from 1 September
>
> Article I: The Constitution of the Free City of Danzig is cancelled with immediate effect.
>
> Article II: All legislative and executive power is in the hands of the head of the State.
>
> Article III: The Free City of Danzig with its territory and population shall immediately form part of the territory of the German Reich.
>
> Article IV: Until the Führer makes a definite decision about the introduction of German Reich law, all legal provisions of the Constitution remain in force as they are at the moment of the issue of this constitutional law.

Forster then requested Hitler 'to agree to this constitutional law and to carry out the re-incorporation of Danzig by a law of the German Reich'. Lastly, Forster assured Hitler of Danzig's 'eternal gratitude and everlasting faith'.[154] In response, Hitler dispatched the following telegram in acknowledgement of Forster's initiative:

> I accept the proclamation of the Free State of Danzig concerning the return to the German Reich.
>
> I thank you, Gauleiter Forster, and all Danzig men and women for the resolute loyalty which you and they have preserved for so many years. Greater Germany greets you with an overflowing heart. The law for reunion is ratified forthwith. I appoint you herewith as head of the civil administration of Danzig.[155]

Also that morning, two letters by Hitler to Mussolini were transmitted to Mackensen at the German Embassy in Italy. The first message, sent by telegram at 11 a.m., was brief:

DUCE:

I thank you most cordially for the diplomatic and political support which you have been giving recently to Germany and her just cause. I am convinced that we can carry out the task imposed upon us with the military forces of Germany. I do not therefore expect to need Italy's military support in these circumstances. I also thank you, Duce, for everything which you will do in future for the common cause of Fascism and National Socialism.

ADOLF HITLER[156]

The second communication, telephoned in twice just minutes before noon—once by Ribbentrop at 11:50 a.m. and again immediately thereafter by Senior Counsellor Theodor Kordt—provided an explanation (albeit distorted) of recent events to Mussolini. Hitler blamed the Polish Government for refusing to send to Berlin a plenipotentiary and for instead ordering general mobilization and perpetrating a slew of guerrilla attacks across the German–Polish border. Since the Poles had resorted to force, he would respond in kind:

To the Italian Minister President, Benito Mussolini.

The latest attempt by Britain at mediation has also failed. I had once more declared myself ready to solve the problem between Germany and Poland by way of negotiations. For two whole days I have waited in vain for a Polish negotiator. Instead:

1) Polish general mobilization has been declared, and

2) A series of further intolerable acts of terrorism have been committed. Last night alone there were fourteen more cases of frontier violation, three of which were very serious. In these circumstances, after having repeatedly warned Poland against continuing such acts, I have now decided to answer force with force.

Hitler thanked Mussolini for his offers to act as intermediary between the Germans and Poles, but expressed the view that owing to the Polish Government's obstinacy, such efforts would almost certainly have been futile. If the Polish Government had sincerely wished to come to terms with the Reich Government, they would have done so. But they were absolutely unwilling to compromise on anything, let alone return to Germany what rightfully belonged to her. And on top of everything else, the ethnic Germans in Poland were being mistreated. Therefore he and the

German *Volk* would prosecute the war unremittingly and put an end to the Polish problem on the Reich's eastern frontier once and for all:

> Come what may, I will carry through this struggle with all the fanaticism of which I and the German people are capable. I thank you, Duce, for all your efforts. I thank you in particular also for your offers of mediation. But from the start I was skeptical about these attempts, because the Polish Government, if they had had even the slightest intention of solving the matter amicably, could have done so at any time. But they refused even to embark on any true understanding which, as all things stood, would have involved concessions on their part. For, after all, it was not Germany who took away something from Poland, but Poland from Germany; and conversely, it was not the Poles in Germany who were maltreated, but the Germans in Poland. For this reason, Duce, I did not want to expose you to the danger of assuming the role of mediator which, in view of the Polish Government's intransigent attitude, would in all probability have been in vain.
>
> Come what may, National Socialist Germany will ensure, in one way or another, that that state of peace and calm shall also come to her eastern frontier which we happily enjoy on all our other frontiers.
>
> ADOLF HITLER[157]

And so a second Great War, more desperate and more devastating than the first, had begun. The German–Polish conflict would broaden to span the European Continent once the British and French Governments declared war on Germany on 3 September, and the conflict would reach worldwide proportions with America's entry into the war in December 1941.

Over the course of the years 1933 to 1939, Hitler had forged the majority of his countrymen into a unified, truculent mass ready to fulfill the age-old Teutonic dream: the acquisition by conquest of *Lebensraum* in the East for the German *Volk*. Beginning 1 September 1939, the peoples of Europe were to experience a horrendous nightmare lasting five years, eight months, and seven days that was to culminate in the deaths of some 42 million European souls, both military and civilian, and in the tragic destruction of countless centuries-old European cities and towns renowned for their rich culture and irreplaceable artifacts.

# Appendix A

## The German–Polish Agreement, 26 January 1934

The German Government and the Polish Government consider that the time has come to introduce a new phase in the political relations between Germany and Poland by a direct understanding between State and State. They have, therefore, decided to lay down the principles for the future development of these relations in the present declaration.

The two Governments base their action on the fact that the maintenance and guarantee of a lasting peace between their countries is an essential pre-condition for the general peace of Europe.

They have therefore decided to base their mutual relations on the principles laid down in the Pact of Paris of the 17th August, 1928, and propose to define more exactly the application of these principles insofar as the relations between Germany and Poland are concerned.

Each of the two Governments, therefore, lays it down that the international obligations undertaken by it towards a third party do not hinder the peaceful development of their mutual relations, do not conflict with the present declaration, and are not affected by this declaration. They establish, moreover, that this declaration does not extend to those questions which under international law are to be regarded exclusively as the internal concern of one of the two States.

Both Governments announce their intention to settle directly all questions of whatever sort which concern their mutual relations.

Should any disputes arise between them and agreement thereon not be reached by direct negotiation, they will in each particular case, on the basis of mutual agreement, seek a solution by other peaceful means, without prejudice to the possibility of applying, if necessary, those methods of procedure in which provision is made for such cases in other agreements in force between them. In no circumstances, however, will they proceed to the application of force for the purpose of reaching a decision in such disputes.

The guarantee of peace created by these principles will facilitate the great task of both Governments of finding a solution for problems of political, economic and social kinds, based on a just and fair adjustment of the interests of both parties.

Both Governments are convinced that the relations between their countries will in this manner develop fruitfully, and will lead to the establishment of a neighbourly relationship which will contribute to the well-being not only of both their countries, but of the other peoples of Europe as well.

The present declaration shall be ratified, and the instruments of ratification shall be exchanged in Warsaw as soon as possible.

The declaration is valid for a period of ten years, reckoned from the day of the exchange of the instruments of ratification.

If the declaration is not denounced by one of the two Governments six months before the expiration of this period, it will continue in force, but can then be denounced by either Government at any time on notice of six months being given. Made in duplicate in the German and Polish languages.

Berlin, 26 January 1934.

For the German Government:
FREIHERR VON NEURATH

For the Polish Government:
JÓZEF LIPSKI[1]

# Appendix B

## The Reich Defence Law, 21 May 1935

The Reich Cabinet has enacted the following law that is hereby made public:

Part I:
State of Defence

ARTICLE I

The Führer and Reich Chancellor can declare a state of defence for the area of the Reich in case danger of war threatens.

ARTICLE II

(1) With the declaration of a state of defence the entire power of execution devolves upon the Führer and Reich Chancellor. The Reich Minister of War exercises it by his orders.

(2) The Reich Minister is empowered in the carrying out of the power of execution to issue legal regulations which may deviate from existing laws. He can, in order to enforce his regulation, threaten punishments and set up special courts.

ARTICLE III

(1) The Reich Ministers are to observe the instructions of the Reich Minister of War. They remain the highest Reich authorities within their realm of activity.

(2) The Reich Ministers will in case of a state of defence effect the necessary measures and are empowered to issue legal regulations which may deviate from existing laws.

Part II:
Mobilization

ARTICLE IV

(1) If conflict with an external enemy becomes unavoidable, the Führer and Reich Chancellor can order mobilization.

(2) The ordering of mobilization includes in itself the declaration of a state of defence according to Part I, in case the latter is not already proclaimed, without prejudice to the directive of Article VI.

(3) With the ordering of mobilization a state of war in the definition of this law begins.

ARTICLE V

The Reich Ministers will effect the necessary measures in case of mobilization and are empowered to issue legal regulations which may deviate from existing laws.

ARTICLE VI

(1) The Führer and Reich Chancellor will appoint a plenipotentiary-general for war economy to direct the entire war economy.

(2) It is the task of the plenipotentiary-general for war-economy to put all economic forces in the service of carrying on the war and to secure the life of the German people economically.

(3) Subordinate to him are:
The Reich Minister for Economy
The Reich Minister for Food and Agriculture
The Reich Labour Minister
The Reich Forest Master and all Reich agents immediately subordinate to the Führer and Reich Chancellor.

Furthermore the financing of the war effort (in the province of the Reich Finance Ministry and of the Reichsbank) will be carried on under his responsibility.

(4) The plenipotentiary-general for war economy is authorized, within his realm of responsibility, to issue legal regulations, which may deviate from the existing laws.

Part III:
Setting of Penalties and Conclusion

ARTICLE VII

Whoever purposely or carelessly acts in violation of a decree issued by authority of this law will be, insofar as a more severe punishment is not stipulated according to other directives, punished with jail and with fine or with one of these penalties.

ARTICLE VIII

The Führer and Reich Chancellor will issue the necessary legal and administrative directives for carrying out of this law.

Berlin, 21 May 1935

The Führer and Reich Chancellor
ADOLF HITLER

The Reich Minister of War
VON BLOMBERG

The Reich Minister of the Interior
FRICK[2]

# Appendix C

## The Anglo–German Naval Agreement, 18 June 1935

Your Excellency,

During the last few days the representatives of the German Government and His Majesty's Government in the United Kingdom have been engaged in conversations, the primary purpose of which has been to prepare the way for the holding of a general conference on the subject of the limitation of naval armaments. I have now much pleasure in notifying Your Excellency of the formal acceptance by His Majesty's Government in the United Kingdom of the proposal of the German Government discussed at those conversations that the future strength of the German Navy in relation to the aggregate naval strength of the Members of the British Commonwealth of Nations should be in the proportion of 35:100. His Majesty's Government in the United Kingdom regard this proposal as a contribution of the greatest importance to the cause of future naval limitation. They further believe that the agreement as from today between the two Governments, will facilitate the conclusion of a general agreement on the subject of naval limitation between all the naval Powers of the world.

2. His Majesty's Government in the United Kingdom also agree with the explanations which were furnished by the German representatives in the course of the recent discussions in London as to the method of application of this principle. These explanations may be summarized as follows:

(*a*) The ratio of 35:100 is to be a permanent relationship, i.e., the total tonnage of the German fleet shall never exceed a percentage of 35 of the aggregate tonnage of the naval forces, as defined by treaty, of the Members of the British Commonwealth of Nations, or, if there should in future be no treaty limitations of this tonnage, a percentage of 35 of the aggregate of the actual tonnage of the Members of the British Commonwealth of Nations.

(*b*) If any future general treaty of naval limitation should not adopt the method of limitation by agreed ratios between the fleets of different Powers, the German Government will not insist on the incorporation of the ratio mentioned in the preceding paragraph in such future general treaty, provided that the method therein adopted for the future limitation of naval armaments is such as to give Germany full guarantees that this ratio can be maintained.

(*c*) Germany will adhere to the ratio of 35:100 in all circumstances, e.g., the ratio will not be affected by the construction of other Powers. If the general equilibrium of naval armaments, as normally maintained in the past, should be violently upset by any abnormal and exceptional construction by other Powers, the German Government reserve the right to invite His Majesty's Government in the United Kingdom to examine the new situation thus created.

(*d*) The German Government favour, in the matter of limitation of naval armaments, that system which divides naval vessels into categories, fixing the maximum tonnage and/or armament for vessels in each category, and allocates the tonnage to be allowed to each Power by categories of vessels. Consequently, in principle, and subject to (*f*) below, the German Government are prepared to apply the 35 per cent ratio to the tonnage of each category of vessel to be maintained, and to make any variation of this ratio in a particular category or categories dependent on the arrangements to this end that may be arrived at in a future general treaty on naval limitation, such arrangements being based on the principle that any increase in one category would be compensated for by a corresponding reduction in others. If no general treaty on naval limitation should be concluded, or in the future general treaty should not contain provision creating limitation by categories, the manner and degree in which the German Government will have the right to vary the 35 per cent ratio in one or more categories will be a matter for settlement between the German Government and His Majesty's Government in the United Kingdom, in the light of the naval situation then existing.

(*e*) If, and for so long as, other important naval Powers retain a single category for cruisers and destroyers, Germany shall enjoy the right to have a single category for these two classes of vessels, although she would prefer to see these classes in two categories.

(*f*) In the matter of submarines, however, Germany, while not exceeding the ratio of 35:100 in respect of total tonnage, shall have the right to possess a submarine tonnage equal to the total submarine tonnage possessed by the Members of the British Commonwealth of Nations. The German Government, however, undertake that, except for the circumstances indicated in the immediately following sentence, Germany's submarine tonnage shall not exceed 45 per cent of the total of that possessed by the Members of the British Commonwealth of Nations. The German Government reserve the right, in the event of a situation arising which in their opinion makes it necessary for Germany to avail herself of her right to a percentage of submarine tonnage exceeding the 45 percent above mentioned, to give notice to this effect to His Majesty's Government in the United Kingdom, and agree that the matter shall be the subject of friendly discussion before the German Government exercise that right.

(*g*) Since it is highly improbable that the calculations of the 35 per cent ratio should give for each category of vessels tonnage figures exactly divisible by the maximum individual tonnage permitted for ships in that category, it may be necessary that adjustments should be made in order that Germany shall not be debarred from utilizing her tonnage to the full. It has consequently been agreed that the German Government and His Majesty's Government in the United Kingdom will settle by common accord what adjustments are necessary for this purpose, and it is understood that this procedure shall not result in any substantial or permanent departure from the ratio of 35:100 in respect of total strengths.

3. With reference to sub-paragraph (*c*) of the explanations set out above, I have the honour to inform you that His Majesty's Government in the United Kingdom have taken note of the reservation and recognize the right therein set out, on the understanding that the 35:100 ratio will be maintained in default of agreement to the contrary between the two Governments.

4. I have the honour to request your Excellency to inform me that the German Government agree that the proposal of the German Government has been correctly set out in the preceding paragraphs of this note.

I have the honour to be, etc.

SAMUEL HOARE.[3]

# Appendix D

## The Anti-Comintern Pact (The German–Japanese Agreement against the Communist International) and Supplementary Protocol, 25 November 1936

The Government of the German Reich and the Imperial Japanese Government, recognizing that the aim of the Communist International, known as the Comintern, is to disintegrate and subdue existing States by all the means at its command, convinced that the toleration of interference by the Communist International in the internal affairs of the nations not only endangers their internal peace and social well-being, but is also a menace to the peace of the world, desirous of co-operating in the defence against Communist subversive activities, have agreed as follows:

Article 1

The High Contracting States agree to inform one another of the activities of the Communist International, to consult with one another on the necessary preventative measures, and to carry these through in close collaboration.

Article 2

The High Contracting Parties will jointly invite third States whose internal peace is threatened by the subversive activities of the Communist International to adopt defensive measures in the spirit of this agreement or to take part in the present agreement.

Article 3

The German as well as Japanese text of the present agreement is to be deemed the original text. It comes into force on the day of the signature and shall remain in force for a period of five years. Before the expiry of this period the High Contracting Parties will come to an understanding over the future period of their co-operation.

In witness whereof the undersigned, being duly and properly authorized by their respective Governments, have signed this agreement and affixed their seals.

Done in duplicate at Berlin on 25 November 1936—that is, 25 November of the 11th year of [the] Showa Period.

Von Ribbentrop, Extraordinary and Plenipotentiary Ambassador of the German Reich
Mushakoji, Imperial Japanese Extraordinary and Plenipotentiary Ambassador

Supplementary Protocol

On the occasion of the signing today of the agreement against the Communist International, the undersigned Plenipotentiaries have agreed as follows:

(a) The competent authorities of the two High Contracting States will work in close collaboration in matters concerning the exchange of information over the activity of the Communist International as well as investigatory and defensive measures against the Communist International.

(b) The competent authorities of the two High Contracting States will within the framework of the existing laws take severe measures against these who at home or abroad are engaged directly in the service of the Communist International or promote its subversive activities.

(c) In order to facilitate the co-operation of the competent authorities provided for in paragraph (a) a permanent committee will be set up. In this committee the further defensive measures necessary for the struggle against the subversive activities of the Communist International will be considered and discussed.

Von Ribbentrop
Mushakoji

Berlin, 25 November 1936[4]

# Appendix E

## The Hossbach Memorandum, 10 November 1937

*Memorandum*

BERLIN, 10 November 1937

MINUTES OF THE CONFERENCE IN THE REICH CHANCELLERY, BERLIN, 5 NOVEMBER 1937, FROM 4:15 TO 8:30 P.M.

Present: The Führer and Chancellor; Field Marshal von Blomberg, War Minister; Colonel-General Baron von Fritsch, Commander-in-Chief, Army; Admiral Dr. h.c. [*honoris causa*] Raeder, Commander-in-Chief, Navy; Colonel-General Göring, Commander-in-Chief, Luftwaffe; Baron von Neurath, Foreign Minister; Colonel Hossbach.

The Führer began by stating that the subject of the present conference was of such importance that its discussion would, in other countries, certainly be a matter for a full Cabinet meeting, but he—the Führer—had rejected the idea of making it a subject of discussion before the wider circle of the Reich Cabinet just because of the importance of the matter. His exposition to follow was the fruit of thorough deliberation and the experiences of his 4½ years of power. He wished to explain to the gentlemen present his basic ideas concerning the opportunities for the development of our position in the field of foreign affairs and its requirements, and he asked, in the interests of a long-term German policy, that his exposition be regarded, in the event of his death, as his last will and testament.

The Führer then continued:

The aim of German policy was to make secure and to preserve the racial community [*Volksmasse*] and to enlarge it. It was therefore a question of space.

The German racial community comprised over 85 million people and, because of their number and the narrow limits of habitable space in Europe, constituted a tightly packed racial core such as was not to be met in any other country and such as implied the right to a greater living space than in the case of other peoples. If, territorially speaking, there existed no political result corresponding to this German racial core, that was a consequence of centuries of historical development, and in the continuance of these political conditions lay the greatest danger to the preservation of the German race at its present peak. To arrest the decline of Germanism [*Deutschtum*] in Austria and Czechoslovakia was as little possible as to maintain the present level in Germany itself. Instead of increase, sterility was setting in, and in its train disorders of a social character must arise in course of time, since political and ideological ideas remain effective only so long as they furnish the basis for the realization of the essential vital demands of a people. Germany's future was therefore wholly conditional upon the solving of the need for space, and such a solution could be sought, of course, only for a foreseeable period of about one to three generations.

Before turning to the question of solving the need for space, it had to be considered whether a solution holding promise for the future was to be reached by means of autarky or by means of an increased participation in world economy.

*Autarky*

Achievement only possible under strict National Socialist leadership of the State, which is assumed; accepting its achievement as possible, the following could be stated as results:

A. In the field of raw materials only limited, not total, autarky.

(1) In regard to coal, so far as it could be considered as a source of raw materials, autarky was possible.
(2) But even as regards ores, the position was much more difficult. Iron requirements can be met from home resources and similarly with light metals, but with other raw materials—copper, tin—this was not the case.
(3) Synthetic textile requirements can be met from home resources to the limit of timber supplies. A permanent solution is impossible.
(4) Edible fats—possible.

B. In the field of food the question of autarky was to be answered by a flat 'No'.

With the general rise in the standard of living compared with that of 30 to 40 years ago, there has gone hand in hand an increased demand and an increased home consumption even on the part of the producers, the farmers. The fruits of the increased agricultural production had all gone to meet the increased demand, and so did not represent an absolute production increase. A further increase in production by making greater demands on the soil, which already, in consequence of the use of artificial fertilizers, was showing signs of exhaustion, was hardly possible, and it was therefore certain that even with the maximum increase in production, participation in world trade was unavoidable. The not inconsiderable expenditure of foreign exchange to insure food supplies by imports, even when harvests were good, grew to catastrophic proportions with bad harvests. The possibility of a disaster grew in proportion to the increase in population, in which, too, the excess of births of 560,000 annually produced, as a consequence, an even further increase in bread consumption, since a child was a greater bread consumer than an adult.

It was not possible over the long run, in a continent enjoying a practically common standard of living, to meet the food supply difficulties by lowering that standard and by rationalization. Since, with the solving of the unemployment problem, the maximum consumption level had been reached, some minor modifications in our home agricultural production might still, no doubt, be possible, but no fundamental alteration was possible in our basic food position. Thus autarky was untenable in regard both to food and to the economy as a whole.

### *Participation in World Economy*

To this there were limitations which we were unable to remove. The establishment of Germany's position on a secure and sound foundation was obstructed by market fluctuations, and commercial treaties afforded no guarantee for actual execution. In particular it had to be remembered that since the World War, those very countries which had formerly been food exporters had become industrialized. We were living in an age of economic empires in which the primitive urge to colonization was again manifesting itself; in the cases of Japan and Italy economic motives underlay the urge for expansion, and with Germany, too, economic need would supply the stimulus. For countries outside the great economic empires, opportunities for economic expansion were severely impeded.

The boom in world economy caused by the economic effects of rearmament could never form the basis of a sound economy over a long period, and the latter was obstructed above all also by the economic disturbances resulting from Bolshevism. There was a pronounced military weakness in those states which depended for their existence on foreign trade. As our foreign trade was carried on over the sea routes dominated by Britain, it was more a question of security of transport than one of foreign exchange, which revealed, in time of war, the full weakness of our food situation. The only remedy, and one which might appear to us as visionary, lay in the acquisition of greater living space—a quest which has at all times been the origin of the formation of states and of the migration of peoples. That this quest met with no interest at Geneva or among the satiated nations was understandable. If, then, we accept the security of our food situation as the principle question, the space necessary to insure it can only be sought in Europe, not, as in the liberal-capitalist view, in the exploitation of colonies. It is not a matter of acquiring population but of gaining space for agricultural use. Moreover, areas producing raw materials can be more usefully sought in Europe in immediate proximity to the Reich, than overseas; the solution thus obtained must suffice for one or two generations. Whatever else might prove necessary later must be left to succeeding generations to deal with. The development of great world political constellations progressed but slowly after all, and the German people with its strong racial core would find the most favourable prerequisites for such achievement in the heart of the Continent of Europe. The history of all ages—the Roman Empire and the British Empire—had proved that expansion could only be carried out by breaking down resistance and taking risks; setbacks were inevitable. There had never in former times been spaces without a master, and there were none today; the attacker always comes up against a possessor.

The question for Germany ran: where could she achieve the greatest gain at the lowest cost?

German policy had to reckon with two hate-inspired antagonists, Britain and France, to whom a German colossus in the centre of Europe was a thorn in the flesh, and both countries were opposed to any further strengthening of Germany's position either in Europe or overseas; in support of this opposition they were able to count on the agreement of all their political parties. Both countries saw in the establishment of German military bases overseas a threat to their own communications, a safeguarding of German commerce, and, as a consequence, a strengthening of Germany's position in Europe.

Because of opposition of the Dominions, Britain could not cede any of her colonial possessions to us. After England's loss of prestige through the passing of Abyssinia into Italian possession, the return of East Africa was not to be expected. British concessions could at best be expressed in an offer to satisfy our colonial demands by the appropriation of colonies which were not British possessions—e.g., Angola. French concessions would probably take a similar line.

Serious discussion of the question of the return of colonies to us could only be considered at a moment when Britain was in difficulties and the German Reich armed and strong. The Führer did not share the view that the Empire was unshakable. Opposition to the Empire was to be found less in the countries conquered than among her competitors. The British Empire and the Roman Empire could not be compared in respect of permanence; the latter was not confronted by any powerful political rival of a serious order after the Punic Wars. It was only the disintegrating effect of Christianity, and the symptoms of age which appear in every country, which caused ancient Rome to succumb to the onslaught of the Germans.

Beside the British Empire there exist today a number of states stronger than she. The British motherland was able to protect her colonial possessions not by her own power, but only in alliance with other states. How, for instance, could Britain alone defend Canada against attack by America, or her Far Eastern interests against attack by Japan!

The emphasis on the British Crown as the symbol of the unity of the Empire was already an admission that, in the long run, the Empire could not maintain its position by power politics. Significant indications of this were:

(*a*) The struggle of Ireland for independence.

(*b*) The constitutional struggles in India, where Britain's half-measures had given to the Indians the opportunity of using later on as a weapon against Britain, the non-fulfillment of her promises regarding a constitution.

(*c*) The weakening by Japan of Britain's position in the Far East.

(*d*) The rivalry in the Mediterranean with Italy who—under the spell of her history, driven by necessity and led by genius—was expanding her power position, and thus was inevitably coming more and more into conflict with British interests. The outcome of the Abyssinian War was a loss of prestige for Britain which Italy was striving to increase by stirring up trouble in the Mohammedan world.

To sum up, it could be stated that, with 45 million Britons, in spite of its theoretical soundness, the position of the Empire could not in the long run be maintained by power politics. The ratio of the population of the Empire to that of the motherland of 9:1 was a warning to us not, in our territorial expansion, to allow the foundation constituted by the numerical strength of our own people to become too weak.

France's position was more favourable than that of Britain. The French Empire was better placed territorially; the inhabitants of her colonial possessions represented a supplement to her military strength. But France was going to be confronted with internal political difficulties. In a nation's life about 10 per cent of its span is taken up by parliamentary forms of government and about 90 per cent by authoritarian forms. Today, nonetheless, Britain, France, Russia, and the smaller states adjoining them, must be included as factors in our political calculations.

Germany's problem could only be solved by means of force and this was never without attendant risk. The campaigns of Frederick the Great for Silesia and Bismarck's wars against Austria and France had involved unheard of risk, and the swiftness of the Prussian action in 1870 had kept Austria from entering the war. If one accepts as the basis of the following exposition the resort to force with its attendant risks, then there remain still to be answered the questions 'when' and 'how'. In this matter there were three cases to be dealt with:

### *Case 1: Period 1943–1945*

After this date only a change for the worse, from our point of view, could be expected.

The equipment of the Army, Navy, and Luftwaffe, as well as the formation of the officer corps, was nearly completed. Equipment and armament were modern; in further delay there lay the danger of their obsolescence. In particular, the secrecy of 'special weapons' could not be preserved forever. The recruiting of reserves was limited to current age groups; further drafts from older untrained age groups were no longer available.

Our relative strength would decrease in relation to the rearmament which would by then have been carried out by the rest of the world. If we did not act by 1943–45, any year could, in consequence of a lack of reserves, produce the food crisis, to cope with which the necessary foreign exchange was not available, and this must be regarded as a 'warning point of the régime'. Besides, the world was expecting our attack and was increasing its countermeasures from year to year. It was while the rest of the world was still preparing its defences that we were obliged to take the offensive.

Nobody knew today what the situation would be in the years 1943–45. One thing only was certain, that we could not wait longer.

On the one hand there was the great Wehrmacht, and the necessity of maintaining it at its present level, the aging of the Movement and of its leaders; and on the other, the prospect of a lowering of the standard of living and of a limitation of the birth rate, which left no choice but to act. If the Führer was still living, it was his unalterable resolve to solve Germany's problem of space at the latest by 1943–45. The necessity for action before 1943–45 would arise in cases 2 and 3.

*Case 2*

If internal strife in France should develop into such a domestic crisis as to absorb the French Army completely and render it incapable of use for war against Germany, then the time for action against the Czechs had come.

*Case 3*

If France is so embroiled by a war with another state that she cannot 'proceed' against Germany.

For the improvement of our politico-military position our first objective, in the event of our being embroiled in war, must be to overthrow Czechoslovakia and Austria simultaneously in order to remove the threat to our flank in any possible operation against the West. In a conflict with France it was hardly to be regarded as likely that the Czechs would declare war on us on the very same day as France. The desire to join in the war would, however, increase among the Czechs in proportion to any weakening on our part and then her participation could clearly take the form of an attack towards Silesia, towards the north or towards the west.

If the Czechs were overthrown and a common German–Hungarian frontier achieved, a neutral attitude on the part of Poland could be the more certainly counted on in the event of a Franco–German conflict. Our agreements with Poland only retained their force as long as Germany's strength remained unshaken. In the event of German setbacks a Polish action against East Prussia, and possibly against Pomerania and Silesia as well, had to be reckoned with.

On the assumption of a development of the situation leading to action on our part as planned, in the years 1943–45, the attitude of France, Britain, Italy, Poland, and Russia could probably be estimated as follows:

Actually, the Führer believed that almost certainly Britain, and probably France as well, had already tacitly written off the Czechs and were reconciled to the fact that this question would be cleared up in due course by Germany. Difficulties connected with the Empire, and the prospect of being once more entangled in a protracted European war, were decisive considerations for Britain against participation in a war against Germany. Britain's attitude would certainly not be without influence on that of France. An attack by France without British support, and with the prospect of the offensive being brought to a standstill on our western fortifications, was hardly probable. Nor was a French march through Belgium and Holland without British support to be expected; this also was a course not to be contemplated by us in the event of a conflict with

France, because it would certainly entail the hostility of Britain. It would of course be necessary to maintain a strong defence on our western frontier during the prosecution of our attack on the Czechs and Austria. And in this connection it had to be remembered that the defence measures of the Czechs were growing in strength from year to year, and that the actual worth of the Austrian Army also was increasing in the course of time. Even though the populations concerned, especially of Czechoslovakia, were not sparse, the annexation of Czechoslovakia and Austria would mean an acquisition of foodstuffs for 5 to 6 million people, on the assumption that the compulsory emigration of 2 million people from Czechoslovakia and 1 million people from Austria was practicable. The incorporation of these two States with Germany meant, from the politico-military point of view, a substantial advantage because it would mean shorter and better frontiers, the freeing of forces for other purposes, and the possibility of creating new units up to a level of about 12 divisions, that is, 1 new division per million inhabitants.

Italy was not expected to object to the elimination of the Czechs, but it was impossible at the moment to estimate what her attitude on the Austrian question would be; that depended essentially upon whether the Duce were still alive.

The degree of surprise and the swiftness of our action were decisive factors for Poland's attitude. Poland—with Russia at her rear—will have little inclination to engage in war against a victorious Germany.

Military intervention by Russia must be countered by the swiftness of our operations; however, whether such an intervention was a practical contingency at all was, in view of Japan's attitude, more than doubtful.

Should Case 2 arise—the crippling of France by civil war—the situation thus created by the elimination of the most dangerous opponent must be seized upon whenever it occurs for the blow against the Czechs.

The Führer saw Case 3 coming definitely nearer; it might emerge from the present tensions in the Mediterranean, and he was resolved to take advantage of it whenever it happened, even as early as 1938.

In the light of past experience, the Führer did not see any early end to the hostilities in Spain. If one considered the length of time which Franco's offensives had taken up till now, it was fully possible that the war would continue for another 3 years. On the other hand, a 100 per cent victory for Franco was not desirable either, from the German point of view; rather were we interested in a continuation of the war and in the keeping up of the tension in the Mediterranean. Franco in undisputed possession of the Spanish Peninsula precluded the possibility of any further intervention on the part of the Italians or of their continued occupation of the Balearic Islands. As our interest lay more in the prolongation of the war in Spain, it must be the immediate aim of our policy to strengthen Italy's rear with a view to her remaining in the Balearics. But the permanent establishment of the Italians on the Balearics would be intolerable both to France and Britain, and might lead to a war of France and England against Italy—a war in which Spain, should she be entirely in the hands of the Whites, might make her appearance on the side of Italy's enemies. The probability of Italy's defeat in such a war was slight, for the road from Germany was open for the supplementing of her raw materials. The Führer pictured the military strategy for Italy thus: on her western frontier with France she would remain on the defensive, and carry on the war against France from Libya against the French North African colonial possessions.

As a landing by Franco–British troops on the coast of Italy could be discounted, and a French offensive over the Alps against northern Italy would be very difficult and would probably come to a halt before the strong Italian fortifications, the crucial point of the operations lay in North Africa. The threat to French lines of communication by the Italian Fleet would to a great extent cripple the transportation of forces from North Africa to France, so that France would have only home forces at her disposal on the frontiers with Italy and Germany.

If Germany made use of this war to settle the Czech and Austrian questions, it was to be assumed that Britain—herself at war with Italy—would decide not to act against Germany. Without British support, a warlike action by France against Germany was not to be expected.

The time for our attack on the Czechs and Austria must be made dependent on the course of the Anglo–French–Italian war and would not necessarily coincide with the commencement of military operations by these three States. Nor had the Führer in mind military agreements with Italy, but wanted, while retaining his own independence of action, to exploit this favourable situation, which would not occur again, to begin and carry through the campaign against the Czechs. This descent upon the Czechs would have to be carried out with 'lightning speed'.

In appraising the situation Field Marshal von Blomberg and Colonel-General von Fritsch repeatedly emphasized the necessity that Britain and France must not appear in the role of our enemies, and stated that the French Army would not be so committed by the war with Italy that France could not at the same time enter the field with forces superior to ours on our western frontier. General von Fritsch estimated the probable French forces available for use on the Alpine frontier at approximately twenty divisions, so that a strong French superiority would still remain on the western frontier, with the role, according to the German view, of invading the Rhineland. In this matter, moreover, the advanced state of French defence preparations must be taken into particular account, and it must be remembered apart from the insignificant value of our present fortifications—on which Field Marshal von Blomberg laid special emphasis—that the four motorized divisions intended for the West were still more or less incapable of movement. In regard to our offensive towards the southeast, Field Marshal von Blomberg drew particular attention to the strength of the Czech fortifications, which had acquired by now a structure like a Maginot Line and which would gravely hamper our attack.

General von Fritsch mentioned that this was the very purpose of a study which he had ordered made this winter, namely, to examine the possibility of conducting operations against the Czechs with special reference to overcoming the Czech fortification system; the General further expressed his opinion that under existing circumstances he must give up his plan to go abroad on his leave, which was due to begin on 10 November. The Führer dismissed this idea on the ground that the possibility of a conflict need not yet be regarded as so imminent. To the Foreign Minister's objection that an Anglo–French–Italian conflict was not yet within such a measurable distance as the Führer seemed to assume, the Führer put the summer of 1938 as the date which seemed to him possible for this. In reply to considerations offered by Field Marshal von Blomberg and General von Fritsch regarding the attitude of Britain and France, the Führer repeated his previous statements that he was convinced of Britain's non-participation, and therefore he did not believe in the probability of belligerent action by France against Germany. Should the Mediterranean conflict under discussion lead to a general mobilization in Europe, then we must immediately begin action against the Czechs. On the other hand, should the Powers not engaged in the war declare themselves disinterested, then Germany would have to adopt a similar attitude to this for the time being.

Colonel-General Göring thought that, in view of the Führer's statement, we should consider liquidating our military undertakings in Spain. The Führer agrees to this with the limitation that he thinks he should reserve a decision for a proper moment.

The second part of the conference was concerned with concrete questions of armament.

HOSSBACH

Certified Correct:
*Colonel (General Staff)*[5]

# Appendix F

## Operation Otto: The Planned Invasion of Austria, 11 March 1938

Berlin. 11.3.38

The Supreme Commander of the Armed Forces
O.K.W. L I a Nr. 420/38 g.Kdos.

30 Copies,
11th Copy

Referring to: Operation OTTO

TOP SECRET

1. If other measures prove unsuccessful, I intend to invade Austria with armed forces to establish constitutional conditions and to prevent further outrages against the pro-German population.

2. The whole operation will be directed by myself.
According to my instructions:
The Ob.d.H. [Army High Command] will direct the land operations with the 8th Army in the formation and strength suggested to me, and with the attachments of the Air Force, the S.S. and police. (See appendix.)
The Ob.d.L. [Air Force High Command] will direct the air operations with the forces suggested to me.

3. Operational duties:
   *a*. Army. The invasion of Austria must be carried out in the manner explained to me. The Army's first target is the occupation of Upper Austria, Salzburg, Lower Austria, the Tyrol, the speedy occupation of Vienna and the securing of the Austro–Czech frontier.
   *b*. Air Force. The Air Force must demonstrate and drop propaganda material, occupy Austrian aerodromes for the use of further possible reinforcements, assist the Army upon demand as necessary; apart from that, hold bomber units in readiness for special tasks.

4. The forces of the Army and Air Force detailed for this operation must be ready for invasion and/or ready for action on the 12 March 1938 at the latest from 1200 hours.
   I reserve the right to give permission for crossing and flying over the frontier, and to decide the actual moment for invasion.

5. The behaviour of the troops must give the impression that we do not want to wage war against our Austrian brothers. It is in our interest that the whole operation shall be carried out without any violence but in the form of a peaceful entry welcomed by the population. Therefore any provocation is to be avoided. If, however resistance is offered it must be broken ruthlessly by force of arms.
   Austrian units who come over to us, immediately come under German Command.

6. On the remaining German frontiers no security measures are to be taken for the time being.

ADOLF HITLER[6]

# Appendix G

## Operation Green: The Secret Plan for an Aggressive War against Czechoslovakia, 30 May 1938

MOST SECRET

II. Two front war with main effort in the South East (strategic concentration '*Grün*')

1. *Political Prerequisites.*

It is my unalterable decision to smash Czechoslovakia by military action in the near future. It is the job of the political leaders to await or bring about the politically and militarily suitable moment.

An inevitable development of conditions inside Czechoslovakia or other political events in Europe creating a surprisingly favourable opportunity and one which may never come again may cause me to take early action.

The proper choice and determined and full utilization of a favourable moment is the surest guarantee of success. Accordingly the preparations are to be made at once.

2. *Political Possibilities for the Commencement of the Action.*
The following are necessary prerequisites for the intended invasion:

*a.* suitable obvious cause and, with it
*b.* sufficient political justification,
*c.* action unexpected by the enemy, which will find him prepared to the least possible degree.

From a military as well as a political standpoint the most favourable course is a lightning-swift action as the result of an incident through which Germany is provoked in an unbearable way for which at least part of world opinion will grant the moral justification of military action.

But even a period of tension, more or less preceding a war, must terminate in sudden action on our part—which must have the elements of surprise as regards time and extent—before the enemy is so advanced in military preparedness that he cannot be surpassed.

3. *Conclusions for the Preparation of 'Fall Grün'.*

*a.* For the *Armed War* it is essential that the surprise element as the most important factor contributing to success be made full use of by appropriate preparatory measures, already in peacetime and by an unexpectedly rapid course of the action. Thus it is essential to create a situation within the first four days which plainly demonstrates, to hostile nations eager to intervene, the hopelessness of the Czechoslovakian military situation and which at the same time will give nations with territorial claims on Czechoslovakia an incentive to intervene immediately against Czechoslovakia. In such a case, intervention by Poland and Hungary against Czechoslovakia may be expected, especially if France—due to the obvious pro-German attitude of Italy—fears, or at least hesitates, to unleash a European war by intervening against Germany. Attempts by Russia to give military support to Czechoslovakia mainly by the Air Force are to be expected. If concrete successes are not achieved by the land operations within the first few days, a European crisis will certainly result. This knowledge must give commanders of all ranks the impetus to decided and bold action.

*b.* The *Propaganda War* must on the one hand intimidate Czechoslovakia by threats and soften her power of resistance, on the other hand issue directions to national groups for support in the Armed War and influence the neutrals into our way of thinking. I reserve further directions and determination of the date.

4. *Tasks of the Armed Forces.*

Armed Forces Preparations are to be made on the following basis:

*a.* The mass of all forces must be employed against Czechoslovakia.

*b.* For the West, a minimum of forces are to be provided as rear cover which may be required, the other frontiers in the East against Poland and Lithuania are merely to be protected, the Southern frontiers to be watched.

*c.* The sections of the Army which can be rapidly employed must force the frontier fortifications with speed and decision and must break into Czechoslovakia with the greatest daring in the certainty that the bulk of the mobile Army will follow them with the utmost speed. Preparations for this are to be made and timed in such a way that the sections of the Army which can be rapidly employed cross the frontier at the appointed time *at the same time* as the penetration by the Air Force before the enemy can become aware of our mobilization.

For this, a timetable between Army and Air Force is to be worked out in conjunction with the O.K.W. and submitted to me for approval.

5. *Missions for the branches of the Armed Forces.*

   a. *Army.* The basic principle of the surprise attack against Czechoslovakia must not be endangered by the inevitable time required for transporting the bulk of the field forces by rail nor the initiative of the Air Force be wasted. Therefore it is first of all essential to the Army that as many assault columns as possible be employed at the same time as the surprise attack by the Air Force. These assault columns—the composition of each, according to their tasks at that time—must be formed with troops which can be employed rapidly owing to their proximity to the frontier or to motorization and to special measures of readiness. It must be the purpose of these thrusts to break into the Czechoslovakian fortification lines at numerous points and in a strategically favourable direction, to achieve a breakthrough or to break them down from the rear. For the success of this operation, co-operation with the Sudeten German frontier population, with deserters from the Czechoslovakian Army, with parachutists or airborne troops and with units of the sabotage service will be of importance. The bulk of the Army has the task of frustrating the Czechoslovakian plan of defence, of preventing the Czechoslovakian Army from escaping into Slovakia, of forcing a battle, of beating the Czechoslovakian Army and of occupying Bohemia and Moravia speedily. To this end a thrust into the heart of Czechoslovakia must be made with the strongest possible motorized and armoured units using to the full the first successes of the assault columns and the effects of the Air Force operations. The rear cover provided for the West must be limited in numbers and quality to the extent which suits the present state of fortifications. Whether the units assigned this will be transported to the Western frontier immediately or held back for the time being will be decided in my special order. Preparations must however, be made to enable security detachments to be brought up to the Western frontier even during the strategic concentration '*Grün*'. Independent of this, a first security garrison must be improvised from the engineers at present employed in constructing fortifications and from formations of the Labour Corps. The remaining frontiers, as well as East Prussia, are to be weakly protected. But, always depending on the political situation, the transfers by sea, of a part or even the bulk of the active forces of East Prussia, into the Reich must be taken into account.

*b. Air Force.* While leaving a minimum of defensive forces in the West, the Air Force is to be employed in bulk in a surprise attack against Czechoslovakia. The frontier is to be flown over at the same time as it is crossed by the first section of the Army.

(See 5*a*) The most important task of the Air Force is the destruction of the Czechoslovakian Air Force and their supply bases within the shortest possible time, in order to eliminate the possibility of its employment as well as that of Russian and French air forces, should the occasion arise, against the strategic concentration and penetration of the German Army and against the German *Lebensraum*. Next to this the crippling of enemy mobilization, of the direction of the government and Armed Forces, as well as the delaying of the strategic concentration of the Czech Army by attacks on communication installations, mobilization and government centres can be of considerable importance to the initial success of the Army. At points in the frontier area where stronger sections of the Czechoslovakian Army or the depth of the defensive system might make the success of the sudden breakthrough of the German Land-attack questionable, the employment of adequate bomber forces must be assured. Czechoslovakian industrial installations are to be spared as far as the course of operations permits. Retaliatory attacks against the population will be carried out only with my permission. Centres of air defence are to be created throughout Berlin, the central German industrial area and the Ruhr area and gradually prepared even now in an inconspicuous fashion.

*c. Navy.* The Navy will assist the Army operations by employing the Danube-flotilla. For this purpose the flotilla will be under the orders of C.-in-C. Army. As regards the conduct of naval warfare at first only those measures are to be taken which appear to be necessary for the careful protection of the North Sea and the Baltic against a sudden intervention in the conflict by other states. These measures must be confined to the absolutely necessary extent. Their inconspicuousness must be guaranteed. It is of decisive importance that all actions, which might influence the political attitude of the European Great Powers unfavourably, be avoided.

6. *Tasks of the War Economy.*

In the war economy it is essential that in the field of the armament industry a maximum deployment of forces is made possible through increased supplies. In the course of operations, it is of value to contribute to the reinforcement of the total war—economic strength—by rapidly reconnoitring and restarting important factories. For this reason the sparing of Czechoslovakian industrial and works installations—insofar as military operations permit—can be of decisive importance to us.

7. All preparations for sabotage and insurrection will be made by O.K.W. They will be made, in agreement with and according to the requirement of the branches of the Armed Forces, so that their effects accord with the operations of the Army and Air Force.

ADOLF HITLER[7]

# Appendix H

## The Munich Agreement, 29 September 1938

Germany, the United Kingdom, France and Italy, taking into consideration the agreement, which has been already reached in principle for the cession to Germany of the Sudeten German territory, have agreed on the following terms and conditions governing the said cession and the measures consequent thereon, and by this agreement they each hold themselves responsible for the steps necessary to secure its fulfillment:

(1) The evacuation will begin on the 1st October.

(2) The United Kingdom, France and Italy agree that the evacuation of the territory shall be completed by the 10th October, without any existing installations having been destroyed and that the Czechoslovak Government will be held responsible for carrying out the evacuation without damage to the said installations.

(3) The conditions governing the evacuation will be laid down in detail by an international commission composed of representatives of Germany, the United Kingdom, France, Italy and Czechoslovakia.

(4) The occupation by stages of the predominantly German territory by German troops will begin on the 1st October. The four territories marked on the attached map will be occupied by German troops in the following order: the territory marked No. I on the 1st and 2nd of October; the territory marked No. II on the 2nd and 3rd of October; the territory marked No. III on the 3rd, 4th and 5th of October; the

territory marked No. IV on the 6th and 7th of October. The remaining territory of preponderantly German character will be ascertained by the aforesaid international commission forthwith and be occupied by German troops by the 10th of October.

(5) The international commission referred to in paragraph 3 will determine the territories in which a plebiscite is to be held. These territories will be occupied by international bodies until the plebiscite has been completed. The same commission will fix the conditions in which the plebiscite is to be held, taking as a basis the conditions of the Saar plebiscite. The commission will also fix a date, not later than the end of November, on which the plebiscite will be held.

(6) The final determination of the frontiers will be carried out by the international commission. This commission will also be entitled to recommend to the four Powers, Germany, the United Kingdom, France and Italy, in certain exceptional cases minor modifications in the strictly ethnographical determination of the zones which are to be transferred without plebiscite.

(7) There will be a right of option into and out of the transferred territories, the option to be exercised within six months from the date of this agreement. A German–Czechoslovak commission shall determine the details of the option, consider ways of facilitating the transfer of population and settle questions of principle arising out of the said transfer.

(8) The Czechoslovak Government will within a period of four weeks from the date of this agreement release from their military and police forces any Sudeten Germans who may wish to be released, and the Czechoslovak Government will within the same period release Sudeten German prisoners who are serving terms of imprisonment for political offences.

ADOLF HITLER.<br>
NEVILLE CHAMBERLAIN.<br>
ÉDOUARD DALADIER.<br>
BENITO MUSSOLINI.

Munich,<br>
29 September 1938.

Annex to the Agreement

His Majesty's Government in the United Kingdom and the French Government have entered into the above agreement on the basis that they stand by the offer, contained in paragraph 6 of the Anglo–French proposals of the 19th September relating to an international guarantee of the new boundaries of the Czechoslovak State against unprovoked aggression.

When the question of the Polish and Hungarian minorities in Czechoslovakia has been settled, Germany and Italy for their part will give a guarantee to Czechoslovakia.

ADOLF HITLER.
NEVILLE CHAMBERLAIN.
ÉDOUARD DALADIER.
BENITO MUSSOLINI.

Munich,
29 September 1938.

Declaration

The Heads of the Governments of the four Powers declare that the problems of the Polish and Hungarian minorities in Czechoslovakia, if not settled within three months by agreement between the respective Governments, shall form the subject of another meetings of the Heads of the Governments of the four Powers here present.

ADOLF HITLER.
NEVILLE CHAMBERLAIN.
ÉDOUARD DALADIER.
BENITO MUSSOLINI.

Munich,
29 September 1938.

Supplementary Declaration

All questions which may arise out of the transfer of the territory shall be considered as coming within the terms of reference to the international commission.

ADOLF HITLER.
NEVILLE CHAMBERLAIN.
ÉDOUARD DALADIER.
BENITO MUSSOLINI.

Munich,
29 September 1938.

Composition of the International Commission

The four Heads of Governments here present agree that the international commission provided for in the agreement signed by them today, shall consist of the Secretary of State in the German Foreign Office, the British, French and Italian Ambassadors accredited in Berlin, and a representative to be nominated by the Government of Czechoslovakia.

ADOLF HITLER.
NEVILLE CHAMBERLAIN.
ÉDOUARD DALADIER.
BENITO MUSSOLINI.

Munich,
29 September 1938.[8]

# Appendix I

## Decree Regulating the Status of the Protectorate of Bohemia and Moravia, 16 March 1939

For ten centuries the Bohemian–Moravian lands belonged to the living space of the German people. Force and lack of understanding arbitrarily tore them from their old historical surroundings and finally created a source of permanent unrest by incorporating them within the artificial edifice of Czecho–Slovakia. From year to year the danger that a new, appalling menace to European peace would emanate, as had happened once before in the past, from this living space, increased. For the Czecho–Slovak State, and those in power there, had not succeeded in properly organizing the existence side by side of the national groups arbitrarily united within its boundaries and had thereby failed to awaken the interest of all concerned in the maintenance of their common State. It has thereby proved its inmost incapacity to exist and has for this reason now also fallen into actual dissolution.

The German Reich, however, cannot tolerate permanent disturbances in these territories that are so all-important to its own peace and security and also so important to the general well-being and universal peace. Sooner or later the Reich, as the Power most interested and affected, by history and geographical position, would have to suffer the most serious consequences. Self-preservation, therefore, requires that the German Reich should be determined to intervene decisively in favour of the restoration of a basis for a reasonable Central European order and should take the requisite measures. For it has already proved in the course of its historical past of a thousand years that it alone, thanks to its greatness and to the qualities of the German people, can be called upon to solve these tasks.

Filled with the earnest desire to serve the true interests of the peoples domiciled in this living space, to guarantee the individual national life of the German and of the Czech peoples, to benefit peace and the social welfare of all, I therefore decree the following, in the name of the German Reich, as the basis for the future existence in common of the inhabitants of these territories:

Article I

1. The territories which formed part of the former Czecho–Slovak Republic and which were occupied by German troops in March 1939 belong henceforth to the territory of the German Reich and come under the latter's protection as the 'Protectorate of Bohemia and Moravia'.

2. In so far as the defence of the Reich demands, the Leader and Chancellor shall take measures differing from the above in respect of individual parts of these areas.

Article II

Inhabitants of the protectorate of German race shall become German nationals and German citizens in accordance with the provisions of the Reich Citizenship Law of the 15th September, 1935. The provisions with regard to safeguarding German blood and German honour shall therefore also apply to them. They shall be subject to German jurisdiction.

2. The remaining inhabitants of Bohemia and Moravia shall be nationals of the Protectorate of Bohemia and Moravia.

Article III

1. The Protectorate of Bohemia and Moravia is autonomous and self-administering.

2. It shall exercise its sovereign rights within the scope of the protectorate in consonance with the political, military and economic importance of the Reich.

3. These sovereign rights shall be represented by its own organs, authorities and officials.

Article IV

The head of the autonomous administration of the Protectorate of Bohemia and Moravia shall enjoy the guard and honours of the head of a State. The head of the protectorate must possess, in order to exercise his functions, the confidence of the Leader and Chancellor of the Reich.

Article V

1. As trustee of Reich interests the Leader and Chancellor of the Reich shall nominate a 'Reich Protector in Bohemia and Moravia'. His seat of office will be Prague.

2. The Reich Protector, as representative of the Leader and Chancellor of the Reich and as Commissioner of the Reich Government, is charged with [the] duty of seeing to the observance of the political principles laid down by the Leader and Chancellor of the Reich.

3. The members of the Government of the protectorate shall be confirmed by the Reich Protector. The confirmation may be withdrawn.

4. The Reich Protector is entitled to inform himself of all measures taken by the Government of the protectorate and to give advice. He can object to measures calculated to harm the Reich and, in case of danger, issue ordinances required for the common interest.

5. The promulgation of laws, ordinances and other legal announcements and the execution of administrative measures and legal judgments shall be annulled if the Reich Protector enters an objection.

Article VI

1. The foreign affairs of the protectorate, especially the protection of its nationals abroad, shall be taken over by the Reich. The Reich will conduct foreign affairs in accordance with the common interest.

2. The protectorate shall have a representative accredited to the Reich Government with the title of a 'minister'.

Article VII

1. The Reich shall accord military protection to the protectorate.

2. In the exercise of this protection the Reich shall maintain garrisons and military establishments in the protectorate.

3. For the maintenance of internal security and order the protectorate may form its own organizations. The composition, strength, numbers and arms shall be decided by the Reich Government.

Article VIII

The Reich shall control directly the transport, post and telegraph systems.

Article IX

The protectorate shall belong to the customs area of the Reich and be subject to its customs sovereignty.

Article X

1. The crown is legal tender, together with the Reichsmark, until further notice.

2. The Reich Government shall fix the ratio of one to the other.

Article XI

1. The Reich can issue ordinances valid for the protectorate in so far as the common interest requires.

2. Insofar as a common need exists, the Reich may take over branches of administration and create its own Reich authorities therefor as required.

3. The Reich Government may take measures for the maintenance of security and order.

Article XII

The law at present existing in Bohemia and Moravia shall remain in force so long as it does not conflict with the principle of the assumption of protection by the German Reich.

Article XIII

The Reich Minister of the Interior shall issue, in agreement with the other Ministers concerned, the administrative and legal regulations for the execution and amplification of this decree.

Hitler
Frick
Ribbentrop
Lammers

Prague, 16 March.[9]

# Appendix J

## Memorandum from the German Government Denouncing the Anglo–German Naval Agreement, 27 April 1939

When in the year 1935 the German Government made the British Government the offer to bring the strength of the German fleet to a fixed proportion of the strength of the naval forces of the British Empire by means of a treaty [the Anglo–German Naval Agreement], it did so on the basis of the firm conviction that for all time the recurrence of a warlike conflict between Germany and Great Britain was excluded. In voluntarily recognizing the priority of British interests at sea through the offer of the ratio 100:35 it believed that, by means of this decision, unique in the history of the Great Powers, it was taking a step which would lead to the establishment of a friendly relationship for all time between the two nations. This step on the part of the German Government was naturally conditional on the British Government for their part also being determined to adopt a political attitude which would assure a friendly development of Anglo–German relations.

On this basis and under these conditions was the Anglo–German Naval Agreement on 18 June 1935, brought into being. This was expressed in agreement by both parties on the conclusion of the agreement. Moreover, last autumn after the Munich Conference the German Chancellor and the British Prime Minister solemnly confirmed in the declaration, which they signed, that they regarded the agreement as symbolical of the desire of both peoples never again to wage war on one another.

The German Government has always adhered to this wish and is still today inspired by it. It is conscious of having acted accordingly in its policy and of having in no case intervened in the sphere of English interests or of having in any way encroached on these interests. On the other hand it must to its regret take note of the fact that the British Government of late is departing more and more from the course of an analogous policy towards Germany. As is clearly shown by the political decisions made known by the British Government in the last weeks as well as by the inspired anti-German attitude of the English Press, the British Government is now governed by the opinion that England, in whatever part of Europe Germany might be involved in warlike conflict, must always take up an attitude hostile to Germany, even in a case where English interests are not touched in any way by such a conflict. The British Government thus regards war by England against Germany no longer as an impossibility, but on the contrary as a capital problem of English foreign policy.

By means of this encirclement policy the British Government has unilaterally deprived the Naval Agreement of 18 June 1935, of its basis, and has thus put out of force this agreement as well as the complementary declaration of 17 July 1937.

The same applies to Part III of the Anglo–German Naval Agreement of 17 July 1937, in which the obligation is laid down to make a mutual Anglo–German exchange of information. The execution of this obligation rests naturally on the condition that a relationship of open confidence should exist between two partners. Since the German Government to its regret can no longer regard this relationship as existing, it must also regard the provisions of Part III referred to above as having lapsed.

The qualitative provisions of the Anglo–German Agreement of 17 July 1937, remain unaffected by these observations which have been forced upon the German Government against its will. The German Government will abide by these provisions also in the future and so make its contribution to the avoidance of a general unlimited race in the naval armaments of the nations.

Moreover, the German Government, should the British Government desire to enter into negotiations with Germany, in regard to the future problems here arising, is gladly ready to do so. It would welcome it if it then proved possible to reach a clear and categorical understanding on a sure basis.

Berlin, 27 April 1939.[10]

# Appendix K

## The Pact of Steel (The German–Italian Alliance) and Secret Additional Protocol, 22 May 1939

The German Reich Chancellor and His Majesty the King of Italy and Albania, Emperor of Ethiopia, consider that the time has come to confirm through a solemn pact the close relation of friendship and affinity which exists between National Socialist Germany and Fascist Italy.

Since a secure bridge for mutual help and assistance has been established through the common boundary between Germany and Italy, fixed for all time, the two Governments acknowledge anew the principles and aims of the policy previously agreed upon by them, and which has shown itself successful in furthering the interests of the two countries as well as in ensuring the peace of Europe.

Firmly bound together through the inner unity of their ideologies and the comprehensive solidarity of their interests, the German and the Italian people are determined also in future to stand side by side and to strive with united effort for the securing of their *Lebensraum* and the maintenance of peace. In this way, prescribed for them by history, Germany and Italy wish, in a world of unrest and disintegration, to carry out the assignment of making safe the foundations of European culture. In order to establish these principles in treaty form, they have named as plenipotentiaries, the German Reich Chancellor, the Minister of Foreign Affairs, von Ribbentrop, His Majesty the King of Italy and Albania, Emperor of Ethiopia, the Minister of Foreign Affairs, Count Galeazzo Ciano, who, after the exchange of proper credentials, have agreed upon the following terms:

Article I

The Contracting Parties will remain in permanent contact with each other, in order to come to an understanding of all common interests or the European situation as a whole.

Article II

In the event that the common interests of the Contracting Parties be jeopardized through international happenings of any kind, they will immediately enter into consultation regarding the necessary measures to preserve these interests. Should the security or other vital interests of one of the Contracting Parties be threatened from outside, the other Contracting Party will afford the threatened Party its full political and diplomatic support in order to remove this threat.

Article III

If it should happen, against the wishes and hopes of the Contracting Parties, that one of them becomes involved in military complications with another Power or other Powers, the other Contracting Party will immediately step to its side as an ally and will support it with all its military might on land, at sea, and in the air.

Article IV

In order to ensure, in any given case, the rapid implementation of the alliance obligations of Article III, the Governments of the two Contracting Parties will further intensify their co-operation in the military sphere and the sphere of war economy. Similarly the two Governments will keep each other regularly informed of other measures necessary for the practical implementation of this pact. The two Governments will create standing commissions, under the direction of the Foreign Ministers, for the purposes indicated in paragraphs 1 and 2.

Article V

The Contracting Parties already at this point bind themselves, in the event of a jointly waged war, to conclude any armistice or peace only in full agreement with each other.

Article VI

The two Contracting Parties are aware of the importance of their joint relations to the Powers which are friendly to them. They are determined to maintain these relations in future and to promote the adequate development of the common interests which bind them to these Powers.

Article VII

This pact comes into force immediately upon its signing. The two Contracting Parties are agreed upon fixing the first period of its validity at ten years. In good time before the elapse of this period they will come to an agreement regarding the extension of the validity of the pact.

Secret Additional Protocol

On signing the friendship and alliance pact, agreement has been established by both parties on the following points:

1. The two Foreign Ministers will as quickly as possible come to an agreement on the organization, the seat, and the methods of work on the pact of the commissions on military questions and questions of war economy as stipulated in Article IV of the pact.

2. For the execution of Article IV, par. 2, the two Foreign Ministers will as quickly as possible arrange the necessary measures, guaranteeing a constant co-operation, conforming to the spirit and aims of the pact, in matters of the press, the news service and the propaganda. For this purpose in particular, each of the two Foreign Ministers will assign to the embassy of his country in the respective capital one or several especially well-experienced specialists, for constant discussion in direct close co-operation with the responsible Ministry of Foreign Affairs, of the suitable steps to be taken in matters of the press, the news service and the propaganda for the promotion of the policy of the Axis, and as a countermeasure against the policy of the enemy powers.

Berlin, 22 May 1939 in the XVII year of the Fascist Era.[11]

# Appendix L

## The Nazi–Soviet Pact (Treaty of Non-Aggression Between Germany and the Union of Soviet Socialist Republics) and Secret Additional Protocol, 23 August 1939

The Government of the German Reich and the Government of the Union of Soviet Socialist Republics, desirous of strengthening the cause of peace between Germany and the U.S.S.R., and proceeding from the fundamental provisions of the Neutrality Agreement concluded in April 1926 between Germany and the U.S.S.R., have reached the following agreement:

Article I

Both High Contracting Parties obligate themselves to desist from any act of violence, any aggressive action, and any attack on each other, either individually or jointly with other powers.

Article II

Should one of the High Contracting Parties become the object of belligerent action by a third power, the other High Contracting Party shall in no manner lend its support to this third power.

Article III

The Governments of the two High Contracting Parties shall in the future maintain continual contact with one another for the purpose of consultation in order to exchange information on problems affecting their common interests.

Article IV

Neither of the two High Contracting Parties shall participate in any grouping of powers whatsoever that is directly or indirectly aimed at the other party.

Article V

Should disputes or conflicts arise between the High Contracting Parties over problems of one kind or another, both parties shall settle these disputes or conflicts exclusively through friendly exchange of opinion or, if necessary, through the establishment of arbitration commissions.

Article VI

The present treaty is concluded for a period of ten years, with the provision that, in so far as one of the High Contracting Parties does not denounce it one year prior to the expiration of this period, the validity of this treaty shall automatically be extended for another five years.

Article VII

The present treaty shall be ratified within the shortest possible time. The ratifications shall be exchanged in Berlin. The agreement shall enter into force as soon as it is signed.

Done in duplicate, in the German and Russian languages.
Moscow, 23 August 1939.

For the Government of the German Reich:
v. RIBBENTROP

With full power of the Government of the U.S.S.R.:
V. MOLOTOV

Secret Additional Protocol

On the occasion of the signature of the Non-Aggression Pact between the German Reich and the Union of Soviet Socialist Republics the undersigned plenipotentiaries of each of the two parties discussed in strictly confidential conversations the question of the boundary of their respective spheres of influence in Eastern Europe. These conversations led to the following conclusions:

1. In the event of a territorial and political rearrangement in the areas belonging to the Baltic States (Finland, Estonia, Latvia, Lithuania), the

northern boundary of Lithuania shall represent the boundary of the spheres of influence of Germany and the U.S.S.R. In this connection the interest of Lithuania in the Vilna area is recognized by each party.

2. In the event of a territorial and political rearrangement of the areas belonging to the Polish state the spheres of influence of Germany and the U.S.S.R. shall be bounded approximately by the line of the rivers Narew, Vistula, and San.
   The question of whether the interests of both parties make desirable the maintenance of an independent Polish state and how such a state should be bounded can only be definitely determined in the course of further political developments.
   In any event both Governments will resolve this question by means of a friendly agreement.

3. With regard to Southeastern Europe attention is called by the Soviet side to its interest in Bessarabia. The German side declares its complete political disinterestedness in these areas.

4. This protocol shall be treated by both parties as strictly secret.

Moscow, 23 August 1939.

For the Government of the German Reich:
v. RIBBENTROP

Plenipotentiary of the Government of the U.S.S.R.:
V. MOLOTOV[12]

# Appendix M

## Proposal for a Settlement of the Problem of Danzig and the Polish Corridor and of the German–Polish Minorities Question, 31 August 1939

The situation between the German Reich and Poland is at the present time such that any further incident may lead to an outbreak of hostilities between the military forces of the two countries, which have already taken up their positions on their respective sides of the frontier. Any peaceful solution of the problem must be of such a nature that the events which originally brought about this state of affairs cannot be repeated on another occasion, thus causing a state of tension not only in Eastern Europe but also elsewhere.

The causes of this development are to be found in (1) the intolerable demarcation of the frontiers as dictated in the Treaty of Versailles, (2) the intolerable treatment of the minority in the territories cut off from the Reich.

In putting forward these proposals, the German Government are attempting to find a final solution, putting an end to the intolerable situation arising from the present demarcation of frontiers, securing to both parties their vital lines of communication, eliminating as far as possible the problem of the minorities and, insofar as this should prove impossible, rendering the fate of the minorities bearable by effectively guaranteeing their rights.

The German Government feel convinced that it is indispensable that economic and personal damage inflicted since 1918 should be investigated, and full compensation made therefore. Of course, the German Government regard this obligation as binding upon both parties.

The above considerations give rise to the following concrete proposals:

1. By reason of its purely German character and the unanimous will of its population, the Free City of Danzig shall be returned forthwith to the German Reich.

2. The territory known as the Polish Corridor, that is to say, the territory bounded by the Baltic Sea and a line running from Marienwerder to Graudenz, Kulm, Bromberg (including these towns), and then in a westerly direction towards Schönlanke, shall itself decide whether it shall become part of the German Reich or remain with Poland.

3. For that purpose, a plebiscite shall be held in this territory. All Germans who were domiciled in this area on 1 January 1918, or who were born there on or before that day, and also all Poles, Kashubians, etc., who were domiciled in this area on that day or who were born there on or before the above-mentioned date, shall be entitled to vote. Germans who have been expelled from this territory shall return for the purpose of registering their votes. In order to ensure an impartial plebiscite and to guarantee that the necessary and extensive preparations for the plebiscite shall be carried out correctly, an International Commission like the one formed in connection with the Saar plebiscite, and consisting of members appointed by the four Great Powers, Italy, the U.S.S.R., France and Great Britain, shall be formed immediately, and placed in charge of this territory. This commission shall exercise sovereign rights throughout the territory. To that end, the territory shall be evacuated by the Polish military forces, by the Polish police and by the Polish authorities within the shortest possible time to be agreed upon.

4. The Polish port of Gdynia to the extent of the Polish settlement is not included in this area, but, as a matter of principle, is recognized as Polish territory. The details of the boundaries of this Polish port shall be decided on by Germany and Poland, and if necessary established by an International Court of Arbitration.

5. In order to allow for ample time for the necessary and extensive preparations for the carrying out of an impartial plebiscite, this plebiscite shall not take place before a period of twelve months has elapsed.

6. In order that during that period, Germany's lines of communication with East Prussia and Poland's access to the sea may be unrestrictedly

ensured, certain roads and railway lines shall be determined, in order to facilitate unobstructed transit. In this connection only such taxes may be levied as are necessary for the upkeep of the lines of communication and for the carrying out of transport.

7. The allocation of this territory shall be decided on by the absolute majority of the votes cast.

8. In order to secure, after the plebiscite (irrespective of the result thereof), Germany's unrestricted communication with the province of Danzig–East Prussia, and Poland's access to the sea, Germany shall, in case the territory be returned to Poland as a result of the plebiscite, be given an extraterritorial traffic zone running from, say, Bütow to Danzig or Dirschau, for the purpose of building a German motor highway (*Reichsautobahn*) and also a four-track railway line. The construction of the motor road and of the railway shall be carried out in such a manner that Polish lines of communication are not affected thereby, i.e., they are to be overbridged or underbridged. This zone shall be one kilometre in width and shall be German territory. Should the result of the plebiscite be in favour of Germany, Poland shall have the same rights as Germany would have had, to build an extraterritorial road and railway connection in order to secure her free and unrestricted access to her port of Gdynia.

9. In the event of the Polish Corridor being returned to the Reich, the latter declares herself prepared to arrange with Poland for an exchange of population, insofar as conditions in the Corridor lend themselves to such an exchange.

10. Any special rights claimed by Poland within the port of Danzig shall be negotiated on a parity basis in exchange for equal rights for Germany at the Port of Gdynia.

11. In order to avoid any sense of menace or danger on either side, Danzig and Gdynia shall henceforth have a purely commercial character; i.e. neither of these places shall be provided with means of military defence or fortifications.

12. The Peninsula of Hela, which according to the result of the plebiscite would be allocated either to Poland or to Germany, shall also be demilitarized in any case.

13. The German Government, having most serious complaints to make about the treatment of the minority by the Poles, and the Polish Government, considering themselves entitled to raise complaints against Germany, agree to investigate into all complaints about economic and personal damage, as well as other acts of terrorism. Germany and Poland bind themselves to indemnify the minorities on either side for any economic damages and other wrongs inflicted upon them since 1918; and/or to revoke all expropriations or otherwise to completely indemnify the respective person or persons for these and other encroachments upon economic life.

14. In order to free the Germans remaining in Poland, as well as the Poles remaining in Germany, from the feeling of being deprived of the benefits of international law, and above all to afford them the certainty of their not being made to take part in actions and in furnishing services of a kind not compatible with their national convictions, Germany and Poland mutually agree to safeguard the rights of their respective minorities by most comprehensive and binding agreements for the purpose of warranting these minorities the preservation, free development and cultivation of their national customs, habits and traditions, to grant them in particular and for that purpose the form of organization considered necessary by them. Both parties undertake not to draft the members of the minority into military service.

15. In case of an agreement being reached on the basis of these proposals, Germany and Poland declare themselves prepared immediately to order and carry out the demobilization of their respective armed forces.

16. Any additional measures required to hasten the carrying through of the above agreement shall be mutually agreed upon between Germany and Poland.[13]

# Appendix N

## Directive No. 1 for the Conduct of the War, 31 August 1939

SUPREME COMMANDER OF THE ARMED FORCES
O.K.W./W.F.A. NO. 170/39gk CHEFS. L.I.
MOST SECRET

Berlin, 31 August 1939.

8 Copies: 2nd Copy.
Known to Ob.d.M. [Navy High Command]
S.O. only [Stamp] Access only through an officer.

Directive No. 1 for the Conduct of the War.

1. Now that all the *political possibilities* of disposing by peaceful means of a situation on the Eastern Frontier which is intolerable for Germany *are exhausted,* I have determined on a *solution by force.*

2. The *attack on Poland* is to be carried out in accordance with the preparations made for '*Fall Weiss*', with the alterations which result, where the Army is concerned, from the fact that it has in the meantime almost completed its dispositions.
   Allotment of tasks and the operational target remain unchanged.
   Date of attack—1 September 1939
   Time of attack—04:45
   This time also applies to the operation at Gdynia, Bay of Danzig and the Dirschau Bridge.

3. In the West it is important that the responsibility for the opening of hostilities should rest unequivocally with England and France. At first purely local action should be taken against insignificant frontier violations. The neutrality assured by us to Holland, Belgium, Luxembourg and Switzerland should be scrupulously observed.
   The German *land* frontier in the West is not to be crossed at any point without my express consent.
   The same applies to warlike actions *at sea* or any which may be so interpreted.
   Defensive measures on the part of the Luftwaffe should *at first* be confined exclusively to the warding off of enemy air attacks on the frontier of the Reich. In doing so the frontier of the neutral states should be observed as long as possible when dealing with single aircraft and smaller units. Defensive operations should only be permitted over this neutral territory when, where French and English attacking squadrons are operating over neutral states against German territory in considerable force, air defence in the West is no longer assured.
   It is of special importance that the Supreme Command of the Armed Forces should be informed with the least possible delay of any violation of the neutrality of their States on the part of our opponents in the West.

4. If *England and France open hostilities* against Germany, the task of those sections of the Armed Forces which are operating in the West is to uphold, while conserving their strength as far as possible, those conditions necessary for the successful conclusion of the operations against Poland. Within the scope of this duty, damage should be done to enemy forces and their economic sources of supply as far as resources allow. In any case I reserve to myself the order to commence *attack* operations.
   The *Army* is holding the West Wall and is making preparations to prevent its being turned—the Western Powers violating Belgian or Dutch territory in doing so. If French forces move into Luxembourg, the frontier bridges may be blown up.
   In its warfare on merchant shipping the *Navy* is concentrating on England. To intensify the effect of this, a declaration of danger zones is to be expected.
   The Supreme Command of the Navy announces in which areas of sea, and within what limits danger zones are considered expedient. The wording of a public declaration should be prepared in conjunction with the Foreign Office and should be submitted to me for approval through the Supreme Command of the Armed Forces.

The Baltic should be secured against penetration by the enemy. The Commander-in-Chief of the Navy decides whether the approaches to the Baltic should be mined for this purpose.

The primary task of the *Luftwaffe* is to prevent the French and English Air Force operating against the German Army and German *Lebensraum*.

In waging war against England preparations should be made for the use of the Luftwaffe in causing damage to sea transport, the armament industry and troop transports to France. Full use should be made of favourable opportunities to make an effective attack on massed English naval units, especially on battleships and aircraft carriers. The decision regarding attacks on London rests with me.

Attacks on the English motherland should be prepared, bearing in mind that whatever happens, inadequate success with part forces is to be avoided.

A. Hitler[14]

# Endnotes

Introduction

1. Adolf Hitler, *Mein Kampf* (trans. by Ralph Manheim), p. 654.
2. *Hitler's Table Talk, 1941–1944: His Private Conversations* (trans. by Norman Cameron and R. H. Stevens), p. 21.
3. *Mein Kampf*, p. 652.
4. *Ibid.*, p. 675.
5. *Ibid.*, p. 654.
6. *Ibid.*, p. 611.
7. *Ibid.*, p. 627.
8. *Ibid.*, p. 625.
9. *Ibid.*, pp. 619-20.
10. *Ibid.*, p. 620.
11. *Ibid.*, p. 665.
12. *Ibid.*, p. 618.
13. *Ibid.*, p. 620.
14. *Ibid.*, pp. 620-1.

Part I: German Diplomacy and the Inaction of the Western Powers

1. Winston Churchill, *The Gathering Storm*, pp. 56-7.
2. Franz von Papen, *Memoirs*, p. 162.
3. Kurt Ludecke, *I Knew Hitler*, pp. 410-4.
4. *Ibid.*, p. 422.
5. Adolf Hitler, *Mein Kampf* (trans. by Ralph Manheim), p. 668.
6. *My New Order* (ed. by Raoul de Roussy de Sales), pp. 145-6.
7. Hugh Baillie, 'Hitler Declares Germany Wall Against Bolshevism', *Madera Tribune*, 27 November 1935, p. 1.
8. *The German Danger* (ed. by Anthony Eden), no. 1.
9. Max Domarus, *Hitler: Speeches and Proclamations, 1932–1945*, vol. I, p. 317.
10. *My New Order*, pp. 176-81.
11. *The German Danger*, (ed. by Eden), no. 1.
12. *My New Order*, pp. 217-8.

13. Alan Bullock, *Hitler: A Study in Tyranny*, p. 323.
14. Domarus, *op. cit.*, p. 393.
15. *The British War Blue Book*, no. 1.
16. *My New Order*, pp. 234-5.
17. Domarus, *op. cit.*, pp. 433-4.
18. *Mussolini as Revealed in his Political Speeches, November 1914–August 1923* (ed. by Bernardo Quaranta di San Severino), p. 17.
19. Albert S. Lindemann, *Esau's Tears: Modern Anti-Semitism and the Rise of the Jews*, p. 467.
20. *Hitler's Ten-Year War on the Jews* (ed. by Boris Shub), p. 283.
21. Churchill, *op. cit.*, p. 95.
22. John Toland, *Adolf Hitler* (abridged edition), p. 256.
23. J. Kenneth Brody, *The Avoidable War*, p. 122.
24. Thomas B. Morgan, 'Italy Sends Troops To Border', *Berkeley Daily Gazette*, 26 July 1934, p. 1.
25. *Ibid.*
26. *Nazi Conspiracy and Aggression*, vol. IV, no. 2,003-PS.
27. *My New Order*, pp. 280-5.
28. Bullock, *op. cit.*, p. 310.
29. Domarus, *op. cit.*, pp. 510-3.
30. T. L. Jarman, *The Rise and Fall of Nazi Germany*, p. 193.
31. *My New Order*, pp. 296-7.
32. *Ibid.*, p. 297.
33. Domarus, *op. cit.*, vol. II, pp. 631-2.
34. *Ibid.*, pp. 632-4.
35. *Treaty of Peace between the Allied and Associated Powers and Germany*, p. 185.
36. *Nazi Conspiracy and Aggression*, vol. IV, no. 1,654-PS.
37. *The Speeches of Adolf Hitler, April 1922–August 1939* (ed. by Norman H. Baynes), vol. II, p. 1,212.
38. *Nazi Conspiracy and Aggression*, vol. IV, no. 2,292-PS.
39. *Locarno: A Collection of Documents* (ed. by F. J. Berber), no. 31.
40. *Documents on International Affairs, 1936* (ed. by Stephen Heald and John H. Wheeler-Bennett), p. 100.
41. *My New Order*, pp. 309-33.
42. *Nazi Conspiracy and Aggression*, vol. IV, no. 2,261-PS.
43. *Documents and Readings in the History of Europe Since 1918* (ed. by Walter Consuelo Langsam and James Michael Egan), no. 65.
44. Ian Kershaw, *Hitler, 1889–1936: Hubris*, p. 558.
45. Churchill, *op. cit.*, p. 173.
46. 'Text of Mussolini's War Plea', *San Bernardino Sun*, 3 October 1935, p. 2.
47. *Documents on German Foreign Policy, 1918–1945*, series C, vol. IV, no. 485.
48. *Locarno: A Collection of Documents* (ed. by Berber), no. 39.
49. *Treaty of Peace between the Allied and Associated Powers and Germany*, p. 53.
50. *Locarno: A Collection of Documents* (ed. by Berber), no. 12, annex A.
51. *Documents on International Affairs, 1936* (ed. by Heald and Wheeler-Bennett), p. 55.
52. *Ibid.*, p. 161.
53. *Locarno: A Collection of Documents* (ed. by Berber), no. 41.
54. *Ibid.*, memorandum.
55. Heinrich Hoffmann, *Hitler Was My Friend*, p. 84.
56. Bullock, *op. cit.*, p. 345.

57. *Ibid.*, p. 343.
58. Churchill, *op. cit.*, pp. 196-7.
59. *Documents on International Affairs, 1936* (ed. by Heald and Wheeler-Bennett), p. 99.
60. Domarus, *op. cit.*, pp. 781-2.
61. *Locarno: A Collection of Documents* (ed. by Berber), no. 69.
62. Bullock, *op. cit.*, p. 346.
63. Domarus, *op. cit.*, p. 790.
64. *Locarno: A Collection of Documents* (ed. by Berber), pp. v-vi (preface).
65. *The French Yellow Book*, no. 1.
66. *Trial of the Major War Criminals before the International Military Tribunal*, vol. IX, pp. 280-1.
67. Frederick L. Schuman, *Europe on the Eve: The Crises of Diplomacy, 1933–1939*, p. 242.
68. Ethan T. Colton, *The XYZ of Communism*, p. 345.
69. Schuman, *op. cit.*, p. 243.
70. *My New Order*, pp. 438-40.
71. *Ibid.*, p. 410.
72. *The German White Book*, no. 339.
73. 'Mussolini and Hitler Address Vast Throngs', *The Oelwein Daily Register*, 28 September 1937, p. 1.
74. *My New Order*, pp. 428-30.
75. 'Mussolini and Hitler Address Vast Throngs', *op. cit.*, p. 6.
76. *Trial of the Major War Criminals before the International Military Tribunal*, vol. I, p. 11, from the 'Charter of the International Military Tribunal', article 6(a) 'Crimes Against Peace'.
77. *Documents on German Foreign Policy, 1918–1945*, series D, vol. I, no. 19.
78. *Trial of the Major War Criminals before the International Military Tribunal*, vol. XVI, p. 640.
79. 'Demand by Germany for Colonies', *The Argus*, 23 November 1937, p. 11.
80. 'Italy Leaves League of Nations', *The Sydney Morning Herald*, 13 December 1937, p. 9.
81. *My New Order*, pp. 486-8.

Part II: Annexation and Expansion

1. *Treaty of Peace between the Allied and Associated Powers and Germany*, p. 95.
2. *Treaty of Peace between the Allied and Associated Powers and Austria*, p. 19.
3. *Ibid.*, p. 33.
4. *My New Order* (ed. by Raoul de Roussy de Sales), p. 235.
5. *Ibid.*, p. 326.
6. *Nazi Conspiracy and Aggression*, vol. IV, no. 2,367-PS.
7. *The Speeches of Adolf Hitler, April 1922–August 1939* (ed. by Norman H. Baynes), vol. II, p. 1,370.
8. William L. Shirer, *The Rise and Fall of the Third Reich*, p. 320.
9. Joachim von Ribbentrop, *The Ribbentrop Memoirs*, p. x, (introduction by Alan Bullock).
10. *Nazi Conspiracy and Aggression*, vol. III, no. 1,377-PS.
11. *My New Order*, pp. 443-4.
12. Kurt von Schuschnigg, *Austrian Requiem*, p. 18.

13. Dorothy Thompson, 'On the Record', *San Bernardino Sun*, 21 February 1938, p. 12.
14. Schuschnigg, *op. cit.*, pp. 20-32.
15. *Ibid.*, p. 32.
16. Charles A. Gulick, *Austria from Habsburg to Hitler*, vol. II, p. 1,801.
17. *My New Order*, p. 445.
18. Schuschnigg, *op. cit.*, p. 36.
19. *Ibid.*, p. 37.
20. Winston Churchill, *The Gathering Storm*, p. 267.
21. *Nazi Conspiracy and Aggression*, vol. V, no. 2,510-PS.
22. *Ibid.*, vol. VI, C-102.
23. *Ibid.*, vol. VI, C-103.
24. Schuschnigg, *op. cit.*, p. 48.
25. *Ibid.*, pp. 49-50.
26. *Ibid.*, p. 50.
27. 'Heil and Farewell', *The Daily News*, 12 March 1938, p. 1.
28. *Nazi Conspiracy and Aggression*, vol. I, C-182.
29. *Ibid.*, no. 2,949-PS, part L.
30. *Ibid.*, no. 2,949-PS, part N.
31. *My New Order*, p. 467.
32. *Documents on International Affairs, 1938* (ed. by Monica Curtis), vol. II, p. 71.
33. *Ibid.*, p. 72.
34. *Nazi Conspiracy and Aggression*, vol. I, no. 2,949-PS, part W.
35. *Axis Rule in Occupied Europe* (ed. by Raphaël Lemkin), p. 283.
36. *Ibid.*, p. 111.
37. Robert Payne, *The Life and Death of Adolf Hitler*, p. 405.
38. *My New Order*, p. 475.
39. *Ibid.*, p. 478-80.
40. *Adolf Hitler from Speeches, 1933–1938*, pp. 25-8.
41. Gino Germani, *Austria in the Twentieth Century*, p. 113.
42. Alan Bullock, *Hitler: A Study in Tyranny*, p. 435.
43. G. J. George, *They Betrayed Czechoslovakia*, p. 20.
44. *Nazi Conspiracy and Aggression*, vol. III, no. 388-PS, item 2.
45. 'The Carlsbad Points', *The Sydney Morning Herald*, 14 September 1938, p. 17.
46. *Nazi Conspiracy and Aggression*, vol. III, no. 388-PS, item 5.
47. *Ibid.*, item 11.
48. *Ibid.*
49. *Ibid.*, item 14.
50. John W. Wheeler-Bennett, *Munich: Prologue to Tragedy*, p. 67.
51. *Documents on German Foreign Policy, 1918–1945*, series D, vol. I, no. 793.
52. E. E. Bridges, *The International Situation*, pp. 1-2.
53. *Ibid.*, pp. 3-4.
54. *Ibid.*, pp. 5-6.
55. *Documents on International Affairs, 1938* (ed. by Monica Curtis), vol. II, pp. 219-23.
56. 'Powers are Warned Not to Meddle', *Ames Daily Tribune*, 10 September 1938, p. 1.
57. Edward W. Beatty, Jr., 'Göring, Hitler No. 2, Warns World to Keep Hands Off in Central Europe', *The Daily Independent*, 10 September 1938, p. 1.
58. *My New Order*, pp. 512-3.
59. *Documents on British Foreign Policy, 1919–1939*, 3rd series, vol. II, no. 862.

60. *Ibid.*, no. 895.
61. Churchill, *op. cit.*, p. 300.
62. Max Domarus, *Hitler: Speeches and Proclamations, 1932–1945*, vol. II, pp. 1,167-9.
63. *Documents on International Affairs, 1938* (ed. by Monica Curtis), vol. II, p. 213.
64. Shirer, *op. cit.*, p. 388.
65. 'Urges Rights for All Groups', *The Lethbridge Herald*, 21 September 1938, p. 2.
66. *Documents on International Affairs, 1938* (ed. by Monica Curtis), vol. II, p. 225.
67. George, *op. cit.*, p. 66.
68. Shirer, *op. cit.*, p. 392.
69. George, *op. cit.*, pp. 85-6.
70. *Ibid.*, pp. 88-9.
71. *Ibid.*, pp. 94-5.
72. Shirer, *op. cit.*, p. 394.
73. *Ibid.*, p. 395.
74. *Documents on International Affairs, 1938* (ed. by Monica Curtis), vol. II, pp. 232-3.
75. T. L. Jarman, *The Rise and Fall of Nazi Germany*, p. 229.
76. Wheeler-Bennett, *op. cit.*, p. 139.
77. 'Chamberlain Returns to London After Final, Fateful Talk with Hitler', *The Evening News*, 24 September 1938, p. 1.
78. *Documents on International Affairs, 1938* (ed. by Monica Curtis), vol. II, pp. 234-5.
79. *Ibid.*, pp. 235-6.
80. George, *op. cit.*, pp. 131-2.
81. 'Text of Hitler's Violent Berlin Speech', *The Advertiser*, 28 September 1938, p. 26.
82. *Ibid.*
83. *Ibid.*
84. *Ibid.*
85. Shirer, *op. cit.*, p. 398.
86. George, *op. cit.*, pp. 147-9.
87. Churchill, *op. cit.*, p. 315.
88. George, *op. cit.*, p. 163.
89. *Ibid.*, p. 164.
90. 'More About Roosevelt Plea', *Winnipeg Free Press*, 28 September 1938, p. 2.
91. Payne, *op. cit.*, p. 423.
92. *Ibid.*, p. 426.
93. George, *op. cit.*, p. 171.
94. *Documents on International Affairs, 1938* (ed. by Monica Curtis), vol. II, pp. 326-7.
95. *Ibid.*, pp. 328-9.
96. *Nazi Conspiracy and Aggression*, vol. IV, no. 1,780-PS.
97. *Documents on British Foreign Policy, 1919–1939*, 3rd series, vol. II, no. 1,228, appendix.
98. 'Prelude to Bigger Things', *The Courier-Mail*, 3 October 1938, p. 3
99 *Ibid.*
100. Churchill, *op. cit.*, p. 319.
101. *The War Speeches of the Rt. Hon. Winston Churchill* (ed. by Charles Eade), vol. I, p. 25.

102. *Ibid.*, pp. 28-9.
103. *My New Order*, p. 535.
104. *Ibid.*, pp. 535-6.
105. *Documents on International Affairs, 1938* (ed. by Monica Curtis), vol. II, p. 333.
106. Churchill, *op. cit.*, p. 332.
107. *My New Order*, pp. 537-8.
108. *Ibid.*, p. 542.
109. *Nazi Conspiracy and Aggression*, vol. III, no. 388-PS, item 51.
110. *Documents on German Foreign Policy, 1918–1945*, series D, vol. IV, no. 81.
111. *Ibid.*, no. 152.
112. Domarus, *op. cit.*, p. 1,260.
113. Churchill, *op. cit.*, pp. 332-3.
114. *Ibid.*, pp. 333-4.
115. *Soviet Documents on Foreign Policy* (ed. by Jane Degras), vol. III, pp. 308-11.
116. *Documents on German Foreign Policy, 1918–1945*, series D, vol. IV, no. 156.
117. *Ibid.*, no. 158.
118. Jochen Thies, *Hitler's Plans for Global Domination*, pp. 115-6.
119. *Documents on German Foreign Policy, 1918–1945*, series D, vol. IV, no. 168.
120. *Ibid.*, no. 202.
121. Dušan Škvama, et al., *Slovak History: Chronology & Lexicon*, p. 140.
122. *Documents on German Foreign Policy, 1918–1945*, series D, vol. IV, no. 209.
123. *Ibid.*, vol. VI, no. 10.
124. *Axis Rule in Occupied Europe* (ed. by Raphaël Lemkin) p. 354.
125. *Nazi Conspiracy and Aggression*, vol. V, no. 2,793-PS.
126. *Documents on German Foreign Policy, 1918–1945*, series D, vol. IV, no. 236.
127. *Ibid.*, no. 237.
128. *Ibid.*, no. 228.
129. Shirer, *op. cit.*, p. 447.
130. *Nazi Conspiracy and Aggression*, vol. VIII, TC-49.
131. 'German Troops Occupy Prague at 6:30 O'clock', *The Dubois Courier*, 15 March 1939, p. 1.
132. *Nazi Conspiracy and Aggression*, vol. VIII, TC-50.
133. *Ibid.*
134. *Ibid.*, TC-51.
135. *Ibid.*, TC-52.
136. *Ibid.*, TC-53.
137. Churchill, *op. cit.*, p. 349.
138. Neville Chamberlain, *The Struggle for Peace*, pp. 414-20.
139. Piotr Eberhardt, *Ethnic Groups and Population Changes in Twentieth-Century Central-Eastern Europe*, p. 40.
140. *Treaty of Peace between the Allied and Associated Powers and Germany*, p. 117.
141. *Documents on German Foreign Policy, 1918–1945*, series D, vol. V, no. 405, footnote no. 2.
142. *Ibid.*, no. 405.
143. *Axis Rule in Occupied Europe* (ed. by Raphaël Lemkin), p. 444.
144. Ian Kershaw, *Hitler, 1936–1945: Nemesis*, p. 166.
145. *My New Order*, pp. 613-4.

Part III: Preparations for War

1. William L. Shirer, *The Rise and Fall of the Third Reich*, p. 436.
2. T. L. Jarman, *The Rise and Fall of Nazi Germany*, p. 226.
3. *Nazi Conspiracy and Aggression*, vol. IV, no. 2,357-PS.
4. *Treaty of Peace between the Allied and Associated Powers and Germany*, p. 121.
5. *Ibid.*
6. Józef Lipski, *Diplomat in Berlin: 1933–1939*, p. 453.
7. *Ibid.*, pp. 453-54.
8. *Ibid.*, p. 303.
9. *Ibid.*, p. 334.
10. *Ibid.*, p. 466.
11. *Trial of the Major War Criminals before the International Military Tribunal*, vol. III, p. 211.
12. *The German White Book*, no. 329.
13. *Ibid.*, no. 328.
14. *Documents on German Foreign Policy, 1918–1945*, series D, vol. V, no. 119.
15. *Ibid.*, no. 120.
16. *Nazi Conspiracy and Aggression*, vol. I, p. 687.
17. *Documents on German Foreign Policy, 1918–1945*, series D, vol. VI, no. 79.
18. *Ibid.*, no. 90.
19. *Ibid.*, no. 99.
20. 'Note Sent as World Awaits Duce's Speech', *The Lima News*, 26 March 1939, p. 1.
21. *Documents on German Foreign Policy, 1918–1945*, series D, vol. VI, no. 101.
22. Alan Bullock, *Hitler: A Study in Tyranny*, p. 498.
23. *The British War Blue Book*, no. 17.
24. *Ibid.*, no. 18.
25. Shirer, *op. cit.*, p. 467.
26. *The British War Blue Book*, no. 20.
27. *Trial of the Major War Criminals before the International Military Tribunal*, vol. III, pp. 216-7.
28. *Nazi Conspiracy and Aggression*, vol. II, p. 345.
29. Grigore Gafencu, *The Last Days of Europe: A Diplomatic Journey in 1939*, p. 182.
30. *My New Order* (ed. by Raoul de Roussy de Sales), p. 592.
31. *The French Yellow Book*, no. 99.
32. Gafencu, *op. cit.*, pp. 70-9.
33. Nevile Henderson, *Failure of a Mission*, pp. 88-9.
34. *My New Order*, pp. 645-54.
35. *The British War Blue Book*, no. 14.
36. *Documents on German Foreign Policy*, series D, vol. VI, no. 200.
37. *My New Order*, pp. 674-7.
38. Churchill, *op. cit.*, pp. 365-6.
39. *Ibid.*, p. 367.
40. *Ibid.*, p. 366.
41. Churchill, *op. cit.*, p. 368.
42. *The British War Blue Book*, no. 15.
43. *Documents and Readings in the History of Europe Since 1918* (ed. by Walter Consuelo Langsam and James Michael Egan), no. 248.
44. *Nazi Conspiracy and Aggression*, vol. V, no. 2,818-PS.

45. MacGregor Knox, *Mussolini Unleashed, 1939–1941: Politics and Strategy in Fascist Italy's Last War* (1986), p. 40.
46. *Documents on German Foreign Policy, 1918–1945*, series D, vol. VI, no. 433.
47. *Nazi Conspiracy and Aggression*, vol. IV, no. 2,327-PS, enclosure 1.
48. 'Polish Corridor as Battlefield of the Next War', *Chester Times*, 29 June 1939, pp. 1-2.
49. *The British War Blue Book*, no. 35.
50. *The French Yellow Book*, no. 150.
51. *Ibid.*, no. 163.
52. *Ibid.*, no. 168.
53. D. G. Tendulkar, *Mahatma: The Life of Mohandas Karamchand Gandhi*, vol. V, p. 197.
54. *Documents on German Foreign Policy, 1918–1945*, series D, vol. VI, no. 712, enclosure 1.
55. *Ibid.*, no. 712, enclosure 2.
56. *Ibid.*, no. 784, footnote 9.
57. *Ibid.*, no. 718.
58. *Ibid.*, no. 766.
59. *Ibid.*, no. 774, enclosure.
60. 'Force to be Met with Force Marshal Śmigły-Rydz Tells Vast Cheering Crowd', *Medicine Hat News*, 7 August 1939, pp. 1 & 8.
61. *Documents on German Foreign Policy, 1918–1945*, series D, vol. VI, no. 780.
62. *Ibid.*, vol. VII, no. 5.
63. *Ibid.*, no. 10.
64. *Ibid.*, no. 119.
65. *Report of M. Carl Burckhardt, High Commissioner of the League of Nations at Danzig*, 19 March 1940, pp. 14-5.
66. Dale C. Copeland, *The Origins of Major War*, p. 135.
67. Lipski, *op. cit.*, p. 582.
68. Galeazzo Ciano, *The Ciano Diaries, 1939–1943*, pp. 118-20.
69. *Documents on German Foreign Policy, 1918–1945*, series D, vol. VII, appendix I.
70. *Ibid.*, no. 130, enclosure.
71. *Ibid.*, no. 56.
72. *Ibid.*, no. 75.
73. *Ibid.*, no. 79, enclosure (memorandum).
74. *Ibid.*, no. 142.
75. *Ibid.*, no. 159.
76. *Ibid.*, no. 192.
77. *Nazi Conspiracy and Aggression*, vol. VII, L-3.
78. *Documents on German Foreign Policy, 1918–1945*, series D, vol. VII, no. 193.
79. *Ibid.*, no. 200, enclosure.
80. *Ibid.*, no. 200.
81. *Ibid.*, no. 201.
82. *Nazi–Soviet Relations, 1939–1941*, p. 69.
83. *Documents on German Foreign Policy, 1918–1945*, series D, vol. VII, no. 213.
84. *Documents and Readings in the History of Europe Since 1918* (ed. by Langsam and Egan), no. 249.
85. *Documents on German Foreign Policy, 1918–1945*, series D, vol. VII, no. 234.
86. Adolf Hitler, *Mein Kampf* (ed. by Ralph Manheim), pp. 660-1.
87. *My New Order*, pp. 687-8.

88. *The British War Bluebook*, no. 64.
89. John Scott, *Duel for Europe: Stalin Versus Hitler*, pp. 355-6.
90. *The British War Bluebook*, no. 124.
91. *Ibid.*, no. 127.
92. *Trial of the Major War Criminals before the International Military Tribunal*, vol. IX, p. 462.
93. *Documents on German Foreign Policy, 1918–1945*, series D, vol. VII, no. 266.
94. *Ibid.*, no. 265.
95. *The French Yellow Book*, no. 242.
96. *The British War Bluebook*, no. 19.
97. *Documents on German Foreign Policy, 1918–1945*, series D, vol. VII, no. 271.
98. *Ibid.*, no. 277.
99. *Ibid.*, no. 261.
100. *Ibid.*, no. 301.
101. *Ibid.*, no. 307.
102. *Ibid.*, no. 324.
103. *Ibid.*, no. 317.
104. *Ibid.*, no. 341.
105. *Documents on British Foreign Policy, 1919–1939*, 3rd series, vol. VII, no. 349, annex 1.
106. *Ibid.*, no. 349, annex 2.
107. *Trial of the Major War Criminals before the International Military Tribunal*, vol. IX, pp. 463-4.
108. Max Domarus, *Hitler: Speeches and Proclamations, 1932–1945*, vol. III, pp. 1,703-7.
109. *Trial of the Major War Criminals before the International Military Tribunal*, vol. IX, p. 465.
110. *Documents on British Foreign Policy, 1919–1939*, 3rd series, vol. VII, no. 349, footnote no. 7.
111. Shirer, *op. cit.*, p. 573.
112. *Trial of the Major War Criminals before the International Military Tribunal*, vol. IX, p. 466.
113. *Documents on German Foreign Policy, 1918–1945*, series D, vol. VII, no. 354.
114. *Ibid.*, no. 350.
115. *Ibid.*, no. 384.
116. *Ibid.*, no. 384, enclosure.
117. *Ibid.*, no. 384.
118. *Documents on British Foreign Policy, 1919–1939*, 3rd series, vol. VII, no. 514.
119. *Trial of the Major War Criminals before the International Military Tribunal*, vol. IX, p. 468.
120. *Documents on British Foreign Policy, 1919–1939*, 3rd series, vol. VII, no. 514.
121. *Documents on German Foreign Policy, 1918–1945*, series D, vol. VII, no. 417.
122. *Documents on British Foreign Policy, 1919–1939*, 3rd series, vol. VII, no. 493.
123. *Documents on German Foreign Policy, 1918–1945*, series D, vol. VII, no. 421.
124. Henderson, *op. cit.*, pp. 278-9.
125. *Documents on British Foreign Policy, 1919–1939*, 3rd series, vol. VII, no. 508.
126. Henderson, *op. cit.*, pp. 279-80.
127. *Documents on British Foreign Policy, 1919–1939*, 3rd series, vol. VII, no. 514.
128. *Ibid.*, no. 504.
129. *Ibid.*, no. 512.
130. *Ibid.*, no. 519.
131. *Ibid.*, no. 525.

132. *Ibid.*, no. 537.
133. *Ibid.*, no. 538.
134. *Documents on German Foreign Policy, 1918–1945*, series D, vol. VII, no. 461, enclosure.
135. *Ibid.* no. 461.
136. Shirer, *op. cit.*, p. 580.
137. *Documents on German Foreign Policy, 1918–1945*, series D, vol. VII, no. 461.
138. *The German White Book*, no. 466, appendix II.
139. Henderson, *op. cit.*, pp. 284-5.
140. *Documents on German Foreign Policy, 1918–1945*, series D, vol. VII, no. 461.
141. Shirer, *op. cit.*, pp. 584-5.
142. *Documents on German Foreign Policy, 1918–1945*, series D, vol. VII, no. 474.
143. *Ibid.*, no. 476.
144. *Documents on German Foreign Policy, 1918–1945*, series D, vol. VII, no. 478.
145. *The German White Book*, no. 470, item dated 31 August, no. 4.
146. *Trial of the Major War Criminals before the International Military Tribunal*, vol. IV, pp. 242-4.
147. *The German White Book*, no. 468.
148. Shirer, *op. cit.*, p. 582.
149. *The German White Book*, no. 469.
150. *Nazi Conspiracy and Aggression*, vol. VI, C-126.
151. Jarman, *op. cit.*, pp. 241-2.
152. *The British War Bluebook*, no. 107.
153. *Ibid.*, no. 106.
154. *Ibid.*, no. 108.
155. *Ibid.*
156. *Documents on German Foreign Policy, 1918–1945*, series D, vol. VII, no. 500.
157. *Ibid.*, no. 504.

Appendices

1. *The British War Blue Book*, no. 1.
2. *Nazi Conspiracy and Aggression*, vol. IV, no. 2,261-PS.
3. *Documents and Readings in the History of Europe Since 1918* (ed. by Walter Consuelo Langsam and James Michael Egan), no. 65.
4. Frederick L. Schuman, *Europe on the Eve: The Crises of Diplomacy, 1933–1939*, pp. 243-4.
5. *Documents on German Foreign Policy, 1918–1945*, series D, vol. I, no. 19.
6. *Nazi Conspiracy and Aggression*, vol. VI, C-102.
7. *Ibid.*, vol. III, no. 388-PS, item 11.
8. *Documents and Readings in the History of Europe Since 1918* (ed. by Langsam and Egan), no. 215.
9. *Nazi Conspiracy and Aggression*, vol. VIII, TC-51.
10. *The British War Blue Book*, no. 22.
11. *Documents and Readings in the History of Europe Since 1918* (ed. by Langsam and Egan), no. 248.
12. *Ibid.*, no. 249.
13. *The German White Book*, no. 466, appendix II.
14. *Nazi Conspiracy and Aggression*, vol. VI, C-126.

# Bibliography

Books

BELOFF, MAX. *The Foreign Policy of Soviet Russia, 1929–1941*, vol. 2. London, Oxford University Press, 1949.
BRIDGES, E. E. *The International Situation: Central Europe, Czechoslovakia, The Prime Minister's Visit to Herr Hitler*. London, His Britannic Majesty's Government, 1938.
BRODY, J. Kenneth. *The Avoidable War: Lord Cecil and the Policy of Principle, 1933–1935*, vol. I. New Brunswick, Transaction Publishers, 1999.
BULLOCK, ALAN. *Hitler: A Study in Tyranny*. London, Pelican Books, 1963.
CHAMBERLAIN, NEVILLE. *The Struggle for Peace*. London, Hutchinson & Co., 1939.
CHURCHILL, WINSTON S. *The Gathering Storm*. Boston, Houghton Mifflin Co., 1948.
—. *The War Speeches of the Rt. Hon. Winston Churchill*, comp. by Charles Eade. Bombay, Cassell & Company Ltd., 1951.
CIANO, GALEAZZO. *The Ciano Diaries, 1939–1943*, ed. by Hugh Wilson. Safety Harbor, Simon Publications, 2001.
COLTON, ETHAN T. *The XYZ of Communism*. New York, The MacMillan Company, 1931.
COPELAND, DALE C. *The Origins of Major War*. Ithaca, Cornell University Press, 2001.
DOMARUS, MAX. *Hitler: Speeches and Proclamations, 1932–1945: The Chronicle of a Dictatorship*, vols. I-IV, trans. by Mary Fran Golbert and Chris Wilcox. Wauconda, Bolchazy-Carducci Publishers, Inc., 2007.
EBERHARDT, PIOTR. *Ethnic Groups and Population Changes in Twentieth-Century Central-Europe: History, Data, and Analysis*, trans. by Jan Owsinski. New York, M. E. Sharpe, 2015.
GAFENCU, GRIGORE. *The Last Days of Europe: A Diplomatic Journey in 1939*. New Haven, Yale University Press, 1948.
GEORGE, G. J. *They Betrayed Czechoslovakia*. Harmondsworth, Penguin Books Ltd., 1938.
GERMANI, GINO. *Austria in the Twentieth Century*. New Brunswick, Transaction Publishers, 2009.

GULICK, CHARLES A. *Austria from Habsburg to Hitler*, vol. II. Berkeley, University of California Press, 1948.
HENDERSON, NEVILE. *Failure of a Mission: Berlin 1937–1939*. New York, G. P. Putnam's Sons, 1940.
HITLER, ADOLF. *Mein Kampf*, trans. by Ralph Manheim. Boston, Houghton Mifflin Company, 1943.
—. *Adolf Hitler from Speeches, 1933–1938*. Berlin, Terramare Office, 1938.
—. *Hitler's Table Talk, 1941–1944: His Private Conversations*, trans. by Norman Cameron and R. H. Stevens. New York, Enigma Books, 2008.
—. *My New Order*, ed. by Raoul de Roussy de Sales. New York, Reynal & Hitchcock, 1941.
—. *The Speeches of Adolf Hitler, April 1922–August 1939*, vols. I-II, ed. by Norman H. Baynes. London, Oxford University Press, 1942.
HOFFMANN, HEINRICH. *Hitler Was My Friend*, trans. by R. H. Stevens. London, Burke, 1955.
JARMAN, T. L. *The Rise and Fall of Nazi Germany*. New York, New York University Press, 1956.
KERSHAW, IAN. *Hitler, 1889–1936: Hubris*. London, Penguin Books, 2001.
—. *Hitler, 1936–1945: Nemesis*. London, Penguin Books, 2001.
KNOX, MACGREGOR. *Mussolini Unleashed, 1939–1941: Politics and Strategy in Fascist Italy's Last War*. Cambridge, Cambridge University Press, 1986.
LEACOCK, STEPHEN. *Our British Empire: Its Structure, Its History, Its Strength*. London, John Lane the Bodley Head, 1941.
LINDEMANN, ALBERT S. *Esau's Tears: Modern Anti-Semitism and the Rise of the Jews*. Cambridge, Cambridge University Press, 1997.
LIPSKI, Józef. *Diplomat in Berlin: 1933–1939*, trans. by Wacław Jędrzejewicz. New York, Columbia University Press, 1968.
LUDECKE, KURT G. W. *I Knew Hitler: The Story of a Nazi Who Escaped the Blood Purge*. New York, Charles Scribner's Sons, 1938.
MUSSOLINI, BENITO. *Mussolini as Revealed in his Political Speeches, November 1914–August 1923*, ed. by Bernardo Quaranta di San Severino. New York, E. P. Dutton & Co., 1923.
PAPEN, FRANZ VON. *Memoirs*, trans. by Brian Connell. London, Andre Deutsch, 1952.
PAYNE, ROBERT. *The Life and Death of Adolf Hitler*. London, Corgi Books, 1975.
POLLOCK, JAMES KERR. *The Government of Greater Germany*. New York, D. van Nostrand Company, Inc., 1947.
POPE, ERNEST. *Munich Playground*. England, Fonthill Media Ltd., 2015.
RIBBENTROP, JOACHIM VON. *The Ribbentrop Memoirs*, trans. by Oliver Watson, intro. by Alan Bullock. London, Weidenfeld and Nicolson, 1954.
SCHMIDT, PAUL. *Hitler's Interpreter*. England, Fonthill Media Ltd., 2016.
SCHUMAN, FREDERICK L. *Europe on the Eve: The Crises of Diplomacy, 1933–1939*. London, Robert Hale Limited, 1939.
SCHUSCHNIGG, KURT VON. *Austrian Requiem*, trans. by Franz von Hildebrand. London, Victor Gollancz Ltd., 1947.
SCOTT, JOHN. *Duel for Europe: Stalin Versus Hitler*. Boston, Houghton Mifflin Company, 1942.
SHIRER, WILLIAM L. *The Rise and Fall of the Third Reich: A History of Nazi Germany*. New York, Simon & Schuster, 1960.
ŠKVAMA, DUŠAN, et al. *Slovak History: Chronology & Lexicon*, Eng. trans. by David P. Daniel. Wauconda, Bolchazy-Carducci Publishers, Inc., 2002.

TENDULKAR, D. G. *Mahatma: The Life of Mohandas Karamchand Gandhi*, vol. V, 1938–1940. Bombay, Vithalbhai K. Jhaveri & D. G. Tendulkar, 1952.
THIES, JOCHEN. *Hitler's Plans for Global Domination: Nazi Architecture and Ultimate War Aims*, Eng. trans. by Ian Cooke and Mary-Beth Friedrich. Oxford, Berghahn Books, 2014.
TOLAND, JOHN. *Adolf Hitler*. New York, Ballantine Books, 1987.
WHEELER-BENNETT, JOHN W. *Munich: Prologue to Tragedy*. London, Macmillan & Co. Ltd., 1948.
WERTH, ALEXANDER. *France and Munich: Before and After the Surrender*. New York, Harper and Brothers Publishing, 1939.

Documentary Sources

*Axis Rule in Occupied Europe*, ed. by Raphaël Lemkin. Washington, Carnegie Endowment for International Peace, Division of International Law, 1944.
*The British War Blue Book. Documents concerning German–Polish Relations and the Outbreak of Hostilities between Great Britain and Germany on September 3, 1939*. New York, Farrar & Rinehart, 1939.
*Documents and Readings in the History of Europe Since 1918*, ed. by Walter Consuelo Langsam and James Michael Egan. New York, J. B. Lippincott Company, 1951.
*Documents on British Foreign Policy, 1919–1939*, ed. by E. L. Woodward and Rohan Butler, 1st, 2nd, and 3rd series. London, Her Majesty's Stationary Office, 1947–).
*Documents on German Foreign Policy, 1918–1945*, series C. London, Her Majesty's Stationary Office, 1962.
*Documents on German Foreign Policy, 1918–1945*, series D. Washington, U.S. Government Printing Office, 1949.
*Documents on International Affairs, 1936*, ed. by Stephen Heald and John W. Wheeler-Bennett. London, Oxford University Press, 1937.
*Documents on International Affairs, 1938*, vol. II, ed. by Monica Curtis. London, Oxford University Press, 1943.
*The French Yellow Book. Diplomatic Documents, 1938–1939*. Eng. edition, London, Hutchinson & Co., 1939.
*The German Danger*, copy no. 45, ed. by Anthony Eden. 17 January 1936.
*The German White Book. Documents on the Events Preceding the Outbreak of War*. Berlin, German Foreign Office, 1939. New York, German Library of Information, 1940.
*Hitler's Ten-Year War on the Jews*, ed. by Boris Shub. New York, Institute of Jewish Affairs, 1943.
*Locarno: A Collection of Documents*, ed. by F. J. Berber. London, William Hodge & Company Ltd., 1936.
*Nazi Conspiracy and Aggression*, vols. I-VIII and 2 supplementary vols., A and B. Washington, U.S. Government Printing Office, 1946–1948.
*Nazi–Soviet Relations, 1939–1941*, ed. by Raymond James Sontag and James Stuart Beddie. Department of State, U.S.A., 1948.
*Report of M. Carl Burckhardt, High Commissioner of the League of Nations at Danzig*. Official no.: C. 42. M. 38. 1940. VII., Series of a League of Nations Publications, 19 March 1940.

*Soviet Documents on Foreign Policy*, vol. III, ed. by Jane Degras. New York, Oxford University Press, 1951–1953.
*The Spanish Government and the Axis*. Department of State, U.S.A., 1946.
*Treaty of Peace between the Allied and Associated Powers and Germany*. London, Her Majesty's Stationary Office, 1919.
*Treaty of Peace between the Allied and Associated Powers and Austria*. Ottawa, de La Broquerie Taché, 1919.
*Trial of the Major War Criminals before the International Military Tribunal*, vols. I-XLII, Washington, U.S. Government Printing Office, 1947–1949.
*Trials of War Criminals before the Nürnberg Military Tribunals Under Control Council Law No. 10*, vols. I-XV, Washington, U.S. Government Printing Office, 1946–1949.

Newspaper Sources

Numerous archived and digitized newspapers (some existing, some defunct) of American, Australian, and Canadian origin, from the 1930s and 1940s. These include: *The Advertiser* (Australia), *Ames Daily Tribune* (United States), *The Argus* (Australia), *Berkeley Daily Gazette* (United States), *Chester Times* (United States), *The Courier-Mail* (Australia), *The Daily Independent* (United States), *The Daily News* (Australia), *The Dubois Courier* (United States), *The Evening News* (United States), *The Lethbridge Herald* (Canada), *The Lima News* (United States), *Madera Tribune* (United States), *Medicine Hat News* (Canada), *The Oelwein Daily Register* (United States), *San Bernardino Sun* (United States), *The Sydney Morning Herald* (Australia), *Townsville Daily Bulletin* (Australia), *Winnipeg Free Press* (Canada).

# Index